Books by Jerome Gold

FICTION

Sergeant Dickinson (originally titled *The Negligence of Death*)
The Prisoner's Son
The Inquisitor
Of Great Spaces (with Les Galloway)

POETRY

Prisoners
Stillness

NONFICTION

Paranoia and Heartbreak: Fifteen Years in a Juvenile Facility
How I Learned That I Could Push the Button
Obscure in the Shade of the Giants: Publishing Lives Volume II
Publishing Lives: Interviews with Independent Book Publishers
Hurricanes (editor)

PARANOIA & HEARTBREAK
FIFTEEN YEARS IN A JUVENILE FACILITY

JEROME GOLD

SEVEN STORIES PRESS
NEW YORK

A Seven Stories Press First Edition

Seven Stories Press
140 Watts Street
New York, NY 10013
www.sevenstories.com

In Canada: Publishers Group Canada, 559 College Street, Suite 402, Toronto, ON M6G 1A9

In the UK: Turnaround Publisher Services Ltd., Unit 3, Olympia Trading Estate, Coburg Road, Wood Green, London N22 6TZ

In Australia: Palgrave Macmillan, 15–19 Claremont Street, South Yarra, VIC 3141

College professors may order examination copies of Seven Stories Press titles for a free six-month trial period. To order, visit http://www.sevenstories.com/textbook or send a fax on school letterhead to (212) 226-1411.

Book design by Jon Gilbert

Gold, Jerome.
 Paranoia & heartbreak : fifteen years in a juvenile facility / Jerome Gold. -- Seven Stories Press 1st ed.
    p. cm.
 Paranoia and heartbreak
 Includes bibliographical references.
 ISBN 978-1-58322-877-7 (pbk.)
 1. Juvenile detention homes--United States. 2. Juvenile delinquents--United States.
 3. Gold, Jerome. I. Title.
 HV9104.G627 2009
 365'.42092--dc22
 [B]

                                2009002347

Printed in the USA

9 8 7 6 5 4 3 2 1

"So much tragedy."

"Find a level of paranoia you can live with and stay there; develop an infinite capacity for heartbreak."

"This country was filled with violent children orphaned by war."

Contents

Intake

All the time I worked at Ash Meadow I commuted from north Seattle, a one-way drive of thirty-seven and a half miles, forty-five to ninety minutes, depending on traffic and weather. I often considered moving closer, but suspected that as soon as I made the move I would take a different job in a different place, and then I would have to commute or relocate again. So out of superstition, or because I was never certain how long I would stay with the job, I did not move.

To get to Ash Meadow from Seattle I took one interstate south and another east. I went through a tunnel and across a lake and through another tunnel. I drove along the southern part of a rich man's town and the tip of another lake and through a town that was rural the first time I saw it, but is gentrified now, and services Seattle. Then I started uphill, aiming for a mountain with a notch like a missing tooth at its peak, where a locally famous waterfall cuts into it. In the fall, as I headed east, mountains from the Cascade Range rose from the fog like islands from a milky sea.

Approaching the mountains, the gloom of Puget Sound gave way suddenly, sometimes even in winter, to a misty sun over green firs and cedars intermingled with the skeletal branches of poplars on either side of the freeway.

In the spring, along the two-lane feeder road connecting Ash Meadow to the highway, amidst the secondary growth of pine and Douglas fir, were wild grasses and cat's-ears, lupins, white or lilac-colored, bracken and Scotch broom, mayweed and English daisies, and ferns, always ferns: spring wood ferns and sword ferns and lady ferns and others I couldn't name. In late summer, as I turned onto the feeder road, above me on the earthen bank crossing my windshield was a small mountain ash, orange berries growing in clusters between its flat leaves, set among gray-barked firs. During other seasons of the year, I could not distinguish this tree from those surrounding it; only the color of its fruit, orange against the gray-green background, caught my eye.

The institution's campus was home to blacktail deer, Canada geese, both migratory and year-round residents, and a number of other birds: crows, of course, and robins, but also barn swallows in the spring, and red-winged blackbirds and flickers and Steller's jays, as well as an occasional pileated or red-headed woodpecker or sapsucker. Sometimes, in the small lake—a pond, really—just east of the campus, I would see one or two herons standing silently. In the summer, a bald eagle patrolled the lake. Sometimes, among the trees in the more domesticated part of the campus near the administration building and the Health Center and the Social Services building, I saw starlings or cedar waxwings in a flock.

Once, leaving work late at night, I saw a gray owl startle from its perch on a trash container and fly into the night, its flight absolutely silent. Once a hawk dropped a mouse at my feet in the recreation yard behind maximum security. Once I saw a lynx sauntering along the fence enclosing max's recreation yard, as if it owned the world.

I never saw a bear, though others did. There was the story, apparently true, of a bear that tried to get through the steel mesh fence that enclosed the rec yard, sending the residents running, screaming, into the cottage.

Once, coming to work at dawn, I turned onto the highway that connected the interstate to the feeder road and, looking afterward in my rearview mirror, saw a full-grown mountain lion bounding across the road behind me. Once, at night, I saw one daintily picking its way along the shoulder of the road, as if trying to avoid stepping on something wet or sharp. One evening I saw a turkey vulture feeding on unrecognizable road kill. Once I saw a hawk rise from a berm clothed in winter's brown grass, a snake in its talons, the snake so stiff with cold I might have mistaken it for a stick but for the curve made by its nether end bending toward the ground.

There was no fence around Ash Meadow. Part of the campus bordered on wetlands and the impact on the environment of building a fence prohibited it. In the late Nineties, an electronic gate was put up at the entrance to the campus, but it connected with nothing; it was just a gate and you could walk around it. Its construction was a great joke among the staff in the cottages, although the administrators appeared to take it seriously. At least they did not laugh when challenged to explain what it was supposed to accomplish. When the gate worked, it did prevent vehicular traffic from entering unannounced, and it worked most days.

Ash Meadow consisted of thirteen cottages, all but one apparently named for an animal. The exception, Andromeda, the sole mental health unit when I began at Ash Meadow, provided a clue that perhaps they were named for heavenly constellations rather than animals. Each of their names, except for Andromeda—Ram, Eagle, Swan, Peacock, Fox, Bull, Lynx, Wolf, Dolphin, Serpent, Crane, Goldfish—was affixed to a configuration of stars as well as to an inhabitant of Earth.

The institution was built in the mid-1960s to house youth at risk, kids who had some problem with the law, but nothing serious yet, or kids who had not gotten into legal trouble, but who the court believed were headed that way. Thirty and more years later stories still circulated among the residents— we called kids "residents" or "students" or just "kids," not inmates or prisoners—about how, in an earlier time, kids used to be able to smoke and ride bikes out on the feeder road and go into the mountains on overnight camping trips and go skiing and just generally enjoyed more freedom than they had now.

All of this was true. Back in the day, staff took residents hiking and climbing. They took trips to the coast for four or five days at a time. They fished, they skied. Swan, particularly, was into outdoor adventure.

This ended in the late Eighties. Ash Meadow was getting residents who were not considered youth at risk, but were convicted felons. On the outside you had had the emergence of the crack-cocaine economy and the corresponding rise of gangs. By the late Eighties, kids who had been dealing had spent enough time in the life to be caught and convicted, some of them anyway. When I arrived on campus two of the cottages stood empty, but a year later all thirteen were filled, and more. Cottages designed to house sixteen residents housed up to twenty-three.

Over the years the composition of the cottages changed. Andromeda was a mental health unit, originally coed. But in 2000 it became an all-girl cottage, and the boys with more severe mental problems went to Dolphin. When I came to Ash Meadow Dolphin was one of the units that housed older boys. Later it became a second maximum security unit, and then, finally, a mental health cottage.

In the Eighties two sex offender units for boys, Fox and Crane, were established. Bull Cottage also took male sex offenders as well as boys who were not sex offenders. By 2001 Bull dealt almost entirely with sex offenders, and Ram also began taking them. There has never been a girls' sex offender unit at Ash Meadow, though a number of girls committed sex offenses. Female sex offenders were placed in Andromeda or in Peacock or Whale, the girls' units for most of the Nineties. In 1999, Serpent Cottage became a back-up mental health unit for girls.

For most of the Nineties, there were three boys' units, aside from Dolphin and those housing sex offenders. These were Swan, Ram, and Goldfish, the last housing the smallest boys, down to age nine. Although Whale housed girls for most of the decade, in 1999 it became coed, then went entirely to boys. Peacock at that time became coed, as it had been for a short time at the beginning of the Nineties.

Eagle, a coed unit, was the drug-and-alcohol cottage. Kids were transferred there from other units, sometimes even other institutions, for twelve weeks of intensive therapy, both group and individual, and returned to their original cottages or institutions upon completion of the course, called the Phoenix Program, or failure. Sometimes a resident went directly to parole after graduating.

Wolf was the maximum security unit, also coed.

The cottages were spread along the western edge of the lake, then looped south to form an upside-down J when viewed on the map that was given out to visitors. In the space between the northernmost cottages and those west of them were a playing field, an asphalt basketball court, and a volleyball set-up. This area was called "lower court." Lower court and all of the area enclosed by the configuration of cottages was called "lower campus." Farther west by four hundred yards and up a slow hill were the administration building, Social Services, the Health Center, the Security office and Central Isolation, the kitchen, the school, and the gymnasium. This area was referred to by cottage staff as "the hill" or "upper campus" or "up above." To the north of it was another playing field, the "back field." West and a little north of it were the maintenance shops.

Throughout the campus were trees of both indigenous and foreign origin. I recognized the red cedars and ponderosa pines and Japanese lace maples, but I hadn't a clue as to the identity of many of the others. One kind enthralled me every fall as much as it did the first time I saw it. Its oval leaves turned flaming red and kept that color for perhaps two weeks, then gradually descended into a dull purple before dropping to the ground. It was not a maple, at least not any kind that I had seen. I suspect it was not indigenous to North America.

For several years I worked with a man who began his career at Ash Meadow as a gardener in the early Seventies. The gardeners then brought in and planted trees whose origins encompassed the earth. Having these trees there from dozens of countries was part of an educational experience designed to give kids who came from the most constrained environments an expanded view of the world and of their place in it. Twenty-some years later, the gardening crew had been disbanded and my colleague could no longer remember the names of the less common trees. No one could tell me the name or origin of my red tree, the reference books did not show it, and I still do not know its identity.

When I applied for work at Ash Meadow I did not want a job. I had been on active duty for Desert Shield, the build-up to Desert Storm, the first American war in the Persian Gulf, and before that I had spent three years with the Census Bureau, and now I wanted to collect unemployment for a while and do some writing. But my friend Dick Teale asked me what my plans were now that I was out of the army again, and when I told him, he suggested I go out to Ash Meadow, where he worked, and apply. He thought I would like working there.

I really wanted a few months to myself, but he said they wouldn't be hiring until April or May and I'd be one of the first on their list if I applied now. So I called, Personnel sent me an application, and I filled it out and mailed it back. Then someone named Carol Ripito called and asked me to come out for an interview.

Afterward I could not tell how the interview had gone, although Carol had said that she liked to hire people who had lived outside the United States, who had experienced living in another culture. Still, I had no sense of what the job was about other than that it had to do with managing kids who were locked up. Despite its appearance as a summer camp, Ash Meadow was a prison. Carol emphasized that: Ash Meadow was a prison.

It was one of five prisons in Washington that housed juveniles and the only one that had girls. Two of the institutions were work facilities, under contract with the Department of Natural Resources to provide fire fighters during the fire season, and to plant trees and clear brush at other times of the year. Elk Grove and The Rivers, the other two facilities, provided schooling, counseling, vocational training, and, in the case of Elk Grove, an eight-week rehabilitation program for kids with drug or alcohol problems.

A year after I started at Ash Meadow, an agreement was made between these three institutions that Ash Meadow would house the younger boys and Elk Grove and The Rivers would take the older ones. Kids could be transferred from one institution to another, depending on circumstances: if a younger boy was particularly assaultive, he could be moved to Elk Grove; if an older boy was significantly smaller than his peers, or otherwise unable to defend himself, he would be transferred to Ash Meadow.

For purposes of the Juvenile Rehabilitation Administration, the agency that oversaw the state prisons for kids and group homes that received state money, a kid was a kid until he or she turned twenty-one. Thus, a kid who was imprisoned at age sixteen on a four-year sentence would serve all of it as a juvenile. On the other hand, a sixteen-year-old convicted as an adult would serve the first years of his sentence at The Rivers, the most secure of the juvenile facilities, then would be transferred to an adult prison to complete his term.

The crimes kids committed to get to Ash Meadow were the same as those done by adult felons: assault, robbery, car theft, burglary, drug-dealing, rape and molestation, manslaughter and murder, kidnapping. Stan MacEvoy, at Swan Cottage, told me that Ash Meadow once held a counterfeiter. Except for this boy, I heard of no other resident in for a white-collar crime. Almost all of the kids we got came from poverty or near-poverty.

Their sentences ranged from sixteen weeks for a fourth-degree assault to years for first- or second-degree murder, manslaughter, rape, or kidnapping. We also had kids in for as little as a week or two for parole violations. For the most part, those with longer sentences were easier to work with. They soon became thoughtful and introspective. Whereas the kids whose sentences were a few weeks or a few months tended to want only for time to pass quickly, those who had committed the more serious offenses came to accept that the institution was going to be their home, the place where they were going to spend their foreseeable lives. They learned to take school seriously, and they were made to look critically at their relationships with other people, including boyfriends and girlfriends and other members of their gang set, if they were in a gang. Some became cynical if they were not cynical when they came in. And I liked them for this, as did a number of other staff, for we were cynical too.

Many of those who were in gangs were eventually disillusioned, for, although the myth is that youth gangs take care of their own, in fact they do not, not if their own are in prison. Gang kids, as a rule, did not receive mail from their homies, not because we intercepted their letters, as kids accused us of doing, but because there were none. The longer a kid's sentence, the more likely it was that his set would forget him.

Religion was important to the kids, and race and ethnicity. Most were Christian of one denomination or another. Some were Muslim. Occasionally we'd get a Jew. More often, we'd get a Satanist. Most who claimed Satanic beliefs did it to needle staff or get a reaction from other kids, but once I had a boy on my caseload who really came from a family of Satanists, and there were others I heard about. Particular parts of Washington—the southwestern counties and Skagit County, north of King County where Seattle is located—seemed to produce them. And our neo-Nazis came from one part of the state, Spokane and its surroundings, but no other.

There was sometimes tension between blacks and whites, and more often between black kids and Hispanic kids. This tension rarely took a violent form, perhaps because staff were alert to it and quick to suppress any threat of violence. The older the kids, the more likely it was that these tensions would exist, or at least would surface to where staff were able to see indications of them.

Our expectations—the institution's expectations—for these kids were that they would learn to be like us, share our values, get respectable jobs, and avoid illegal drugs, all but marijuana, at least. If they could not, or would not, become like us, our expectation was that they would remain criminals, perhaps spending the greater part of their lives in prison.

The models of deportment we used, the values and aspirations we espoused, were rooted in our own beliefs. A person should show deference to authority, should want to better himself through legitimate work, should meet his obligations to his family. Yet we ourselves, we counseling staff, tended to be antiauthoritarian. We were often contemptuous of those institutions whose officers we encouraged the kids to obey. We were as often divorced as other Americans and as often resented paying child support or resisted paying it. In short, our models, by and large, were not models we lived up to—they were sometimes impossible to live up to—yet we promoted them as offering the only path to well-being and economic and emotional stability.

We were middle class and, for the most part, we came from middle-class or working-class parents. Increasingly, as the Nineties progressed, we were white and female, whereas earlier we had been more diverse, at least in terms of color. This was not accidental. One of the most powerful administrators on campus tended to hire white women in their thirties as lower-level managers. In turn, they hired people who fit into what their idea of a staff team was.

We looked at fear and distrust as illnesses to be treated rather than as functional adaptations to the environments most of the kids came from. Our job was to remake these kids in our own image and then send them back into the world they had come from. Really, I used to ask myself, what else could we do if we did not want them to return to prison? Make them more adept at committing acts of violence? Teach them how not to get caught the next time they do a burglary?

From the beginning I had doubts about what I was doing, at least relative to gang kids. The violence they visited on one another was terrible. But the gangs also offered a sense of belonging and a path to esteem and possibly wealth that was otherwise denied these kids, their disillusionment notwithstanding. If you were successful in persuading a kid to give up gang life, what would you give him to replace it? Crime has always been an alternative route to power and prosperity in America. Without the gang, what would these kids have? Some could make something of their lives without it, but what about the others?

What we did best, I thought, and still think, was simply to remove these kids from their environment and put them in a place where they had a chance to grow up without someone trying to kill them. In a just world, every child would have the opportunity to reach maturity without fear of being killed or brutalized, but that would be another world.

Prior to my coming to Ash Meadow, I had viewed the major events of my life as connected to international or national events: war or social change. All of my children had been born during the Viet Nam era, the last during my years as an activist in the War Against Poverty. My marriage encompassed the years from the early part of the war to its end. Though I had not gone to the war in the Persian Gulf, as I had the one in Viet Nam, I had been on active duty then and helped prepare others to go. I regarded the individual and the family both as victims and as tools of those who promoted their own large-scale agendas.

But as I continued in my job, year after year, I adopted a smaller view. I concentrated on the individual child, still seeing him and his family as at the mercy of powerful forces, but also as actors with volition. A kid could play a role selected for him by people he may not even know, but he could also refuse the role, if he had the strength. He could leave the gang, go to school regularly, suffer boredom, get a legitimate job when he was old enough. These things were possible, if he was strong enough. If, before, I saw the individual essentially as victim, I learned to see him also as determining his own fate, at least sometimes. At least some kids.

Over the years, and especially after I went to work in maximum security, I became more sympathetic, or at least I found myself showing more sympathy to residents, and I gained a reputation among them for being "understanding." I do not know why this should have happened. Perhaps I came to appreciate the fact that kids are limited, more than adults, not only in their options for action, but in their abilities. In max, too, we always had some kids who more properly should have been in a mental health unit.

This book is taken from the journal I've kept since shortly before the Gulf War of 1991. I keep a journal only when I am troubled or need help thinking something through. I journaled during my time in the War Against Poverty, and again when I did anthropological fieldwork. My current journal extends throughout my entire career at Ash Meadow.

Every resident's name and every staff member's name, except my own, has been changed. Many place names have also been changed. I have used other techniques as well to aid in disguising personal identities. In a few instances, I combined minor figures, some of those who appear only once or twice, to make a composite. Two persons portrayed from my life outside of prison are also composites. I used composites for purposes of efficiency only.

Every incident depicted in this book was taken from life. Yet every incident passed through the filter of my mind and pen. Some things, if I was not troubled or intrigued by them, or if something else claimed prior attention, were not recorded. Another journaler, witnessing or participating in the same events, would have had different interests and these would have shown themselves in what he chose to put to paper. I found some things so distressing that, though one of the purposes of my journal was to reduce the level of stress I lived under, I was unable to write about them.

At certain points, the journal reads as if it was written not for myself but for a future reader. In a sense this is true, but I knew the identity of that reader: it was me. I included particular details because I suspected that without them I would later come to doubt something happened that did happen. I had already had that experience. As a soldier in Viet Nam, I did something so outrageous, so unlike the person I later came to believe I was, that I think I would have forgotten it or denied that I could have done it, had I not written about it.

There is something uncanny in the journal, in the way life's themes sometimes converge. During one period I had two boys on my caseload, both of whom had suffered head injuries as small children, both of whom experienced black-outs when very angry, and both of whom had learning disabilities related to the way they processed auditory information. Later I dealt with two kids at the same time who had each been involved with retaliation against a rapist. Then others who feared they had HIV.

I don't have an explanation for these convergences, except to speculate that by becoming sensitive to one kid's dilemma, I was able more easily to detect the same dilemma in others.

The reader should know certain things about me. My academic training was in history and anthropology. Although I received a PhD in the latter, I never afterward worked in academia, never applied for a college or university position. I know this about myself: I distrust authority, and while I do well at the edges of a hierarchy, I am not meant to be an integral part of it.

I own and operate a small literary press and have run it for twenty-five years at this writing. I have written several books of fiction, nonfiction, and poetry. I fought in Viet Nam and, as I indicated earlier, was on active duty during the build-up to the first American war in the Persian Gulf. I was an unpaid organizer in the War Against Poverty.

As a child living in Los Angeles in the late 1950s, I had some exposure to youth violence and gangs. While I wasn't in a gang, I knew of them and knew kids who joined with others to do burglaries or robberies or to defend themselves against bigger kids or to beat up other kids.

Most of my experience of violence, at least the most intense part of that experience, has come from my participation in war. Since my return from

Viet Nam, I have been interested in the emotional and psychological impact of violence and how this plays out later in life.

Some of my history has directly affected my understanding of what I saw and experienced at Ash Meadow, some indirectly. I do not think my literary activities had much to do with Ash Meadow, but the reader should know of them in order to make sense of some of the journal entries I have included.

A final note: Readers who like a neat wrap-up in books will not find it here. Many staff and most residents came and went in a comparatively short time. The job wasn't for everyone, and some staff left within a few years, or a few months. Kids were released and, for the most part, I did not hear of them again. In short, people arrived, you got to know something about them, and they disappeared. Seldom was there resolution to personal conflicts. Resolution is the stuff of fiction; this book is as close to the experience of life as I could make it.

Part One: Life as an Intermittent

1991

SATURDAY, FEBRUARY 16: Started work at Ash Meadow last Tuesday. Got briefed by Kathy, the Director of Personnel, who told me: "If you have a conflict with a superior, you'll lose."

Well, that's good to know. Actually, she wasn't being antagonistic. She was simply informing me of one of the facts of life at Ash Meadow. But I wonder, does she say that to every new hire?

Most of last week was orientation. I spent Tuesday with Security, Wednesday and most of Thursday at Crane Cottage, a sex offender unit, and Friday at Wolf, maximum security. Tomorrow I work a six-hour shift at Wolf.

Staff styles—and kids—differ between Crane and Wolf Cottages, but one thing they, and, I assume, the entire Ash Meadow campus, have in common is a firm authoritarian structure: the counselors are *in charge* of the kids. The counselors—at least one of the two I saw in each cottage—engage in slight put-downs of the kids. This, I think, works to establish or maintain a social distance between staff and residents, as the kids here are called, at least officially.

At Crane, George, a counselor, had a verbal confrontation with Jamie Small, a resident, at the door to Jamie's room. It was loud enough for me to hear it in the living room. The issue, George told me afterward, was that Jamie had been advising other residents as if he were a counselor, and he,

George, was taking that pseudo-status away from him. Jamie had appropriated it, George said; it was not something that had been awarded him.

On returning to the living room after locking Jamie in his room, George said, "I feel good! I always feel good after a one-on-one with Jamie!"

Later in the evening another resident, Peter Mertz, had a committing offense group. A C.O. group is something like an encounter group where one kid makes a kind of public confession of the crime or crimes he committed that brought him to Ash Meadow, and the other residents and staff question him. It's done according to a prescribed formula. That is, the kid doing the group answers specific questions that another resident or a staff reads to him. Following the answer to each question, residents and staff may ask others that are not on the list. When these are exhausted, the reader goes on to the next question.

Peter admitted to having molested his younger brother and sister and, in a foster home, to having beaten the shit out of a boy his own age with the help of two other boys. The beating included injuring the victim's genitals. Peter had held the victim's legs so one of the other boys could rape him, but, for reasons Peter doesn't know, the boy decided not to.

Peter said he doesn't feel bad about what he did to this boy. He said doing it made him feel happy. "You know, like when you're beating somebody up, you feel happy."

For most of the other residents, happiness as a response to hurting somebody was foreign.

Peter had attempted suicide twice, once by drinking a bottle of whiskey as fast as he could, "hoping to make my heart overreact," and once by jumping off a bridge. He contemplates suicide often.

Last night, talking with Mick, one of the counselors at Wolf, I said that cottage staff were also imprisoned insofar as they had to adhere to the same authority structure as the residents.

He agreed. He said that in his case it was beneficial because he had become more responsible than he was before he came to work here. He is a Juvenile Rehabilitation Counselor 2 and has been at Ash Meadow for five years. I'd put him in his late twenties, maybe thirty.

In *The Seattle Times* is a reprinted story from the *Los Angeles Times*. An infantry battalion commander is giving his troops a pep talk, preparing them for battle. He's telling them not to fear being afraid, and tells them, from his own experience, what fear feels like, how it tastes. And then he tells them: "Not a whole lot of kids here whose dads are anesthesiologists or justices of the Supreme Court. We're the poor, black kids from the block and Hispanics from the barrio. We're just as good as the rest, because the honest thing is, that's who I want to go to war with—people like you. And you guys will do great."[1]

Reading that last line, I started to cry. I had to put the paper down.

FRIDAY, FEBRUARY 22: Worked Swan Cottage yesterday evening with Stan, a retired teacher who has been a counselor at Ash Meadow for eight years, and Bill, a young guy with experience at Woodbyrne, a sister institution, and in Iowa before that. Stan said his philosophy is not to tell the kids anything. "As far as I'm concerned, they eat, go to the bathroom, and sleep. That's all." He talks a lot harder than he is.

Bill told me that when he first came to Ash Meadow he read case files to acquaint himself with the residents. One of the kids kept asking him if he had gotten to his yet. Finally Bill, who had been reading them in alphabetical order, skipped to the S's and read this kid's.

This boy and another had paid a five-year-old for his little sister. They raped her, beat her, then kicked her and left her for dead in her yard. (She survived, at least physically.)

Bill said that after reading the file he couldn't look at the kid without remembering what he had done.

I told Bill that I had known a woman who had been gang-raped, then had one of the rapists murdered. The county attorney had refused to prosecute her.

"Maybe there's some justice after all," Bill said.

He said he didn't like working with sex offenders because he knew they would get out and do the same type of crime again. A burglar getting out and committing more burglaries is one thing; someone who rapes children is another. Bill said he didn't want to feel so hopeless. This sense that rehabilitation does not work seems to be pervasive among the staff at Ash Meadow.[2]

SATURDAY, FEBRUARY 23: The ground war—Desert Storm—began today. Almost unbelievable that it is happening. All those people. All that suffering.

Earlier today I read Peter Matthiessen's "The Blue Pearl of Siberia" in the *New York Review of Books*. He talks about the hundreds of thousands of seals in Lake Baikal that were killed for meat, fur, and blubber, and says the slaughter continues at a rate of 6,000 a year.[3] What struck me was not outrage at the killing of all those animals, such that they are approaching extinction, but the use of numbers to represent . . . what? The life experience of each and every one of them? You feel outrage from a distance; terror is what you feel when the killing is upon you; horror—hopefully—when you witness it. Numbers are what you use to distance yourself even from outrage.

War is planned and conducted by administrators, military and civilian, who manage numbers, not at all concerned with the lives those numbers represent, unless one of them is a son or a son-in-law or a brother. But, as that battalion commander last week noted, you don't find the children of Supreme Court justices in the infantry.

THURSDAY, FEBRUARY 28: Ceasefire in effect in the Persian Gulf as of midnight last night.

SUNDAY, MARCH 3: Played racquetball today with Tim Silver. Talked about the Gulf War. He made the point that our beating the Iraqis does not mean we have the ability to impose our will anywhere in the world. We had a much tougher time in Panama. In Kuwait and Iraq we did not face any urban fighting, the Iraqis were poorly led, and their army apparently had been broken by the war with Iran. In Viet Nam, the NVA and VC had a cause, a program, and leaders who were superior to ours.

I said I could not have guessed the amount of damage the bombing would do to the Iraqi army. The NVA soldier we interrogated at Plei Me said he had been through two B52 strikes on his way down from the North. He had been afraid, but he noted that his unit had taken hardly any casualties from them. The Iraqis took such terrible casualties because they were stationary and we knew where they were.

Tim said he was once within 800 meters of a B52 strike in the Hobo Woods. He looked up and he saw the bombs falling and he didn't know where they would hit.

THURSDAY, MARCH 14: Worked Swan Cottage with Mike Collins. I said, "These kids are not here to get their just desserts, they're here to learn to live under adult authority." I actually used the expression "just desserts." Mike agreed.

Swan is one of the cottages that gets older boys. There are three gangs represented here: Bloods, Crips, and Sureños. The Bloods and Crips are from Seattle and Tacoma, respectively, and the Sureños are from Yakima and Tri-Cities.

SATURDAY, MARCH 16: Played racquetball with Tim this morning. I told him about the eleven-year-old who is in Ash Meadow for having raped several little girls. The boy himself had been raped by his father, who is in prison now—he had raped all of his children.

Raquel, one of the staff in Goldfish Cottage, where the boy is housed, told me he had written a note to her, handing it to her himself instead of leaving it for her to find, in which he detailed what he would like to do to her sexually. The other staff were angry and wanted to punish him. (Actually, they would have said "consequence" him, the word used as a euphemism for punish or punishment.) But Raquel understood that the boy was trying to tell her he loved her—she's old enough to be his grandmother, and is maternal in her interactions with the kids—and that he was saying the only things he knew that would express what he felt. These were probably what his father had said to him in order to rationalize his abuse, and the boy had believed that they were a part of love.

"And you enjoy that?" Tim asked, alluding to the work I do at Ash Meadow.

"I'm fascinated by it."

"Isn't that the same thing? I couldn't do that kind of work." Then he said, "You still think you can make a difference."

This was an allusion to a number of discussions we've had about the futility of trying to make people into something they don't want to be. I denied his accusation—it did come across as an accusation—but Tim didn't believe me, and deep, deep down I knew he had hit the nail on the head.

TUESDAY, MARCH 26: White kids make up almost all the sex offenders. Why is that? Carol Ripito says that, unlike other kids doing crimes, sex offenders don't get caught in the act by a policeman. The police or CPS is called by a family member or a neighbor. And while white families will give up their children to the authorities, non-whites don't trust the legal system enough to turn their children over to it.

Another observation: below the age of, say, thirteen or fourteen, almost all of the kids at Ash Meadow are white. Age fourteen and over, the kids are disproportionately African American, Hispanic, and Native American—disproportionate to their numbers in the general population of Washington.

SUNDAY, MARCH 31: I told Tim at racquetball this morning that I have a suicide watch tonight over an eleven-year-old who is very determined. "I can't believe the things we, as a species, do to ourselves," I said.

"I don't know why you can't believe it. I believe it. I don't understand it, but I believe it," Tim said. Then he said: "I can't believe you can't believe it."

MONDAY, APRIL 15: Took a couple of kids to an off-campus doctor's appointment. In the waiting room, one said he would be getting out in either August or November, his minimum/maximum release dates.[4] The other asked him how far apart those months are. "I don't know my months," he said.

WEDNESDAY, APRIL 17: About my job at Ash Meadow: As an intermittent, I do not know the kids nearly as well as the regular staff in the cottages do. I go from cottage to cottage, shift by shift, not really establishing roots in any of them. Unlike regular staff—or "permanent" staff, as they are called—I am not briefed on what is going on in the cottage. While I read the log, most information is passed on verbally at shift change. At shift change, if intermittents are present, we are generally ignored. We are usually not even introduced to other staff by those who know us. Yet we are expected to perform as regular staff do.

Okay. Enough.

TUESDAY, MAY 7: Watched a tape of ABC's *Eye of the Storm* in the Wolf classroom. Wolf and Andromeda Cottages, maximum security and mental health, respectively, have their own classrooms, satellites of the main school on upper campus. Each has two classrooms side by side in a single building about the size of a doublewide trailer. This building is at one end of a fenced, asphalted, recreation yard, and is separate from the cottage.

Eye of the Storm is a documentary, made in 1970, about a third grade class's introduction to discrimination, in this case, discrimination based on eye color. The point of the exercise was to have the students experience at least some of the effects of discrimination and to highlight discrimination's irrational foundation as well as how damaging it is. All of the third grade students were white.

After the video, during a discussion of what the long-term results of the exercise might be, Hollis, a black kid, said the third-graders would be racists when they grew up anyway.

Going back up to the cottage for lunch, another kid called me a "white bastard."

SATURDAY, MAY 11: Worked Wolf today. A kid went off on the floor and we—the two regular staff, an intermittent named John, and I—put him in the isolation cell located beside the staff office. It's called a "quiet room," perhaps sardonically. It's made of concrete and steel and is anything but quiet when a kid is going off in it.

He isn't a big kid and he wasn't trying to hit anybody, but he was yelling and posturing and he resisted going into the cell. He kept yelling, "You're messin' with Albert! This is Albert you're messin' with!"

I shouted at him over his yelling: "Albert! Is this getting you what you want?"

He actually went still for a few seconds, as though he was considering what I'd said, but then went back to yelling and kicking.

"I guess it is," I said.

Dennis, one of the regular staff, laughed. I had Albert by the back of the neck and Dennis was trying to wrap up his legs. The others were handcuffing him. I'd guess his age at twelve or thirteen.

TUESDAY, MAY 14: Wolf again. I was watching two kids clean up the kitchen after lunch when one kid punched the other. I pressed my panic alarm and ran into the kitchen. The kids were grappling, trying to position themselves to get a punch in, and I wrapped an arm around each of their necks and sat down, pulling them to the floor with me. Robert, one of the regular staff, came in and grabbed the larger one and led him off to the quiet room. I sat with the other one on the floor until they were gone. I had my arm across his chest and could feel his heart racing like a high-speed engine.

Dennis told me later that this kid has a heart problem and is expected to die before he reaches adulthood unless he has surgery, which his father will not authorize. Nevertheless, he's constantly antagonizing other kids. This time, the kid he pissed off is a kid with organic brain damage, one of the more impulsive kids in a cottage filled with impulsive kids, but also one of the most likable. I noticed a scar on his scalp when I took him down. Dennis said it was from a beating his mother gave him, possibly the origin of the brain injury.

FRIDAY, MAY 24: Worked Swan tonight. Wolf's alarm went off and I ran over, leaving Stan alone with the Swan kids. Bob and another staff from Goldfish were already there, along with three guys from Security, by the time I arrived. It was Albert again, screaming as he was being placed in the quiet room, "You're messin' with Albert! This is Albert!"—the same thing he was yelling a couple of weeks ago when John and I and the two permanent staff put him in.

Back at Swan, Jimmy Jackson started yelling as he vacuumed the living room carpet after supper, "The Lord is stupid! He's stupid!" A new kid, Eamon, was offended.

The argument began during dinner when Jimmy said he didn't believe in God because God had never done anything for him. Eamon pointed out that Jimmy was denying God, not disbelieving in Him. So Jimmy started throwing insults at God.

SATURDAY, MAY 25: Here's some background on Albert, the kid at Wolf who goes off so much. When he was six months old he fell out of a window and was in a coma for several months. According to the medical diagnostic in his file, his later behaviors are "typical of closed system injuries." However, his mother had been using cocaine when she was pregnant with him, and this, too, may be at the root of his behavior. He is Ash Meadow's first crack baby; we are expecting more as kids born of mothers who used crack in the Eighties get older. Also, his mother has been in and out of a number of mental hospitals for reasons unknown to us, so there may be yet another component to Albert's behavior.

He has been raised by his mother and grandmother, who reinforce his idea that he is society's victim. He is black and poor, certainly, but it is not in his best interest to dwell on it. He blames other people for his behavior: "See, Dennis, what she made me do!" he shouted when, angry at another staff, he broke the teeth out of his pick and threw them around his room.

Once I told him to go inside from the recreation yard after he hit Hollis in the eye during a basketball game. He started yelling about the other kids not playing by the rules, but I wouldn't be distracted. Guido, another staff, came out of the cottage to assist me. Albert told him: "I want to hit you, Guido. I'd like to hit you. And him!" Pointing at me. "I want to kick his ass!"

He takes up so much of staff's time, and he is so disruptive, that he dominates the cottage. He belongs in Andromeda, and in fact was there, but was transferred to Wolf because he is unpredictably violent.

I find it very difficult to write about him. The problem—my problem—is that I find him so hateful. But as obnoxious as he is, his head injury, presumably the cause of his behavior—or his mother's addiction, or his genetic make-up—is not something he brought on himself. Yet, as much as I might want to sympathize with him, I see him as too dangerous for me to risk this kind of emotion on.

Because of him, Nels Nelson, Joe Brown, Ronnie Berry, Arthur Manning, and Theodore Patterson—six of the sixteen residents in Wolf, all six of whom have assaulted staff here or in county detention—Wolf staff have good reason to be paranoid. Just yesterday an intermittent found a weapon, two nails protruding from either side of the plastic shell from a ballpoint pen, in Nels Nelson's room. Nels said he got it from Joe Brown. Today Dennis showed me another, this one with only one nail extruding.

Wolf uses two intermittents now on swing shift instead of the one they're authorized, an indication that both staff and the administration see the situation in the cottage as, if not critical, at least dangerous enough to justify paying extra staff.

The paranoia at Wolf affects both regular staff and intermittents. A couple of weeks ago I worked an afternoon with Dennis and Shirley. Shirley and I were watching the floor while Dennis was talking with one of the kids in the staff office. Shirley and I watched the kids and they watched us. Shirley and I looked at each other. Although she was a permanent staff, she had little more experience than I had. I wished Dennis was on the floor. I hadn't realized how much I relied on him. The atmosphere on the floor was so tense that it seemed as though we were all, kids and staff, connected by invisible wires—pluck one and everybody would go into immediate and violent action. I thought that if I turned away for a second, the kids would be all over me or all over each other. I could see fear on Shirley's face too. We cleared the floor.

The kids went to their rooms, seemingly surprised by what we were doing. Some were laughing. I knew even before we got them locked in that we had made a mistake, that whatever Shirley and I thought was about to happen was not going to. We had invented a fantasy and believed it was real.

Nobody is armed here except some of the kids . Not even Security staff carry a weapon. You have to rely on knowledge—knowing something about fighting and how the body can move under duress—and size, though some kids will have size on you. Generally, two or more staff will team together to handle a kid, but this does not always happen. It *should*: it allows the kid to save face when he's taken down and, because his pride is intact, he may not struggle so hard. Also, because he's outnumbered, he may prefer to avoid a physical confrontation.

If a situation looks like it's about to escalate into something physical, or if it is already physical, staff will clear the floor. That is, one of the staff will yell, "Clear the floor!" Kids are supposed to run to their rooms, close their doors behind them and sit on their beds until staff tell them that the situation is normal again. Almost always, kids will go to their rooms as they should. Then one staff goes around, locking the residents' doors, while the other two staff deal with the kid who is the problem.

Sometimes a situation will demand that all staff remain on the floor. For example, they may have two kids who are a problem on the floor at the same time. Or they may want to box one kid in without touching him, and so they'll work together, adjusting their positions relative to the resident, to try to persuade him to go to his room or to submit to going into the quiet room. But generally the rule is two staff on one kid and the third staff locking the other kids in.

An exception occurred last Wednesday. I was working Wolf with Dennis and Cherry, another permanent staff. Lunch was over, the work details had been done, and the kids were in their rooms waiting to be brought out for the start of the afternoon session of school. All three of us staff were on the floor when Dennis decided to go into Zone 2 to talk with Arthur Manning. Cherry went into the staff office to get a cup of coffee.

From where I was by the staff desk, I could see Dennis leaning against the wall opposite Arthur's door. I could not see the door but I did see a trapezoid of sunlight on the floor in front of Dennis, so I knew the door was open. I looked away and when I looked back, Dennis was gone. There was no sound. Cherry came out of the office and I told her Dennis had been swallowed up by Zone 2. She said she would see what was going on and she walked nonchalantly into the zone. She disappeared, apparently into Arthur's room, then reappeared and walked with the same seeming nonchalance toward me. She had a small, odd smile on her face. She said, "I think you'd better go down there."

I ran into the zone ahead of her. Arthur was on his stomach on his bed. Dennis was straddling his back, his knees pressed against Arthur's ribs, his hands doing something, I couldn't figure out what, with Arthur's head. Arthur's arms were free and he was struggling, but because Dennis was sitting on his back I couldn't get Arthur's arms together to handcuff him. I grabbed his right arm and put a wrist lock on him and he stopped moving. I looked back and saw that Cherry had wrapped up his legs. It was obvious that Arthur wasn't going to go anywhere we didn't want him to go.

Dennis asked Arthur if he was ready to go to the quiet room and he said yes, but when I eased the pressure on his wrist, he tried to break loose. I applied it again, and again he was still. This time he agreed to allow us to handcuff him and to take him to the quiet room. We cuffed him and though he resisted walking to the quiet room, he was being more of a nuisance than a danger and we dragged him along until he agreed to walk. I think it was fun for him.

Afterward I asked Dennis what he had been trying to do with Arthur's head. He said, "I figured if I could control his head, I could control his body." He seemed absolutely convinced of this so I didn't say anything. It had begun when Arthur tried to push his way past him when they were talking and Dennis pushed him back into his room and wound up grappling with him so that he couldn't get a hand free to press his body alarm. It was a good thing I noticed his disappearance.

SATURDAY, JUNE 1: Rough night at Wolf. Guido, Dennis, John, and I were on. Robbie Kelso was in our quiet room when we started the shift, but was soon moved to Central Isolation, relinquishing his spot to Kurt Prince when Kurt went off in his room. He and Albert and Ronnie Berry all went off at the same time, yelling and pounding on and kicking their doors. We sent Albert and Ronnie to Central immediately, then sent Kurt to Fox when he wouldn't stop banging on the quiet room door. It's often a good idea to put a kid in another cottage's quiet room. Deprived of the opportunity to perform for his own cottage mates, he'll usually calm down faster.

Robbie is out of it. He was singing a song about being insane that he'd apparently made up. One of the other kids says Robbie's crazy.

Dennis found a handmade knife, a "shank," on the kitchen floor. We locked everybody down, then searched every kid for weapons. We made each one strip, then searched his clothes and his room with a metal detector. Didn't find any more.

My own feeling about the strip search is that, with the metal detector, it wasn't necessary, and it degraded the kids. But maybe that was the point. Staff were afraid and angry and needed to feel that they (we) were in control.

Something happens in Wolf that seems not to happen in other cottages, at least not as much: kids will shit or piss in their rooms, apparently to retaliate against staff for a perceived injustice. Robbie does this, but for reasons we don't understand.

FRIDAY, JUNE 7: In Fox there is a fourteen-year-old sadist. A partial transcript of his interrogation by a detective is in his file. The detective asks the kid why he took so much more time with one little girl than with the other children he'd molested. "Because she took so long to cry," the boy says.

I looked through the window in his door as he slept surrounded by five stuffed bears of various sizes.

WEDNESDAY, JUNE 12: Worked swing shift at Bull Cottage. Saw a sixteen-year-old sucking his thumb. He's big and, at first glance, seemed composed, sure of himself. But when he went to bed his thumb went straight into his mouth.

SATURDAY, JUNE 15: Martin Hill, a boy at Swan, asked me if I was married. I said no, but I had been. He asked if I had any sons. (Interesting that he didn't ask about daughters. He asked specifically about sons.)

I said two.

He asked their ages and then asked if I saw them.

I said yes.

"That's good," he said.

I told Gigi about some of the kids at Wolf shitting and pissing in their rooms. She said adult prisoners will also do this. She used to work at Monroe.

SUNDAY, JUNE 16: Teasing, I believe, is used to assert dominance. Having worked at Wolf through a very rough time, I find that I tease the kids there, and in other cottages, almost constantly now. It's a kind of aggression.

WEDNESDAY, JUNE 19: Worked Swan again. Travis, one of the residents, punched the window in his room a couple of days ago, breaking it and cutting his hand. He was complaining today that his hand still hurt. He thought he might have a piece of glass in it. Will, another resident, said, "Let me see it."

I thought he was going to look for the glass; I'm sure Travis thought so too. Instead, Will squeezed his hand, hard, even after Travis told him to stop. Will apologized, but he was laughing as he was making his apology.

After lunch I took some kids out in front of the cottage to shoot hoops. Suddenly Louie sat down on the big cedar stump near the driveway.

"I'm in jail," he said.

I laughed. "Where did you think you were?"

"I just realized it. I can't leave if I want to."

He was really upset. He asked to go back in the cottage and I unlocked the door and let him in.

Bill—not Will the resident, but Bill the staff—told me later that Louie is serving a five-year sentence for first-degree robbery. It's his second offense.

FRIDAY, JUNE 21: At Swan Cottage today:

Eamon: "How do you know this isn't a dream? How do you know this isn't somebody else's dream?"

Travis: "Dream? This is a nightmare. This is God's nightmare."

Jimmy (dancing around, feigning punches): "Punch him in the chest. He'll know if it's a dream or not."

Eamon has only one lung. He's also very effeminate and doesn't deny being homosexual, making him an easy target for several of the other boys, including Jimmy.

SATURDAY, JUNE 22: I had several of the Swan kids out in front of the cottage, shooting hoops, tossing a football, enjoying the sun. Dusty Trudow was telling how he had robbed the Seven-Eleven or Circle K or whatever it was. Although his tone was jocular, he went into such detail in his description of the crime that his listeners, me included, were bored to the point of walking away. But when he said his gun was not loaded, Martin and Travis perked up. Travis told him he was stupid, and Martin asked, "What would you have done if the police had come?" as if it would have been better to shoot it out with the police than to give himself up. Dusty was caught because he was video-taped by a store camera.

Later, as we were about to go back inside, Ben Green told me he was in Ash Meadow for having shot someone from another gang. When the kid was lying on the ground he went over to him, shot him again, and spat on him.

"I don't know why I did that," Ben said.

I asked if the kid had died.

"Nuh uh."

"You were lucky."

He said he knew and he said again, "I don't know why I did that. Why I shot him or why I spit on him. I wasn't even mad at him."

He'll be getting out within the next couple of months. He's got to be wondering what his life is going to be like.

THURSDAY, JUNE 27: At Wolf this evening, Albert asked for a book to read in his room. The library is in the staff office at the far end of the aisle leading to the bathroom. I brought out several paperbacks, but Albert said he'd already read those. I took him into the office and had him look at the books himself. Something made me turn around, and when I did, Tatyana, a large, very aggressive girl, was standing behind me. She said Cherry had sent her in to ask me for some Tylenol. So I had Albert on one side of me and Tatyana on the other in a very narrow aisle, and now Tatyana decided that she wanted to look at the books too. I was trying to get both kids out of the office, raising my voice, when Cherry appeared at the door and helped me herd them out. She was laughing, and when I stepped out of the office I saw Guido laughing, too. They had sent Tatyana in knowing that I already had my hands full with Albert. It was a joke, but I was pissed. Two of the most volatile kids in the cottage. I'm still angry as I write this.

FRIDAY, JUNE 28: Worked swing shift at Swan. The kids were down by nine-thirty. At ten-thirty Stan and I were checking on kids and giving head calls when I shined my flashlight in Tussant Fisher's room. He was standing by his window. I asked him if he needed a head call. He said no, and I went on to the next room. Then he called me back. "Shine the light on me." I did, and he started doing a little dance like something you would see a chorus line do in a 1930s movie, singing, "I'm in the spotlight now!"

Cracked me up. I told Stan about it. He said Tussant's elevator doesn't go all the way to the top floor. That cracked me up too.

SATURDAY, JULY 6: Worked fourteen hours in Wolf yesterday. Albert asked to talk with me and I spent nearly an hour with him at the door to his room. He goes home to his mother on the twenty-seventh. He's worried that he'll swear at home—he says he never swore until he came to Ash Meadow—and that he won't be able to control his temper and that he'll slam things down or throw things. He says he never did those things before either, although, he pointed out, he is here for an assault. "I hurt somebody bad," he said.

This hateful little thirteen-year-old with all these anxieties, working so hard to please (who? His mother? Us?), now that he's getting out. It's a completely different view of him from the one I've had.

SUNDAY, JULY 7: Joe Brown at Wolf asked me to bring him something to read yesterday, something about black people. I went to The Magus today and picked up a collection of stories by James Baldwin.

Joe and Albert find it hard to believe that I don't have a TV, that I prefer to read. Joe said he didn't know what he would do without a TV.

MONDAY, JULY 8: There is something symbiotic in the relations between residents and staff. They learn what each other's buttons are and how to push them. Either side can escalate and force the other to escalate. Either side, if given the opportunity, and having the inclination, can back away, so that *usually* the other will back off too.

TUESDAY, JULY 9: When somebody asks me what I do for a living, I answer, "I work in a prison for short people."

WEDNESDAY, JULY 10: Worked Swan last night. Martin Hill, Louis—the kid who three weeks ago began to comprehend that he's in prison—and a third kid, Donnie Dorset, whom I don't know very well, went AWOL while at the gym with John Loring, a Swan swing-shift staff. I stayed back with Gigi and John joined the search crew.

THURSDAY, JULY 11: The AWOLs were caught at three-thirty this morning as they were walking into town, about eight miles west of Ash Meadow. John Loring spotted them and called the police and our own Security staff. The search was called off at two a.m., but John had continued on his own.

Louis was transferred to Elk Grove, a sister institution, later this morning. Martin and Donnie were transferred to Wolf.

Speaking of Wolf, I'd been hearing rumors from the kids that Tatyana slapped Cherry. I asked one of the Security guys about it. He said it was true. Tatyana's been in Central Isolation, at her own request, for the last three days. I suppose she's afraid of retaliation by Wolf staff, or maybe some of the kids who have attached themselves to staff.

THURSDAY, JULY 18: Worked Wolf, seven to three. Albert, doing laps with the other kids during P.E., ran ahead of Tatyana, lowered his shorts and underwear, and mooned her. She broke out laughing. I thought it was funny too, but I made him go inside. He became belligerent, at one point punching me on my hip. He had warned me not to touch him, and I hadn't, but I did move in close to him and he may have punched me out of fear. Shirley thought he was just being aggressive. Dan Fried, the P.E. teacher, and I finally got him into his room.

MONDAY, JULY 22: Worked Wolf again, three to eleven. Albert, instead of going to his room at his bedtime, began walking around the cottage, "wandering," as we call it. At one point he went into the staff office but came back out when I rushed in behind him. When he came out, Cherry grabbed him and I moved in on her right. He was trying to twist away from her, but also to stay away from me. We finally got him into his room; I pushed him in and Cherry closed and locked his door.

We got off shift at the same time. Walking out to the parking lot, I said, "Sometimes I just hate coming to work."

"So do I," Cherry said.

That surprised me. I hadn't realized Albert had the same effect on her.

THURSDAY, AUGUST 1: Called Tim Silver to see if he wanted to play racquetball this weekend. We haven't played since May. I called him once in June, but he said his back was bothering him. Same thing today, but it isn't his back. It's his wife. The last time I saw him we went to his place for a cup of coffee after we played. She quizzed me about Ash Meadow; she seemed angry with me for working there.

SATURDAY, OCTOBER 5: Talked with Royal Jones at Dolphin Cottage this evening. I met him at Wolf when he first came to Ash Meadow. He's a Crip, here because of his involvement in a drive-by shooting.

He was talking with some other kids in the living room about the money to be made from selling drugs. I reminded him of a conversation he and I had in Wolf last spring. I had pointed out, and he had agreed, that his love for his mother was in conflict with his loyalty to his gang. (She wanted him to stop gangbanging.)

He took a different tack from the one he took six or seven months ago. He acknowledged that the conflict in his emotions existed, but he said now that his mother is white and doesn't understand what gangs are, that they are like family. But she's beginning to understand, he said.

I said maybe she already understood, and maybe that's what makes her unhappy: she sees her son choosing a different family from the one she wants to be to him.

Anyway, Royal said, it would be hard for him to work for three or four dollars an hour, knowing he could be making a thousand or two thousand a day from selling crack. He said he had never sold crack to a pregnant woman though.

"What?" I said.

"I never sold crack to a pregnant woman," he said again.

"Do you ask every woman you sell to if she's pregnant?"

He didn't answer.

"You don't know who you're selling it to because you don't know what becomes of it after you sell it. Maybe the guy you sell it to shares it with his wife or girlfriend."

"We never thought of that," a kid sitting beside him said. But Royal didn't say anything.

SATURDAY, OCTOBER 26: Took some kids from Swan to the back field to play soccer against some kids from Fox. Cherry brought over the Fox contingent. I had forgotten that she'd transferred to Fox. We were standing together, watching the game, and she said, "Sometimes I forget they're just kids. And then I see them playing and I find myself enjoying seeing them having fun. And then I think, 'He raped his sister.'"

MONDAY, OCTOBER 28: Talked at length with a kid at Wolf. He was released from Ash Meadow only a week ago, violated his parole, and is back. He's a predatory sex offender. He's back because he tried to rape another boy in a public restroom. He may be transferred to Monroe, he said.

He and his girlfriend have a child and he wants to help raise it, but he's afraid now that he will not get to. He said he just can't control himself. Once a month he'll be overwhelmed by the desire to assault someone—I assume he meant sexually assault—and everything they taught him at Fox just doesn't work when he feels this way. He can feel it coming on, every month, and it's just too strong for him. He prays to God to stop it but it just keeps happening. He believes God has abandoned him because he is evil.

The boy was crying. I told him I didn't know what to say that would help him. He said that was okay, and thanked me for listening to him. When I stood up he was still crying.

Dennis had been listening to us. Later, after the kids were locked in their rooms and we had a chance to talk, he told me that he's pretty sure the kid will be transferred to an adult facility: if not Monroe, then another one. He's being held at Wolf until somebody decides what to do with him.

He asked me if I'd noticed an unusual smell in Zone 2. I said I had and that the kids in that zone were complaining about it. Dennis said it was body odor and that it came from this boy. He was clean; he showered every day. But he had this terrific odor. Not always though, not consistently, only sometimes.

SATURDAY, NOVEMBER 9: Doug Little and I took the Swan kids to the swimming pool this morning. Afterward, leaving the pool, one of the kids, Richard Quiroga, tried to close the sliding glass door opening to the outside on me. I let Doug know, but he dismissed it as my faulty perception. (I'm only an intermittent, after all.)

After lunch I took some kids out in front of the cottage to shoot hoops. Ready to go back inside, I turned my back on them to unlock the door. When I turned around again, Richard was standing behind me, his fists clenched, so angry he was shaking.

"You've got to be kidding," I said. I opened the door and he went inside, followed by the others. Writing this now, I remember how silent they all were. In fact, it was the silence I sensed behind me that caused me to turn around before I'd opened the door. I think now that if I had delayed Richard may have hit me from behind, believing I would not know who had done it.

After we went inside, Richard got Doug's attention and they went into the staff office while I watched the floor. When Richard came out of the office he stopped and faced me and then punched the glass window behind me, his fist going past my shoulder. The punch was clearly intended to miss me, but was also intended to frighten me. Doug shouted, "Clear the floor!" and all the kids scattered to their rooms. He followed Richard into the zone and locked him in. He told me afterward that Richard would be transferred to Wolf for that, "that" being his attempt to intimidate staff. I have to say that I felt vindicated when Richard punched the window.

Gigi came in at three. After hearing about Richard, whom she likes, she told me that when he was small, his father would punish him by putting him in a bathtub full of scalding water. On another day I might have sympathized with Richard, but today I said only, "So what?"

SUNDAY, DECEMBER 1: Worked a day shift at Andromeda with Lollie and Kris, two permanent staff. We talked about a girl who had been at Whale Cottage and has since gone on to a group home. She's attending college now. I remember her, a small, dark-haired woman. I say "woman" rather than girl because she was already nineteen or twenty when I met her and was much more mature, in her thinking and expression, the way she carried herself, the way she responded to other people, than any of the other residents at Ash Meadow that I've met.

She was at Ash Meadow for having murdered her father. He came into the kitchen one morning and she shot him. She always said she didn't know why she did it. I believe she really did not know.

Kris and Lollie said she had been neither physically nor sexually abused, but they believed she had been emotionally abused by her father, although there is no evidence to indicate he had mistreated her. Kris said she mentioned the girl's father to her once and she could tell by her expression that she was still terrified of him. It was obvious that both Kris and Lollie are fond of her—they said so—and were trying to excuse the murder by saying she had reason to kill her father. I like the young woman too, and I hope she gets good things for herself, but let's not blame her father for his own murder.

I think I can generalize here. If staff like a kid, they will either suspend moral judgment on him (or her) or look for a way to excuse the offense. For example, they'll say the kid is a victim of society—Michael Collins at Swan Cottage uses this one—or of a dysfunctional family, as Kris and Lollie believe, in this case. If staff do not like the kid, they will see the kid as hopeless, beyond rehabilitation, and deserving of even more punishment than he or she is getting.

Daniel Mallon murdered a man because the man "looked funny" at him and Daniel was carrying a gun. Daniel can be charming. He is popular with his teachers and with staff. They recognize that he has worked hard to change his behavior so that it is less aggressive—at least it appears to be less aggressive. When Daniel is charming, I wish him well. But I have seen another side of him: aggression in the guise of competitiveness. This includes not only outplaying an opponent in football, basketball, ping-pong, or whatever, but in humiliating him afterward by rubbing his victory in his opponent's face. While other boys in Swan do this too, I detect a kind of malice in Daniel that transcends what I see in the others.

When I see Daniel in his cruel mode, I have doubts that his charm is sincere. But when I am charmed by him, I do not doubt his sincerity. In short, when I like him, I wish him well; when I do not like him, I do not wish him well, and, in fact, feel he deserves worse than he has gotten so far.

1992–1993

For almost two years I hardly wrote in my journal. Perhaps enough of the novelty of Ash Meadow had worn off that I did not feel I needed a journal to help me make sense of what I saw. But I do retain a number of memories of that period.

I was working a day shift with Security and we got a call to go to Wolf. When we went into the cottage, Dennis was swearing and kicking a trash can across the living room. I asked what was going on and Mick said, "Nothing. Dennis is just going off."

Dennis had just hurt a kid. The boy had been hurt before: he'd had his collar bone broken when Security took him down and one of the Security staff fell on top of him. The boy had a pin holding the bone together and it stuck out like a misplaced tack through his skin. It had a dull metallic sheen, like tarnished aluminum. He liked to show it to people he hadn't already shown it to. This time, in taking him to the floor, Dennis had twisted the boy's torso; when we arrived the boy was handcuffed and crying, not from rage but from pain.

We all liked him. He was a mental health case who would have been in Andromeda had there been a bed for him. He was not mean, and was often amusing. Once when he was in Wolf's quiet room he yelled out to the other kids: "Don't let them brainwash you! They're trying to brainwash you! If you let them, they'll brainwash you!" and laughed in an affected, maniacal way.

Of all the kids in the cottage, he was probably the only one who had heard of brainwashing, though certainly the others understood that staff pressed them to think differently, to behave differently.

Eamon, the boy who wondered if we weren't all living in a dream, got out and went to New Jersey to live. He would call Swan occasionally to talk with Stan, his former case manager. He said he was going to Princeton, and maybe he was. Stan had liked him and so had I, but one of the staff who worked in Swan when Eamon was there was homophobic, and Eamon had suffered emotionally because of him.

Again working Security, I once picked up a very small ten-year-old from Social Services where he had just processed in. Walking out to the van for the ride down to Goldfish, he looked up at me and asked in a tiny voice: "Are you mean?"

Early in August 1992 I was bringing the Swan kids back to the cottage from school. I was the only staff, and I was at the rear of the line of kids. I had a radio in my right hand. One of the boys, Brendan, was talking to me, but I was focused on the fifteen boys walking ahead, watching for movement that would signal a threat or the start of a fight, so I wasn't paying attention to him. Another boy, Ezekiah, dropped back, said a word or two, then fell in beside Brendan.

I told Ezekiah to walk ahead of me where he belonged. He started to argue about my allowing Brendan to walk with me, but not him, and then Brendan snatched the radio out of my hand and ran. I thought he was trying to make a joke and had crossed the line separating fun from something else, and I yelled at him. He turned, and when I saw his face I knew he was not joking.

I shouted to the rest of the kids to get down to the cottage fast, and then I saw Ezekiah running after Brendan. But as Brendan continued on up the road, Ezekiah ducked into the woods. Another boy ran over to him and tried to talk him into coming out, telling him he was making it hard for everybody else.

I unlocked the door to the cottage and herded kids inside, including the one who had tried to talk Ezekiah into coming back. Mike Collins, the other staff on duty, had seen Brendan run and was already on the radio to Security. We locked all of the kids in their rooms and monitored the radio. Ten minutes later Ezekiah returned to the cottage escorted by Carol Ripito and Herman Boats, the cottage director.

Brendan had run to the end of the road and into the small lake east of the campus. The water was too shallow to swim and the bottom was thick with silt. Plowing his way through the thigh-deep muck, he was moving slowly enough that one of the Security staff decided to go in after him—an act for which, for years afterward, he was known as "Swampman." Swampman gaining on him, Brendan crawled out of the water on the far side where one of the Recreation staff was waiting. Brendan lunged for him and tried to strangle him, but he was exhausted and easily held down until Swampman arrived and handcuffed him.

Brendan spent a couple of months in Wolf, then returned to Swan, until he again ran away. This time he was gone for three days, although he apparently never left the grounds. Instead, he hid in the woods during the day and came out at night to collect food that kids from other cottages would pass to him from their bedroom windows. When he was caught he was sent to Elk Grove, which was, at least by reputation, a harder place to do time.

I was working a graveyard shift in Whale and had the radio on. Suddenly the duty nurse's voice came over: "Panic alarm in Bull! Panic alarm in Bull!" I could hear the high squeal of the alarm as it came over the speaker in the health center, then the two Security staff talking as they raced their vans to Bull. Then I didn't hear any more.

After I got off shift I stopped by the Security office. The Security guys were congratulating Ronnie, the young woman who had been working Bull. They were hugging her, patting her back and shoulders, and telling her how courageous she had been, how proud they were of her. She was beaming.

Doing her rounds that night, checking each room, she had discovered a boy hanging by a sheet from his window latch. Although staff are told during orientation that they are not to enter a kid's room when alone, even if they see an apparent suicide, Ronnie hit her body alarm and went in. She held the unconscious boy up, relieving the pressure on his neck, until Security arrived to cut him down and give him CPR. She was a hero, a real one.

As I recall this a decade and a half later, I remember admiring her and feeling happy for her happiness and her discovery that she could perform well under duress, but I felt nothing for the boy she had saved. To me, he was an abstraction.

Two years before, a boy—I'll call him John—had killed himself using a similar method. The coroner determined that it was an accident. John probably wanted only to achieve semi-consciousness by cutting off the oxygen to his brain. This was something kids did, using a variety of things—sheets, towels, clothing—to half-strangle themselves for a quick high. But he vomited, and unable to get air, panicked and ran toward the door, perhaps to bang on it to attract help. The shoelaces he had tied around his neck caught him, and he fell back and down, breaking his neck.

I had been working at Ash Meadow only a few months then, and felt nothing about his death. I felt bad for the staff on duty at the time. I knew all three and liked them all. Dick Teale, John's case manager, was the man who originally suggested that I apply for work at Ash Meadow.

I did not know John, and like the boy who tried to kill himself two years later, he was, for me, an abstraction. I emphasize this because a few years later everything had changed. But in 1991 and again in 1993, neither John nor the other boy found their way into my journal.

One young woman did make her way in.

TUESDAY, OCTOBER 20 (1992): Last night I worked eleven to seven at Whale. At about six this morning a young woman called. She gave her name as Sharon Ruykeyser. She said she was calling from Yakima. She asked to speak with Paul or Chip or Joan. She had been a resident in Whale in 1986 and '87 and she wanted to talk with someone she knew. She asked if Paul or Joan or Mark were working, apparently recalling the schedule from five years ago. When I told her that no one had come in yet, her voice dropped and I could feel her sadness through the wire. I asked if she was all right.

She was not. She had shot up three-quarters of a gram of heroin last night. Her body had jerked while she was still shooting; she thought she probably would have died if her body had not jerked. This was her first time with heroin.

She's a crack and powder cocaine addict. She weighs less than a hundred pounds now, she said. She's five feet five inches tall and she weighs ninety-six pounds. She had an interview at an International House of Pancakes and the manager said he would call but he hasn't. She's sure it's because he could tell by looking at her that she's a crack addict. She might be able to get work as a barmaid, but she doesn't want to be a barmaid again. She used to bring in fifty dollars a night just in tips but she doesn't want to be a barmaid again.

Yakima is a drug seller's heaven, she said. Crack is everywhere. If they recognize you as an addict, dealers will offer it to you anywhere—just going out for a pack of cigarettes, in the store, in the parking lot, everywhere. She had just moved there from Spokane and the move was one of the worst mistakes of her life.

The doctor at the hospital where she was taken for the overdose told her that in his opinion it was not too late to save her. He didn't mean only from the heroin, but from crack too. But she knew she had to save herself, that nobody else could save her.

She's twenty-three now. She was released from Ash Meadow in 1987 when she was eighteen. She had her second child while at Ash Meadow. She took the rap for her boyfriend because he had prior convictions. He assaulted someone during a robbery and she took the rap for him.

She asked if Paul or Mark had come in yet. I told her I didn't know either of them. She said Mark was short, had a red beard and looked like Abraham Lincoln. Paul was the kind of guy where you could be throwing furniture around and screaming, and afterward he would say, "I hear you. And I love you."

She said she doesn't want to be a bad mother but when she works as a barmaid she tries to sleep in the morning and the kids get up and she's always yelling at them, "Be quiet! Mommy's trying to sleep! Be quiet!" and this is why she doesn't want to work as a barmaid. Although now she's so thin she doesn't think anybody would hire her anyway.

She's afraid of dying—the heroin frightened her—and she feels very, very ashamed of how she's neglecting her children. Since she returned from the hospital last night she's been vomiting up whatever she eats. "There's puke all over the house."

She'd lifted weights when she was in Eagle Cottage where she'd spent three months working on her drug problem. She and some boys would work out in the weight room at the gym while the other kids played basketball. One of the staff said it was inappropriate for her to be working out with the boys in a room by themselves because she was the only girl there. So Paul opened weight training to all of the girls. But Sharon was the only one who wanted to lift weights. As it shook out, she and one boy worked out with weights while the others played basketball. "Basketball was big," she said.

"It still is," I said.

"Is it?" She laughed. I think she was glad that something had remained the same.

She wondered again why she had shot up with heroin when cocaine was her drug. It finally occurred to me that she had tried to kill herself. She took the heroin *because* it was not her drug.

At six-forty, Caroline, one of the regular staff, came in. I wrote out on a bit of scratch paper that I was talking to a potential suicide in Yakima, and would she please call a social worker to go over to this woman's house. (It did not occur to me that social workers would not be available at six or seven in the morning or that they would not be the people to handle this kind of affair anyway.)

I asked Sharon if she would mind if I sent a social worker over to talk with her. She said that would be good but how would I do that unless I left the phone I was talking to her on. She was afraid of my leaving her even for a minute. I told her another staff, Caroline, had come in and she would call on another phone while I stayed here. Sharon said she didn't know Caroline. I asked her to tell me her address. I wrote it down and passed it to Caroline.

We continued talking. She got sick again and excused herself and threw up while I stayed on the line. We had just started talking again when she said someone was at the door. She asked me if I could hear him banging. I said I could and that she should answer it. Only a second had passed when I heard from a distance, "Hey! It's a cop!" Then she was on the phone. "You said you were going to send a social worker, but it's a cop!" I could hear him pounding on the door and shouting, "Mrs. Ruykeyser? All you all right? I'm here to help you!"

"Sharon," I said, "I don't know why they sent a cop. I thought they were going to send a social worker. But listen to him. He's only trying to help you. If you don't like him, then don't open the door."

"All right. I'll listen. I'll be right back."

The banging stopped. I heard her talking with the cop, then she was back on the phone.

"It's all right. He seems nice. I let him in."

I heard his voice as he came nearer.

"He seems really nice," she said again. "I'm going to go now. Thanks for talking to me. Or letting me talk to you."

She hung up.

It was a little past seven now. Another staff had come in and I was able to leave. Before I left, I filled Caroline in on what had happened before she arrived. When I told her that I had been afraid that Sharon would kill herself, Caroline said the real danger was that she would kill her children, believing that she was sparing them the suffering that the world would inevitably cause them.

Walking out to my car I saw Carol Ripito and stopped to talk with her. I told her about Sharon. Carol remembered her. Paul left Ash Meadow several years ago, she said. She agreed with Caroline that the greater danger was to Sharon's children.

I went home and went to bed and I did not get out of bed for two days except to use the bathroom and to call in sick for a shift I was scheduled to work.

Three days before Sharon's call I had seen a robin alight among four or five crows on the tarmacked surface of the parking lot in front of my apartment. Immediately the crow nearest it struck it twice on the head with its beak. Then a second crow hit it and the robin's legs collapsed and the two crows alternately hammered it until long after it was dead. The other crows had moved off and had been joined by still others who had descended from the cottonwood and the cedars at the edge of the parking lot and seemed content to observe. But when one of the robin's legs separated from the body, a third crow joined the first two in eviscerating the dead bird.

The memory of this coupled with my thinking on Sharon and I saw her in the robin's situation. By misjudgment or by circumstance, she had landed in the wrong situation and she was going to die while the rest of us watched.

On Thursday I realized I was hungry and I got up and ate something. It was around noon. I was functioning again.

Part Two: Swan

1993

In August 1993 I began work at Swan Cottage as a full-time, permanent employee, a Juvenile Rehabilitation Counselor 2, or JRC2. I had been on the hiring register for several months, but had had to wait until a white male veteran had left—two had just retired—before I could be hired. I worked swing shift and had Thursdays and Fridays off. My duties included managing a caseload of up to five residents, interacting with and monitoring all of the kids in the cottage (twenty-three when I started there), conducting treatment groups, acting as a surrogate parent, breaking up fights, and innumerable other things that were considered necessary for case management or the functioning of the cottage. As a rule, I worked with one other staff, either Stan MacEvoy or Rob Gorey. Gigi had left for a job in parole and Bill had gotten a cottage director's slot in another institution.

On my first night I had my back turned to the residents while I made a phone call for a kid. I heard, or felt, something and spun around to see two boys slugging each other in the middle of the living room. I shouted "Clear the floor!" and caught one of them as the kids ran to their rooms and Rob came out of the office where he had been talking with a boy on his caseload.

I told the boy I'd caught to sit down, and I stood over him while Rob locked the other kids in. When he got back, the boy, Jonas, told us that the other kid had come up to him when he saw my back was turned and said, "Who's for blue [the color associated with Crips]?" Jonas stood up, saying "I am," and they went at it as the rest of the cottage watched.

Rob and I talked to a couple of the other kids and they corroborated what Jonas told us. We gave Jonas and his antagonist twenty-four hours OP. Jonas did not object, but Beanie, the other boy, did. He denied he'd fought Jonas and said he hadn't seen anybody fight.

FRIDAY, OCTOBER 29: At PC Tuesday, Herman told me to create a treatment group to be called "Alternatives to Violence." He said it can be anything I want it to be, and I can do anything I want to do in it, though I have to run it by him before starting it. He told Sara Willey to come up with a cottage Youth Group, distinct from campus Youth Group, but modeled on it.

Sara and I had questions that Herman wouldn't answer, telling us to work it out ourselves. Herman is clearly not good with the specifics of a thing. He probably knows this. He has something in mind though, a goal of some sort. It sounds to me like there may be some political maneuvering involved at the administrative level.

Sara, I'm guessing from the tenor of her questions, doesn't want to do Youth Group. And I? I couldn't stop my mind from racing. My idea is to explore the role of violence in these kids' lives, the violence they've done and the violence that has been done to them.

SUNDAY, NOVEMBER 21: Cottage student elections! And what a fine time we had! For president, Reggie Greene versus J.P. Prince—eight to five in favor of Reggie. But wait! There's also a vote for Michael Jackson. That makes fourteen votes with thirteen kids voting. But wait again! Tony Hunter says he didn't vote! That makes fourteen votes with twelve kids voting.

I toss out the election. It has to be done over. I tell the kids that if this happens again, there will be no more student government. The second time around, J.P. gets seven votes, Reggie six! Several of the gang members are stunned—J.P. has no gang affiliation. Reggie says, "Hey, man, I was supposed to win." I shrug. I think of Tammany Hall and the Chicago political machine.

To students' complaints—Bernie Higham, Beanie's brother, doesn't like secret ballots; Tony and Reggie both say Reggie should have won—I say, "Consider this a lesson in democracy. This is how it's done when you vote for president."

Vicente says they're all felons, they won't be able to vote. I respond with: "If you're clean as adults, your records as juveniles will be sealed. Or do you intend to do crimes as adults?"

To which Beanie tells me to stay out of his personal business.

WEDNESDAY, DECEMBER 1: Yesterday Bernie got a major bust—up to twenty-four hours OP, loss of level and the privileges that go with it, his room stripped of everything but his essential clothing and bedclothes—for fighting at school.

The day before, Vicente got one for provoking a fight, according to the incident report. Vicente said a kid named Michael, from Dolphin Cottage, asked him how he tagged his gang's initials. Vicente showed him: VxCxVx, using small x's instead of periods. Michael asked him why he had crossed out the C (the C, in Michael's mind, apparently, standing for Crip). Vicente said he hadn't, but Michael said he was going to cross out the V, thereby signifying that Vicente should be killed. This is just talk, as Vicente knows. Nobody is going to kill him, not, at least, while he is at Ash Meadow.

After class, Michael and Louie, also from Dolphin, went up to Vicente and gave him some shit about crossing out the C. Vicente shoved Louie away from him. This was seen by a teacher and Vicente got a major bust. Okay.

So yesterday, in class, Bernie throws a pencil across the room, goes to pick it up, and knocks Louie's hat off. This results in the fight that got Bernie his major bust. It should be noted that Bernie and his brother Beanie are Vicente's co-offenders—that is, all three were convicted of committing the same crime, first-degree assault. They are also in the same set.

Back in the cottage, John Loring decides it is not a good idea to have three residents who are co-offenders and in the same set living in the same zone, and he informs Bernie that he has to move to Zone 1. Bernie says he's not going to. John and Rob Gorey march Bernie through the cottage and put him in Zone 1, Room 2. After a while Rob notices the letters VCV on Room 2's window. They are made with blue tape. Rob says Bernie is not supposed to have blue tape, as he is in a stripped room. Rob calls Security and asks them to search Bernie. Security comes over—Dennis, who used to work at Wolf, and Newt Smith, who started working at Ash Meadow only this year—and they open the door. Bernie hands over what remains of the roll of tape, and they tell him they're going to strip search him because they don't trust him not to be hiding more tape.

I was not present for most of what occurred afterward. I left the room because I didn't want to embarrass Bernie further by my presence. But I went by twice to see if they needed additional help. The first time, Bernie was standing with his back to the wall, facing Dennis and Newt. Rob stood away, by the door. Dennis was telling Bernie that he had the choice of voluntarily stripping or of getting stripped by them. Dennis said, "Come on, Bernie," almost pleading with him. Bernie was afraid; you could see the moisture in his eyes and in the set of his mouth. But he shook his head no. I left.

A couple of minutes later, Sara shouted "Clear the floor!" I repeated the call and she and I locked the kids in their rooms. Then I went back down to Room 2. Bernie was struggling. Dennis and Rob held him belly-down on his mattress while Newt pulled off Bernie's pants and underpants. If this were an adult prison and these men convicts, I would have thought I was witnessing a rape. Bernie was trying not to cry, but blubbering nonetheless. Sara walked in and Newt screamed at her, "Get out of here!" and she turned and left.

It was terrible. Bernie was humiliated, and Dennis and Newt understood his sense of being degraded and hated their role in it. Dennis said, as they were stripping him, "We don't like to do this, but it's our job."

I went back out to the living room to wait with Sara. Soon the three men came out of the zone. Dennis came over to me and said something again about hating it, but it was his job. I told him that he and Newt did fine, trying to imply that they shouldn't hold this against themselves.

Dennis said, "Well, at least we know he doesn't have any more tape."

"He'll tell his friends that it took three of you to hold him down," I said.

"That makes it a win-win situation."

After Dennis and Newt left, Rob and Sara and I sat on the ping-pong table. (It's made of plywood and rests on top of the billiard table.) Rob said it was beyond him why somebody would refuse to strip when it was obvious we had the ability to overpower him.

Later Bernie marked up his wall with writing extolling the glories of his gang. Neither Rob nor Sara nor I suggested we take the pencil from him.

At dusk I turned on the light in his room. He asked me to turn it off, and I did. When I checked on him a half-hour later, I found that he had concealed himself in the large shelf space beside his door. I told him I couldn't see him and he showed his arm in the beam of my flashlight. From then on I would shine the light into his room through the window in his door and he would flash his arm or his leg.

WEDNESDAY, DECEMBER 8: Peter Chaple told me that his mother used to beat him and his sister and his brother with a wooden paddle. "Like a short oar, but heavier," he said. This was about a year ago when his sister was twelve or thirteen and his brother was five. His sister moved out into the streets where she felt safer, Peter said. He has since lost track of her. They were both sexually abused by their stepfather. He said his stepfather made him watch while he raped her.

He's afraid his mother will continue to beat his little brother. At this point I told him that I am required to tell Herman what he, Peter, told me about himself and his brother and sister having been abused, and that Herman might have to inform CPS. Peter went very still, his face becoming wood.

I asked him why he was upset. Because, he said, he was afraid his brother would "get lost in DSHS," just as he had, and Peter would never see him again. He would rather his brother remain at home. When I asked if he thought his brother may have been sexually abused too, he said no, because his brother's father—that is, Peter's stepfather—really loves him.

TUESDAY, DECEMBER 14: As other kids were beginning their after-dinner details, Peter Chaple sat down at a table in the dining room with a plate of food, announcing that it was his third helping. He appeared happy. I told him dinner was over, but he just kept eating and smiling up at me and talking conversationally, as though I hadn't said anything. I told him three or four more times that dinner was over, but he ignored me and continued to eat. He told me how much weight he had gained since coming to Ash Meadow and grabbed some flab around his middle and laughed.

I asked, "How many demerits do you want?"

"Four," he said. "Give me four."

I cleared the floor. Rob locked the other kids in while I stayed with Peter. Then Rob came over to the table and I explained what was going on. Rob told Peter that dinner was over. He said this several times just as I had.

Finally Peter said he would take his supper to his room. He started to stand up, holding his plate. Rob snatched it out of his hands. Peter tried to get the plate back and Rob put him in a double hammerlock. He got Peter into the living room and folded him over the back of one of the stuffed chairs so I could get his shoes off before putting him in the quiet room, a precaution against residents' using the laces to hang themselves, or stuffing a shoe into the toilet to flood the room. Peter was screaming. As I started to pull his shoes off, he tried to kick me and I crossed one leg over the other and pressed down and removed one shoe. Then I reversed his legs and pressed down again and took off the other shoe. Then I called Security. Candace answered the call but said Security was involved with something somewhere else.

Peter was still screaming and struggling to get loose from the hold Rob had him in. I told Rob we should put Peter in the quiet room ourselves. We did, with Peter trying to break loose all the way to the cell.

By now his screams were incoherent. At first, when Rob bent him over the chair, he was just yelling and swearing at us, normal, everyday stuff, what you would expect when you've overpowered a kid and he knows that all he's got left is his voice. But now he was hysterical. He continued to swear at us but the rest of what he was saying was gibberish, words in any order, making no sense at all, and sounds that weren't words.

In the quiet room we had trouble getting him onto his stomach and keeping him there long enough for us to get out and close the door. Finally I slipped out and Rob came rushing out behind me. I closed and bolted the door. Peter was still screaming, focused now on Rob, yelling at him to "Get out! Get out of here! Get out!" He kept on, saying he would kill Rob as soon as he got the chance.

Rob said, "Okay. I'm going, Peter. Look. I'm leaving the office. Calm down." And we went out into the living room. And Security arrived.

After work I met Gigi for coffee. We've been getting together occasionally for coffee or a movie. I told her what happened with Peter. She asked, Why didn't we let Peter take his dinner to his room in exchange for a minor bust?

Good question. I got a little defensive, but she was right. It hadn't occurred to me. It would have meant our relinquishing control of the situation, but really, except for the time we were holding Peter down, we weren't in control. Actually, I'm talking about dominance, not control. Or control through dominance.

TUESDAY, DECEMBER 21: Only today did it occur to me that Peter Chaple probably associated Rob's bending him over the chair last Tuesday with his stepfather's raping him.

1994

WEDNESDAY, JANUARY 5: Sara and I showed a tape of a Maury Povich show on gang violence to the cottage. Povich had Bill Cosby on as a guest. The show was apparently taped during the last presidential campaign. Cosby got into an argument with a young man I took to be a youth worker: Cosby wanted people to vote, and the youth worker said that voting was not worth his or anybody's time. Of course, underlying the idea of voting is the idea of being part of society, or committing oneself to becoming part of it.

The young man was adamant that voting doesn't matter because one politician is like another; none can be trusted to do what they promised during the campaign. I don't think he saw things in terms of social commitment or an obligation to society, or the absence of these. I think he simply did not see any relationship between gangs on the one hand, and the abstraction called society on the other. What he saw was people, politicians who have their own interests, interests that do not include doing anything to alleviate the social and economic conditions that promote gang violence. Maybe that's what he saw; maybe there's too much of myself in that last sentence.

Anyway, after we watched the tape I broached the idea of voting with the kids. Those who responded at all, three or four of the twenty we have in the cottage, said there isn't much sense in it; anybody you voted into office would serve only himself anyway. They assume that all politicians are so corrupt as to want only to enrich themselves, and to hell with everybody else.

SATURDAY, JANUARY 8: Got a new kid, Tommy Whitacre, on my caseload. He's in for residential burglary. He's fourteen. I talked with him for only a few minutes today. I told him my goals for him were: 1. After he left Ash Meadow he wouldn't do any harm to anyone else, and 2. he would live his life in such a way that no harm would come to him. He said he understood.

I told him that he is safe here, that nobody is going to shank him or beat him up. I could see his body relax when I said this, and he smiled for the first time. He's a skinny kid, but sinewy; he might lose a fight, but he'll do some damage.

Then I told him that if anybody does assault him, he is to tell staff. His face became wary again, and the tension returned to his body so that the slump he had allowed himself disappeared and he sat erect. He had no questions, and I had no more time to talk with him.

TUESDAY, JANUARY 11: I told Terry MacArthur that he is the most impulsive kid I've ever met. He said, "I don't consider myself impulsive. I just make decisions faster than other people."

I told John Loring what Terry said. John said, "That's the kind of thing that makes it worth coming to work."

WEDNESDAY, JANUARY 12: A "sherm" is a marijuana joint or a tobacco cigarette soaked in formaldehyde, allowed to dry, then smoked. It's called a sherm because "it hits you like a Sherman tank." It makes a person feel more powerful, "like you can do anything."

SUNDAY, JANUARY 30: Tommy Whitacre was angry but wanted me to coax him into telling me why. He was angry with himself, he said, because he was trying for his Level One last week but got a minor bust, thereby ruining his chance to get his level, at least this week. He feels he let the cottage down by remaining on CR, because they want to have a social next Friday and Herman said that everybody had to be off CR before they could have it. I told him he would probably make his level on Tuesday unless he screws up again.

Tommy used both drugs and alcohol frequently before he was locked up. He says he also huffed gas. His mother is a recovering alcoholic. His brother, ten years older than he, uses various drugs; Tommy used to be his supplier. His sister doesn't use anything.

Tommy says he did all of his crimes after having ingested drugs. He doesn't think about doing a crime until he is messed up. (But all of his leisure time on the outs was spent drugging or drinking, so he must have thought about doing crimes a lot.) He believes that his brain does not work like other people's. He spaces out and hallucinates. When he's bored and not doing anything, he sees "tracers," secondary images of people as they walk by, out of the corner of his eye. He says he has blackouts and believes these are related to his alcohol and drug use. He would like help in dealing with his drug-and-alcohol problem.

FRIDAY, FEBRUARY 4: We are asking these gang kids to be more courageous than we should reasonably expect them to be, more than any adult I know would be. We are asking them to break with their support networks on the outside, or to be agents for change among them.

Imagine an environment in which every person, those you know and those you don't, is or may be a threat, in which every person you meet is capable of killing you and may want to. Except for your homies. (What does that remind you of? Viet Nam during our war there. At least my experience in Viet Nam.)

Given that environment, which is the one these gang kids come from, I submit that they have adapted well to it, or they would not have lived to be fifteen years old. That environment is not going to change any time soon, and we send kids back out into it all the time. We try to soften them, to get them to separate themselves from the only people who will help them stay alive. Maybe what we should be doing is teaching them how to be better killers, fine-tune their adaptation to the world they live in.

Grant Williams runs Youth Group, a campus group composed of gang kids from various cottages. The primary purpose of the group is to intervene in conflicts that would set one gang against another. Youth Group owes its existence to a gang fight at the school last year. The secondary purpose of the group is to learn to use skills other than threat, intimidation, and violence to accomplish what they want to accomplish.

A kid Grant was close to—call him James—was paroled last year. He was home a few days when another kid came to his house and told him so-and-so was looking for him to settle a problem they'd had before James went to prison. So-and-so was at a gas station now, waiting for him. James went to the gas station to try to convince his old enemy that he wanted no trouble, that they could work their problem out through negotiation. As a sign of good faith, he went to the gas station unarmed. His enemy shot him in the heart.

Grant says he wonders all the time if he made a mistake with James. If he had not taught him to resist his impulse for violence, James might be alive still (though he might have killed his enemy, I would add).

SATURDAY, FEBRUARY 5: Danny Beck—a really sweet kid, thoughtful, considerate, a nice kid to have around—told me that when he gets angry enough, he does a drive-by. But he has to be very angry. He doesn't have to be angry at the person he shoots at, he just has to be angry. Shooting somebody, at least shooting at somebody, relieves this anger. Vicente told me the same thing: what relieves his anger is not actually shooting someone, but shooting at him, and sometimes not even shooting at someone, but just shooting.

I just reread the first sentence of the last paragraph. It reads like sarcasm, when you consider the remainder of the paragraph. But I didn't mean it as sarcasm. He really is a sweet kid.

SATURDAY, FEBRUARY 19: At the gym this morning, Tommy Whitacre had a problem with another kid. I don't know what the problem was, but it led somehow to Tommy's threatening a staff.

Tommy says he remembers everything leading up to the threat but doesn't remember making it. He thinks, though, that he did it, because staff say he did.

He says he's had blackouts before. Both his mother and his sister have told him he hit them, and he's been told that he hit other people too. He says he has no memory of any of this.

I want to point out that when Tommy told me about the burglary, his committing offense, he admitted to a lot more than he was charged with. So I don't think he's into denying responsibility for what he does. Also, when small, he was severely beaten more than once by his stepfather. On one occasion, the beating included a pistol-whipping. On another, he was knocked unconscious when his stepfather hit him with a two-by-four. I reported all of this to the medical staff.

SUNDAY, FEBRUARY 27: At dinner I saw Charlie Lewis turned around in his seat in the dining room so that he was facing the table behind him. I asked him which table he was sitting at.

"I was just blowing my nose," he said.

"You turned around to blow your nose at someone else's table?"

"It's rude to blow your nose at your own table."

MONDAY, FEBRUARY 28: Tommy filled me in on the events leading to his arrest. A day or two earlier, he and a friend had been walking when a kid pulled up, got out of the car, aimed a gun at Tommy and said he was going to kill him. Tommy was hungover from a night of huffing gas and just started walking toward the guy, not caring if the guy shot him or not. The guy again threatened to shoot him and Tommy told him to do it, he didn't care.

But then his friend jumped the guy and together they beat the shit out of him. Tommy hit him in the head with a rock and they took his gun.

Later that day or the next, a carload of kids drew up beside Tommy and his friend and got out of the car. Tommy had the .22 he had taken in the burglary—this is the burglary for which he was convicted—and began to fire, letting off thirty-two rounds at them, though not hitting anyone. They ran without shooting back. (I asked him what they were doing while he reloaded; the .22 could not have held thirty-two rounds. He said they ran but left their car. After they had gone he shot it full of holes.)

Still later, he was firing the same gun out of his apartment window into a vacant lot when the police came. They found the gun, traced it to the burglary, and Tommy was charged. He was shooting into the lot because it made him feel good.

His sister was arrested a couple of weeks ago for possession of four ounces of marijuana. She spent a night in jail. Although Tommy had supplied his brother with drugs, he had protected her from them when he was on the outside. He feels he can't protect her now.

This evening Stan, standing at the back door, said: "Listen." It was the frogs from the small lake behind us. It was the first time this year that we heard them. "It's spring," Stan said.

SATURDAY, MARCH 5: Tommy says he's always angry—every day. There is always something or somebody to make him angry. He's afraid that someone will disrespect him enough that he will assault him. He ruminates about getting back at people who have disrespected him.

I asked if he got pleasure from his anger. He does. He said that when he wants to fight, he'll goad his opponent into hitting him so he can go wild. He likes to get hit because it releases this wildness. Afterward, he says, he feels good.

TUESDAY, MARCH 8: Tommy stopped going to school when he was in the fourth grade because gang kids would chase him and sometimes beat him up on his way to school. Once they caught him and dropped a rock on his head. He has a scar from this. He has other, smaller, scars on his forehead from another beating he took.

We talked a little about the old-style gangs and how gangs have changed and how they haven't. I was surprised that he'd heard of the White Fences of East L.A., zip guns, switchblades, and the other accoutrements of 1950s and early '60s gangs. His first stepfather told him about all of this. His stepfather had dealt drugs with the White Fences and the Hell's Angels.

WEDNESDAY, MARCH 9: Did a Life Story with Michael Fuentes. He's in for Assault 2. He threatened to stab another kid, and did shoot him in the shoulder with a BB gun.

He's done worse. He shot someone in a drive-by, though he did not kill him. He did it in retaliation for a drive-by that boy's set did on Michael's set.

Michael said that, if he loses a fight or if it's inconclusive, that night or the next day or soon he will look for the kid he fought, and if he has a gun, he will come up behind the kid and put the gun to his head as a warning. If he does not have a gun, he will come up behind the kid with a baseball bat and hit him in the head with it and beat him unconscious. He has done some very bloody work this way. He does this to get respect, "to teach him not to mess with me." But he does not like to think about these things, he said. In fact, he looked upset, even ill, when he talked about them to me.

What he does think about is the possibility of someone getting back at him by harming his family. "I think about it all the time."

He says, though, "When I get mad, I'll go crazy. I'll just blank out." This does not happen every time he gets angry, but it does happen sometimes. He was like this even in elementary school. (Another one!? Another kid who has blackouts? How likely is it that I would get two on my caseload at the same time?)

Michael said he can predict the future during a blackout. He'll have episodes of headaches first, and dizziness. They may be days or months apart. Each subsequent episode increases in severity until finally one will drive him unconscious. This happens only when he is sober, not when he has been drinking or using drugs. He gets blackouts from drinking too, but does not have visions then.

He knew that his father would die. During a blackout he saw his uncle coming to tell his mother that Michael's father had gone. Some time later he saw his uncle come to the house and he knew without being told that his father was dead.

While in another blackout, he saw his sister in a hospital room and knew that she was going to die. Months later, he and his mother visited her when she was in a coma shortly before she died, and the scene was as he had envisioned it. This was about a year and a half ago. He has had this type of blackout since he was a small child. They last, he thinks, from fifteen minutes to an hour.

He has not had a vision since the one about his sister, but he does get feelings. He knew, for example, that he would be arrested and convicted for his offense.

Michael's mother has been clean for about five years, but he remembers her and her friends going into the bathroom of his house to shoot up. He would search the bathroom for needles afterwards so he could break them. His father and his grandmother, his mother's mother, used to tell him that his mom was no good. (Immediately after saying this, he looked so hurt that I asked him how he felt. He said he wanted to cry.)

When his mother needed drugs she would go crazy, beating her children with a cooking pan or an electrical cord or whatever else was handy. Michael had once seen his father chase her with a knife after having forced his way into the house by breaking a window with his bare hands. Michael himself used to chase his sisters with a knife.

He remembers that once, after his parents had separated, his father came by with either a BB gun or a real one to scare Michael's mother so she wouldn't see other men. Michael was afraid he was going to kill her.

His father would sneak over to the house to see him sometimes when his mother wasn't home, and Michael often ran away from home so he could stay with his dad. Once they stayed at his uncle's house; once they lived in a car. Michael's father died homeless, probably from the effects of alcoholism. Michael was five or six years old the last time he saw him.

I asked Michael if he could remember a time when he felt loved by his parents. He said he felt loved when his mom got off drugs and got her children out of foster care, where they had been placed owing to her abusing them and her inability to take care of them. Michael was in four different foster homes, going from one to the next because of his violent behavior. When he and his brother and sisters returned to their mother, they didn't know each other.

His mother is a different person now, he says. She's off drugs, she has a job, she goes to church, she's calm.

I asked him if he knew he was behaving toward other people as his father had behaved towards his mother.

He asked what I meant.

I pointed out that his father had threatened his mother with a gun and he, Michael, had shot one boy in a drive-by and another boy with a BB gun.

He didn't see a connection.

I reminded him that he'd seen his father go after his mother with a knife, and that he himself had chased his sisters with a knife.

Again he denied seeing a connection.

I asked him if he'd ever broken a window with his bare hands.

He laughed and said he had, and then was silent.

I asked him if he thought he belonged at Ash Meadow.

"No one belongs here," he said.

"Where should criminals be then?"

"Kill me," he said.

"Kill you?"

"Kill them. They should be killed. They should be tortured. This is like a day camp."

SATURDAY, MARCH 13: Tommy used to sell drugs—crack, dust—to his mother. He told me once before that he supplied his mother with drugs; he hadn't told me that he sold them to her. He once considered killing her. He didn't want to tell me why when I pressed him—he was clearly upset—but finally he said he was angry with her for "always calling the police on me" because of his violence.

He said he misses the violence, even the times he was beaten up. He misses the rush. He stabbed somebody in the arm once.

I told him that it stops being fun when your friends start getting killed, and he told me that his closest friend was sitting beside him when he was killed in a drive-by. Tommy grew upset again, talking about this, and he changed the subject.

Drugs make things brighter, he said. Even so, he wants to go through the Phoenix program. He's been enjoying his good health since he's been at Ash Meadow, lifting weights, playing basketball.

He never sold drugs to children, he said. I told him he was rationalizing: children got drugs from the people he sold them to. He said that was true and admitted that he'd once given crack to a pregnant woman in exchange for sex with her daughter. But the girl wanted to have sex with him anyway, or so she told him.

FRIDAY, MARCH 25: Went with Leah [my daughter] to see a play based on Tillie Olsen's story, "I Stand Here Ironing." Waiting for it to start, I said, "A large number of kids in my cottage have tortured small animals."

Leah burst out laughing. She said she was imagining me saying this on being introduced to somebody for the first time.

MONDAY, MARCH 28: The frogs are out in force now. Tommy says they keep him awake. He puts his pillow over his head, but it does no good.

WEDNESDAY, MARCH 30: Last night the frogs were loud! LOUD!

SATURDAY, APRIL 16: Came in to work today after two weeks of training at the Juvenile Services Academy. As soon as I stepped inside the cottage, I knew something was wrong. I heard Tommy Whitacre say "Uh oh." He looked at me, forced himself to smile, then moved away to join some other kids in the living room. It was probably his reaction to seeing me that alerted me.

There were a couple of kids in the cottage that I didn't know; they had come in while I was gone. Neither seemed to take much notice of me. Thinking about it now, I realize that this in itself was odd. Usually kids check staff out when they don't know them, or haven't seen them for a while. But when I said hello, they hardly looked at me. Maybe this was bothering me, too. For the next couple of hours I continued to feel uneasy.

Right after dinner, before we started clean-up details, Tommy asked to talk with me privately. He said it was important. I took him in the staff office. He told me that he and the two new kids had been planning on going AWOL tonight. While I was at the academy, a female intermittent had worked my shift. They had thought she would be working tonight too. Their plan was to push her into the office, rip her body alarm off her neck, overpower her, take her keys, and lock her in the quiet room. Then they would let themselves out of the cottage. But then I walked in, and Tommy decided not to go through with it.

He said he didn't want to attack me. I told him I appreciated it. I wasn't being sarcastic.

He said he went to the other two and told them he wasn't going to go through with it, though they tried to convince him to. He told them he was going to inform staff.

I asked if they knew what we were talking about now. He guessed that they probably did. I looked out the office window: details seemed to be going okay. Stan was sitting on the ping-pong table at the far side of the cottage, observing.

I asked Tommy if he was worried about what these two kids might do to him for snitching. He said he wasn't worried; they weren't going to do anything.

I asked him why he wanted to run. He didn't know why. He'd thought through the plan a number of times and had concluded that they would be caught shortly after getting out of the cottage.

"What about Stan?" I asked. "What were you going to do about him?"

"I don't know. Nobody talked about him."

I felt myself staring at him. Finally he laughed and looked away.

He said he thought from the way I looked at him when I came into the cottage that I already knew about it.

I asked if he understood that he and the other two would be placed off program and put on Tables. The others would go to Wolf since they had not said anything to staff, but most likely he would not have to go to max. He said he understood.

I took him to his room and locked him in. By this time it was quiet time and all of the kids were in their rooms. I told Stan what Tommy had said. We brought the other two boys out, one at a time, and questioned them. One denied everything. The other said he would have told staff but he knew Tommy was going to do it.

I left a message on Herman's voice mail about what had happened and what Stan and I were doing about it. The rest of the evening was quiet.

In April I became co-facilitator of a treatment group called Male Survivors of Sexual Abuse, commonly known as Survivors' Group. More accurately, I began a six-month apprenticeship under Carol Ripito, who had been conducting this group for several years.

Once a week for an hour and a half, six to ten boys drawn from the various cottages gathered after school in the conference room in the Administration Building. They were recommended for the group by their case managers, then were interviewed individually by both Carol and me. During the interview we told them what would be required of them if they chose to participate in the group: very little, actually. They would have to attend meetings, but it would be their decision whether or not to confide in the other members.

The idea behind forming the group was to show how sexual victimization contributed to kids' criminal activity. Carol said she'd taken some heat over the years for doing this group. Some people, including some staff here at Ash Meadow, were offended by her treating criminals as victims. "But how did they get to be criminals?" she said. "They weren't born wanting to commit crimes."

She warned me that at some point in each twelve-week cycle the kids would ask us why we were doing this group. What they really wanted to know was whether or not we had been sexually violated, too. She told me this before our first group meeting so I would have time to prepare an answer. What she always told them, she said, was that the group was about them, not about her, and they should focus on how their experience as survivors related to their committing crimes. I told them that I was once in love with someone who had been sexually abused, and while I was not able to help her, I wanted to try to help others who were also victims—I used the word "survivors," as Carol had—of abuse.

SATURDAY, APRIL 23: Tommy says that although other kids in the cottage make fun of him when he talks about this, he's been thinking about his future and what he can do so he doesn't get involved in doing crimes again.

He says, too, that he's starting to like his life at Ash Meadow, and that scares him.

SATURDAY, APRIL 30: Tommy said: "I really fucked up some people's lives." Good. Remorse is good. John Loring said that Tommy is the kind of kid you want to take home with you and adopt. I agree.

SATURDAY, MAY 7: Bernie Higham was shipped to Elk Grove today. Why him and not another kid, I don't know. I assume it was to separate him from his brother, Beanie. I didn't particularly care for Bernie, but I didn't dislike him either. I have felt sorry for him ever since we had him strip-searched.

In return, we got a kid named Terence Starbuck. Apparently Elk Grove initiated the exchange because of Terence's (unspecified, at least to me) "mental health issues." Ash Meadow is better set up to deal with mental health problems than Elk Grove is.

SUNDAY, MAY 8: Michael Fuentes is fearful of just about everything. He uses intimidation to conceal that fear from himself and to advertise himself to others as someone to stay away from. He told me that he is not afraid of anyone on this campus. That is silly. He does not try to bully kids larger than himself, only smaller or weaker kids.

His mother has distanced herself from him, telling him he is responsible for his own decisions now. He was near tears as he related this to me.

MONDAY, MAY 9: Yesterday Michael told Terence Starbuck to give him his, Terence's, belt, or he would punch him in the mouth. Terence refused. Michael said he would shank him unless Terence gave up the belt. Terence refused again but went to his room and wouldn't come out, even for dinner. At the time I didn't know what had happened. All Terence told me at first was that he wanted to go back to Elk Grove and he would do anything to get there. "People here disrespect each other," he said.

After dinner Danny Beck told me that several kids were planning on going off. He mentioned Jonas Henson, Charlie Lewis, Michael Fuentes, and Colin Turner. While I was talking with Danny in the staff office, Colin told Stasha, the intermittent working with Stan and me, the same thing, but added that he had decided not to go off because Johnny Brunson had said he was going to tell staff.

Stasha and I compared what the kids had told us, then Stan suggested we gather the residents together in order to clear the air about the plot. We let the kids out of their rooms and brought them into the living room. I had hardly told them why they were here together when Michael began complaining about people who snitched. He looked directly at Johnny Brunson. I shouted "Clear the floor!"

On their way to their zones—Michael to Zone 2, Johnny to Zone 1—they threw words back and forth. Stan was walking behind Michael, I behind Johnny. Then Michael broke and ran over and punched Johnny. They started swinging, and both Stan and I hit our body alarms. Stan took Michael to the floor and I pulled Johnny away into the kitchen.

The fight was obviously over—they were silent rather than talking trash to each other—and Stan and I locked them in their rooms. When I came out of the zone, Security had just come through the door.

Later, when Stan and I had a chance to talk, we figured that neither kid really wanted to fight. Michael was performing for the rest of the cottage and Johnny was only defending himself. Once Stan put his hands on him, Michael seemed only too glad to be taken down, and Johnny didn't resist at all, instead assuring me that he wasn't going to do anything more.

Today Michael admitted that the idea of going off was his. He said he didn't know why he wanted to, or why he wanted other kids to go off with him. I know why: it was a test to see if he could get them to do what he wanted them to do.

WEDNESDAY, MAY 11: Michael did his apology group today for assaulting Johnny Brunson and threatening to shank Terence Starbuck. The cottage did not accept his apology. Neither kids nor staff trust him. I told him to write out a plan detailing how he intends to earn back the cottage's trust.

Michael said there were only two kids who said they would wait to see how he behaved before they would accept his apology.

Yeah, I said, but the cottage as a whole voted against him. And staff agrees with them.

Michael seems to think that if he just avoids attracting staff's attention, this whole thing will blow over. I'm certain that he wants to intimidate as many residents as he can into voting for him next time. I doubt that we'll dissuade him from wanting to punk other kids, but we may convince him that the price he has to pay for doing it is too high.

SUNDAY, MAY 15: Michael threatened to shank another resident. He doesn't even have a shank; it's the threat that counts, both to Michael and the kid he's targeting. I told him that sooner or later, if he persists in trying to intimidate other people, somebody is going to hurt him or worse. He understands this but doesn't think he can stop.

I told him to make a plan for staying out of trouble after he's released, but he seemed at a loss.

Stan says at least a couple of times a month: "These kids don't make plans. They live by accident." Lots of ways that second sentence can be taken, all of which are probably true, at least in Michael's case.

TUESDAY, MAY 17: Marie Klein, the school psychologist, says Tommy has an audio-memory disability that prevents him from hearing everything that is said. As a result he gets distorted information. I'm reluctant to put much emphasis on this. The only times I have known him to distort information have been when he is angry. In fact, he's quicker than most kids to comprehend the meaning behind what somebody is saying. I have watched for signs of distortion and questioned him from different angles to be certain he understands what has been said. I've been especially aware of the possibility of information distortion with him because I know that Michael Fuentes often does not accurately perceive what is going on around him, and Michael's and Tommy's backgrounds, even including blackouts, are so similar.

WEDNESDAY, MAY 18: Dean Savage did his Life Story with me this evening. This included an account of how his girlfriend was shot by a friend of his who was loaded on drugs and playing with a gun he said was empty.

I asked Dean if it was hard for him to talk about her. He said it was, but didn't say anything more. I waited for a second or two, then said, "Well, I'll sign your level move-up form," leaving him with his sadness. God. It was the end of my shift and I just wanted to go home. Am I tired? Raquel, at Goldfish, says cottage staff burn out after ten years. Am I already there? I certainly didn't do Dean any good.

SATURDAY, MAY 21: Tommy talked about labeling—he must have learned that word in school. He said that because people labeled him a criminal, he caught the attention of other criminals with whom he then began to associate, and this made him want to do more crimes.

"Are you saying that in order to keep from doing crimes, you have to stay away from people who do crimes?"

"Yes."

"Can we call that progress?"

He laughed. The kid has a great laugh, and he wants to please me.

SUNDAY, MAY 22: Yesterday during clean-up after supper, Peter Chaple punched a pane out of his window. J.P. Prince told Stan, who looked in on Peter and then came back to the office where I had been giving out meds and told me that Peter had indeed broken his window and was bleeding. I opened the blood-spill kit, put on the gloves, had Mike, the intermittent working with us, help me into the gown, forewent the mask and boots, and started for Peter's room with Mike tying the gown behind me as I walked. At Room 5, I motioned for Mike to hang back and then I unlocked the door.

Peter was sitting on his bed, his back against the far wall. His left arm was extended, palm up. There were fresh cuts on it. Blood was seeping from them, but not badly. He often cuts on his left arm. His right hand was pressed against the side of his neck. I thought he might have cut his neck or stabbed himself and was trying to stanch the bleeding now. I could see dried blood on his hand, but this must have been from striking the window. The right side of his head and torso were in shadow. A second or two had passed since I'd opened the door. I was still standing in the doorway. I asked Peter what was wrong, then stepped inside.

I saw now that he was holding a shard of glass against his neck, and I drew back. I was afraid that if I tried to take it from him by force, he would go ahead and cut through the muscle and the artery before I could stop him. I said, "Come on, Peter. Give it to me."

He pressed the glass hard against his neck. He was terribly frightened. His pupils were dots the size of pinpricks. He stared at me with such intensity that I thought perhaps he couldn't see me. Suddenly he made a quick downward motion with his right hand and I heard something tear. Before I could move, he put the glass to his neck again. I saw no new blood.

"Peter, I'm going to sit down over here. All right?"

He didn't respond and I sat down beside him on his bed. He was watching me. I called to Mike. "Can you give me some help here?"

I didn't know what I was going to do, but I did not want Peter to cut himself again. Then—I don't know why; I could think of nothing else to do—I grasped Peter's left hand and pressed it gently. As though he had been waiting for this specific signal, he threw the glass down on the bed. I told Mike to pick it up, then told Peter to turn his head so I could see his neck. He did. He had scraped it raw but it was not bleeding.

Then Security was there and Peter went with them. Before they left, one of them asked me if I was all right, and I nodded yes. After everybody had left I continued to sit there. Finally I forced myself to stand up and I walked out of the room.

After I got off shift I went up to Central Isolation to talk with Peter. He said he thinks of suicide all the time. Constantly. Tonight just seemed, for no particular reason, the right time to do it. He broke out his window six weeks ago, he said, and had intended to kill himself then, but staff came into his room before he could do anything.

WEDNESDAY, MAY 25: Michael Fuentes will go to Apple Park Group Home on June 1 for a month of drug and alcohol treatment. If he graduates,

Herman and I will consider releasing him when he's completed his minimum sentence.

I talked with him today. He says he's always angry, but he's not always aware that he's angry. No shit.

SUNDAY, JUNE 5: Tommy Whitacre's behavior has deteriorated over the last ten days. He's come close to fighting a number of times. He told me his older brother, Morgan, has become addicted to crack. Though Tommy sold crack, he never used it himself. He believes Morgan's girlfriend got him started because she's on it. What makes it worse is that the dealer Tommy used to sell for is the one who sells it to Morgan.

Tommy mentioned the movie *South Central.* I have not seen it. He said he identifies with the protagonist, who goes to prison for upholding his set, then is ignored or forgotten by it. The set turns his brother on to drugs in the protagonist's absence. But the latter makes something of himself while in prison, and the movie apparently has a happy ending, as American movies do.

Tommy believes it's possible to make himself over. He says he wants to be educated. He wants knowledge. But school here is boring, as it was for him on the outs. He does read novels—the mass market variety. I suggested he use the school library to gain knowledge outside of the classroom. He liked that idea. In a way, he's lucky: he knows how to read. Not every kid we get does. On the other hand, he isn't able to retain the rules of arithmetic.

I asked him why he hadn't confided in staff about his brother instead of letting it eat at him.

"You don't know how hard it is for me to say my brother's a cluck," he said.

SUNDAY, JUNE 12: When Tommy and I talked last Sunday, he told me of his concern about his brother's addiction to crack. I wrote this in the cottage log. Now several staff and teachers have urged him to talk to them about his family problems, and he doesn't want to. Plus, he feels I betrayed his trust.

I told him that I regret the consequences of putting this information in the log, but that I believe I was right in doing it. Staff had seen that his behavior had changed suddenly, but had not understood why, and I thought his learning about Morgan's addiction explained why. (I do regret having put this stuff in the log. Even as I was writing it, I felt I was betraying him. I certainly did not expect staff—and his teachers! How did they hear about it?—to hound him the way they have.)

Changing topic, in a way, Tommy said he's been trying to do well, but when he falls short of his personal goals he gets angry with himself, and then other kids begin to irritate him. He said some staff—he wouldn't tell me who—have told him they're disappointed in him for not having become a cottage leader, "as though I still couldn't get to be one."

SATURDAY, JUNE 18: Tommy had a feedback group today. Afterward, I pointed out to him the similarity between his peers' feedback and staff's loggings on him; to wit, his increased frustration at inconsequential things, his intimidating some of the other kids, the fluctuation in his behavior between acceptable and unacceptable.

He said he's afraid of the person he was on the outside. He considers the old Tommy bad, and although he tries to suppress him, he keeps resurfacing. He regards that Tommy as the real Tommy, and the Tommy he is now, the nice kid, as a fraud.

I asked him how he thought the old Tommy came into existence. He said it was what he was taught by his father (meaning his first stepfather). I told him that beneath what he calls the bad Tommy is an even older Tommy that the bad one was built on top of. Several weeks ago, Marie Klein commented to me that someone must have loved him at some time in his life, and I had mentioned this to him. Now I reminded him of what she had said.

He wished he could remember who it was, he said. Possibly it was his sister.

I said my point was that Marie saw a warmth in him that indicated he's able to love, and she thought he must have learned this by responding to someone's love for him.

He said he had no idea who it was.

WEDNESDAY, JUNE 22: Shortly before I arrived at the cottage this afternoon, Tommy had a blackout during which he grabbed Colin Turner, apparently intending to hit him. Eric Warner grabbed him from behind and pulled him away. Tommy says this is the first blackout he's had in the six months he's been in Ash Meadow. (Is this true? He reported having a blackout, or something like it, on February 19.)

This evening I got him to describe how he feels as he approaches a blackout. He says that for a couple of weeks prior, he'll have a growing sense of unease. (His behavior began to change for the worse about a month ago.)

He'll lose his appetite and become increasingly irritable. He'll get severe headaches. He'll misinterpret other people's actions, ascribing intentions to them that may not be true, so that he'll believe he's being threatened or disrespected when he may not be. He'll want to fight, though he may not have selected someone to fight with. After the blackout, he'll feel relaxed and have a sense of well-being.

He says he's had pressures on him that he hasn't had before: finding out his brother is a cluck; learning that his sister was raped last year by a member of his set (he had not told me this before); realizing that his mother is just not very stable, and that she'll never have a good job; and anxiety about going into the Phoenix program.

He says that although he feels good following a blackout, he doesn't want to have them. He'd like to make a rep for himself when he gets out so he'll be respected in a nonviolent, non-gang way.

Is he conning me? I don't think so. Grant Williams told me that Tommy has been mediating problems between rival sets on campus on his own. (Grant has been trying to persuade Tommy to join Youth Group, but Tommy has resisted.)

TUESDAY, JUNE 28: Yesterday in Survivors' Group, within Colin Turner's hearing, but not Carol's or mine, Peter Chaple insulted Colin's sister. Also, according to Colin, Peter mouthed "Fuck you" to him.

During group, Peter accused Colin and Charlie Lewis of talking about confidential stuff to kids who are not in the group. Back at the cottage after the session was over, I asked both Colin and Charlie if this was true. Both denied it. Colin thinks Peter made it up, that no one is talking out of group. This is possible. Both Carol and I, during group, asked Peter to be specific about what had been said, but Peter wouldn't, or couldn't. In my experience with Peter, he gives specifics when asked, if he knows them.

Also in group yesterday, Peter said he had molested younger children, and that he was not ashamed of having done it. As I write now, I can see the malice on Peter's face as he said this, the smirk that challenged Colin and Charlie to do something. For whatever reason, Peter wanted to hurt them.

And he did. They took Peter's admission hard. Both had considered Peter their friend and had trusted him. Colin was raped a year ago by a homie, so trust does not come easily to him. Charlie was sexually abused by a babysitter, and others, too, I'd be willing to bet, in the dozen or so foster homes he was in. He has said he gets "confused" when sex offenders talk about their offenses because he remembers seeing a friend raped in foster care. I'm inclined to think the friend Charlie says he saw was himself, and the confusion he feels is a kind of paralysis he may have experienced during his rape.

On the other hand, he sees survivors of sexual abuse as victims and feels compassion for them as such. So if a survivor is also an offender, Charlie may indeed feel confusion about where to place his sympathies. But there is no question that he was angry with Peter yesterday.

Carol believes Peter; she thinks Colin and Charlie violated the group's commitment to confidentiality. I do not believe Peter. In any event, Carol has ended the group. She said it's the first time in twenty years that she's cancelled a group, but it can't be continued unless everyone in it trusts everyone else. And that's not the case now.

WEDNESDAY, JUNE 29: Tommy told me that somebody intends to "do something" to my food. "Somebody" has observed that I leave my dinner unattended on the table while I check details, lock kids in after they've finished eating, or answer the phone. I didn't ask who Somebody is because I didn't want to put Tommy in the position of having to choose between loyalty to me and the prisoner's code of not snitching. Besides, I'm sure it's Tony Brown; I've noticed him watching me. He's angry with me because I've given him several demerits recently.

THURSDAY, JUNE 30: Last night Colin Turner was chattering behind me. I wasn't paying attention until I heard him say (about me): "Hold on, he's ignoring me. Wait till he's done ignoring me."

SATURDAY, JULY 2: Gigi told me this morning that she misses the emotional involvement of working with juveniles, although when she was at Ash Meadow she would often go home after her shift and cry.

I realized today, probably from talking with her, that what I like about working with these kids, particularly kids with gang backgrounds, is that I get to experience again some of the emotions I felt in Viet Nam, and some of the sensations.

Michael Fuentes is back after bombing out of Apple Park for "refusing treatment." He said today that he intentionally failed at Apple Park because he wanted his maximum sentence and was afraid that if he graduated he would get less. He said also that he was not comfortable with "sharing" in treatment groups, meaning he did not want to reveal things about his life or family to the other residents at Apple Park because he did not trust them not to use his disclosures against him some day.

This is a common feeling among the kids we send to the Phoenix program or Apple Park, especially the gang kids. One reason for it is that some of them have committed crimes other than those they've been convicted of, and don't want to be charged with them. A second reason is that there may be kids from rival sets in the group who will use, in one way or another, any information they can get about their enemies. Still a third reason is that gang kids' trust can be won, if at all, only over a long period of time, at least several months, and they do not spend enough time at Apple Park (one month) or in Phoenix (three months) to give over their trust. Michael said that, other than me, the only person he can talk openly to is a girl he knows from the outside who is in Peacock Cottage now.

When I told him he would get his maximum—August twenty-fourth will be his release date—he was visibly relieved. He had been afraid we would still give him his minimum, which would have put him out of Ash Meadow this Thursday. He said his girlfriend will be getting out a month before he does.

SUNDAY, JULY 10: Michael says he's had bad headaches the past few days, the kind that precede a blackout. He's also experienced some dizziness. He's especially concerned because he's had a dream three times in the last three nights of his brother being shot to death. (Remember that visions sometimes accompany his blackouts.) He called his mother after he'd had the dream a couple of times and she said his brother had been to a fortune teller, who told him that he would be killed soon.

I asked Michael if he believed it was inevitable that his brother would be killed. He said no, that he knew of another kid who had been told by a fortune teller that he could save himself by keeping a small bag of secret ingredients on his body and by giving up gang life, and he had not been killed.

I asked Michael if he would give up gang life if he believed it was the only way to save his life. First he nodded yes, then he said, "I'd try to."

I asked if he thought he could stay away from gang life after he gave it up, if he did. "They'll come after me," he said, meaning that his enemies would want to kill him even if he left his gang, and that his gang offered some protection against them.

I allowed him to call his brother tonight, to warn him.

TUESDAY, JULY 12: Michael was seen by a psychiatrist today. The psychiatrist said his headaches are caused by stress.

THURSDAY, JULY 14: When I was an adolescent I wanted to know first-hand the tragic side of life. I romanticized tragedy and fantasized about how people are changed, having experienced it, and how I would be changed, having witnessed it. Now I spend most of my conscious hours in the midst of tragedy and I wonder not if there is an end to it, for I know there is not, but how much more of it I will be able to handle.

SUNDAY, JULY 17: Tommy had been angry with his sister for not having told him earlier that she'd been raped, but she said during a phone call the other night that she did tell him, right after it happened. He does not remember this but he believes her. He thinks she may have told him during one of his blackouts.

During the same call she complained that her boyfriend had been hitting her. Tommy considered going AWOL so he could beat him up and protect her. But he realized that if he escaped, he would not be able to help her anyway, because he would be on the run.

I pointed out that, although he says he wants to avoid gang life, he still has the impulse to retaliate for what someone does to him or to someone he cares for: he wanted not only to protect his sister from her boyfriend, but also to beat him up for what he'd already done.

Tommy agreed, and said he still wants to beat him up.

I said, "I can understand, and even agree with, the idea of protecting your sister. I have a sister too. But to apply this idea to covering the back of a friend who's getting ready to fight, is part and parcel of gang mentality, as we staff call it."

He said that was so, but said, too, that it's hard to give up. He said he would feel that he was betraying his friend if he did not cover his back. Besides, staff do the same thing.

Uh oh, I thought. Here it comes.

He said, "Whenever you have a problem with a kid, you lock everybody in their rooms and then you gang up on him when he's alone. When one of you goes into a zone, another is watching. If you have to take a kid out of his room, it's never just one of you goes in, it's always two or three of you, or you call Security and they go in. You cover each other's back just like we do. You're not setting a very good example, Jerry."

"Shit," I said.

Tommy laughed. He was enjoying this.

"I can't find a way out," I said.

"There isn't one."

"Here's one. When we do it, we're not trying to hurt anybody. We're just trying to maintain control."

"But sometimes you do hurt a kid. And that's all I try to do too, is control somebody so they'll do what I want them to do."

"All right, you've got me. I need time to think about this. I'll get back to you on this one."

"Next time we talk."

"Maybe not next time, but soon."

"Next time."

He was really enjoying himself. I was glad to see him win something for once.

TUESDAY, JULY 19: I have to say that I am really surprised at, and pleased by, the difference in Michael since he went to Apple Park. He told me after he came back that he was working to change himself, but I didn't believe him until I talked with him today. He says it's because of a boy he met at Apple Park. Alex. Alex had been able to leave gang life.

Michael is convinced now that his own gang doesn't care about him, that he's just a number to them, someone to inflate their ranks. If they cared about him, he said, they would not pressure him to drink or smoke weed. But he knows they will. He knows, too, that it will be difficult to resist them. They'll say he isn't down. He's determined to resist, though he doesn't know if he'll succeed.

He needs these talks with me, he said, to alleviate his anger. He knows he uses anger to cover the anxiety he's feeling now.

When we got him back from Apple Park I didn't want to talk with him; I'd given up on him. Still, I went through the motions of conversation. But it's apparent now that he's made a tremendous gain—it shows that if you persevere, even after you've given up hope, something may come of it yet. Isn't this what courage is? To continue in the face of despair?

I told Michael that I knew it must be terribly hard for him to do what he's doing, and that I admire him for trying so hard. His face took on a shine with what I believe was happiness, the only time I've seen him happy. "Thank you," he said.

MONDAY, JULY 25: Rob said that during his drug-and-alcohol group this evening he told the kids he was afraid of reading the paper someday and learning that one of them had been killed. He started to cry and the kids responded by trying to comfort him. Listening to him, my eyes began to fill.

TUESDAY, JULY 26: Tommy refuses to be intimidated by either peers or staff, he says. He acknowledges the superiority of staff's power, but does not accept that staff or anyone else is superior to him as a person.

I told him I agreed with him, but he said that other staff, some of them, would not agree. He likes Stan though; he thinks Stan is funny.

THURSDAY, JULY 28: Last night Dean Savage asked if he could talk to me. I took him into the staff office, and he started just as soon as he sat down. He said that when he's swimming his ears ring, and this reminds him of what he heard after his girlfriend was shot. Sometimes he'll look at something inanimate and it will start moving and become his girlfriend.

The first time he told me about the night of his girlfriend's death, he thought he had loaded the gun and placed it on the couch beside him; then the other kid picked it up and shot his, Dean's, girlfriend.⁵ But now he remembers what really happened. It's coming back to him bit by bit, he said. He loaded the gun and placed it on his lap. His friend picked it up. I think the implication of the gun's being on Dean's lap is that he could have refused to let his friend take it, but didn't. An alternative theory would be that Dean himself shot his girlfriend, but he's not able to remember that part yet. He obviously feels guilty about something. Whether his guilt is related to his failure to exercise control over his gun or to something else, I don't know.

After he told me his latest version of the shooting, he told me this: several months later he needed money to buy some drugs and went with an older boy—Dean is only thirteen now—to rob a convenience store. At the store they looked at magazines until all the customers left, but just as Dean and the other boy approached the clerk another man walked in. He stayed for what Dean guessed was about an hour, reading magazines.

At this point, I thought, Uh oh, this kid's going to confess to something. I broke in on him and reminded him that if he gave me enough information about a crime to take it to the police, I was required to do that, and indeed, I would do that. I said, too, that if he told me about a murder, I would have to inform the police even if I did not have specific details on it.

Dean said he understood, but he wasn't going to confess to anything. Then he said his buddy kept telling him, "Do it," meaning Dean should go ahead and hold up the clerk, but Dean said he didn't want any witnesses. Finally Dean got angry because the man wouldn't leave. He went over to the magazine rack and shot him in the face. Afterward the man was still alive, and the older boy shot him again. Then the two of them ran without even taking any money.

I broke in again. I asked Dean if he understood that he had just confessed to what appeared to be a murder.

He looked shocked. "I did not!"

"You said you shot somebody in the face and then your buddy shot him again. It sounds to me like you probably killed him."

"He was still alive after I shot him!"

"All right," I said.

He continued. It was as if once he opened up, he couldn't stop. Later that night he went to a friend's house. She was watching the news on TV. She was crying because some boys had just shot her uncle. Dean looked at the TV screen and saw a picture of the girl's uncle. It was the man Dean had shot. Dean said to her, "I hope they get those kids."

Dean told me he feels guilty about having shot his friend's uncle. Also, the older boy was caught, and Dean is afraid the boy will implicate him. The boy is facing twenty years.

After talking with him, I went into Herman's office and briefed him on what Dean told me. Herman said if the kid is looking at twenty years, it's probably murder. He gave me the phone number of the chief of police of [the city where Dean lives]. The chief was out of town. He'll call me back when he returns.

FRIDAY, JULY 29: I told Gigi that working at Ash Meadow puts me in the same frame of mind that war did: I have a little edginess, a little meanness, a little more awareness. Brings out a little of my PTSD.

Gigi said working at Ash Meadow reminded her of her drinking days, and that's why she liked it.

SUNDAY, JULY 31: Tommy got four demerits today over petty issues that he built up into issues that were not so petty. The reason is that he's doing well—so well, in fact, that he's afraid he's fallen too much under our influence here at Ash Meadow, and therefore felt impelled to do something in order to be able to see again the boy he used to be before he came here.

He says he doesn't know who he is now, and has no feel for where he's going. He says he becomes afraid when he thinks like this, and he was never afraid before. Staff tell him to plan his life, to find something he wants to do and work toward it. But he doesn't know what he wants to do. Also, he says, sometimes he thinks that all of his effort to make himself a better person may be wasted. That is, he may become a better person, but it won't have any effect on his life. Yet he can't keep from trying to improve himself.

Fascinating kid.

MONDAY, AUGUST 1: Michael Fuentes is worried about getting out. He'll be released on the twenty-fourth. He says he's been thinking about suicide. He's thought about it before. He would take a bunch of pills because that's how his sister killed herself. He gave me a commitment not to try to kill himself, and to seek out a staff to talk to when he feels angry.

THURSDAY, AUGUST 4: I talked with a detective yesterday from [the town Dean Savage is from]. This is the same detective who investigated the shooting of Dean's girlfriend. Another detective is handling a case in which a kid named Renquist shot a man who was sitting in his car behind a convenience store. Renquist said two guys were with him. One was named Hopper; Renquist has not given the name of the other one. This happened last December. Dean doesn't remember exactly when he did his shooting, but his girlfriend was shot in November and he shot the man in the store sometime after that.

After the phone call I went up to Social Services to talk with Carol Ripito; Herman was out sick. I told her about Dean's confession. I told her that I felt

I was in an ethical bind because I'd talked with a detective after telling Dean I would not, if he was not specific about the details of what he'd done.

Carol said I'd done the right thing, and now what I had to do was tell Dean what had transpired with the detective. I was to inform him that he did not have to talk with the police if they asked him to. If he chose to talk with them, he had the right to have a lawyer present. If he wanted a lawyer, Ash Meadow would get him one from Legal Services. Carol told me also not to discuss the case further with him.

At quiet time I brought Dean into the office. I asked Rob Gorey to be there too so I would have a witness to my telling Dean of his options. I did this, and then I told Dean about my conversation with the detective and what he had told me about the Renquist shooting.

Dean said I had told him that he had not said anything to me that was detailed enough for me to go to the police.

I told him I had talked it over with Herman, and Herman said that because it might be murder, we had to report it.

Dean said it wasn't murder. He had just found out that the man had not died. But, he said, he was glad Renquist was in trouble, because it was Renquist who had snitched on him, getting him sent to Ash Meadow. It was Renquist who beat that kid down, and then told the police that Dean had done it. (Dean is in for Assault One.)

Apparently he wasn't involved in the Renquist shooting. Dean says he was on house monitor in December. This would be easy enough to verify, as he knows. But the police have no other shooting that resembles the one he described.

SUNDAY, AUGUST 7: Michael says he's been feeling good lately. When his anxiety—he says "anger"—becomes too much for him, he goes to his room and cries. Then he feels better. But he's afraid that after his release he may ignore all his good intentions and revert to gangbanging. He misses the pleasure he's gotten in the past from brutalizing other people. He tries not to think about his friends who have been killed.

MONDAY, AUGUST 8: Yesterday I wrote out three questions for Michael to answer. Today he gave me back the list of questions and his responses. I had him do this exercise more for my education than for any other reason. I've corrected his spelling.

Question: What do you think about when you think about beating someone up? What do you see in your mind?

Answer: I think about hitting him in his head. I see me hitting him. I see me beating him down and kicking him.

Question: What do you feel when you see those pictures?

Answer: I feel pumped up.

Question: Are these feelings the same as those you feel when you are really beating up on someone?

Answer: I don't know. I guess I can say yes because I feel pumped up (on both kinds of occasion), and no because I feel more powerful (when actually beating somebody up). And I feel like no one can beat me. And I feel like I am better than everyone else 'cause I beat him down.

THURSDAY, AUGUST 11: When Dean talks about gang violence now, he says it's fun. When he first told me about shooting the man at the convenience store, he said he wished there weren't any guns or drugs. Now he likes talking about guns. He seems more self-assured. His adolescent awkwardness disappears when he talks about guns. "An AK-47 will take your head off very nice," he said in Alternatives to Violence.

SUNDAY, AUGUST 14: Tommy is driven to dominate his peers, though not necessarily by violence. He told me today that he enjoys letting people know when they're wrong, meaning when he's certain he's right but they are not, because it makes him feel powerful. I warned him that small victories now might cost him later.

Writing about him now, his desire to dominate, I recall being told by [a member of one of the most prominent families in Seattle], "I know about myself that I'm driven to dominate other men of my age group."

Gee. If Tommy had been born into money, think what he might have become. What might Michael have become if he had been born rich?

TUESDAY, AUGUST 23: Herman told us at PC that Tony Hunter—we released him four or five months ago—is one of the three boys who shot up that Beacon Hill apartment. The story of the shooting was in the paper yesterday or the day before. They killed a seven-year-old girl. Apparently they got burned by the girl's mother in a drug deal and they went and shot up her apartment. They missed the mother, got her daughter while she was sleeping.

I haven't written much about Tony here. I'm not sure why. Maybe because his original offense was so appalling that I didn't want to think about it or him. Carol Ripito said that what he did was one of the worst crimes she's read about in the twenty years she's worked here. She was talking about the account of the crime that was in his file. Herman and Sara, Tony's staff, saw him as a person without conscience, without remorse or empathy. Herman said there was no hope for him. Most, maybe all, of us staff despised him for what he had done to that girl. But sometimes, in Alternatives to Violence, I saw a crack in the facade of hardness, of consciencelessness. All of this was before he killed that other little girl on Beacon Hill.

I don't know what to say about him. There is nothing else I want to say.

WEDNESDAY, AUGUST 24: Michael Fuentes was released today. Tommy Whitacre goes to the Phoenix program tomorrow.

SATURDAY, AUGUST 27: Had coffee with Ron Dakron and Marilyn Stablein at Larry's Market yesterday. Ron told us about once having been in a writer's group. He told the others in the group, "Sorry, I don't accept criticism." But he said he was willing to give criticism. It really pissed them off.

I saw a young woman standing at the counter. "She looks like someone I know. Murder One."

MONDAY, AUGUST 29: Herman put Reggie Greene on my caseload. We just got him back. He ran from a group home. I can't say I'm looking forward to working with him. It's obvious that Herman likes him. There is something of the bully about Herman and there is something of the bully about Reggie, too.

WEDNESDAY, AUGUST 31: Last night I was in the craft room with five kids, conducting Alternatives to Violence, when I heard "Clear the floor!" I got the kids in the group locked down, then went out on the floor. Fran Sikora and Roy Burns were standing together in the living room. Both are new staff. Fran replaced Sara, who quit in June. All the kids had been locked in their rooms.

What had happened was this: Terence Starbuck wrote a sexually graphic letter to one of his teachers, probably as a satire—I doubt that he intended to mail it; he's not stupid—and showed it to Charlie Lewis. Fran saw Charlie reading it, glanced at it over his shoulder, and took it from him. She gave

Charlie a demerit and Terence a major bust and sent him to his room. Terence began carving on his arm with a pencil and Fran cleared the floor. I didn't ask why she cleared the floor; I attributed her decision to her being new.

I called Security and they took Terence to the health center. I called Herman at home and left a message that I was going to place Terence on SPL III. Then I called the O.D. She agreed with my decision to place Terence on suicide watch.

When Security brought Terence back, I had them put him in the quiet room. He wanted to go to his room, but I refused because I wanted him close by and away from Charlie, who was in the room next to his. After Security had gone, Terence tore the bandage off his arm and ripped up his shirt. He punched and slapped himself in the face, then began to bang his head on the concrete floor.

I called Security but they said they did not have the authority to put a kid in restraints. I asked them to move Terence to Central Isolation, where he could be observed by the nurses. They said no, as I thought they would, because the nurses don't want to be responsible for monitoring a kid on suicide watch.

I knew that Terence's psychiatrist had changed his meds, and I called the health center to ask them what I could expect from Terence in terms of behavior. Dorothy said Terence's psychiatrist was not available and she did not have the authority to prescribe medication. (But I hadn't asked her to prescribe a med. I only wanted to know what I could anticipate from the boy.) She did say she would call Dr. Arens, our medical doctor.

I called Security back to strip Terence, as I was afraid he would use his clothes to hang himself. Security took his clothing, although Terence insisted he did not intend to kill himself, that he had torn his shirt up only because he wanted to. As he stripped, he shouted, "I'll get you for this, Jerry! I'll kill you, Jerry!" We left him in his undershorts.

As soon as the lights from the security van disappeared, he went back to banging his head while yelling that he was going to kill me, alternating this now with crying and asking, "Why are you doing this to me, Jerry?"

Fran and Roy had been gone for some time, their shift having ended, when Dorothy called back. She said Dr. Arens refused to change the prescription Terence's psychiatrist had authorized. Arens had called the psychiatrist and the latter told him that Terence would stop banging his head when it began to hurt.

"His forehead is all welts now, and he's bleeding. He's crying and he's still banging his head. The psychiatrist is full of shit."

"Think of it this way, Jerry. Graveyard shift comes on soon and then it won't be your problem."

"We don't have a graveyard tonight. I'm working all the way through."

"I'm sorry."

"Yeah. Thanks anyway."

The screaming and crying, the head-banging and the threats lasted until four in the morning. I wondered if he would damage his brain more than it was already damaged. Once or twice I wondered if he was going to bash himself until he died. When he was quiet I gave him a mattress and a pillow without a case. He wasn't aggressive now, but he asked again as he lay down why I had done this to him.

SATURDAY, SEPTEMBER 3: A new kid, Tyee Horgan, on my caseload. Early childhood spent in a crack house. His mother sold it, his father used it. Tyee says his mother is straight now.

She used to beat him when he was small. Eventually she became "uncomfortable"—that's the word he used—with hitting him, so she got a woman friend to do it. She drove a VW bug, and he remembers hearing it as it pulled into the driveway when she came to beat him.

His mother cried when he was committed to Ash Meadow, but told him she would rather he was here than on the streets, because he's safer here. He agrees.

He's a Crip. He says he's shot at three people in gang-related incidents and believes he shot one boy in the leg. He's also used a baseball bat on other kids. He likes the feeling of power he gets when he assaults someone. But he doesn't want to bring younger kids into his gang; he doesn't think smaller kids should be in a gang.

He steals cars for their components and to impress girls. "Girls go for guys who have cars," he says. He likens stealing and driving a car to getting dressed in new clothes and showing them off.

MONDAY, SEPTEMBER 5: Carol told me she won't be able to do Survivors' Group anymore; her administrative duties have increased and she no longer has the time. She said she's done this group for almost twenty years and hated to give it up, but she can't do everything.

This means that there will no longer be a campus Survivors' Group. I'll be starting one up in my own cottage, just for our residents.

THURSDAY, SEPTEMBER 8: Had a bowl of soup at Burgermaster this afternoon. Laurel and Freida, two middle-aged women who are regulars, were sitting at a table next to mine. Laurel looked over at me and said, "But Jerry would have a different point of view, wouldn't you, Jerry?

"What's that?" I said.

"Freddie says sex offenders should be castrated."

"I have a friend who knows somebody who was castrated and he says he doesn't have any desire for sex anymore," Freida said.

"What would you do about the 40 percent of offenders who are female?" I asked.[6] I was alluding to a conversation Laurel and I had some months ago.

"I don't accept that!" Laurel snapped.

"I can't imagine how someone without a penis could be a sex offender," Freida said.

SUNDAY, SEPTEMBER 11: Tyee and I were talking in the staff office this afternoon. I don't remember what I said, but what I said was not as important as the fact that I raised my voice. Tyee looked directly into my face and said, "You motherfucker. I'll kill you."

I stood up and told him to head down to his room. He walked slowly and I walked behind him at the same pace. When he got to his room he walked in without hesitating and I locked the door behind him.

After supper I went down to talk with him. He said he knew he had twenty-four hours OP, but wanted to apologize. I accepted his apology, then asked him why he threatened me. He said that when I shouted at him—Had I shouted? I don't think I did—I reminded him of his father, who used to yell at him when he was small.

It's interesting that he knows why he reacted as he did. I don't expect this kind of understanding from either a kid or an adult.

SATURDAY, SEPTEMBER 17: I talked with Hedda Levy, Reggie Greene's counselor at the group home he ran from. She described him as street smart, but immature. She said he was kicked out of school for "a sexual episode." (He told me he was caught in the boys' bathroom with a girl who was fellating him. He said she had agreed to go into the bathroom with him and that it was her idea to give him a blow job. But then she told her parents that he had forced her.)

I told Hedda that Reggie said he had smoked weed while on leave from the group home to attend his sister's funeral. (She and her boyfriend had been murdered while sitting together in his car.) Hedda said that, in fact, Reggie had smoked regularly while at the group home. He lies constantly, she said.

SUNDAY, SEPTEMBER 18: In the last week Tyee has received two major busts and two minor busts, all resulting from his rage spilling out. One of his major busts came from threatening me last Sunday. Then he got a minor bust for going too far in teasing two girls at school. They were teasing him too, alluding to his skinniness and his stammer. His response was to throw one girl's history of prostitution in her face, and to ask the second girl, within other kids' hearing, about her miscarriage.

He told me that the girls deserved to be hurt because they had hurt him. He did acknowledge that he had overreacted to the comparatively small hurts they had inflicted on him.

MONDAY, SEPTEMBER 19: Reggie Greene said that Tony Hunter had asked him to go with him and the two other boys on the Beacon Hill shooting where that seven-year-old girl was killed. Tony and Reggie are in the same set. Reggie said he almost did it because he wanted to avenge his sister's murder on someone, he didn't care who. But he decided to spend the night with his girlfriend instead.

WEDNESDAY, SEPTEMBER 21: Tyee told Candy, our newest staff, not to point her finger at him. His tone got him a demerit. Later he told me that Candy pointing at him as she spoke reminded him of his mother. His mother beat him as recently as a month before he came here, he said. (But he told me earlier this month that his mother had stopped beating him, had assigned his beatings to a friend of hers.) She and the young woman who is his child's mother both beat on him. He says he loves his mother even though they don't get along. He hates his father, who also beat him, but he loves him too, Tyee said.

SATURDAY, SEPTEMBER 24: Today was Family Day. Parents were invited to come to the cottage, talk with staff, visit the school, talk with their kids' teachers, etc. I had the chance to watch Tyee and his mother together. He tries to manipulate her sense of guilt. He alluded, one after another, to incidents where he had gotten the short end of the stick: promises she'd made, but not kept; things she'd said she would buy him, but hadn't; ways in which she had favored his sister over him. She responded hardly at all to his accusations.

She told me, when Tyee was in the bathroom, that she is not going to put herself through anything like what she went through with him before he got locked up. Which means, I think, that she doesn't want him to live with her again.

Tyee is the only kid on my caseload who had a parent show up today. Of the twenty kids in the cottage, the parents of five came.

MONDAY, SEPTEMBER 26: Reggie has been seeing Deirdre Holser, our chaplain, for help in dealing with his grief. It comes from multiple sources: his father is in prison; his mother was invalided in an auto accident; his sister was murdered only a few months ago; and several members of his set have been killed in the last two years. On the outs, Reggie's method of dealing with his emotions was to get loaded on marijuana. There is a period of four months following his sister's death of which he has no memory, he says. Now, without marijuana, he has to experience his emotions, and he is frightened by what he is feeling and by how powerful it is.

One of his agonies revolves around the issue of June's baby: is it his or someone else's? (June is the girl he spent the night with instead of going on the Beacon Hill shooting with Tony Hunter.) But I wonder if June really had a baby, or if Reggie has made up a story so I'll allow him to call her. He says it was about a year ago that she was pregnant, but then she had a miscarriage.

I called the hospital Reggie told me she'd gone to and the records clerk said that June had been in at the time Reggie said she had. The symptoms the clerk read off did indicate that June had a miscarriage.

So where did this nine-month-old baby come from that Reggie says June has? He says he has seen the baby twice, both times when he was on the run from the group home. He says she looks like June's mother. He says he both does and does not want to know if the baby is his.

MONDAY, OCTOBER 3: Tyee had a feedback group for his Level I today that must have been terribly painful for him, although he did not say so. Other kids told him in the plainest terms that they did not like him. Rob noted that he makes enemies when he can't make friends, just to get attention. (Tyee acknowledged this was so.)

He told me that he knows he is going to fail, though he does not know at what. He believes his relationship with his mother is at the root of his feeling worthless, and believes, too, that he cannot break free of her. He did get his level.

WEDNESDAY, OCTOBER 5: Reggie has a talent for organizing people to do what he wants them to do. I told him he could be a Malcolm X or a Martin Luther King. He said he isn't a Malcolm X or a Martin Luther King: they were assassinated and he doesn't want that to happen to him. Later in our conversation he said he'd rather be killed for something he did wrong than for doing what was right.

SUNDAY, OCTOBER 9: Reggie is upset that June has not visited him, and possibly has not been honest with him. Is the child his or not? How does she account for claiming both a miscarriage and a birth? Why hasn't she shown him a birth certificate? (I had authorized her visiting him, as she is purportedly his child's mother. I would also like to hear her answer these questions myself.)

Another topic. When we were talking a few days ago, Reggie commented that he'd rather be killed for doing something bad than for doing good. Today I gave him the assignment to write an essay explaining why. Hopefully this will give me a clue as to how he makes decisions.

SUNDAY, OCTOBER 16: I pointed out to Tyee that his demerits usually result from rudeness or disrespect toward staff. His response was that staff deserve it because they disrespect him. Also, he doesn't like certain staff, i.e., Candy. He does recognize that his rudeness is self-defeating: he wants to go for his Level 2, but knows he won't get it unless he changes his behavior.

He pointed out, though, that his behavior has improved. I agreed.

Reggie turned his essay in today. He said it's easier and takes less time to earn respect by gangbanging than by doing good. Also, if he was killed while involved in a crime, he would feel he deserved it, but not if he was killed while trying to do good.

Underlying his thinking, I believe, is his assumption that he's not going to have a long life.

MONDAY, OCTOBER 17: Reggie came back to the cottage just before dinner from grief-and-loss counseling with Deirdre and asked to eat alone in his room. He came out in time to do his detail, then asked to talk with me.

Deirdre has been guiding him in grieving for his sister. Reggie is torn because he promised his sister, after her death, to kill her killer—he's certain he knows who he is—and to finish his education and make a success of himself as she had wanted him to do. He realizes now that he cannot do both. Deirdre wants him to write his sister a letter apologizing for not being able to do it all. As we talked, he cried, at one point giving himself over entirely to this conflict. He sobbed as he said, "I don't know, man. I don't know, man," while I held his hand.

Later this evening we had an AA/NA meeting in the cottage. Reggie talked about his dilemma, then told the others that he had decided not to kill the man who murdered his sister. He said his sister would not want him to because if he did, it would mean the end of his education, and therefore the end of his ability to achieve legitimate success in the world. Also, he said, if he killed that man his, the killer's, family would suffer, and Reggie did not want anyone to suffer as he has been suffering.

At this point, Rick Blue stood up and walked over to me. My immediate thought was, How dare you walk away when Reggie is going through this? But something was on Rick's face and I took him into the office. As Reggie had, now Rick cried. He had sworn to get the boys who killed Arne, his best friend, but now, because he didn't want to return to prison, he wanted to break his promise. He felt he was betraying Arne.

TUESDAY, OCTOBER 18: Rick asked me if I was proud of him for making Student of the Week. A kid is eligible for Student of the Week if he has three days out of seven during which he received no demerits. I told him yes, I was proud of him.

He asked if I was proud of everybody, for whatever reason. I said no.

"Good," he said.

Another kid without a father.

WEDNESDAY, OCTOBER 19: Stopped in traffic on the way to work, I had this fantasy. Two guys are in a car stopped behind another car at a light. The crosswalk is filled with pedestrians. The driver of the car in the rear blasts his horn. Of course, the car in front cannot move forward without hitting the pedestrians. The driver of the car behind blasts his horn again. "I just love this," he says to the guy in the passenger seat.

THURSDAY, OCTOBER 20: Tommy Whitacre returned from the Phoenix program today. He "coined," meaning he graduated, plus a little more. While it's possible to graduate without coining, to get your coin—a medallion, actually—you have to have achieved what the Phoenix staff call "a certain spiritual level." I'm glad for him and I'm proud of him. He's eligible to go to a group home now.

SUNDAY, OCTOBER 23: Reggie told me he's been edgy lately. I've noticed it too. He had stomach pains earlier today. He had them last Monday, too, during grief-and-loss with Deirdre. Not knowing what else to think, I'll attribute them to his ongoing conflict over his sister's death, and his commitment not to seek revenge, but his desire for it nonetheless.

FRIDAY, OCTOBER 28: I look at the kids here at Ash Meadow as I once looked at the professional soldiery I was a part of: they are outcasts, in refuge from society. Sometimes, in my thoughts, I call them "my little soldiers."

Social commentators wonder where little gangsters get guns. They steal them. The decal homeowners put on their front door that says, "This house protected by Smith and Wesson" may as well be an advertisement. What it says to the kid is "Burglarize this house and take the guns." The bumper sticker that says "When guns are outlawed, only outlaws will have guns" has it exactly backward: when guns are outlawed, outlaws won't be able to get them either. But guns won't be outlawed, not in these United States.

If this were another country, or if we lived in another time, we might worry about the poor stealing guns from the rich and killing them, or the police who protect them, with those guns. But this is the United States. Here the poor kill each other.

SATURDAY, OCTOBER 29: Tommy's brother was in an automobile accident. He has damage to his brain such that he has lost his ability to walk and much of his ability to speak. He told Tommy that he will have to learn how to perform these functions and others as if he were a child again. Talking to him on the phone, Tommy cried openly.

His sister is using drugs and drinking to the extent that their mother is caring for her two children. Tommy loves her deeply but he is afraid she will drag him down with her, so he intends to keep his distance from her. This is not easy for him. I once asked him who in his life has loved him without qualification. The only person he could think of was his sister.

MONDAY, OCTOBER 31: Yesterday I took Reggie and Tommy out for pizza and a movie, a rare treat, one for only the best-behaved kids. After the pizza we were in the parking lot, walking out to the car, when we heard the whine and squeal of a car accelerating fast. Reggie spun around, trying to locate the source of the sound. He said, his hand over his heart, signifying its own acceleration, "That's the sound a car makes when it's coming around for a drive-by."

Coming out of the movie, Reggie asked Tommy, "Did you see that guy looking at me?" meaning maddogging him. I don't think this happened. I think Reggie sees life in terms of threat, real or potential. The theater is in an affluent suburb, and what Reggie was looking for was not there, at least not on a scale large enough to see it at a glance.

In the lobby earlier, he and Tommy were commenting on the insignia on the varsity jackets some of the older teens were wearing. They were trying to figure out what gangs these kids belonged to.

TUESDAY, NOVEMBER 1: Tommy left for Ridge Vista Group Home this morning.

WEDNESDAY, NOVEMBER 2: We interrogated the entire cottage this evening, one kid at a time, about cheeking meds. Reggie swore to Rob—"I put it on my dead sister"—that he was not involved.

But he was involved: other kids knew he was, and told us. Apparently he got some Prozac from Charlie Lewis, took a little for himself, and gave the rest to Jonas Henson, who ate some and crushed and snorted the remainder. "I wanted to see what it would do," Jonas said.

Reggie has betrayed his sister's memory. I wonder how he thinks about that. What lies does he tell himself? The grief is real, nonetheless.

He's lost his level, of course.

SATURDAY, NOVEMBER 5: I began a reading group at the cottage this evening. What this means is I invited whichever kids wanted to listen to me read Rebecca Brown's *The Gifts of the Body*. The book evoked such emotion in me that I thought it might be a good vehicle to introduce, or reintroduce, compassion to some of these guys. I have half a dozen kids in the group, including Jonas Henson and Colin Turner. I wasn't surprised that Colin wanted in—books are important to him—but Jonas' wanting to be read to did surprise me.

I expected some of the kids to leave once they understood that many of the characters are gay, but none did, not one. They were enthralled, as I was, by the issues of death and bereavement brought out in the book, and by the primal simplicity with which Rebecca tells the stories. It was a great experience, reading to these guys and seeing how caught up they were in the stories. I read only a couple tonight. I'll read more as I have time.

MONDAY, NOVEMBER 7: I talked with Reggie about his lying concerning his involvement in the unofficial med distribution last week. He tried to turn the conversation to the subject of drug use, saying that only he can refuse to do drugs—no one and no treatment can do that for him.

Fine, I said, but the lying is a separate issue.

He claimed he did not say to Rob "I put it on my dead sister." What he really said, he told me now, was "'at's on my sister" and "I fut it on my sister."

Okay, I said, but by saying "'at's" instead of "that's" and "fut" instead of "put," he allowed Rob to believe he was putting it on his sister when he wasn't. He knew he was lying, but hoped Rob would believe he was not. That's the way a child lies, I said.

I told Reggie he had disrespected himself and had betrayed his sister. He acknowledged that he had and that even before talking with me today he had decided not to lie again, but to admit his guilt when caught—unless he's caught doing something on the outs that's illegal.

MONDAY, NOVEMBER 14: Back in the cottage after grief counseling, Reggie told me he's never felt this bad. It has to do with his sister's death, of course. His behavior has become childish in some respects; he whines and he taunts other kids. A couple of months ago staff saw him as one of the more mature kids in the cottage, if not the most trustworthy. Now he says that if he was on the outs, he'd beat somebody up to relieve the stress he's feeling.

TUESDAY, NOVEMBER 15: This evening in Alternatives to Violence I had the group do an exercise in which one person talks while another listens. The group was to focus on the listener, asking themselves, Does he use body language to encourage the speaker? What does his facial expression say? Does he refrain from interrupting? I placed two chairs in front of the group. I sat in one and I had Roy Rogers sit in the other, facing me. (Roy Rogers is really his name. Honest! But he's never heard of Roy Rogers or Dale Evans or Trigger. And he's not related to Les Rogers, who was here about a year ago.) I demonstrated what I wanted by talking to him, or trying to. Unfortunately he couldn't keep from hamming it up. He'd make his eyes go googly, then make exaggerated snickers, then cross his arms and lean back in his chair, stern-faced. Finally I told him to go back to his seat and I called Jonas Henson up.

Jonas was a very good listener. I told him that I was anxious about reading the last story in *The Gifts of the Body* to the kids in the reading group because I cried when I read it for myself, and I wasn't sure I was willing to allow myself to cry in front of the kids.

Then it was Jonas' turn. He talked about how worried he was about leaving Ash Meadow. He told me of his problems with girls, how he gets high by beating them up, how only drugs and beating up females make him so high. He was worried he would do something that would get him sent back to Ash Meadow or to another institution.

Now Roy wanted to talk. Charlie Lewis agreed to listen. Roy talked about feeling hopeless. Nothing seems to be working, he said. None of the treatment we've provided has changed him. He still feels impelled to do the things he did before he came to Ash Meadow. He said he's just going to reoffend and be caught and be sent back and be let out and reoffend and be sent back, like his father and his brothers and his uncles and cousins.

This was supposed to be an exercise in listening, but all of us, the kids and I, were caught up in the stories rather than checking out the listener.

FRIDAY, NOVEMBER 18: The other day I told Gigi about a time when I was a child in Chicago and Bonnie and I and our mother went shopping. It was cold and rainy and we stopped for lunch at a restaurant, probably as much to get in out of the weather as to get something to eat. I ordered chicken soup, but when I tasted it I pushed it away. Maybe it was too salty or too watery, but in any case I didn't eat it. When the waitress came back, she took the soup away, saying, "He needed this like he needs a hole in the head."

At that point, or so I told Gigi, I pulled out my Uzi and shot the waitress, shouting, "Die, bitch! I'm from the future and you're dead!"

And Gigi yelled, "The meek shall inherit the earth!"

SATURDAY, NOVEMBER 19: Tyee needs a hearing aid. I have been trying for weeks to persuade him to wear one. The health center will get one for him if he'll use it. A few days ago, he agreed. I was delighted and didn't try to conceal how I felt. Today he said he does not want to wear a hearing aid after all.

I told him that the reason he doesn't want one is because all his life people have pointed out to him how different he is—he stammers, he has poor diction, too many teeth, he's skinny and, in terms of verbal I.Q., he's the most intelligent kid our school psychologist has ever tested—and a hearing aid would be one more thing to make him stand out. I told him I believed the embarrassment he would feel at first would be worth the longer-term benefits of wearing one. This conversation, I know, is going to go on and on.

Actually, I need a hearing aid. Knowing this, I still don't get one. But I'm not skinny and I have the right number of teeth.

SUNDAY, NOVEMBER 20: Reggie had his feedback group today for move-up to Level 1. It was obvious during the group that he was trying, by posture and gesture, to intimidate some of the other kids. Although he was supposed to remain silent when the others commented on or criticized his behavior, he responded to one of them as if the latter had no right to speak. Reggie would have gone on if I hadn't stopped him.

In the office he claimed he was unaware of his body language, but said he came at Willie as he did because Willie was playing with him and he didn't like it.

Reggie demands deference from other kids. This is really, I think, what his problem with Willie was: Willie was not being properly deferential.

MONDAY, NOVEMBER 28: Tyee earned himself two major busts in three days. He lost his level and ended up on Tables. I asked him which one of Satan's spawn had gotten hold of him and he went off about how Jacob French isn't as tough as he makes himself out to be. Tyee will be going to Apple Park for drug-and-alcohol treatment soon; he's very nervous about it.

Reggie will also be going to Apple Park. Date not set.

WEDNESDAY, DECEMBER 7: Rob showed me a flyer inviting soldiers to apply for sniper training at Fort Lewis. A friend of his sent it to him as a joke. Rob is a hunter.

I told him I had known only two snipers. One was all right. The other was a battalion surgeon who liked to go out beyond the perimeter and snipe when he was off duty.

Laughter just tumbled out of Rob's mouth. "That'll unplug that artery!"

SATURDAY, DECEMBER 10: I asked Tyee if he feels he's changed in the time he's been at Ash Meadow. He went on for half an hour. What a surprise! Among the things he said:

He's learned to accept it when someone says "No."

He's learned empathy.

He realizes he can't smoke weed or chill with his old homies because if he smokes weed he'll commit crimes, and if he chills with his homies he'll smoke weed.

He understands that some of the things his mother did she did simply to obtain food to feed him and his sister.

He doesn't know why Swan staff do what we do, but he sees some of the effort we and his teachers have made on his behalf and he is determined to complete high school and go to college because he feels indebted to us, and making something of himself is the only way to repay us.

He understands that violence, in most cases, is not necessary and he believes he can avoid it.

I was quite touched. I believe he spoke sincerely. However, he was OP for the day for having gone off this morning.

MONDAY, DECEMBER 12: Reggie tells me he's forced to be a leader, whether or not he wants to be, because of his personality. He thinks he can be a leader for either good or ill. He thinks that what he should be is a leader for good.

SUNDAY, DECEMBER 18: Last night Reggie heard another resident make a derogatory remark about Candy under his breath. Reggie, affecting a joking manner to disguise his informing, asked Candy if she'd heard what the kid said. Candy gave the boy a major bust, and then, because Reggie had laughed, rebuked him. Reggie argued, but it was obvious that Candy was angry and his insistence only alienated her more, which further frustrated him.

He was frustrated, he told me later, because he had tried to do the right thing but was punished for it. He asked me if I had ever had a time in my life when no matter what I did, it was wrong. He said that even as he was arguing, his mind was telling him he was making a mistake, but he couldn't shut himself up.

Reggie is trying hard to change himself. He's right, though, when he says most staff look at him through the filter of their history with him. But after all, his habit of belaboring his point, of trying to win it over and over again, is something that continues to put us off, because we suspect he's just lying over and over again. Even so, remembering how he was a year ago, and comparing that memory with how he is today, I have to say he's made progress. He agrees.

WEDNESDAY, DECEMBER 21: Relapse. In horseplay at school, Tyee snapped a girl's bra and grabbed her wrist hard enough to bruise it. His pattern is that at some point in banter —mutual ranking, for fun—or horseplay, Tyee makes a quantum leap and says or does something hurtful. He says he's joking but that others don't perceive he is. A part of his pattern is that he doesn't at first accept responsibility for what he's done. We've been through this before.

SUNDAY, CHRISTMAS DAY: A Christmas card from the kids on my caseload was in my box when I came in today. The illustration on the card showed three kids singing to a collie puppy. The kids are blond and rosy cheeked. Reggie and Tyee are black, though Rick is kind of blond. I don't think I look like a puppy.

Inside, Tyee wrote: "Jerry: you a coo staff & if I had my choice of staff I'd still pick you. I'll always remember you. You have helped me realize who I really am and what I need to do so I won't reoffend. Thanx. Have a marry Christmas."

Rick: "Jerry: I know that we've had our ups and downs. But I just want to wish you a merry Christmas. Thanks for being there for me."

Reggie: "Jerry: I appreciate all the work we have done 2-gether and I am glad I have you for a staff. Merry Christmas."

I was immensely moved. Rick confided to me that the card was his idea. Reggie overheard him and said, "What do you mean?" and pretended to be angry. Rick laughed and said, "Okay, it was your idea."

When I thanked Tyee for the card, he claimed the idea for himself.

I told Stan I had gotten a card from my kids and he looked at me like I was crazy. "Why would they do that?" he said. "Imagine that. Getting a Christmas card from your caseload. How are you raising these children, Jerry?"

TUESDAY, DECEMBER 27: Tyee left for Apple Park today.

WEDNESDAY, DECEMBER 28: Reggie says he's determined to be a success. He wants people to remember him. He believes God gave him Tony Hunter as an example of what might happen to him if he does not change. June showed up just as he was getting into a car with Tony. Only a girl could have kept him from going with Tony, he said. He believes God sent June to him that day.[7]

1995

SATURDAY, JANUARY 7: Reggie learned today that his "auntie," his mother's closest friend who sometimes cared for him when he was younger, died in a fire last week. She was not burned to death or asphyxiated, but died of a heart attack while trying to save her smallest children who, unknown to her, were already safe.

His sister's murder, his father's imprisonment, his homies being killed, and now this. This kid's losses go on and on.

SATURDAY, JANUARY 28: Came to work today, and who should be there but Tyee Horgan. In a yellow suit and a shit-eating grin. I knew he'd be returning from Apple Park soon but I didn't expect to see him in yellow. On Thursday, with only hours to go before graduation, he'd allowed himself to be goaded into a fight, so he was sent back to Ash Meadow without graduating.

Why the grin? I think he was glad to see me.

FRIDAY, FEBRUARY 3: Reggie Greene off to Apple Park for drug-and-alcohol treatment.

MONDAY, FEBRUARY 13: A couple of weeks ago Tyee received hearing aids, one for each ear. His stammer, in the short time he has been using them, has almost disappeared. He began to gain weight at Apple Park and actually looks like a young man now instead of a skinny kid. He seems to have more self-confidence and has been a lot less volatile.

SATURDAY, FEBRUARY 18: Colin Turner talked to his mother tonight. Afterward he slammed the phone down in its cradle and went to his room. He looked on the verge of tears. Jonas Henson and I had both been watching him, and Jonas asked if he could go down to Colin's room and talk to him. I agreed.

After a while I followed Jonas into Zone 4. Colin was saying that his brother Knute was in Crane Cottage now, a sex offender unit. Colin said Knute had never been taught what men are supposed to do because their father left when they were so young. Colin himself had had to learn from his homies.

On the outs, he said, he robbed people, he did burglaries. Sometimes he had more money than his mother. His brothers looked up to him, but his mom was always hitting him, whether he did right or wrong. Now she dumps on him for being locked up.

"I'm not stupid," Colin said. "I knew I was doing wrong." But his family was poor and he wanted the things other kids had.

The cause of his upset tonight was his feeling that his family is disintegrating and there is nothing he can do about it. His sister is going to marry a soldier and then they'll be going to Germany to live. "Nothing is as important as family," Colin said.

SUNDAY, FEBRUARY 19: Tommy Whitacre went AWOL from Ridge Vista Group Home, was caught and returned to Ash Meadow last week. After he was apprehended Ridge Vista wanted to send him to another group home in Spokane where his mother lives, but Tommy said he wasn't ready for that. For what? For—I think—dealing with the trauma of life as his family lives it.

Yesterday, at the beginning of my shift, I gathered all the kids together in the living room and explained that the only people on duty would be an intermittent and me, so if there was any problem in the cottage, we would lock down the kids on Tables and CR. Tommy said nobody could keep a kid from kicking someone's ass if he wanted to. This was in response to my suggestion that the cottage police itself so no one has to be locked down.

Later I heard a shout from a kid—I don't know who—in the living room.

I looked up and saw Tommy and Joe Voit by the ironing board maddogging each other. Tommy had the iron in his hand. I went over to them, told Joe to step back, and took Tommy over to the ping-pong table. It would have been better to take him into the office, but that would have left Mike, the intermittent, on the floor alone with the rest of the cottage.

Tommy refused to tell me what happened between him and Joe, so I told him to go down to his room. He got angry. He said the problem was over and there was no need for me to send him down. He had slipped into what staff call the "gang stance," which is also a martial arts defensive position, and his hands were half-closed. I pointed this out to him.

"I'm mad," he said.

"All the more reason for you to take a time-out."

"For the rest of the night!"

"That's right."

Finally he went to his room. Mike locked him in. I asked Joe what had happened. He refused to tell me and I sent him down too.

After all the kids were locked in for the night, Tommy asked to talk with me and I took him out of his room and brought him into the staff office. He said that while he was ironing, Joe reached across to grab his own shirt from the back of a chair. Tommy told him not to reach over the iron like that and Joe called him a "little kid." Tommy got ticked, and Joe, to save face, mad-dogged him back. That was when I stepped in.

But that was not what he wanted to talk about. He'd been having bad dreams. And he'd been thinking a lot. The dreams and the thinking were about his old life on the outs.

An old girlfriend, Amelie, is in Peacock Cottage now. She's someone he used to use sexually. He wasn't very kind to her, he said. Until he saw her this past week, he thought about his past only occasionally. But seeing her brought his past back to him in a rush.

She's been telling other girls about some of the things he did, and since most of his friends are girls, he's afraid of losing his friends. He told Amelie he had changed, that he's completely different now. She told him that she still loves him. She misses the things he used to do to her.

But that was not what he wanted to talk about either, though it was close. He'd done a lot of things, he said—"I did what I had to"—but what most haunts him is what he did to a man who raped his sister. Shooting wouldn't have been as bad, he said.

His mother was raped a couple of weeks ago. Now he thinks, What could I do that wouldn't make things worse? He doesn't want to go to prison again. He said he realizes now that he can't be with his family and also take care of himself.

He said he deserves to be punished for the things he's done to people and he believes that Amelie's telling other girls about him, and their resulting fear of him, is punishment, but only a part of what he has coming to him.

I think he wants to confess to a murder, probably of the man who raped his sister. This is hard for him. It is hard for me, too. I don't want him to confess because I don't want to report it. I don't want to think of him spending his life in prison.

TUESDAY, MARCH 7: Reggie returned from Apple Park a few days ago. He says he learned a lot about himself there. He seems more centered now, more certain of who he is. He also seems more tolerant of residents who used to irritate him.

But there are some things about him that haven't changed. You never know how much of the truth he's telling you, or what is a distortion, or if everything is a lie. It's difficult to see how his dishonesty will benefit him if he ever has the chance to live in an environment different from the one he grew up in. I've been trying to clue him about other ways of approaching the world: Not every other young man wants to harm him.

MONDAY, MARCH 13: Tonight I listened in on Rob's drug-and-alcohol group as I was writing a treatment report in the cottage director's office. I heard Tommy say how angry he was and that he was unable to get rid of his anger, how little things he hadn't noticed before set him off now. He said that when he was at Ridge Vista he was smoking marijuana three or four days a week. The implication was that he was using marijuana to subdue his anger. I missed what he said next, but then heard him tell someone that staff are obligated to inform the police if you confess to a crime. Somebody said something, then Tommy said that someone—meaning, I'm certain, Michael Collins; I know Tommy's been talking to him—has been pressing him to go to the chaplain, but he wasn't sure he wanted to do that. Rob told him then that he needs to find someone to talk to, but not to tell him any of the details of the crime.

When the group was over, I took Tommy into the office. I told him a story

I had heard when I was in Viet Nam. "Tony" was part of a seven-man team whose mission was to snatch a North Vietnamese soldier and extract information from him. They did, but after twelve hours of "interrogation"—that is, torture—the prisoner died.

I told Tommy that I may or may not be Tony. This was my gift to him, an offering of a kind of intimacy, of presumed knowledge about me that I did not ordinarily give out. It was a lie in that someone else was Tony, but I allowed Tommy to believe what I knew he would.

"I figured that," he said, meaning he assumed I was Tony.

I suggested that, if he wanted, he could tell me a story about a friend of his. Then I waited. After several minutes during which he would start to say something, then stop, then laugh nervously, then start again, he told me about a friend of his, also named Tony.

[I am not going to recount here what Tony did. What he did was bad, and it was done in retaliation for something that had been done to someone he loved.]

Afterward, when Tony had doubts about what he had done, his homies told him that he couldn't have done anything else, that he had done what was right. But they looked at him differently now, as if he was different. And Tony's not sure he wouldn't do it again if faced with the same situation.

This, of course, is what's troubling Tommy now, other than his own memories: he believes that, like Tony, he will do something terrible again if he accepts responsibility for the safety of the women in his family. As he can't protect them, all he can do is take revenge on those who violate them.

THURSDAY, MARCH 16: I cannot look at a car filled with teenage boys now without the apprehension that they have guns. When I see a boy in a restaurant or a theater or on the street, I look at how his pants wrap around his legs to see if he has a gun in his pocket, and check out the length of his coat to determine whether it's long enough to conceal a sawed-off shotgun or an Uzi.

WEDNESDAY, MARCH 22: A scene I fantasized while stuck in traffic: Doctors, nurses, wounded soldiers fleeing a battle that is overrunning a hospital. Artillery shells exploding. One soldier, his right arm and left leg in plaster, is hobbling along, carrying a nurse, uninjured, on his back, she shouting instructions at him. Two other soldiers, wearing the blue shirt and light cotton pants of army hospital patients, but seemingly healthy, carry a doctor in whites—he is also uninjured—on a stretcher, the doctor sitting up and calling out orders.

SUNDAY, MARCH 26: Tommy said he has to prepare himself to lose his mother because someday she's going to die. He said he doesn't know what he'll do when he loses her. This fear of loss—Rick Blue said the same thing about his own mother a few months ago.

MONDAY, APRIL 10: During grief-and-loss counseling last week, Reggie said, Deirdre told him that June did have a miscarriage and that the baby he saw with her was a friend's. I asked Reggie how Deirdre would know this, but he didn't answer. He just shrugged and got a smile on his face of a kind I hadn't seen before.

Today he told me June broke up with him and he's feeling bad.

SUNDAY, APRIL 16: I was entering the intersection at 15th Northeast and Northeast 80th to make a left turn when a woman stepped into the crosswalk, seemingly on impulse. I'd seen her on the sidewalk, but she'd appeared to be waiting for the light to change so she could cross on 80th.

I stopped to let her cross. The driver behind me—a long, white Cadillac, a middle-aged man driving—honked, as if to tell me I should run the woman down because he was in a hurry! He was making faces and waving his arms; I could see him in my mirror. I flipped him off. I thought of getting out of my car and going over and kicking his door in, but I didn't; I stayed in my car and waited for the woman to leave the crosswalk.

MONDAY, APRIL 17: Reggie was interviewed for Fessendon Group Home last Thursday. Yesterday I talked to him about doing a relapse plan in case he starts using again. He said he knew what he needed to do—attend lots of AA/NA meetings, talk to supportive friends—but he didn't know if he would do it. I'm taking him to Fessendon next week.

TUESDAY, APRIL 18: At PC Rob told us that several of the kids last week had unbolted a chain from the trampoline at the gym and brought it back to the cottage. Last week was spring break and we had filled the kids' time, at least in the morning, with gym activities. Fran had been monitoring them, supposedly. They had worked on it with their fingers for three days and she hadn't noticed a thing. She hadn't seen one of them stuff it into his pants, and hadn't asked him, on the walk back to the cottage, why he was limping. It is a large, heavy chain, and he limped to minimize its rattling and because of its weight. Fran did not try to defend herself.

It's interesting that Rob brought it up. Apparently Herman knew about it, but, gathering from Rob's tone and the fact that he was looking at Herman while ostensibly speaking to Fran, had not intended to say anything to the rest of us.

After Rob finished, nobody said anything. This is so serious that a staff could be so oblivious as to endanger the entire cottage, both kids and staff, that it's almost incomprehensible. If kids are bringing weapons into the cottage, or manufacturing them, they are doing it because they are afraid of other kids. I said this and Herman agreed.

If some kids have weapons, others may have them too. I said we need to search the cottage—soon. Meaning now!

Herman said he'd already had the day staff do a search. They hadn't found anything.

I asked if they had known about the chain. I was beginning to wonder if I was the only staff in the cottage who hadn't known.

Michael Collins said Herman had told him. John Loring said he hadn't known there was a special reason for the search; he had treated it as run-of-the-mill.

Nobody else had known. And that is a problem, our not knowing that the kids may be armed or that something is happening to make them afraid. And part of the problem is that not only Fran, but Herman concealed it from us.

Herman said Fran will have to undergo retraining relevant to cottage security and that Rob will be in charge of it. I'm sure Rob will do his damnedest, but the idea of retraining is just a way to mollify staff. Herman must know how we feel. Most of us, maybe all, would like to see Fran fired.

TUESDAY, APRIL 25: Drove Reggie down to Fessendon in Tacoma today. He seemed reluctant, mainly, I think, because this is the town his sister was murdered in. But he said he'd try it.

SATURDAY, APRIL 29: Gigi was over yesterday. We talked about Darlene Lauder. Darlene came from an all-American family. She's smart, athletic, and blond, and her parents and brothers are the same. But she murdered an elderly woman in a burglary that went awry.

Darlene reminds me of Daniel Mallon, the boy who shot a man to death a few years ago because the man had looked "funny" at him.[8] Daniel was also bright, blond, athletic, and seemingly without conscience.

Gigi said maybe we could introduce them to each other.

I said, "Maybe they could find an old woman who looks funny."

SUNDAY, APRIL 30: Reggie called from Fessendon. He sounded bored.

TUESDAY, MAY 23: Herman and I talked about Tommy today. He was involved in a contraband exchange. Colin Turner gave him candy in return for chewing tobacco, which Tommy was to get from Derek Burk, who, Derek said, had gotten it from Charlie Lewis. Charlie was transferred to Elk Grove last week, so it's convenient for Derek to say he got it from him. On the other hand, it would be like Charlie to have had it in the first place, and to exchange it for—who knows what.

Originally Tommy told Herman he was not involved in the exchange. When Herman found out that, in fact, he was, he told Tommy that there was "no honor in a dishonorable action." Tommy may have felt he was protecting his friends by lying, but the lie was "dishonoring"—so saith Herman as reported by Tommy. I love these Hermanisms. They sound great to teenage ears, but mean so little to adult.

I had told Tommy only a couple of days before all this came to light that while the positive aspect of "gang mentality," as we staff call it, is the strong caring for the weak, a negative aspect is that this is a trap for both. The weak learn to expect this protection and resent the strong when they withdraw it. I had been talking, obliquely, about Tommy and the relationships he's established in the cottage. Only after our conversation had ended did I realize he could also interpret what I said as a model for his relationship with his family, his mother and sister anyway.

Herman and I agree that gangs are paramilitary, feudalistic organizations. Our military experience and our similar academic studies—his were in sociology, mine in anthropology—enable us to see the social aspect of them. And, of course, both of us remember the terror in being on the receiving end of our enemy's rage, and the feeling of satisfaction in releasing our own. Both of us identify, to a degree, with these kiddie gangsters.

TUESDAY, MAY 30: Thinking about Reggie Greene. I don't think his prognosis is good. After he went to Fessendon, I talked with Deirdre about him. Although Reggie believes he accomplished a lot in grief counseling with her, Deirdre is less sanguine. She says that the emotional numbing he's used to deal with his losses has prevented any significant breakthrough.

There's no question that Reggie can be dangerous. He was dangerous on the outside before. But perhaps he won't be as dangerous as he might have been had he not spent time here. I can never know this, of course, but in a job that requires some kind of faith, or self-deception, to continue doing it, this little bit is probably not too harmful. (God, did I write that? There's a lot packed into that little sentence that I wish was not there.) I am certain that his grief counseling resulted in his decision not to avenge his sister's murder, and that he will try to abide by this decision.

By the way, Deirdre told me too that June did not have Reggie's baby—that, in fact, she never had a baby.

I said Reggie had told me that. I asked how she had learned the truth.

She said she hadn't learned it on her own, but had suspected it. When she confronted Reggie, he confirmed it. According to him, June had a miscarriage, but she and Reggie decided to pretend she'd had his child so that I would allow him to talk with her on the phone.

Did June finally break up with him?

Deirdre said she thought so, but knowing Reggie, you never know what to believe.

WEDNESDAY, JUNE 28: One effect of working at Ash Meadow is coming to doubt my own values, my notions about what is right and what is wrong, what is deviant and what is not, what can be explained in terms of culture or class and what cannot.

I've been thinking a lot about Tommy. Like some others—Colin Turner, Reggie Greene—he seems to have a desire for a kind of balance in his life, for payback even when he is the one who might have to pay. His behavior can be so self-destructive. I wonder if eventually he will not simply kill himself. He is in a lot of pain, no question, and he thinks often about the guy he, or "Tony," killed. Perhaps I should have encouraged him to confess.

SUNDAY, AUGUST 6: A few months before Colin Turner came to Ash Meadow he went to a party with some homies. He got drunk and also smoked some marijuana. He was unable to defend himself, and his homies stripped him and threw him on his stomach and four of them held him while a fifth raped him. The humiliation was bad enough, but the fact that his homies did it to him made it much worse.

Colin says another homie shot the rapist as payback, but I suspect that this is not true. It doesn't sound the same as when he talks about being raped; there is no emotion in his mention of the shooting. Also, it makes a package that is too neatly wrapped to have happened.

Last week the Victim Awareness group watched a movie titled *The Rape of Richard Beck*. It's about a hard-case police detective who is raped, and how this experience changes his life. At the point in the movie when the detective is being raped, Colin asked me if he could go to his room. I said yes. After a couple of minutes I went into the zone and found him sitting on his bed, crying. "Why'd they do it?" he asked.

"I don't know, Colin."

"I don't understand why they did it. They were my homies."

After a while he stopped crying. He looked grim. I asked him if I had to worry about his trying to kill himself. He laughed and said no. I told him he could come out when he was ready and I went back out on the floor.

Yesterday afternoon I overheard him telling a joke in the living room. Its punchline was "I gotta go pack my shit," and it referred to anal intercourse. Colin and the other kids were laughing. When he saw me—the joke belittled gays and Colin knows I don't approve of that kind of humor—his laughter broke for a fraction of a second until he could see how I was going to respond. He saw that I was not going to say anything, and he turned away and continued laughing.

At quiet time I went to his room and told him that if he wanted to talk more about what happened to him, I'd be willing to listen. As far as I know, I'm the only staff in the cottage he's talked to about having been raped.

He thanked me, but said he didn't want to have to think about it. He'd rather stuff it. He understood that his anger built up until he couldn't stand it any longer, and then he'd explode. He'd experienced that and knew it would happen again. But he'd rather explode every so often than have to think about what his homies did to him.

MONDAY, AUGUST 14: Tommy was paroled today.

MONDAY, SEPTEMBER 4: Charlie Hicks attempted suicide last night. He had an early bedtime for having gotten too many demerits. I checked on him about seven-thirty and found him standing on his bed, trying to tie a looped strip of cloth, probably torn from a shirt, to the grate of the air vent in his ceiling. I opened his door and demanded the cloth. He handed it over but he wouldn't come down off the bed. I yelled out, "Clear the floor!", hit my body alarm, and stayed with him until Security arrived to place him in our quiet room.

Later, after he had finished yelling about how dumb I am, that he had no intention of killing himself and that I had placed him in the quiet room for no good reason, he told me he really did want to kill himself. He said he was frustrated at not doing well in the cottage—"I just get in trouble"—and the other kids are constantly putting him down.

I think this kid has been through something that has just destroyed his sense of himself as someone worthwhile. He admits to having been physically abused, but he may have been sexually abused too. Once when we put him in the quiet room, we had him strip, squat, and cough, as is our procedure, and a pencil dropped out of his ass. It had not been sharpened, so obviously he had not intended to tag the quiet room walls with it. He's fat and unhappy and his mother brings him candy.

THURSDAY, SEPTEMBER 7: A café where I go for coffee provides 2-percent low-fat milk as an alternative to half-and-half or creamer. The 2-percent comes in a waxed, ten-ounce carton, several of which are placed near the coffee urns. When one carton is finished, the customer simply opens another. A fantasy follows:

I'm opening a carton when a small, orange-haired woman comes up beside me. She asks, "May I use that?" Although her words are inoffensive, the tone of her voice is demanding.

"Wait your turn!" I snap. In my mind is the thought that I am the one opening the carton and she should wait until I have used it.

An alternative ending: I am annoyed as I open the carton, and I think she should wait until I have used it. But I'm surprised by her aggressiveness and I give it to her after I've opened it. She spits in it and hands it back, grinning.

SATURDAY, SEPTEMBER 16: I haven't seen Gigi in over a month. The last time she came over she got violently angry. The only sense I could make of what she was saying was that she was jealous of the closeness between my daughter and me. She said some pretty vicious things about Leah. At one point she threw some dishes on the floor. One bounced back up against her leg. She burst into laughter and I thought the episode was over. She'd been like this before, but this time was the worst. Then she shouted at me, "So our relationship is just fucking!" I didn't say anything, though by now I was intensely angry, too. I went into the bedroom, locked the door, and put my hands over my ears, trying to block out her screaming. Eventually she left. After she had gone, the silence that remained was a pure, sweet pleasure.

This morning I received a note in the mail from her. She said she had tried to goad me into hitting her, that that was what the screaming was about. "Every relationship is about power," she wrote. Then she became afraid that I would come out of the bedroom and actually hit her, and that was when she left.

The last paragraph of her letter was erotic. She told me she missed me, my smell, the way I slept, and so on. I'm not going to see her again.

WEDNESDAY, SEPTEMBER 27: I called Wilt Jones, Tommy Whitacre's JPC, to see how Tommy's doing. He's had a couple of dirty UAs: marijuana. He's living with his mother, who is having her own problems staying clean.

SATURDAY, OCTOBER 14: Tommy is back on a parole violation. Carrying a concealed weapon, dirty UAs, possession of drug paraphernalia. His lip is cracked where he got hit during a fight.

SUNDAY, OCTOBER 15: On stepping into the cottage, I noticed immediately that a boy on CR status and wearing an orange jumpsuit, indicating that he is an AWOL risk, was playing ping-pong. Michael Biddle, who was supposed to be on Tables, was in the living room, watching TV. I announced that CRs would not be playing ping pong but would be restricted to the living room, and Tables kids would be at Tables.

"Has Fran gone home?" Derek Burk asked.

A few minutes later I sent Ricky Arden to his room. After he kicked his door I put him in the quiet room. I asked Fran, as a "nonisolating staff"— i.e., one who did not participate in placing him in isolation, that is, the quiet room—to review him before she left for the day.

I moved Ricky into the quiet room at 3:40. Fran talked with him from 3:50

to 4:05, then, to my amazement, took him out of the quiet room and returned him to his room. She said he had committed himself not to go off in his room again.

I told her I'd asked her to review him, to see if he understood why I'd moved him to the quiet room and what he needed to do to be allowed out of the quiet room; I hadn't asked her to take him back to his room.

She reiterated that since Ricky had made a commitment to handle his room, she felt justified in taking him back. She said that when we put one of our residents in another cottage's quiet room, we always take him back after he commits to handling his room.

That was so, I said, only after he had spent at least half an hour being quiet, showing us that he is in control of himself.

She said Ricky had been quiet for half an hour.

No, I said, he'd been talking with her. He hadn't even been in the quiet room for half an hour. I told her she didn't have the authority to release Ricky from the quiet room after I had placed him there. That's where we left it. I was so angry I couldn't speak anymore, and I walked out of the office. It's clear to me that Fran let Ricky out of the quiet room to retaliate for my having sent the kid in orange back to the living room and the kid on Tables back to Tables.

Fran is the same person who, two weeks ago, after I'd placed Ricky on SPL III and taken his shoelaces, gave them back to him without telling anybody. The kid was on suicide watch, for Christ's sake!

She's also the person who, last April, by her inattentiveness, allowed some of the kids to smuggle a chain from the gym into the cottage. They had spent three days unscrewing the bolts that secured it to the trampoline while she was supposedly monitoring them. She hadn't a clue as to what they were doing. (But what if she had? What if she saw no harm in their taking the chain? Either version could be true.)

TUESDAY, NOVEMBER 7: Tommy was returned to parole today.

THURSDAY, NOVEMBER 9: I heard that Reggie Greene ran from Fessendon Group Home. Herman says it had to do with a girl.

THURSDAY, NOVEMBER 23: Rob told me that Julio Bitford, a kid I knew when I was an intermittent and one of the few I have disliked, was recently sentenced to 103 years. Rob said he thought Julio had been involved in an armed robbery in which a police officer was killed, though Julio had not killed him.

Interestingly, I heard about both Reggie and Julio from some of the kids before anyone else told me. The kids hear about life on the outs from their parents when they visit or call, or from friends who write them.

The kid who told me about Julio said that at his sentencing Julio got angry at the judge, demanding to know how he could give him 103 years when he hadn't killed anybody, but give his co-offender, who did kill the officer, only eighty-four years. Okay, said the judge, I'll give you eighty-four years, too.

The kid telling me the story laughed when he told me the last part.

WEDNESDAY, DECEMBER 20: Found out that Tommy Whitacre is doing time at Woodbyrne Youth Center, a sister institution, for possession of a weapon. James Pickle, one of our new kids, said that Richard Wain, who had been on John Loring's caseload, has been stabbed to death. Rob told me he'd heard that Willie Gonzalez, who was on mine, has also been killed.

Last night Joe Voit refused to get out of bed to attend Victim Awareness. I went into his room to try to talk him into coming out. Suddenly he sat up and punched the wall, startling me. The next thing I knew, my hands had come up in a defensive move and Herman was in Joe's face. I hadn't even known Herman was behind me.

In a moment Joe was on his feet, and then Rob was also there and got Joe in a straitjacket hold. I got Joe's legs to keep him from kicking Rob, but this threw Rob's hold on him out of balance and left Joe some room to squirm and we had to carry him out of his room and into the quiet room.

We laid him down on the floor and he began banging his head, alternately screaming and swearing, and making another noise like an animal's roar that he combined with his screams. He reminded me of when Peter Chaple became hysterical when Rob and I took him down, but Joe wasn't hysterical. Herman became afraid that Joe would try to kill himself and told him to take off his shirt and pants. Joe just kept screaming and roaring and banging his head on the floor, so we lifted him up as he struggled, trying to break loose, and pinned him like a moth in a display box against the wall.

By this time the scuffle had been going on for ten or fifteen minutes and we adults were at a loss for what to do next. Finally I grabbed Joe by the back of his neck and pressed the side of his face against the wall and started talking so he could hear me. I told Herman that we could probably get by with taking the kid's belt and socks and just patting him down instead of stripping him. I asked Joe if he would agree to that. "Yes-s-s-s," he said, the word coming out like a snake's hiss as it might be heard in an animated movie. I couldn't tell if he hissed out of anger or another emotion, or because the way I held his face against the wall prevented him from speaking clearly.

We took his belt and socks—his shoes had been left in his room—gave him a pat-down, and, one by one, backed out of the quiet room. As soon as the door was closed, he went off again. Not a wonderful experience for any of us. Not the kind of thing you come away from feeling spiritually uplifted.

THURSDAY, DECEMBER 21: Donald Jackson is a new kid on my caseload. He's been in Ash Meadow for several months, but was just transferred to Swan from Bull Cottage; I don't know why.

He says he lived with his brother Paul, a crack dealer, last year. Donald's file does not mention this brother.

He says he's been raped twice, once by his drug dealer and once by a guy who got him drunk after inviting him to his apartment. Both rapes occurred within the last year. He described them. The first sounds like rape, although he was paid afterward. The second time may or may not have been. He certainly set himself up, and it may have been an instance of prostitution. Both cases, as noted, were associated with either drugs or alcohol.

I asked him if he'd been tested for HIV, and he said he had been, here at Ash Meadow. The health center said he had not been tested. I do believe Donald lies sometimes.

He admits molesting his brother Michael, but says he wouldn't do it again because "it hurt him so much the first time." My sense is that if Donald did it again, it would be *because* it hurt his brother so much the first time.

Donald says he and some friends, while drunk, burned down a shack that was inhabitated, although the inhabitant, an elderly man, got out. Donald admits also to singeing the fur on cats and dogs and burning Michael with a cigarette.

SATURDAY, DECEMBER 23: Donald has agreed to be tested for HIV. We staff will not be privy to the results, but at least he will know whether or not he is positive. And there is always the possibility that he will tell someone if he is, and then we would know. (But, even so, how would we know whether or not he was lying?)

I warned him against lying to me. I told him it is a thing with me personally: I hate being lied to. I told him, too, that it is cottage policy to give a resident a minor bust and up to twelve hours OP if he is caught lying. Donald said he understood.

He talked a lot about his drug use. He likes opiates. His father and stepmother were both heroin users, but are apparently clean now. Donald said his dad introduced him to heroin, helping him fix the first time.

I asked why his father wanted him to do heroin. Donald said his dad told him he wanted him to understand why he used it. After the first time, he encouraged Donald to use it for his own pleasure. Donald says he's used it twelve or thirteen times, but never felt addicted to it, in that he never had withdrawal symptoms like he did with crank.

He says he began drinking and drugging when he was twelve. He's fourteen now. A younger brother introduced him to marijuana, which he doesn't like, and his mother introduced him to alcohol, which he does like.

Donald's mother committed suicide about a year and a half ago. He had been living with her until shortly before her death. A month after she died he tried to hang himself. He told me he did it so he could be with her.

1996

MONDAY, JANUARY 1: Donald Jackson says his stepmother beat him with her fists and slammed him against the wall from the time he was seven until he was twelve. At twelve he was large enough to intimidate her, and she stopped beating him. When he threatened her, she told him she would call the police if he hit her.

He says he did his first crime when he was ten: he beat a kid with a bicycle chain for making kissing noises and gestures at him. Donald says, too, that he fought with a kid at Bull Cottage who called him a fag.

I called Bull. Donald's former counselor there did not remember the incident, but said Donald does have some concerns about his sexual identity. No shit.

This confusion about, or denial of, his sexual identity, together with his drug use and the fact that he was introduced to hard drugs by his father, plus his stepmother's abusiveness and his mother's suicide, makes me less than optimistic about Donald's future.

He was well "therapized" at Bull. He knows the buzz words and uses them to conceal his emotions. He dissimulates. There is a pattern: he will say something, I will disagree, then he will agree with me as though we had been in accord all along. Then I will ask him to do something and he will ignore me. He has not started his autobiography, which I told him to do a week and a half ago. He has not been tested for HIV.

I told him he will not get a level promotion if he does not do the assignments I give him.

TUESDAY, JANUARY 9: I've noticed in Alternatives to Violence that when one of the videos we watch depicts a woman being slapped, some, but not all, of the kids in the group laugh. I've found that those who laugh have seen their mothers similarly mistreated. It's uncanny how consistent this is. What I mean by "consistent" is that it's true 100 percent of the time. (Those who do not laugh may or may not have seen their mothers beaten.)

What clued me in to this was a conversation I had with John Cash (named after the singer?). He told me that when he was four or five he saw his mother and stepfather arguing. He started to cry and ran into his room, his mother following him. His stepfather came in after her and asked her what she thought she was doing.

"I'm comforting my son," she said.

He said, "Oh yeah? I'll show you how to comfort him." Then he beat her up.

John said he had been afraid that his stepfather was going to beat him up, too. Now, he said, he was ashamed of having been afraid for himself, even if he was only five then.

I speculate that when a kid laughs at the video, he is releasing the tension caused by a remembered sense of powerlessness, that is, his inability to help his mother. But I think, too, that over time he may come to resent his mother for having been too weak to defend herself, and him, from being beaten. If this happens, he may also come to identify with the person harming her, for this person is clearly stronger than she is, and if he identifies with the bully, then he, the kid, can be strong too, strong enough not to be hurt by people powerful enough to hurt his mother (or him).

At first, when I ask kids why they laughed at the video, they invariably say that it's funny—the expression on the actress' face, the way the slap came so unexpectedly—and insist, no matter how I frame the question, that they laughed for that reason alone. And when I ask how many of them ever saw their mother beaten, I can see them searching their memories by the way their eyes move. The faces of some, when they've found what they were looking for, become set and grim. Others—their eyes seem literally to bounce away from what they don't want to acknowledge. Yet eventually they do acknowledge it, if not within the hour or so that the group lasts, then by the next session.

Will the video, my probing, and their facing their memories deter them from brutalizing women? Maybe. In some cases.

WEDNESDAY, JANUARY 10: Donald has his C.O. group coming up. I went over the questions with him. He seemed to be honest when it came to the facts of what he did, but he avoided accepting responsibility for his actions, insisting it was the booze plus bad company that led him to do the burglary.

SUNDAY, JANUARY 14: First conversation with Ron Lafitte, a new kid. New to Swan, that is; he spent several months in maximum security. Apparently he was quite a problem there until recently. He's in for Robbery One. He and two adults held up a convenience store. He says he was forced to participate because a faction of his gang believed he had burned them on a drug delivery he made for them. His share of the money from the robbery would go to reimburse them. He says if he hadn't gone along with them, they would have killed him. After the hold-up he was given twenty dollars and a carton of cigarettes. This much is in his file. His account matches the information there. He says his gang still has a hit out on him because he hasn't paid them everything he owes. He remains committed to his gang in spite of the fact they intend to kill him.

He says he's very intelligent, and he seems to be. He's also loquacious in a kind of free-association style. Taking a little from my conversations with Tommy Whitacre, I said that something about him shows that someone in his life loved him. I asked who that might be, besides himself.

He laughed and said I was weird. "Everybody loves me," he said, as though that should be obvious.

Ron's father is in prison for having abused his children. He has an older brother in Elk Grove and another one serving time in a federal prison. He also has an older sister who is not in prison.

Their father used to beat the brother who is in Elk Grove, but he also beat Ron sometimes. Their father used to force the kids to read the Bible after supper until late at night. If they fell asleep, he beat them. He would quiz them on their reading, and if they gave a wrong answer he beat them then, too. Ron's brother would distract their father when he got angry with Ron, and that is how this brother was beaten so much more than Ron was. Ron hasn't said much about his other brother yet, the oldest of the three. I don't know where he was when all of this was going on.

Ron and his brother, the one who is in Elk Grove, lived with their mother and her husband after their father went to prison, but they fought with their stepfather and eventually went into foster care.

SATURDAY, JANUARY 20: Donald will have to do his C.O. group again. The other kids felt, and I agreed with them, that he was not taking responsibility for the crimes he did.

He seems not to feel remorse. His assault charge was for burning his brother with a cigarette. Donald says he feels no emotion at all about it. When I asked him later why he did it, he said he didn't know. I think he does know, but he doesn't want to tell me or anyone else.

During the group he accused the other residents of confusing him when he gave contradictory answers to their questions. He said his motivation for the burglary was to steal stuff so he could get drugs. But when he was asked again, he said it was to get something to eat and to get out of the cold for a while.

I talked with him for an hour and a half tonight. He said that when I shout at him I reduce his self-esteem and this makes him angry. (I don't believe I shout at him, but I do speak bluntly to him. He may perceive that I don't like him.) This child has certainly worked hard to turn the ideas he's learned here at Ash Meadow to his own advantage: I "shout" at him, therefore I am responsible for his anger and his loss of self-esteem.

He gets angry too, he says, when other kids belittle him. I suppose we can say, then, that his anger provides a way for him to regain his self-esteem, to feel potent.

I get the sense that all of this, the stuff about self-esteem and anger, is something he's giving me because he hopes to get something from me in return. And that something is a roommate. He wants one, he says, so he'll have someone to talk with and play cards with. He's lonely, he says. I believe that. But there's no way I'll agree to his sharing a room with another kid.

I turned the conversation back to the notion of responsibility. I told him he needs to accept responsibility for his behavior so he can gain control of his life. And to do this he needs to believe he's capable of gaining control of his life. If you refuse to take responsibility for yourself, you are saying you are not capable of living your life independent of those who will control you. You might consider doing enough crimes when you get out that you will spend the rest of your life in prison, I said.

He responded by saying he likes getting into fights on the outs, even when he gets beaten up. He stabbed a kid in the arm once, but wasn't caught, he said. It was a thrill to stab him because he did it for revenge, and it was another thrill to get away with it.

So much for my little lecture on responsibility.

SUNDAY, JANUARY 21: Ron told me that his father was sent to prison because some of his, Ron's, siblings told CPS that he had sexually abused them. Ron says they lied, and they lied in order to please their mother, who was angry with him for having hit her.

The last time Ron and I talked he told me his father had beaten him and his brother, and he said that while he was unhappy about being taken away from his father, he had been happy to get away from the beatings. When we talked today, he passed over the beatings as if they meant little, or nothing at all. But later in the conversation he reiterated how much he loves his brother for having taken their father's beatings so that he wouldn't have to. Ron said he cries when he and his brother are getting ready to do something dangerous, because he is afraid his brother will get hurt. He said he would die for his brother. He said that while other kids say things like this, that they would die for someone, he means it.

He said he'd been involved in several shootings. Here I think he was trying to con me. Earlier today I had seen him watching me, studying me. I'm sure he made a conscious decision to try to con me, to see whether I would buy in. I doubt that he's shot anyone as he claims to have done, though he may have tried to.

Last week he told me the reason he got only twenty dollars and a carton of cigarettes from the robbery was because he did not shoot the store clerk when the others told him to. Today when he was going on about all the gunfights he'd been in, I said it sounded like a movie, not something told from experience. He ignored me and went on talking.

FRIDAY, JANUARY 26: Robin and I walked in Discovery Park yesterday. We saw three flickers at the edge of the open field west of the parking lot. They were feeding on the ground along with the thrushes. We saw Bohemian waxwings a little farther on, in some bushes at the edge of the trail. And perched on a high, bare tree was an immature bald eagle, already quite large. A crow was trying to worry it, but it was not worried. Finally the crow set down on a nearby limb. It looked miniscule beside the other bird. Oddly, its size compared to the eagle's, and its sitting there so complacently, reminded me of Reggie Greene, and I began to laugh. Robin asked me what I was laughing at, but all I could say was that the crow reminded me of someone I knew.

I hadn't seen Robin in eight or nine years, then ran into her at a Safeway. We were in graduate school together. She recently separated from her husband, her children are grown. I'm not sure what is going to happen between us, if anything. She says she's looking for companionship. Working with these kids, I've learned not to take anything anybody says at face value.

SUNDAY, JANUARY 28: James Pickle told me last night: 1. Reggie Greene fell for a woman with money he met while he was at Fessendon and went AWOL to be with her. They're in Chicago; 2. Aaron No Bear, who was in Swan Cottage three or four years ago, was shotgunned and lost part of his colon and a piece of his hip bone; 3. Jack Bergeron (a kid in Ram) is doing time for an auto theft that James did. Jack thought that because he had no record, he would get fifteen days, while James, with his record, would get a year or two. So Jack confessed and got two years; 4. Michael Fuentes is doing four years at Elk Grove—armed robbery and assault. The assault was apparently pretty savage; 5. Michael's younger brother was jumped out of his set. He's doing good, James said.

Where does James get all this stuff? I know he talks to his father frequently. Is his dad a clearing house for information on kids we've had at Swan?

MONDAY, JANUARY 29: Donald blathered for two and a half hours about everything he could think of. He does this when he approaches a topic he doesn't want to talk about, yet he does want to talk about it. What he did and didn't want to talk about was his life with the man from whom he got his drugs and with whom he lived. I had thought Donald was living on the streets—that is, going from one friend to another as he wore out the hospitality of each—before he was arrested, but he was actually living with just this one guy. This is one of the guys who, Donald said, raped him.

Why did Donald choose today to tell me about this part of his life with drugs? He had just had a call from his father, who told him he was going down to California for a few months to get away from his own drug dealers. He said he wants to get straight. Donald is contemptuous of his father for thinking he can outrun his addictions.

WEDNESDAY, JANUARY 31: Ron talked about joining Islam. He alluded to two friends, the older brothers of Josiah, Ron's former friend. Josiah identified Ron to the hit men who came for him as the kind of person who, yeah, might keep a little money from a drug sale for himself. Ron believes Josiah said this out of fear for himself. Still, he and Josiah were close once, and although Ron says he can never trust him fully now, he would like to be close to him again. Josiah took the place of Ron's brother when the latter went to Elk Grove.

When Ron mentioned Josiah's brothers, he used the word "friends," but I think he meant something more like mentors or guides: they were the ones who introduced him to Islam. One of them blames whites for everything bad in the world. The other says the first one is crazy, that he blames whites for what he himself does.

Ron does seem sincere in his faith—or perhaps his wanting to have faith. He said he's read most of the Qur'an and intends to read it all.

THURSDAY, FEBRUARY 1: Nels, a staff at Ram Cottage, told me yesterday that Jimmy Mills, a Ram resident, said he'd seen Reggie Greene in Seattle after he ran from Fessendon. According to Jimmy, Reggie did go AWOL to be with a woman—Mike Carter's brother's ex-girlfriend. (Mike Carter is a former resident of Swan and is from the same set as Reggie.) This version sounds more likely than the one that had him going to Chicago—Nels said another version had it as Detroit—with a wealthy older woman.

TUESDAY, FEBRUARY 6: Tom Ballou, in Alternatives to Violence, told us that when he was three he witnessed a fight between a black man and a Mexican. The black man was winning until the Mexican pulled out a knife and stabbed him, ripping his gut open. Then he made a cut across the black man's forehead and, with his fingers, tore the skin from his face. This is Tom's earliest memory. "You see that when you're three or four years old, it leaves an impression, you know?"

SATURDAY, FEBRUARY 10: I called Shannon Jackson, Donald's grandmother, to try to find out what's become of Donald's father. Donald has been after me to call; he says his grandmother won't talk to him.

Shannon said Donald's father and stepmother left for California last week. She referred to Richard—her son, Donald's father—as a sociopath. She said when he's angry he'll punch holes in the wall, throw cans of pop at his children, drag them by their hair. Obviously Donald's behavior sometimes replicates his father's, and she has told Donald this. She said, too, that there's a warrant out for Richard and his wife. The warrant pertains to Michael, Donald's brother, but Shannon doesn't know, or wouldn't tell me, what it's about.

She believes Donald feels guilty about his mother. Her last child, born shortly before her suicide, was born with Fetal Alcohol Syndrome and spina bifida. (Donald has not mentioned this child, his half-brother, to me.) Donald accused her of injuring the child by her drinking, but she denied that drinking had anything to do with the baby's condition. Donald told her that if she didn't stop drinking he would never see her again. Shannon thinks Donald did speak with his mother once more before she died, but blames himself for her death nonetheless.

Shannon has not visited Donald because she recently had back surgery. When she's feeling better, she said, she'd like to have family counseling with him here at Ash Meadow. She doesn't know why he would think she doesn't want to talk with him. When I offered to put him on the phone, she declined, saying her back was bothering her.

MONDAY, FEBRUARY 12: I asked Ron last week to imagine a situation on the outs where he would be tempted to do something that could get him in trouble, and then to figure out a plan to keep himself from doing it. Here is what he came up with.

"My brother asks me to help him jack this other guy's jacket and I tell him, 'No, it ain't worth it. We might get into trouble and plus you already have a jacket.' And he'll say, 'I no but I want another one. We won't get caught. Your just afraid, ain't you?' And I'll say, 'Yeh, that's it. I'm just afraid' and he'll say, 'I no you are a punk.' And then he'll try to make me believe that I owe him something. He'll say, 'I did this in the past for you and you still owe me. You no that, right?' And I'll say, 'I'll pay you in a different way.' And then he'll say, 'Don't even talk to me, punk. Your a little bitch. Scared to jack one little jacket' and it'll go on like this for a wile and then he'll finally forget and apologize to me and the same thing will happen again."

Here is Ron's plan for staying out of trouble.

"I plan to go to a full day of school all day every day.

"I plan to get me a legal job.

"I plan to think about my victim before I do another stupid thing.

"I think all of this can be done if I give up the drug and alcohol life."

It all sounds reasonable until you consider that his brother and his friends will be pulling at him to go along with them, and he doesn't have anybody in his life he respects who will tell him not to.

TUESDAY, FEBRUARY 13: Wonderful day today. Herman takes away the minor busts Roy and I gave Johnny Longtree and Michael Biddle last night when they wouldn't stop shouting out of their rooms. This morning Oscar Gonzalez told Herman he was the one making all the noise. He was lying, probably to indebt the other boys to him, and Herman bought it. Now Herman refuses to listen to my objections that Oscar lied to him. Herman says I need to find out what was really going on, as if Roy and I were not here when it was going on. Typical fucking Herman.

Then Fran tells me that even though Donald Jackson is on Tables status, she will continue to allow him special privileges. She has been permitting him to play ping-pong with the non-Tables kids (but only Donald: other kids on Tables do not get to play ping-pong) when I am not here, and she has been letting him sit in the living room to watch TV. She says if I do not want Donald to have special privileges, I must write a justification for my decision in the log and she will consider it.

Remember, Donald is on my caseload, not hers, and she is not my supervisor. *But* she has Herman's ear. Why does she want to cut Donald slack, but not the other kids on Tables? She says it's because she feels sorry for him. I don't believe her. I think it's because he's my kid and the other Tables kids are not.

John Cash: "I like to see people in as much pain as I am."

SATURDAY, FEBRUARY 17: This afternoon I looked up from the staff desk to see Juan Reece and Johnny Longtree grappling on the floor. Stan and I separated them; I held Johnny and Stan got Juan. I was so focused on Johnny, I didn't even know at first who the other kid was. Johnny continued to yell out threats at Juan, so we had Johnny moved to Ram's quiet room.

What happened was this: Johnny, who was off-program, was let out of his room to get a mop, broom, and bucket to clean it, because he had trashed it earlier. Going back and forth to the mudroom, where we keep the cleaning supplies, he simply walked past the mudroom and came around behind Juan, who was sitting at Tables, and punched him in the back of the head. This was especially hateful because Juan is suffering badly from AIDS, though neither Johnny nor the other kids know it. (Actually staff are not supposed to know it either—state law prohibits our being told—but it's obvious: the lesions, the recurring fever, the weight loss and lack of appetite.) Still, everybody knows Juan is sick with something. Of course, that's why Johnny went after him: Juan would be easy. And Johnny, who, when he was smaller, was punked by a number of kids, has gotten taller and heavier and wants to build a new reputation.

All of this happened while other kids were being visited by their relatives. The visitors seemed to enjoy it.

TUESDAY, FEBRUARY 20: Donald Jackson approached me again about having a roommate. He accused me, again, of not trusting him. He claimed he had a roommate at Bull six weeks after he got there. He said he didn't remember what I told him the last time he asked for a roommate. I had told him I could not justify rooming a sex offender, even one who was not adjudicated, with another kid when there are other rooms available. I gave him this answer again.

Then he said I'm mean because I won't let him play ping-pong when he's on Tables. I reminded him that he is supposed to decline to play when Fran or any other staff tells him he may, but he had asked Michael Collins on Sunday to let him play. I may be mean, I said, but he has to show himself to be trustworthy before I will allow him any privileges such as ping-pong.

Then he asked me why staff don't trust him. I asked him if he was joking. He laughed and said he was. Then he said Fran trusted him. I kept silent.

He volunteered that he hit Joe Voit a couple of weeks ago—which is why he's on Tables now—because Joe had made fun of his stutter. Then he said he really didn't know why he hit Joe.

THURSDAY, FEBRUARY 22: Had a long talk with Ron Lafitte last night. He's a "high profile" kid, meaning the crime he committed was serious and it attracted a lot of media attention. His intense anger had not been apparent, though Herman told me it was there, until last night. I listened to him for two hours, including an hour after I was off shift. He's angry, angry, angry— at the judge who sentenced him; at Ash Meadow; at the schools he attended, at least the school administrators who he believes are racist; at anybody who keeps him from doing what he wants to do. Or so he comes across.

But, he has a cottage detail that pays him fifty cents an hour. He's conscientious about getting his work done on time. He says money he earns means something to him; it isn't like spending someone else's money. I infer that he wants to be part of the economic mainstream, but feels he's kept out. He's right, of course.

He's saved 115 dollars. "It's like having fifteen dollars," he said, because he doesn't want to drop below 100 dollars. "A hundred dollars isn't very much."

SATURDAY, FEBRUARY 24: Donald Jackson has been on SPL III since Thursday, when he punched out a window and used the broken glass to cut his arm. Today he asked for a shaver. After I refused to give it to him, he told me he had intended to cut his wrist with the blade.

Donald's constant theme is that nobody loves him. His grandmother, whom he assaulted, has not visited him, her reason being a severe back problem. Donald says yes, she has a back problem, but if she wanted to, she could pop a couple of morphines and then come up.

He says he wants to die so he can be with his mother. He's certain he would be with her because people who kill themselves all go to the same place. He insists he's not threatening to kill himself just to get attention; he really means to do it. He says he never thought about suicide until after his mom did it. He would like to go by drowning. That would be perfect, he says. When he was nine he fell off a pier and almost drowned. It was like a high, he says. His father saved him.

TUESDAY, FEBRUARY 27: I think I've mentioned this before, but it occurs to me (again) that Donald Jackson is not able to decide just about anything for himself, nor to evaluate anything as either good or bad. When he talks about the events in his life, and I ask him if something was good or bad for him, he says it was both, and in equal parts. When we play ping-pong, he often adjusts his grip on the paddle again and again, even as the ball is upon him. In conversation, he waits for me to express my opinion or make a judgment; then, usually, he will agree with me. Or he will offer his opinion, then change his mind when I give an opposite opinion. Then he will deny he changed his mind, or he will plead that he was confused by what I had meant, or by something else.

He is extremely jealous of the time I spend with Ron, the only other kid on my caseload now.

Me: "Find a level of paranoia you can live with, and stay there."

Stan, of a Boeing executive who used to be his neighbor: "Nice guy, for being as smart as he is."

SUNDAY, MARCH 3: Last Wednesday I gave Ron the assignment to write one or two pages on what gets him angry. Here is what he gave me today.

"When I fill angry I try not to show it at first because sometimes it can be a sign of weakness. They'll no just what to do to get me going and at times I let em but I think I handle it well. But when I get mad at a peer I sometimes try and hurt them in some way. Then I wait for em to attack me and say something that will set me off. That's why I say sometimes I set myself up for things. Now sometimes on the outs I won't want to fight but they no they can get me mad. On the outs I'm use to fighting other people to prove my point. I love violence and continue to hurt people simply because they won't stop when you tell em you don't like things. I try not to show my anger for another reason also. It's because sometimes I fill like I can let it all just build up until someday I get mad enough to let it all come out so I'll do more damage to another person. I get mad when I see my friends doing work they don't even get payed to do. [He is talking about cottage details: cleaning the cottage.] When I think about it a lot I get angry. It looks like modern day slavery so that's why it's such a big issue to me. I believe we should stick together and work together and it makes me mad when staff try and get kids to be on there side. It also makes me mad when the staff say one thing but do another. Now these are most of the things that make me less happy, more angry."

MONDAY, MARCH 4: Last night I got Donald out of his room about nine-fifteen, talked with him for an hour or so, then played ping-pong with him until almost eleven. He enjoyed both the talk and the game.

Today I talked with his grandmother. She believes it was Donald's father rather than Donald who molested Michael, but that Donald got Michael to say it was him. She thinks Donald confessed to it in order to hurt his stepmother. The reason Shannon suspects Richard is that she learned a few days ago that he molested his sister when they were young.

Ron lost his level today. He wrote in a letter to someone on the outs that he intends to kill someone when he's released. Security caught the letter before it was posted. I informed Ron that until Herman or I tell him otherwise, his mail and his phone calls will be monitored.

TUESDAY, MARCH 5: Donald told me that he did not molest his half-brother. He said Michael came to him after watching a television program on "bad touching" and said he had been touched that way. Donald asked him who had done it and Michael said it was a big man. He thought it was their father, but he wasn't sure. Donald also thought it was their father, but because he did not want him to go to prison, he told Michael to say that he, Donald, had touched him.

This does not make sense. Why wouldn't Donald have told Michael not to say anything at all? But maybe Shannon is right: Donald wanted to hurt his stepmother.

He said his conversation with Michael occurred in late July two years ago in a hotel in Anaheim where they were staying while on a trip to Disneyland. The molestation occurred before that. Donald said he was living with his grandmother when Michael was molested.

WEDNESDAY, MARCH 6: I asked Ron who he was talking about killing in his letter. At first he denied having said he was going to kill anyone, but then he admitted that he was referring to the person who told the police where he was. It was a full day before he and the guys he robbed the store with were caught. They were hiding out in an apartment. Someone—Ron believes he knows who—told the police where they were.

I told him he was going to have to convince me that he had put his intent to get revenge, if not his desire to do it, behind him before I would approve him for a level move-up again. I reminded him how much time he had left to do.

At 5:05 I left a message for the CPS worker in Seattle who is handling Donald's case to the effect that Donald now says he did not molest his half-brother, but believes his father did it.

The caseworker called back within half an hour and referred me to CPS' main office. I called there and was referred to CPS in Palm Springs, where Richard and Margarite Jackson and their son Michael supposedly are staying. I called Palm Springs at 6:25, 6:40, 6:50, and through the evening, but no one answered. I called the Palm Springs Police Department and they referred me back to CPS.

SATURDAY, MARCH 9: Conversation with Ron goes like this: he expresses his opinions, then when you respond, he shuts you out. He does this by forcing himself to think about something unrelated to what you are saying. Sometimes, he says, he will think about music, going over the lyrics of a song in his mind. Sometimes he actually hums to himself while you are talking. He was trained in this technique by some of the older members of his set.

He must fear his own doubt. Doubt may lead to a change in his thinking. He is so invested in his gang—he feels it's all he has—that he is afraid of being disloyal, or being perceived as disloyal. This fear, of course, is reinforced by his gang's accusation that he stole from them. He wants to regain their trust.

SUNDAY, MARCH 10: Ron gave me a . . . I would call it an explication of his relationship with his gang. I'm not sure why he wrote it; I didn't ask him to. He may feel that if I understood more, I would be more sympathetic toward him. Or maybe he was trying to clarify something for himself.

To synthesize: he says most kids join the organization—he, like Reggie Greene, calls Folk an "organization" rather than a gang—as a way of finding protection from other gangs or from other people who would harm them. While some branches of Folk see themselves as just another street gang, others see themselves as seeking a kind of unity. Ron says when he joined the Nation of Islam he was already in Folk. The same people who introduced him to Folk later encouraged him to become a Muslim. Both Folk and Muslims believe in caring for the neighborhoods they live in.

When he joined the Folk he was looking for something that had meaning. He wasn't interested in something that just went around and started trouble and made enemies. He wanted to belong to something that offered unity.

Folk is not about crime, although most of the members choose to do crime. But, he says, "I think no matter where you're from you can still have enemies. You can still get killed. If you don't become where you're from"—that is, join the gang your neighborhood identifies with—"or don't make friends with gang members, you have a higher chance of being messed with because you're saying you hate their beliefs. Even if you do not say it like that, you're putting em down.

"We have a thing on our block that is known to all the Folk. It's called D.W.T.C. In a good way it means Devastation, Wisdom, Taking Control. And in many ways our elders support us."

MONDAY, MARCH 11: Someone finally answered the phone in Palm Springs' CPS office—a woman named Debby. Debby said she needs the date of birth for both Richard and Margarite Jackson. I called Shannon and she gave them to me. I left this information on Debby's voice mail. Palm Springs CPS now has voice mail.

Elsewhere on the Donald Jackson front: Donald said today that he began using drugs only after his mother's suicide. It was after his own suicide attempt and a day of smoking marijuana that he lost his temper with his grandmother and pushed her and threatened to kill her. He admitted today that she had done nothing to provoke him.

TUESDAY, MARCH 12: Since last fall a volunteer named Matthew Plumber has been coming to the cottage a couple of times a month, sometimes once a week. Over the holidays he didn't come at all; I think he went out of town. Before he left he brought in some very nice, expensive ping-pong paddles as a Christmas gift for the kids. I warned him that the kids would destroy them. They would pick at the rubber and the foam until the paddles were down to the wood, not out of malice but from a sort of general anxiety that seems to pervade Ash Meadow.

Matthew said it was all right, the paddles were theirs. If they destroyed them, then they simply wouldn't have them to play with. Despite what he said, I didn't see Matthew as someone who gave something so that someone else could have it. I saw someone who, in his own mind, continued to own what he gave away. What I saw was a person who used a gift to indebt someone to him. But I suspected, too, that he did not know this about himself.

In fact, when he came back after the first of the year and saw that the paddles were in no better condition now than those we'd had for years, he was upset. He tried to disguise what he felt with nonchalance, then allowed it to show by telling me what he had paid for the paddles. Then he shrugged and turned away. He was more than upset; he was angry.

He did not come around for a few weeks, but then resumed his visiting pattern. He seems to have a different agenda now, though I'm not sure what the original one was. Last month when one of the kids got a major bust and was placed on twenty-four OP, Matthew wanted to let him bake a cake before going to his room. I said no. Matthew responded with "Aw, come on, Jerry, let him have this before going off-program."

Yesterday Donald Jackson was very angry with me and had been for a couple of hours. When he is like this, I do not allow him to talk to me because he will go on without let-up, sometimes for hours, and even then he will not be satisfied. Instead, I wait until he comes down from his anger. Then he can articulate what he wants and we can talk.

But during after-supper details, Matthew, seeing that Donald was angry, invited him to talk, then told Donald he should talk to me. Even though Donald told him that I did not want him to talk to me, Matthew insisted. I overheard much of this, but was absorbed in monitoring other kids' movement as they were doing their details. Donald approached and, before I could say anything, began to vent. He got angrier and angrier as he spoke, threatening to get a lot of major busts, without specifying what he would do to get them; to refuse to attend Survivors' Group; to spend the remaining fifteen months of his sentence locked down. Finally I sent him to his room.

Immediately following this, and before I could say anything to Matthew, he went up to two African-American kids who were sitting together at a table and said, "What's up, Boy?" He bent over them and looked into their faces, challenging them to respond. One of the kids was Ron Lafitte. I don't remember now who the other kid was. I was watching Ron; he is one of the most dangerous kids in the unit. Plus, he had just lost his level again and was not in the best of moods.

I said, "What did you say!"

"I was just joking," Matthew said. "The kids know that. Don't you?" He looked at them, that odd, challenging smile on his face again. The one kid hesitated, then nodded slowly and stood up and left from the table. Ron stared at Matthew for a long time before he broke eye contact and looked away.

I do not know why, but obviously Matthew intends to create a little havoc here in the cottage. He may be doing academic research. He told me once that, following his divorce, he decided to go back to college and is, in fact, a student now. Or his actions may be owing to a psychological quirk. But he does go out of his way to make a difficult situation worse. And he seems to have an instinct for those kids who are particularly vulnerable at the moment, and a propensity to goad them into acting out. I might have thought it's me he's really after, using the kids to get at me, as Fran will, but John Loring told me that Matthew does the same kinds of things when he's here during John's shift.

WEDNESDAY, MARCH 13: Matthew came in today. It's unusual for him to come in twice in a week but he said he found himself with some free time and thought he would drive up to Ash Meadow. I used the opportunity to confront him about the "boy" incident a couple of days ago. He said it was humor.

I asked him to tell me what was funny. He did not answer, saying only that humor has "a paradoxical connotation."

I asked what his agenda was. He said he had no agenda, but believed that "caring, trust, and respect" comprised a better way to manage residents than "structure, discipline, and consistency." (He actually said this, as though the two sets are mutually exclusive.)

I asked how calling a kid "boy," especially a black kid, showed caring and respect.

"We've already talked about that," he said.

I cited a number of times in which he had told kids to do the opposite of what staff told them to do, e.g., telling a kid he could talk in line on the way up to school; telling a kid who had just got ten twenty-four OP not to go to his room yet because they were going to bake a cake. I asked if his version of caring and trust included subverting cottage staff's authority.

He glared at me for a second or two, then said, "Of course not," and walked away.

THURSDAY, MARCH 14: I went by Everett Greiman's shop and bullshitted with him for a while. He said that when he was about ten he would see his parents beating on each other. In the morning they would behave as if everything was fine. He still has nightmares about it, he said.

Then he told me that a few days ago he and Baxter, his dog, an old terrier, were sitting on the curb outside the shop, basking in the sun, when two guys came out of the bar across the street. They crossed over and the younger one—Everett figured he was barely old enough to drink legally, if he was that old—kicked Baxter as hard as he could, "as if he were a football."

"Whoa!" Everett said. "Why'd you do that!"

The guy flipped him off. "Fuck you," he said to Everett. "Fuck you," he said to Baxter. He pulled a knife out of his back pocket.

"Whoa," Everett said quietly. He sat where he was.

This is why he doesn't own a gun, he said. If he owned a gun he would have shot that guy.

SATURDAY, MARCH 16: Richard, Donald Jackson's father, called him from Palm Springs tonight. Richard told him he's no longer using heroin and neither is Margarite. Richard said, too, that he got a job in a warehouse, driving a forklift. Donald was very up after the call, and optimistic about his father and stepmother.

MONDAY, MARCH 18: In Alternatives to Violence tonight, Tim Pendleton told us his father committed suicide. Tim said he did it because he had been in Viet Nam. Tim was small when it happened and did not know his father well, but that was what his mother and grandmother said. The shot woke him up.

Jorge Garza said he witnessed a stabbing when he was small.

We talked about how difficult it could be for the individual to know if violence is legal or illegal. I gave an example of a village being destroyed and the villagers shot; I used My Lai as the model. The kids' response was that if the soldiers were commanded to do it, it was legal.

I said it's illegal to obey an unlawful order. Soldiers are supposed to be able to think for themselves and to evaluate a situation accurately, regardless of what their commanders tell them. Soldiers are responsible for their own actions when it comes to violating the law.

As I hoped it would, this discussion led to another one, this one about gang violence. Tim said the violence in his life—seeing his father after he shot himself, finding dead guys, the victims of gang shootings, lying in the flower bed in front of his house—has imposed limits on the way he is able to live, although he doesn't know exactly how.

WEDNESDAY, MARCH 20: Ron talked more about the robbery. The guys he owed money had seen him walking on the street and had taken his gun and made him get in their car. They went into the Seven-Eleven, threatened the store clerk with a shotgun, told Ron to start grabbing stuff, then got out and into the car. Ron had gotten upset and one of the others had called him "suckah" and asked if he hadn't ever done a robbery before. "Not like that," Ron told him.

Recounting this to me, he seemed to go into shock, his lips going blue, his hands fidgeting, the muscles in his legs jumping—I could see his thighs in spasm under the cloth of his pants.

In an earlier telling, Ron said he had held the shotgun and the others had wanted him to shoot the clerk, but he had refused. In that version, he had had some control over what they were doing and refused to make it worse. In this version, he admitted that he had been intimidated into going along and was frightened during the robbery. Confessing his fear to me, I think, shows a level of honesty that he would not have been able to reach a few months ago.

He had not wanted any of the money they'd stolen, but the others insisted, so he took what they gave him—twenty dollars. He says now that he does not want to continue in the criminal life.

MONDAY, MARCH 25: Yesterday Joe Voit threatened to kill Roy Burns. For reasons none of us know, he has become fixated on Roy. We moved him into the quiet room, where he would have his own toilet and would not have to be let out to use the head.

Angel Ramsey, an intermittent, was working with us. Herman had been in and had told Angel that under no circumstances was he to let Joe out of the quiet room. No sooner had Herman left than Joe asked Angel for a head call and Angel, having already forgotten what Herman told him five minutes before, and apparently having forgotten also that there is a toilet in the quiet room, let Joe out.

Joe walked directly to where Roy was sitting at the staff desk on the far side of the living room, picked up the telephone and swung it at him. Roy blocked it with his arm. Angel, having realized what he had done, came bounding across the floor and took Joe down. He and Roy together got Joe back into the quiet room.

I had been in the craft room with some kids, doing an Alternatives to Violence group, when the alarm went off. By the time I got the kids locked down, Roy and Angel were escorting Joe to the quiet room. Once Joe was locked in, Roy briefed me on what had happened and I called Herman at home.

Herman wanted to know why we hadn't slammed Joe and why Roy hadn't taken Joe down himself. It sounded like Herman wants us to start slamming kids, that is, to cause more pain than necessary in taking them down. But if someone gets hurt, a staff or a kid, will Herman accept responsibility for having set us up so that the injury could happen? No. This reminds me of Viet Nam, where higher-ranking officers (read "managers") wanted things done, but would not put anything in writing. They left it to the troops to do the dirty work, then denied having given the order for it or even having knowledge of it, when someone found out.

Why does Herman want us to slam kids? I think it's because he feels he does not have control of the cottage. This, at least in part, is because he spends so little time here. He's gone for up to a week at a time, he comes in for a day or two, acts the bully with staff, then leaves again. I think that when he sees staff responding to him he feels in control again. And I think he wants us to slam the kids because he would then feel that staff, not the kids, control the cottage. He dominates staff, staff dominate kids: he wants evidence that these relationships are real.

Joe Voit was transferred to Elk Grove today.

WEDNESDAY, MARCH 27: I talked with Shannon Jackson, Donald's grand-mother, a couple of days ago. She said Donald told her during a telephone call that she is a terrible person and a morphine addict. She would like to have family counseling here with Donald. She said Donald wants to talk with her about his father, but she will do that only in counseling. I doubt she'll come to counseling. She's never been here to visit him, in spite of her intentions.

Tonight Donald and I were playing ping-pong. On the last point—he'd lost badly—he hit the ball with all his power directly at me, forcing me to duck. He was smiling happily. Of course he said it was an accident. The smile did not leave his face even as I sent him to his room and locked him in. He made it clear that a demerit and an early bedtime were a small price to pay for making me flinch.

SUNDAY, MARCH 31: John Cash: "I have this dream—I dream it a lot—that I have parents and my brother and sister live with us, and I go to school and

I do good in school, I get good grades and I come home and my mother's there and she gives me a hug and my brother and sister are there and they give me a hug, and I deliver newspapers and I go out and deliver my papers and make money and people respect me, I'm respectable.

"It's never been that way. It never will be. I have another dream, it may be a flashback. I'm sitting on my bed, crying, and my mother comes in and she's drunk, I smell beer on her breath, and she hugs me and my stepfather comes in and asks her what she's doing. 'I'm comforting him,' she says, and he says, 'Comforting him? I'll show you how to comfort him.' And then he begins to hit her and he beats her up and then he beats me up.[9]

"I wish somebody would kill me. Every time I've tried to kill myself, I've failed. I can't even kill myself right."

TUESDAY, APRIL 9: When Tim Pendleton came to us a few months ago, Herman called the entire cottage together and told everybody about Tim's injury, that he'd had some damage to his skull when he was younger and that another head injury might kill him. Herman warned the kids not even to think about hitting him, no matter how angry they might get with him. (Actually, he's fairly easy to get along with.)

Last Thursday, Donald Jackson filled a water bottle, then hit Tim in the back of the head with it. He knew about Tim's injury, he even told Michael Biddle afterward that he knew. Herman said assault charges will be filed against Donald. He was transferred to Wolf Cottage.

Matthew was in today. He smiled as though he were my best friend. He said he would be coming in only a few times more. He graduates in June and he's planning on doing something else then, maybe leaving the Northwest.

MONDAY, APRIL 29: One waitress to another at Burgermaster, a restaurant where I hang out: "If I wasn't so chicken, I'd commit suicide. I had an aunt that did. I didn't know her. She was a great aunt. She had brain damage."

WEDNESDAY, MAY 1: Last night after Alternatives to Violence, Cal Reed asked to talk to me. I was hoping, as I took him into the staff office, that he wasn't going to confess to something I didn't want to report. But it wasn't anything like that.

He was concerned about his laughter, which he sees as sometimes inappropriate. He laughs at things he finds funny, but which other people do not.

For example, when Ron Lafitte told him his, Ron's, mother was dead (not true, by the way), Cal laughed. But last night when Pang-li talked about the death of his cousin and how Pang thought he'd seen his cousin's ghost, Cal got scared, although the other kids were enjoying the story. He's afraid of ghosts, especially the ghost of the boy he killed.

He said he's told other kids that you'll go crazy if you look into the eyes of the person you've killed as he's dying. He doesn't know who told him that, but he's repeated it, even though he's not sure it's true. Darlene Lauder told him she doesn't feel bad about the woman she killed; if she allowed herself to, she'd go crazy, Cal said she said.

I suggested that insanity was not really what he and Darlene were talking about. Rather, they would be confronted with themselves, with trying to deal with what they did, without the defense of telling themselves that it wasn't so bad, or that it's over now, or that they don't feel bad about it. Cal thought that was true.

I asked him if he honestly believed that Darlene has no regrets, not only about having to serve time, but about having killed a woman who had tried to befriend her.

Cal thought Darlene did feel bad, or she wouldn't have said she didn't.

But he does fear the supernatural. He remembers seeing his father beating his mother on a night he saw one of "the Freddy Kruger movies" (*Halloween?*). Now he associates his father with Freddy Kruger. When Cal was small, he would dream of fearsome beings that he believed might kill him. He would wake up, telling himself they would be gone now, but they would still be there. One looked like R2D2 in *Star Wars*.

Even now, he said, he keeps his body covered when he sleeps. He doesn't even hang a leg out of bed. And he sleeps with his back to the wall.

We never did talk about his odd laughter.

THURSDAY, MAY 2: Michael Collins: "*Somebody* has to love these kids."

WEDNESDAY, MAY 8: I reviewed a video, a TV documentary, *Bangin' in Little Rock*, I think it was called, to see whether it's appropriate for our kids to see. It's about Bloods and Crips in Little Rock, Arkansas. I felt despair watching it. Went outside where some of the kids were shooting hoops, just to be near them, as though my presence could protect them. Cal Reed, Ron Lafitte, Pang-Li, Larry Street—"My little soldiers," I thought.

What about them reminds me of soldiers? I think it's the weariness and paranoia I see in them, the sense that death may snatch them at any moment. Watching them play. Despair—theirs and mine—and laughter.[10]

MONDAY, MAY 13: Last night, toward the end of Student Government, Ron Lafitte, the president, asked if anybody had anything else to bring up. William Lee mentioned that Stan drew German soldiers on the back of the day sheets. He did not say there were also staff cars in the pictures. For Stan, the car is the thing; the soldiers provide backdrop. Stan likes to sketch older cars, back to Model A's and T's.

William asked if anyone besides himself was offended. Cal Reed jumped in and put the question to Angel Ramsey, who will be working as a temp with us until Herman can find someone to fill his slot. Cal's question to Angel was this: "As a Jew, what do you think about Stan drawing pictures of Nazis?"

Angel: "I think he's a neo-Nazi."

I could not believe he said that. I just stared at him. He saw me looking at him and said, "That's what I think."

I cannot exaggerate the pandemonium that followed: the kids had manipulated a staff into "defecting." Pang-li said, "What you draw is who you are." When I told him that was b.s., he said one of his teachers had told him that. Another kid, which one I cannot remember now, said something similar.

By now, the meeting had devolved into a bitch session. Two or three kids complained that staff do not look hard enough to find the things kids lose. Justin Swallow said he had lost something in his pocket and staff hadn't looked there.

Kids were so caught up in complaining that they ran out of time before they could nominate anyone for Student of the Week. They asked for more time, but I refused to give it. After all but the highest-level kids were in their rooms, the four who remained out decided to nominate kids themselves. No, I said, the entire cottage had to vote, not just the higher levels.

They decided then to put in everybody's name and let staff decide. The rule is that Student Government nominates up to three kids, from which staff select one—I didn't accept the nomination of the entire cottage.

After most of the kids were locked down and the issue of Student of the Week dealt with, I called Herman at home and told him about Angel's remark. Herman asked me to write out what had happened in a memo and put it on his desk.

While I was on the phone in the office, Roy commented to Angel that it's quite an accomplishment to be able to talk with two feet in your mouth. Angel claimed that what Cal had asked him was "What would you do if you found Nazi pictures in somebody's room?" Angel also denied that he had said what both Roy and I heard him say, and asked Cal to vouch for him. But Roy walked away before he could hear what Cal might say.

Tomorrow at PC I will recommend that we dissolve Student Government, then begin again with an education program to train at least some of the kids in the purposes of government. I will also recommend that we dispense with the notion of Student of the Week until a new student government is set up.

TUESDAY, MAY 14: PC accepted my recommendations. As I knew would happen, I was appointed to train kids in the functions of government and to help them establish a new one. Oddly, when I told the kids this, there was almost no response. Maybe they expected worse.

SATURDAY, MAY 18: Angel didn't work yesterday but called in and talked to Roy. He said Herman had shown him the memo I wrote, adding, "This is what your peers think of you," as if Angel were a child.

Had I known Herman was going to show him the memo, I would not have written it, or I would have written it differently. I thought I was writing for Herman's information only.

Angel told Roy I should have been more sympathetic toward him because, after all, we are both, Angel and I, Jewish.

"Jesus Aitch Christ," I said when Roy told me this. Then I said "Sorry" because I'd forgotten he's the son of a Christian preacherman. Still, he laughed.

MONDAY, MAY 20: Last night I sat Ron, Cal, Pang-li, William Lee, and Tim Pendleton down in the living room to begin to train them in how to conduct a meeting. I began by saying that there can be no more staff bashing. That was as far as I got.

Ron said Student Government was for students to express their feelings, and student issues arose from those feelings. He rejected my idea that he was imposing his feelings on the other students. Pang-li took the position that staff should stay out of students' business. Cal tried to talk Ron into being more flexible because they were in danger of losing Student Government. But when he saw that Ron wasn't going to bend, he said that because "staff," meaning Angel, agreed with the kids about Stan being a Nazi, the kids were also speaking for staff when they expressed their feelings.

Ron said the students elected him to represent them, and he would express their feelings to staff regardless of the consequences. He said I had come to this meeting with my own agenda, and again dismissed the notion which I'd reiterated, that he also had an agenda, which was to impose his anger on Student Government, then say he was representing students' feelings.

TUESDAY, MAY 21: I got Ron his Level 3 today. That's how I put it to him, that I—*I*—got it for him. Staff voted for me, not for him, and I've spent *my* credibility with them by doing this for him. And now, if he's going to continue as president of Student Government, he has to conduct its meetings according to procedure, in which I will train him.

If he refuses to do this, if he encourages or permits even one more episode of staff bashing, he may be able to establish his integrity, as he might put it, but Student Government will be ended for good and there will be no more Students of the Week. The price of his integrity, then, is students' losing privileges rather than gaining more. A hard lesson, to be sure, but, hell, he did a robbery he didn't want to do because he'd decided that his life was worth more than somebody else's money, or even somebody else's life.

I said all of this to him. We'll see how things go on Sunday.

SUNDAY, MAY 26: Student Government went smoothly. William Lee tried again to get the other kids stirred up by saying Stan owed them an apology for having drawn German soldiers, but Ron ignored him and Cal, apparently working in concert with Ron, quickly introduced a different topic. William seemed confused and said nothing more. There are three candidates for Student of the Week.

MONDAY, MAY 27: Had Memorial Day off. Went with Robin to the Nisqually Bird Refuge. Saw a blue heron rookery, the herons croaking and clattering in their nests, sounding like wooden planks clapping against each other. Flying, they look like an artist's rendering of pterodactyls. Also saw a single snow goose among some Canada geese, and, on the mud flats, a curlew.

We had a five-and-a-half- or six-mile walk. After racquetball yesterday with Roy Burns and a run the day before, I'm a little tired today. But it was a sunny day, and Robin was good company, and I feel very, very good.

William Lee tonight: "When I was a kid we didn't have brains. And we were grateful. We didn't have fingers either. We had to grow our own. We had to steal our teeth from the tooth fairy."

Justin Swallow: "If you fart on somebody, is that assault?"

TUESDAY, JUNE 4: In Alternatives to Violence tonight, Ron told about a gang killing he said he'd heard about but had not participated in. I suspect that some of what he said was made up, but that it was true essentially. Again I am struck by this yearning to confess some of the kids have, even when they don't know they want to.

If the story is true, and if Ron was actually involved in the killing, it would help explain why he doesn't have much empathy for people: he doesn't allow himself to. He cannot permit himself to identify with his victims, so he seeks a kind of psychic numbness. Writing this, I'm reminded of what Cal told me about his conversation with Darlene Lauder.[11]

Tom Ballou said during the group that he expects, and wants, to return to a life of violence—he likes that adrenalin high. He said he doesn't think about getting hurt. He acknowledges the possibility of his own death, but figures he'll go wherever his friends are, Heaven or Hell, and if there is nothing after life, he won't care.

I suggested the possibility that he might be crippled rather than killed.

"In that case, I'll just have to keep a gun handy." In order to kill himself, I assume he meant.

Both he and Ron said that, for them, time slows down when their adrenalin is pumping, everything looks "fake," as in a movie. I was reminded of my own experience of running out of an ambush, convinced afterward that I had actually seen the bullets passing my left leg.

They made the point that what violence, at least gang violence, is all about is dominance, though they didn't use that word. It's about not allowing others to be your equal, except for your homies, of course. This, I think, explains how Ron or Michael Fuentes could beat somebody down or shoot somebody who is unarmed and think it's right to do it: it assures, at least in the short term, that you and your homies will prevail over him.

The idea of dominance explains too, I think, why gangsters respond so readily to authoritarianism, though they despise authority. It is the violence, actual or potential, that attracts them, especially when it is personalized. They want to be able to see who is ordering them around, to size him up— "check him out," they would say—to see what he has beneath the surface, what knowledge he owns. This is how you have to live if you are going to survive in the world.

My little soldiers.

MONDAY, JUNE 10: Ron *seems* to be changing. He says he is still a gangster, "but . . ." He says he needs to learn how to listen to others. He says he wants to know more, and admits the possibility that gang life is too restrictive, if for no other reason than that your enemies may prevent you from moving to where you want to go and meeting people you might want to meet.[12] We discussed the possibility of his going to a group home, and he asked me to consider one not in Seattle, so he isn't drawn into the life again.

His brother will be released from Elk Grove soon. Ron says his brother's big issue is their dad and the beatings their dad gave him. But, Ron says, his brother is beginning to be able to forgive their father.

TUESDAY, JUNE 11: Cal Reed in Alternatives to Violence this evening (I had to coach him not to tell us when or where it happened, nor to use real names): "It began—we went to a dance. One of my homies said something to this girl and she, you know, she said something too. She was laughing. We didn't know she was with this other—these other boys. And one of them called my friend a nigger. And he came over to us and he told us that this Mexican called him a nigger. And I got hot. And I wanted to get them, the Mexican guys. We could see them grouping up and talking just like we were doing, so we knew something was going to happen.

"They left, then we did. We walked out into the parking lot. My homie who was talking with the girl was walking ahead. He was in front of us maybe fifty or seventy-five feet. And they were waiting by their car. And they shot him—pop pop pop—a twenty-two. In the shoulder. Then they took off in their car and we got in our car and followed them to a park about a block from this elementary school where they stopped. And we stopped.

"They must not have figured that we had guns too, probably because we didn't shoot back when they shot at us—shot my homie. But that was because our guns were in the car. They were stupid. They only had the double deuce. We had two trey-eights and a twelve-gauge shotgun. We shot them, all but one. We shot at him but he was lucky. There were a couple of girls—the one and then another. The boy we shot in the front with the twelve-gauge recovered fully. I'm just joking. The others were just shot in the arm, in the shoulder, in the leg.

"I don't know what we could have done different. Maybe not done anything when they called my homie a nigger. But when we were putting the guns in the car before we went to the dance we talked about killing somebody that night. I knew I was going to kill somebody that night."

TUESDAY, JUNE 18: New kid on my caseload—Terry Voight. He's here on a charge of malicious mischief. He is a nonadjudicated sex offender, meaning he has admitted to committing a sex offense but was not charged with it. He "touched" his sister.

He says he was molested by an older cousin who also molested several other children in the family. This cousin has been arraigned.

Terry says he has a problem with lying. He attributes it to trying to escape the consequences of doing something wrong. I think it may also be related to his having been abused.

He was a skateboarder on the outs. He talks about skateboarding the way the other kids talk about basketball. He knows the names of the famous and not so famous skateboarders, what each is noted for, what kinds of boards they use.

He says he's not into gangs because gangsters get shot. But he is into Satanism. He says he became a Satanist because he couldn't stand the principal, and also some of the teachers, at a Christian school he attended.

MONDAY, JUNE 24: Terry has a swastika scratched on his left hand, which the other kids have noticed. They accuse him of being "down for Hitler."

He tells me he molested other little girls besides his sister. This is in his file. He's had quite a lot of treatment to help him to understand and control his impulses; he admitted touching other kids during a treatment group on the outs.

He says he was angry with his parents when he molested his sister. But, he says, his counselor on the outs thought there was something going on with him in addition to his being angry. He says that when he gets out he doesn't want to do again what he did. He *hopes* he doesn't do it again.

WEDNESDAY, JUNE 26: Carol Ripito came down to the cottage to talk to Herman about something and I took the occasion to say goodbye to her. She's leaving Ash Meadow to head up a psychiatric unit elsewhere. I'm sure she doesn't want to leave; she's spent all of her career here. But the superintendent retired several months ago, and even though Carol filled in as acting superintendent, JRA selected someone else for the permanent position.

I wished her luck and told her I had learned a lot from her during the time when we co-facilitated the campus Survivors' Group. I told her I was going to miss her. She was touched, I think, and thanked me.

I know Herman has had his problems with her, but I've always respected her and had confidence in her judgment. I *am* going to miss her. Herman will report to Don Martino now.

SATURDAY, JUNE 29: Last Wednesday Ron came up to me in the office as I was getting ready to give out meds and asked, "Is it true you're black? Willie Bolles says you are." He was grinning, but I think it was a real question.

I said, "I used to be but I changed my religion."

Both of us laughed like hell. I don't know what I meant. I've been turning it over in my mind since, but I still don't know.

TUESDAY, JULY 2: Ron was depressed because Herman told him that he would not recommend him for a group home any time soon. Herman said he was still too invested in his gang. Ron says he wants to get out, and that he doesn't consider it likely he'll commit more crimes when he's out. He seemed to feel a little better after we talked.

FRIDAY, JULY 5: I've talked with Tom Ballou privately a few times in the last couple of weeks. He has initiated all of our talks.

In Alternatives to Violence he said he knows he will return to a life of violence when he's released. He says he thinks about it all the time, dreams about it, fantasizes about doing it. He's shot several kids, although he hasn't killed any, as far as he knows. Violence, doing violence, provides him more pleasure than any drug, he says. And he can control his high by the amount of violence he does. (He assumes, when he says this, that he is in control of his life, but he once remarked: "I've got a better grip on the mudroom [detail] than I do on my life.")

He's grieving the loss of his friends who have been killed. Also, I think, he's looking for meaning to assign to their deaths. In one of our talks he told me how quickly they went. "They would just be gone. I never got to say goodbye to them." The importance of saying goodbye is something he learned in Grief-and-Loss Group.

But when he said "They would just be gone" I recalled my own post-war experience when I was trying to come to terms with the loss of almost everyone I had been close to. Eventually I had to acknowledge that their lives were meaningless because their deaths were. And, as their lives had no meaning, neither had mine.

What would have given their lives meaning? Had they been accepted by their society, instead of being outcasts because they were soldiers, their deaths—their lives—would have been meaningful. Meaning is conferred by other human beings; there is no intrinsic meaning to life that we know of. Tom once said, "I don't regard myself as antisocial. I'm with other people when I do my crimes." For him, meaning is conferred by the society of outlaws.

But if he longs to resume the violent life, he is also afraid of returning to prison. That is how he expresses it, as a fear. In prison he is cut off from his homies. On the outs, living the life of violence, he can, in a sense, be in communion with them until he is caught again, or killed.

WEDNESDAY, JULY 10: Terry seems to be getting along better with the other residents. Some, like Michael Biddle, try to intimidate him, but he admits that he does things to make kids want to get back at him. (He has been caught reading other kids' mail. He puts down their mothers.) He is in both of my groups, Survivors' Group and Alternatives to Violence, and does quite well. He is thoughtful and more open, especially about having been raped, than I thought he would be.

SATURDAY, JULY 13: Ron says he isn't sure he wants to leave Ash Meadow because he'll miss the friends he's made here. This is a theme running through his life—loyalty: to his brother, to his gang, to the friends he made here. He has a difficult time breaking up with a girl even when she humiliates him with her infidelity, as the girl in Peacock he is going out with does. His need to attach himself to someone is his bane.

He says he will remain straight for the six months he's on parole. After that, he'll see. He wants money because he wants "things," and he wants financial independence. He has not ruled out crime as a way to get all that.

This idea that kids here have of "going out" with someone is kind of moving. They hardly ever have a chance to touch each other; never is it sanctioned. Yet they talk to each other and write each other through the campus mail, visit each other in their respective cottages if staff in both approve, and declare that they won't go out with anybody else, as if they are true lovers. In a way, I suppose, they are, as much as they can be. I have heard of kids having sex, but it would be pretty rare that they could find a place and enough time together outside of staff's view to do it. Perhaps it isn't too different from when I was a kid and boys and girls went steady.

Oh yes, it is. Groping makes all the difference in the world.

MONDAY, JULY 15: Terry was the focus of a group tonight wherein the other residents confronted him on his proclivity to touch their butts, his racial slurs, and his antagonism toward them. They know that Michael Biddle and William Lee bully him—Michael because Terry is a white boy without friends, so it's safe to torment him, William because Terry is a sex offender and William was molested when he was small—but the others who don't bait or harass him object to his taking out his anger on them. For example, Terry fears getting beaten up by Michael and William, so he picks on Cal, who, he knows, will not hit him (because Cal sees Terry as beneath him; Terry is not in a gang).

Terry's "oppositional disorder," as his psychiatrist labels it, is real. He consistently does the opposite of what is expected of him, or, if he does comply, he will make a show of reluctance. He has no insight into why he is oppositional, but agrees that he is.

About his butt-patting: he does not discriminate between male and female butts. A few weeks ago, Bev, Rob's wife, came by to drop off some paperwork. She's the supervisor for Peacock, the girls' cottage next door to ours, and does the shift scheduling for both cottages (in return for which Rob does the payroll for both). She was bent over the staff desk, talking with Rob, when she suddenly straightened up and turned and demanded, "Who did that?"

Terry, who had just walked by, denied he did anything, but no one else had been near enough to goose her. He was punished, of course; I don't remember how many hours he had to spend in his room. But, God, it was funny—goosing the supervisor's wife! Even Rob laughed about it—later, of course, after Bev left and Terry was in his room.

TUESDAY, JULY 16: On July fourth, three of our kids, allowed out in front of the cottage to shoot hoops, ran away. They were caught and sent to Wolf. One of them, Morris Workman, had been with us for only a couple of months, and he was on my caseload. The only thing about him that impressed me was that he lied about everything that he seemed to think he could get away with lying about, no matter how trivial.

Herman told us today at PC that last Saturday Morris put a sharpened pencil to a female staff's neck and told Benny Roche, the other staff on duty, to give him his keys and alarm. Benny didn't, but didn't press his alarm either. Then the female staff—I don't know her name—collapsed at Morris' feet. Morris attacked Benny, who hit him back, breaking his supraorbital bone.

I told Ron tonight that I'm going to recommend that he serve three months more than his minimum—three months less than his maximum. He was upset; he'd been counting on getting his minimum. He'd been working hard to keep from getting in trouble and he feels now that it's been for nothing.

Although I told him he could still get his minimum if he graduates from the Phoenix Program or from Apple Park, he doesn't want to try. He remains heavily invested in his gang and I think he feels that drug-and-alcohol treatment would challenge his beliefs, and this frightens him.

He feels betrayed and I feel as though I betrayed him. He cried. He's angry and I feel terrible.

WEDNESDAY, JULY 17: More on Morris Workman. He apparently organized a couple of other kids at Wolf to attempt an escape with him, as he did when he planned his escape from Swan. The plan at Wolf was for the other kids to use mop handles to assault Benny while Morris took down Ruth Monroe and got her keys. Benny and Ruth were the only staff on duty. When the time came to do it, Morris grabbed Ruth from behind and stuck a sharpened pencil to her neck, but instead of going after Benny, the other kids ran to their rooms.

Morris warned Benny not to hit his alarm and told him he would kill Ruth unless Benny gave him his keys. (I don't know what happened to Ruth's keys.

Maybe Morris didn't want to relax his grip on her so she could get them out of her pocket.) Benny did not press his alarm, but tried to negotiate with Morris for Ruth's life. While they were talking, Ruth's legs gave out and she fell to the floor, leaving Morris exposed. He punched Benny (I don't know what became of the pencil) and Benny hit him back, breaking his jaw and the orbital bone at the side of his eye. I heard that Benny hit him hard enough to knock the eye out of its socket, but this may be only wishful thinking on the part of the staff who told me about it.

SUNDAY, JULY 21: Ron asked to talk with me and I took him into the staff office. He doesn't seem as angry as he did a few days ago. Instead, he appears very sad.

He's trying to come up with a way to get his minimum sentence. He does not want to go to drug-and-alcohol treatment. He's afraid of being required to confide his beliefs and life experiences to other kids in the treatment groups. I remember that Tommy Whitacre and Michael Fuentes felt the same way.

WEDNESDAY, JULY 24: Ron had his 60-percent board this afternoon.[13] Herman presided, since Don Martino didn't show up. This seems to be par for the course for Don. The same thing happened when Stan had a 60-percent board last week.

Ron got his minimum plus three months. Herman told him after listening to Ron plead his case that his gut feeling was that Ron should get his maximum, but he would go with my recommendation.

Ron cried again. I noticed that his voice gets thin when he's approaching tears. Again I felt terrible.

MONDAY, JULY 29: Terry was tried in Cottage Court today. Witnesses were Tom Ballou, Michael Biddle, Cal Reed, and Pang-li. The charges were racial ranking, poor hygiene, and instigating fights.

About racial ranking: Terry said Pang was saying something in Khmer and other kids were laughing, presumably at the sounds Pang was making as none can understand Khmer, so Terry mimicked Pang, trying to be humorous. He did not regard what he did as racial in nature, he was only trying to win the other kids' acceptance. But Pang and Tom, close friends, did see it as racial.

The bad hygiene: This is probably true. Terry did not try to defend himself. Many kids who have been sexually abused employ poor hygiene in an effort to keep people away from them.

Instigating fights: I couldn't figure out what this meant except that he gets kids angry at him. He may be trying too hard to fit in. As with the Pang-li incident, he sees kids laughing at something and so he does something that he hopes will make them think he's funny, but instead they get angry with him.

He said Michael Biddle has hit him several times, and today tried to hit him with a broom. He said Michael has threatened to hit him with his ring hand. Michael does this, Terry said, when Fran is on duty, because she doesn't see anything.

There's a real possibility that Terry has been made into the cottage scapegoat.

WEDNESDAY, JULY 31: Talked with Ron. He's "hella mad" about his 60-percent board. He says one of the staff—he wouldn't say who—had told him that if his behavior was good, we would give him his minimum; we would have to. Because we didn't, he feels we've been playing him, that is, being dishonest with him, getting him to trust us, then betraying him. I hadn't known he was basing his hopes on what another staff had told him.

When Herman and I told him how much time he was going to have to serve, we told him, too, that if he completed the Phoenix Program or the program at Apple Park, he would get his minimum. He said then that he would refuse to go.

Today he asked me about the two programs, how they differ, where Apple Park is, etc. But when I began talking about them, he interrupted me and said he didn't need drug-and-alcohol treatment, that it was a waste of time for him. We'll see.

SUNDAY, AUGUST 4: New kid, Tyrone Wiley, came over from Wolf. Anxious about his new cottage, he asked me if Stan is a Nazi. The damage Angel has done! Goddamn him!

SUNDAY, AUGUST 11: Ron told me this evening that he would be willing to go to Apple Park for drug-and-alcohol treatment, but not to Eagle Cottage, which runs the Phoenix Program, because he doesn't want to go through treatment with girls. Eagle is co-ed, Apple Park is not. He says it's hard for him to concentrate when he's around girls.

SUNDAY, AUGUST 18: Terry got a minor bust yesterday for hitting Michael Biddle in the face with a basketball. He told me Michael punched him in the stomach first, but he did not tell this to Fran, who busted him.

Later, in his room, he was tapping on his window and one of the staff cued him to stop. Then Michael, in his room, tapped on his window. When staff came into the zone, Michael said it was Terry who had been tapping. Terry was moved to the quiet room where, a few minutes later, he tried to strangle himself with his socks after having wet them in the toilet. Placed on SPL II, he went into mood and behavior swings, alternately crying and swearing, sitting morosely in a corner of the quiet room or pounding the metal door.

He stabilized early today and his suicide level was reduced to III. He is back in his room now. He claims not to remember having tried to kill himself.

On Wednesday his foster parents will visit him. He just found out—this will be the first visit he's received from anyone since he's been here—and he's so excited he can't sleep.

THURSDAY, AUGUST 22: Here is what I think I know about Terry Voight. His parents divorced when he was a year old. He went to live with Fred Voight, who, Terry believed, was his father. Terry's psychosexual evaluation says that his mother was neglectful and a substance abuser. These were apparently the reasons he was not placed with her.

When she was married to Fred she had an affair with Daniel Voight, Fred's brother. Terry is the product of that affair. At age six, Terry learned that Daniel was actually his father and went to live with him and his family. He stayed until he was twelve, when, following a beating by Daniel, he ran away. He was placed in foster care for three months, then returned to Daniel's house. For the next two years he alternated between his father's home and foster care.

At age three he was raped by three cousins at a family reunion. This information comes from Terry; there is no documentation on this. The reunion was a yearly occasion, and from age three to age five Terry was raped by these three boys every year. When he was five he was raped by his half-brother. At age eleven, Terry molested two of his cousins, ages eight and six. At thirteen he molested his half-sister, age two.

He was sent to a mental health facility and spent three months there. According to a report done by this agency, Terry disclosed that he had initiated sexual contact with six children aside from his sister. These include two younger boys. Terry has admitted to me that he had contact with four girls, but has not mentioned the two boys.

He has had difficulty in getting himself accepted by the other residents in Swan Cottage. On three occasions that I know about, he has touched another resident's ass. (And, of course, he goosed Bev.) This behavior has distanced him from the other kids and has also worked to establish him as the cottage scapegoat. He's had problems especially from one of the lower-functioning kids. Until Terry came to Swan, Michael Biddle had been picked on by several of the other residents; now he is Terry's special tormentor.

Terry has used racial epithets to hurt or anger his peers. He does this when another resident teases or taunts him. He does not seem to instigate misbehavior, for the most part, but responds disproportionately to others' victimizing him.

He is in Ash Meadow on a fifty-two- to sixty-five-week sentence for malicious mischief. Yesterday his foster parents—that is, the last set of foster parents he lived with—visited him. They appear to genuinely like him, but were realistic: when Terry said he wanted to live with them again, Mr. Sanders told him that if there is a bed available when he is released, they would like to have him back. If not, Terry will have to go somewhere else.

SATURDAY, AUGUST 24: I asked Terry why he likes Jimmy Mills, considering Jimmy is black. Terry said Jimmy is nice to him, and protects him from other kids.

"That says a lot for him, doesn't it? Especially when you think about some of the things you've said to the black kids. Calling them 'nigger' and all."

Terry agreed.

"Why do you think Jimmy puts up with it?"

"I don't call *him* 'nigger'."

"All right. Here's what I want you to do. Whenever you're tempted to call a kid a nigger, I want you to visualize Jimmy Mills. I think if you can do that, then maybe you'll be able to get past some of this racist crap. Do you think you can do that?"

"I'll try." About a beat and a half passed. "Can I call some of the white kids 'nigger'?"

WEDNESDAY, AUGUST 28: Terry Voight, about the toilet in his zone being stopped up: "Help! I've fallen in and I can't get out!"

MONDAY, SEPTEMBER 2: Ron is angry about having to attend the drug-and-alcohol group here in the cottage. He says it's boring. He says now that he doesn't want to go to Apple Park because he has the feeling that even if he graduates, Herman and I won't give him his minimum.

I asked him where all this anxiety had come from, but he just went on and on.

LATER: Last week (August 22 and August 23), the *Seattle Times* reprinted a couple of articles by Gary Webb from the *San Jose Mercury News*. In them Webb shows, convincingly, how crack cocaine was introduced to the United States by the CIA in order to finance anti-Sandinista forces in Nicaragua.[14] It's an appalling story, but anyone who believes it could not be true must have been born within the last five years. I gave the articles to Ron to read.

I wanted him to see that by dealing crack, which he has done, he has placed himself in the position of doing the dirty work of the very authority he despises, and who is obviously the enemy of black development. After all, crack was sold, at least initially, to blacks, not to whites. And how many of the CIA's decision makers in this instance did Ron suppose were black?

This evening, some time after his rant about attending drug-and-alcohol group, I asked him what he thought about those articles I gave him. He said he saw the connections I had talked about, but said, too, that he didn't want to feel bad by regarding himself as contributing to the destruction of the black community. He preferred to focus on the money he could make and to ignore the larger issue.

When I pressed him on how he could reconcile selling crack to the people he says he wants to help, or BGD's involvement in the drug trade with its claim that it wants to foster community development—BGD stands for Black Growth and Development as well as Black Gangster Disciples, Ron had told me, and I threw this back at him now—he distracted himself, and reassured himself, I think, by reciting his claims to the "knowledge" OGs from the BGD had imparted to him, and the meaning of the BGD symbols. I might have been listening to a fundamentalist, so successfully had he closed his mind.

This is typical of Ron. Under pressure of unwanted knowledge, he withdraws behind the shield of cant and ritual that BGD taught him.

TUESDAY, SEPTEMBER 10: Last night Ron sat in the living room with everybody else during Drug-and-Alcohol Group, but hardly spoke. When Rob asked him a question, he responded with a word or two or said he didn't know the answer.

I took him into the office and told him that at PC staff would be considering whether or not to allow him to keep his level. I told him, too, that he was behaving like a child, but that the child he was when he came to Ash Meadow is gone. I told him he is afraid of growing up and resists it by falling back on his childhood behavior. I told him he is using the idea of being true to himself as a crutch: the self he's being true to is a kid who no longer exists, the kid he used to be. I was angry but I think what I said hit home. He was listening.

LATER: At PC we took Ron's level from him for his refusal to participate in Drug and Alcohol Group. He says he doesn't care, but he does. When I told him, he made fun of PC's decision and of staff decisions generally, but he did this in a semi-whisper so other staff couldn't hear.

WEDNESDAY, SEPTEMBER 11: It occurs to me that Ron really hasn't fit in anywhere in his life with the exception of his gang, and even that is questionable. He has difficulty reading and he is not athletic. He doesn't have much confidence in himself except to do the things he thinks his gang would expect of him.

MONDAY, SEPTEMBER 23: Terry told me he molested his sister once, not three times, as his file has it. He did it on an occasion when a baby-sitter was taking care of them. His sister asked him to change her diaper. He took it off and placed his hand on her vagina. She started to cry—he thinks she was afraid—so he stopped.

He says he didn't know what to do sexually, but he wanted to get back at his parents. What he knew about sex he had learned from his cousins, some of whom had also molested, or raped, small children, including Terry.

He describes Daniel Voight, his biological father, as being physically abusive, hitting him with a belt at the least provocation, or with no provocation Terry could understand. His father overreacted to Terry's misbehavior, he feels. He says he knows that at times he behaves much as his father does. His father also goes out of his way to irritate people.

TUESDAY, SEPTEMBER 24: On Saturday there was a near fight at the gym. Fran had the kids up there to play basketball, but according to them, she was doing some sort of paperwork and was not watching them.

Tonight, for my Alternatives to Violence group, I called together Tyrone Wiley, Cal Reed, Ron Lafitte, Willie Bolles, Johnny Longtree, and others to dissipate the tension in the cottage, which I felt but which Fran and Michael Collins said did not exist. Nothing had been logged on this incident. I had picked up some allusions to it by overhearing the kids talk.

Hostilities on the court began because Cal and Tyrone had been having problems for several days—they wouldn't tell me the nature of these problems—and Cal decided to play rough against Tyrone during the game. He figured Tyrone would get angry, but, afraid of Cal, would find or manufacture an excuse to hit Michael Biddle or Donny Mack. These are two very irritating kids. Cal dislikes Michael especially because Michael used to punch him, then run away before Cal could hit him back.

Ron did not know of Cal's plan, but was also rough with Tyrone. When he saw Tyrone getting mad, he told him to chill. But Tyrone was remembering how he had been beaten up on the outs by "South-enders," BGD from the Rainier Valley in Seattle—Tyrone is a BGD from the Central District—and saw what was happening at the gym as similar in its beginnings. On the earlier occasion he had been too young to defend himself, but now he was determined to fight back, and moved toward Ron.

Johnny Longtree stepped between them and tried to separate them, but Tyrone told Johnny to stay back unless he wanted some too. Ron heard Tyrone say "too" and moved in closer. But then Cal moved in and told Ron to step back. He told Tyrone that if he hits anybody, "there will be a whole lot of blows coming down on your body." And then Willie Bolles, very much larger than Tyrone and even Cal, moved up "so that I'm suckin' his lower lip," Tyrone said—he liked this phrase and said it twice more, laughing between expressions—and Tyrone pushed him back. This, apparently, was when Fran noticed something unusual and stepped in. Fortunately.

Like Cal's story of the shooting following the dance,[15] we see several actors, each with his own experience in mind as well as a personal history that places him in the particular situation—that is, in the gym at Ash Meadow—performing his role as he expects himself to perform it. But we see, too, that each boy's memory of his earlier experience does not allow him to anticipate others' behavior, although he believes it will: Tyrone is not about to be jumped (unless he strikes first) and Cal's prediction that Tyrone will go after Michael Biddle or Donny Mack is inaccurate.

SUNDAY, SEPTEMBER 29: Terry's behavior has been very good. He hasn't received a demerit in a week. He's in a pretty good frame of mind, suffering his disappointments, if not well, at least not badly.

He told me a little about his grandfather. This was Daniel's and Fred's father, and the father of the uncle whose children raped Terry. His grandfather would call the girls in the family boys and the boys girls. He would refer to a boy as "she" and a girl as "he." Given the soft sexual boundaries in Terry's family, his grandfather's allusions should probably be considered both cause and symptom.

SUNDAY, OCTOBER 13: Terry blurted out this evening that the reason he touched his sister was that he knew she would tell her parents and they would believe her. He said he wanted to be forced to leave his father's house because he was afraid of his father and was angry with him and his stepmother for giving his sister more attention than they gave him, and he could not on his own bring himself to leave. As he talked, it was clear that he felt some emotion, but there was also something calculating about his telling me. The explanation that his father and stepmother gave his sister more attention is too pat, especially the way he phrased it.

Recall that Terry has been diagnosed as having Oppositional Defiant Disorder. Recall, too, that he idolizes Charles Manson for his antiauthoritarianism, and that he's in Ash Meadow for painting an anarchy symbol on an American flag out of dislike for the government. What drives him, it seems, is his desire to desacralize society's, or authority's, cherished symbols and to draw attention to the fact that he is doing it. And what would disturb his father and stepmother more than his violating their small daughter?

SUNDAY, OCTOBER 20: Talking with Terry this evening, I brought up again his offense against his sister. I said he has a pattern of getting angry with someone, then of releasing his anger on someone else who is more vulnerable than the person he is angry at. Molesting his sister fits that pattern.

He agreed and said he hadn't thought of it before.

We talked about his drug use on the outs. He said he isn't going to use again, except possibly cigarettes. I gave him an application for the Phoenix Program.

TUESDAY, OCTOBER 22: Ron says he feels as if both his family and his homies have abandoned him. He has not heard from his homies at all, and only occasionally from his family. His brother is talking about going to Florida, when he's released from Elk Grove. Their dad, who will be getting out of prison a little after Ron's brother does, will also be going there.

WEDNESDAY, OCTOBER 23: Ron talked to his brother Marion on the phone tonight. Marion lived in Chicago, then moved to Florida where he lives with their grandmother. Ron's other brother, Marlon, gets out of Elk Grove tomorrow. Marion said he's going to take Marlon back to Florida with him. Their father will be living with them.

Ron says Marion told him not to trust anybody but his family. He said not to trust even his homeboys, because they will betray him. He reminded Ron that he's in Ash Meadow because his homeboy snitched him out. Ron says Marion is an OG who is now trying to steer clear of his gang, the Disciples.

I haven't seen Ron so excited. He says he can't believe how much love he's feeling for his brothers. (He hasn't seen Marion in eight or nine years.) He says he feels sorry for anybody who doesn't have family.

It's difficult to figure out what exactly is going on. For example, Marlon can't leave Washington without the permission of his parole officer. Is he planning to run once he's out? Does he even know that Marion intends to take him to Florida? But anything that will reinforce Ron's loyalties to his family as opposed to his gang is all right with me.

TUESDAY, OCTOBER 29: Last week I got the administration's approval for Ron's brothers to visit him. Marlon was released from Elk Grove on Thursday and Marion was in the area too. Today at PC Herman told us that on Friday they did indeed visit. They came in and, even before they sat down with Ron, they started throwing gang signs at the other residents, essentially daring anybody to represent his gang. Herman said that from now on a person has to have been out of prison for at least six months before he can visit Ash Meadow.

I asked Stan, who had worked Friday night, if he saw anything like what Herman said happened. Stan said he had not. But Ron told me it was more or less true. His brothers had thrown gang signs until he asked them to stop because he didn't want any trouble after they left. But their attitude, the whole tone of their visit, had obviously scared some of the kids. Marlon and Marion had mad-dogged some of them, talked to some as if they were lower than low.

Well, it was my mistake. It did not occur to me that anything like this would happen. Herman, to his credit, took the view that it was an honest error in judgment on my part and that we need to ensure that nothing like this happens again. Ron, when I talked with him, seemed embarrassed by his brothers' actions.

WEDNESDAY, OCTOBER 30: This evening Willie Bolles asked to talk with me in the office and asked me also to call Martin Lyons in. I thought there might be a problem between them that Willie wanted to talk out, which would have been odd because they are cousins and are close. But as soon as we were in the office, Willie put his arms around Martin and said, "Martin, I'm so glad you're not out there."

Then Willie told me their cousin David was smoked a few days ago. He was shot, then his throat was cut. It's that part, the cutting of David's throat when he was helpless, that most upsets Willie. He and Martin are convinced that a war between BGD and Norteños will start soon over David's murder. While they don't know who killed him, they are certain Norteños did it, and even though David was a Crip, his family is BGD. Willie told how once when he and David were kickin' it, David said that if he ever got smoked, Willie would have to get them back. "Aw, man, I don't even want to hear it," Willie said, meaning he didn't want to think about David getting killed.

Martin said his mother understands that he'll need to be strapped when he goes home. (He'll be paroled on the first of December.) At least, he'll need to have guns in the house because of the danger of Norteños coming to his house to kill him. He lives only four blocks from their turf. His mother doesn't want him to carry a strap when he's out of the house, though, Martin said.

Both boys say they are worried not so much for themselves as for their families who might be hurt because they happen to be in the house when somebody does a drive-by, or because they happen to be with one of them when someone shoots at him.

Both Willie and Martin said it's the gangbangers who haven't done their time yet—as though serving a prison sentence, even in "baby prison," is a rite of passage—who are all hot to retaliate for David's murder. But as I listened to these boys, I could see that they, too, are intensely angry.

Imagining how their lives may be when they get out, Willie said that even if he runs away when his rivals accost him, they could shoot him as he runs. Or, if he gets away and, trying to protect Martin, doesn't tell him, and then he, Willie, gets killed later, Martin would find out that Willie had been accosted the first time and feel that Willie hadn't trusted him.

Or, Willie said, he could be trying to avoid trouble but then someone could disrespect David's memory and Willie would have to go head to head with the guy until one of them was hurt "really, really, really, really bad" and had to be hospitalized. Or, if Willie was carrying a gat, he could shoot the guy.

Both he and Martin are afraid of getting caught up in a gang war. They are afraid of leaving Ash Meadow, Martin especially, because he'll be out in a month and people will still be hot over his cousin's death. Willie is refusing to go to a group home because the group home Fran, his staff, wants him to go to is near his home and he wants to avoid going home for as long as he can.

SATURDAY, NOVEMBER 2: Willie Bolles: "I wish I had never been born so I wouldn't have to die."

Ron talked a little about his brothers. It's obvious that he was impressed by them and admires both of them. Marion's mouth, he said, was half-filled with gold, and he wore gold jewelry. But Ron says he's not certain he'll go to Florida when he gets off parole. His brothers won't be staying with their father and grandmother, but in another town. Where he goes will depend on where Marlon is when it's time for him to make up his mind. Where Marlon goes, there goes Ron.

Cal Reed asked me if Martin Lyons could supervise his shaving from the bathroom doorway. We don't allow more than one kid at a time in the head. Cal has never shaved before. This is how they learn—from other kids who have an ounce more of experience than they have themselves.

SUNDAY, NOVEMBER 3: Willie told me that another cousin of his and Martin's had confessed to killing David. It's hard for him to accept, and hard for Martin too. They don't know why he did it. He was high, maybe, they think.

MONDAY, NOVEMBER 4: We learned today that Ron's brothers, after they left here on Friday, went into Seattle and went amok. "Amok" means they stole a car, robbed a convenience store, hijacked another car, pistol-whipped the driver and kidnapped the woman he was with. As it turns out, she is the wife of [a city official].

Ron already knew about it—Herman had told him—when I came to work. When we talked he seemed dazed, but was also, I thought, trying to numb himself. He expressed concern for Marlon especially, saying neither he nor Ron knew Marion that well—it had been years since either had had any contact with him. He said he'd had no idea . . . Then he said how "stupid" they had been. He said he hoped nothing bad had happened to the woman. He couldn't imagine them hurting her, but said again that he didn't know Marion very well. Throughout all of this he seemed emotionless, appearing to think with detachment, expressing himself clearly, although with some bewilderment. Then he began to cry. He said Marlon had betrayed him. Ron loved him so much and was so looking forward to being with him again, and then he had to do this, and now Ron would never see his brother again except to visit him in prison, if he could.

I suggested he write Marlon a letter, telling him how he felt. He didn't have to mail the letter, although he could if he wanted to, but it might help him just to write it. Ron said he would.

WEDNESDAY, NOVEMBER 6: Terry's been in the Phoenix Program for a week now. He has Felicia as his staff. That's good. She'll mother-hen him. He's worried that the program will be too hard for him, and asked if he might still get his minimum sentence if he doesn't graduate. That's the arrangement we have: he gets his minimum if he graduates. I told him I do not doubt that he will graduate.

WEDNESDAY, NOVEMBER 13: I visited Terry over at Eagle Cottage. Last weekend his biological father, Dan, and his stepmother, Cindy, visited him for family counseling. The weekend before, his uncle Fred and his wife Kathy visited him. It appears that all family members who have had a parental role with Terry are trying to support him. The exception is Terry's biological mother, who has had no contact with him since he was seven.

Terry is still unsure of his ability to get through the Phoenix Program. He resisted telling the other kids there about himself, so that Felicia finally told them during a treatment group that Terry is a sex offender. She told Terry to tell them what he did, but Terry refused, saying he wasn't ready. Of course, he's catching flak from them, both for being an SO and for refusing to talk about it.

MONDAY, NOVEMBER 25: Terry has been at Eagle for almost a month. He's still worried that he won't graduate. He said he feels inside that he won't. I told him that everybody in the Phoenix Program feels that way. He believes the staff are singling him out. I said that maybe they want him to open up about his sex offenses and they're trying to goad him into it. (They do and they are; I've talked with Felicia.) He said he's afraid to because he's already been targeted as an SO and he does not want to make things worse.

WEDNESDAY, DECEMBER 4: Terry told me that, to him, the animals he tortured were the people who had abused him. The animals did not represent these people but *were* his tormentors. He would see the faces of the cousins who had raped him on the faces of the animals and he would say to them: "How do *you* like it?" He sometimes had flashbacks of his own abuse experiences while he was torturing them.

Other times he saw the animals as monsters, and hurt them before they could hurt him.

He said that sometimes now when he is having a flashback, a staff or another resident will say something to him and he will visualize the face of one of his abusers on that person and respond with anger. If this is true, it explains his tendency to overreact to his peers' antagonistic remarks.

He said, too, that sometimes he has flashbacks of his father, Daniel, beating him and threatening to kill him.

WEDNESDAY, DECEMBER 18: Terry told me today that he was intensely angry with his father for having raped him. This began when he was sent to live with Daniel when he was seven and continued all the time he lived there. He said he told a school counselor but she accused him of lying in order to get his father in trouble.

Drove home from work in a night snow. The air sparkled like mica.

1997

THURSDAY, JANUARY 9: Ran into Tony Deacon at the QFC. We were in graduate school at the same time. We weren't intimates, but it was good to see him and we made plans for dinner next week.

FRIDAY, JANUARY 17: Met Tony Deacon and a friend of his visiting from California, Hector something, at a place on Roosevelt this evening. Hector was much impressed with himself, talked about fighting in karate tournaments. He didn't mention any he didn't win. He was interested in publishing and I told him about Leonard Chang's success with his book, *The Fruit 'n Food.* I described the plot and told him that it's based on an incident that happened in Queens.

Hector said he wasn't surprised the book is a success, because of how close-knit the Koreans are. He went on and on about Korean clannishness and how wealthy they are and how the men are controlled by their women. He said a Korean woman hit him once and "I decked her." When other Korean women objected, he told them that their husbands beat them, so . . . (He did not finish the sentence.) When they said American men were not supposed to beat women, he told them that he is *African*-American—he emphasized "African" in telling the story—and he would hit any woman who hit him. "Oh," he said they said. "That's right. He's *African*-American. We should be careful with him."

At some point I started laughing. I think this would have been during his harangue about Korean clannishness and wealth, because I was so surprised at hearing such crap, especially from someone I had just met, but also, I think, I was embarrassed for Tony, who, I assumed, was discovering something about his friend. Tony said nothing but sat with his arms crossed, an almost imperceptible smile fixed on his mouth. I think I was laughing from nervousness, too, because Hector's speech sounded so much like the anti-Semitic diatribes I've heard.

When he finished with the Koreans, Hector went on to how his view of sex was different from that of Euro-Americans'. I started laughing again—here was this professor of sociology boasting about his sexuality and talking about an entire group, a composite of other groups, as though he could account for how they think.

After we'd finished eating I apologized to Tony but said I had to be at work early. As I was sliding out of the booth, Hector asked, "What do you do?"

"I work in a prison for short people."

I had forgotten, but maybe I hadn't, that Hector is only about five feet six or seven. I don't expect to see him again, perhaps not Tony either.

WEDNESDAY, JANUARY 22: Herman told me that Willie's and Martin's cousin who had confessed to killing their other cousin last October had lied. It was a gang killing, West Side versus East Side Crips, and the cousin who confessed was apparently trying to show that his loyalty to his set superceded his loyalty to his family.

SATURDAY, JANUARY 25: Terry graduated from the Phoenix Program on Thursday. He's so proud, and rightfully. Not every kid graduates. Plus, he got his coin, meaning he attained a level of promise uncommon even among program graduates. His posture has improved, he's carrying himself like a human being instead of a beaten puppy. It's great to see him this way. I'm proud of him.

WEDNESDAY, FEBRUARY 12: Alternatives to Violence last night. Several kids said they liked to get hit in a fight because it made them fight harder. (I remember Jonas Henson said this too.) I asked David Warne if he'd ever had his nose broken. He said yes, and admitted he hadn't liked it.

I think the pleasure they get from fighting harder, if it is pleasure ("working harder," they say, "for my 'hood"), is linked to their submission to their OGs and to the idea of their 'hood as a kind of gang community. Sort of the way patriotism works for inexperienced soldiers and stay-at-home civilians. Most of these kids are wannabes rather than weathered gangsters.

But after the group had ended, Montague Miller asked me if I knew what a "curb bite" was. He mimicked a guy with his teeth open against a curb, then another guy stomping on his head.

TUESDAY, FEBRUARY 25: I called John Parish, Terry's probation officer, to let him know we'll be releasing Terry in May. John said Terry's father has mentioned sending him out of state to live with relatives when he is released, but has not provided anybody's name yet.

I said Terry told me that Daniel raped him soon after he went to live with him, and continued this kind of abuse all the time Terry lived there.

John was surprised but said this explained why Daniel was so controlling. He said that when Terry started talking to mental health workers in a sex-offender treatment group he was participating in about his cousins' abusing him, Daniel pulled him out of the program.

John is concerned about Sharlo, Daniel's small daughter (and Terry's victim). Sharlo's mother would have no idea of what was going on. He asked me to try to persuade Terry to file charges against Daniel, and said he was certain his own office would prefer charges also. He asked when Terry first disclosed his father's abuse.

I said he first mentioned it to me in December, but had told me, too, that he had disclosed it at Eagle. I'd thought staff there had filed a CPS report, but I learned only yesterday from one of them that they had not because Terry had asked them not to.

WEDNESDAY, FEBRUARY 26: I talked with a Shannon Gore at CPS. She said John Parish had already reported that Terry had been abused by his father. She told me she would record that I called to confirm that the alleged abuse had been reported.

LATER: I told Terry that CPS would be investigating his father's relationship with him and also with Sharlo. Terry said that all of that between Daniel and himself is in the past. He'd forgiven his father. He said Daniel did not actually rape or molest him, but only forced him to take a shower with him, and only one time.

I reminded Terry that he told me a couple of months ago that his father began molesting him shortly after he went to live with him and that it continued as long as they were living in the same house.

Terry said he remembered saying something like that, but he had been talking about Daniel's having physically abused him. Terry said he lumped the physical and sexual abuse together when he talked about Daniel.

I asked Terry if it was not true, as he had told me, that he had disclosed in a treatment group in Eagle that he had been sexually abused by Daniel. Terry said this was true, but he insisted now that Daniel is really "a nice guy" and he doesn't want to make any trouble for him. Terry said he's afraid that Sharlo will be taken away from Daniel.

I asked if he thought Daniel might be abusing Sharlo. Terry said no, because if Daniel were, Sharlo would tell her mother. (I didn't say anything about how often a mother will acquiesce in or even abet her child's abuse. Terry was distraught enough.) I asked him if he would believe Daniel was abusing Sharlo if a CPS investigation showed he was. Terry said he still would not believe it because Daniel loves Sharlo and would not abuse her.

"Didn't he love you?" I asked.

Terry was crying silently, huge tears rolling down his face. I forced myself to focus on his mouth, the lips so compressed they had turned white, in order to keep from crying myself. He shook his head no: Daniel had not loved him.

I let some time pass, then I asked him how I was supposed to know when he was telling the truth if he said one thing in December and another thing now. Hadn't he told other residents that Daniel had abused him?

Terry said he had been talking mainly about his cousins. He admitted using the word "abuse" but said he hadn't defined what he meant by it. He said now that Daniel had physically abused him but had not sexually abused him.

I let it go. I had had enough, and Terry had had more than enough. Let CPS work it out.

WEDNESDAY, MARCH 26: Terry was interviewed by a King County detective yesterday. The detective is investigating the possibility of Terry's half-sister, Sharlo, being sexually abused by Daniel, their father. Also, the detective is investigating the possibility that Daniel sexually abused Terry.

Terry says now that he did. Once Daniel forced him to shower with him. Another time Daniel was in a rage because Terry had lied to him about something—Terry doesn't remember what—and he took Terry out in the garage.

At this point, Terry stopped talking and stared at the floor, the flesh around his eyes swelling, his mouth growing white with tension.

"He raped you," I said as gently as I could.

Terry nodded his head.

He's afraid that if Daniel finds out he told the detective all of this he'll go into one of his rages again. More important, Terry says, his family, even the tiniest ones, will turn against him (i.e., against Terry). He said he needs his family so he'll have someone to talk to.

He said Daniel told him that the problem between them is that Terry lies to him. Terry accepts that he is at fault in this, but he said he lies to Daniel because he is afraid of him. He said that he doesn't want to lie to Daniel anymore. But he wishes the detective hadn't taped his interview with her. Without the tape he would be able to lie his way out of Daniel's rage.

In spite of all this, Terry said he wants to live with Daniel again because that way he'll have his family.

TUESDAY, APRIL 1: Ron left today for a group home in Seattle. Fran tells me there is a warrant out for Martin Lyons. He's been missing meetings with his parole officer.

WEDNESDAY, APRIL 2: Went to the Children's Justice Conference in Bellevue today. It was all right. The attendees were earnest people troubled by the work they are doing. The speakers were glib. I did meet a woman I found myself attracted to. Unfortunately she lives in Spokane.

SATURDAY, APRIL 5: Terry feels much better about having talked to the detective last week. He's decided after all that he wants to live with his foster parents.

SATURDAY, APRIL 12: I called Mary Corning tonight. She's the woman I met at the Children's Justice Conference two Wednesdays ago. She said she had just been looking through some papers and found an old date book from 1971. On April 12, 1971, she lost her virginity to one Paul Shelton. An important date.

Then she said she didn't know why she was telling me this. I swear I could feel her redden over the phone.

"Well, I guess it *was* an important date," I said. I was trying to lessen her embarrassment. She changed the subject. We talked about our respective jobs.

SATURDAY, APRIL 26: I talked with Mary Corning again. Four hours on her nickel, as she pointed out. She said she sometimes cannot help seeing herself as the oppressor in relation to these kids. She's a JPC, a juvenile parole counselor, or parole officer. She said that what she tries to do is stamp them out in the mold society wants them in.

I agreed: that's what all of us in the system try to do, if we are doing our jobs right. But I rationalize what I do by taking the view that I'm trying to keep them from coming back to Ash Meadow or going to Elk Grove or The Rivers. And what I have to teach them may help them. Usually this rationalization works for me.

Mary said she agreed, and offered, too, that there is no getting around the fact that they did things to get sent to prison.

LATER: Yes, yes, yes, I agree with her, but for all my argument about teaching kids how to survive in society such that they don't come back here—i.e., to Ash Meadow; I am at home as I write this—I have to recognize that sometimes my rationalization doesn't work. I deal with a disproportionate number of black and Hispanic kids—disproportionate to their numbers in society—whose familes are impoverished, who almost always come from single-parent families, whose mom or dad or both have a drug or alcohol problem, whose mom or dad themselves may have served time or are serving time. So let's face it: society doesn't love these kids and wants them exactly where they are: in prison. And I am society's representative. I am the father society wants them to have, even though I despise society for all the reasons the best of my generation despises society. So, however I want to see myself, I do represent oppression.

SATURDAY, MAY 3: Had my hair cut today at the place in the University District I always go for a haircut—I don't know the name of it. A new barber, affable, in his forties, I would guess. He recently returned from L.A. after a year and a half there. Grew up on Queen Anne Hill, lived on Capitol Hill. Asked me what I did.

"I work at Ash Meadow."

His eyebrows went up.

"I won't ask you if you know my friend," he said.

"Staff or resident?"

"He was an inmate out there."

"Some get out and do all right."

"Do you remember, a few years back"—his voice drops, his eyes shift to the guy nearest us, another barber who is sitting in his chair, his attention on the street beyond the window—"a couple of kids . . ." and then he describes a killing, a manslaughter case that was notorious when it happened and still is. One kid served less than six months in detention. The other came to Ash Meadow.

"I know him."

"How was he there?"

"He was all right. He could be really sweet."

"He's my son. I didn't know I had a son until he was seventeen. Then his mother called me and told me she was pregnant with my kid when she got married. She didn't call me until after he got out of Ash Meadow. How was he out there?" he asked again.

"He was all right. He was angry that he got two years when his co-offender got only a few months." I saw something on the barber's face, a kind of doubt, and I said, "Of course, the victim's family might not think two years is enough."

The barber shook his head. "Two years isn't enough. He should've been there until he was twenty-one."

He said he wanted his son to go to barber college, but the kid was already invested in a gang and just wanted his father to give him money. The barber said he hadn't seen his son in about four years. He asked me if they look alike. They do, and I said so. He seemed pleased. We shook hands. "My name's Victor," he said. "I hope I see you again."

SUNDAY, MAY 4: Roy tonight got David Warne and Terry Voight going in a grape fight after most of the kids were locked down. He hit Terry with a grape on the back of his head, then, when Terry turned around, pointed at David. Terry didn't do anything, so Roy threw a grape at David and pointed at Terry. David threw one at Terry and Terry yelled that he didn't do it and threw one at Roy. I just tried to duck those that were thrown at me and pretended that I wasn't involved. But as soon as I had a shot at Terry's back, I let him have it. Grapes were all over the floor and were rolling into the zones. Philip Burl yelled out from Zone 1, "Hey, there's a grape rolling under my door. Oh no! It's a drive-by fruiting!" Cracked Roy and me up. It's always nice to have an evening snack that can serve more than one purpose.

WEDNESDAY, MAY 7: Last night during Alternatives to Violence Luis Contreras talked about a couple of robberies he did. He said he always wanted to knock the victim out to gain time for his getaway. This was when he and his homies would rob a store.

I asked him if he wasn't concerned that he might kill someone without meaning to. He said he knew how to do what he was doing, that he could knock somebody unconscious and all he would have afterward was a headache. But he admitted he had not considered that he might kill somebody without intending to.

But his last crime had nothing to do with robbery. He beat somebody with a bat, not caring if he killed him or not, just wanting to hurt him. And he did: he crippled the man. Luis said the guy had approached him about buying a girl. He told the the guy to wait, that he would get someone. The guy said,

"What about her?" pointing at Luis' sister. They were at Luis' house and the man was pointing past him into the living room. So Luis got a bat and beat the guy down. He was a young guy who had a wife and three children. This came out at the trial. Luis had not met him before he came to Luis' house.

There is always a larger context to a crime. Or to any event.

SUNDAY, MAY 11: I just read Joanna Catherine Scott's poem about her Filipino driver whom she had to fire because he had infectious tuberculosis.[16] She was a diplomat's wife, and there was an embassy rule: "No tubercular locals may serve in a diplomat's house." He had wanted to emigrate to the United States. Some time after she fired him, she reconstructed the remainder of his life in Manila, where he had worked for her. He was swindled out of his severance pay by another man. When he threatened to kill this man, the driver's wife and child were beaten. Finally, giving up hope of going to America, he took them back to his natal village.

It is a story of injustice, of life's being unfair. But why should we think life ought to be fair? I think of Ron Lafitte, coerced into robbing a store in order to pay off a debt, getting for himself a carton of cigarettes and two years in prison. The entire sequence of events leading to his imprisonment was a series of unfairnesses. Should we expect life to be different for ourselves, we who are more privileged, who are more fortunate?

Whether or not we should, we do. We hope, we believe, that we can insulate ourselves from injustice. Injustice is for people who cannot afford to buy insulation. If we thought the same rules apply to us as to them, we could not bear it; we would deny it was true. We *do* deny it.

Ron may be enraged at the unfairness in his life. (He is, actually. He, too, expected something different. Even at the age of fourteen, he is disappointed.) But he also regards each day as a challenge, one harboring potential or threat, filled with problems that have to be confronted. How is he different from us? Well, a problem not dealt with may bring his death, or the death of someone he loves.

WEDNESDAY, MAY 14: In the craft room this afternoon during Survivors' Group, Terry began staring at the chalkboard behind me. He wanted me to turn and look at it. I was irritated because he was distracting me from what Cory was saying about confiding to other kids what his grandfather had done to him, and I refused. Finally Terry was so insistent that his "vision" was on the chalkboard that I did look . . . and saw only a large smudge of chalk dust. Terry went up to the board and, with his finger, drew a girl's face and a four-fingered hand—one thumb, three fingers—on the board. I asked him if he had expected me to see that concealed in the chalk dust. He said yes. He came back to the table the three of us were sitting around and put his head down.

Later in the session he told us how he had gone to his school counselor after his father had beaten him. She told him he'd have to show his butt to the principal before they would believe him. Terry did. There were bruises on his butt, but the principal said there was no evidence of abuse.

Still, at some time Terry did catch CPS's attention. Daniel told him that if he told CPS what was going on, that is, his beating and raping Terry, Daniel would kill him. So when Terry was interviewed by the investigator, he told her he had lied earlier, that Daniel had not beaten him.

When he said he lied to CPS, Terry began to cry. He said he was worried now about what Daniel was doing to Sharlo. This was the first time he'd expressed concern about her. In the past he said he thought she was safe, that Daniel was angry with him, not her. I wonder now if what Terry drew on the board was a portrait of Sharlo. (And the four-fingered hand?)

At dinner he ate little, if anything. He stared at the wall. Other kids kept trying to see what he was looking at. I thought he was only trying to draw attention to himself. He'll be paroled on May 30, and he's been anxious and increasingly needy. A few days ago he followed me around like a puppy, even bumping into me when I stopped suddenly. When I told him that if he pissed on my foot I would give him twenty-four OP, other kids laughed, but he didn't get it. Still, at dinner tonight I wondered if something was wrong with him; even for Terry, this was strange behavior.

He had craft-room detail after supper. A few minutes into details, Pang-li told me Terry was drawing on the chalkboard. Pang-li was smiling, out of unease, I think, and shaking his head. I went into the craft room and found Terry drawing small figures and faces with a piece of chalk. These, I thought, were his "demons," to which he sometimes alludes in our talks. I left him to it.

But soon Larry Street came out of the craft room and said Terry was "tweakin'." I went back and found him stretched out on his back on top of a table. I had been concerned about how the other kids were taking all of this, weighing their discomfort against what I felt was Terry's need to be with people. But now I got him to his feet and took him out of the craft room. I asked him if he wanted to go to his room but he said he wouldn't feel safe in his room. I had him sit in the living room and I told Stan and Julia Park, an intermittent working with us for the evening, that I didn't know what was wrong with Terry but we needed to keep an eye on him.

Then I called the health center and talked to Dorothy. She asked if he was on meds. I told her yes, Paxil, but these behaviors were new. The side effects I'd noticed before were his complaining about being tired, his skin appearing clammy, and his teeth chattering uncontrollably at times. Dorothy said there was really nothing she could do, that it sounded like he was having a mental breakdown. All she could suggest was to put him in his room or, if he became agitated, the quiet room. She said this happens all the time, kids having mental breakdowns. (This was news to me. I've worked here how long? Six years?) All we can do is isolate them. But I didn't want to isolate Terry—he said he felt unsafe in his room.

I went back into the living room to try to talk with Terry. After a moment he leaned over to his left and turned so that he lay on his back on the chair, his feet still on the floor. His eyes were open. He was staring past me. His pulse was strong, he was breathing, but his eyes didn't blink and his facial expression was empty. It didn't change when I passed my hand in front of his eyes. I took his wrists to pull him into a sitting position, but when I felt how limp his body was, I eased him down again, afraid that he wouldn't be able to sit up by himself. I heard Julia groan behind me.

I called Dorothy again. When I was waiting for her to pick up the phone, I asked Stan to clear the floor. Now Herman came out of his office and went over to where Terry was lying down.

Dorothy said there was nothing she could do but offer her sympathy. She personally suspected that Terry was reacting to the Paxil, but the psychiatrist who had written the prescription would not be in until next Tuesday and was not otherwise available. Dorothy said her sister once had a similar reaction to Paxil, which is why she believed it was the culprit.

Meanwhile Herman was working with Terry. He had gotten him to blink his eyes. It was Terry's first movement in several minutes. "They get tired when you don't blink, don't they?" Herman asked. Terry gave the slightest nod. It was his second movement. Herman gradually pulled Terry up until he was sitting straight. Then Herman sat down beside him and told him he wanted him to stand up. "For me," Herman said. Terry, slowly, slowly, seemingly with terrible effort, stood up. His back was bent, his shoulders forward, his elbows back and up. He stood silently like that, staring emptily. I moved to help him, but Herman put his hand up, signaling me to hold back. He told me later that he wanted Terry to make the effort, to exercise his will. Now he put his hand on Terry's shoulder and began talking to him. Touched him and talked to him.

Dorothy called back. She said she'd talked with Dr. Arens. She had called him at home. He said we should talk to Terry, that he could hear us, and touch him in order to keep him "in touch with reality."

Herman, still talking softly with Terry, patting his shoulder, his back, asked what Dorothy had said. "Do exactly what you're doing," I said. "He can hear us. We should touch him and talk to him."

After a while, Herman had Terry sit down again. Terry stared at the wall, or perhaps at the ceiling where it met the wall. Herman asked what he saw there. "Demons," Terry said. It was the first thing he'd said since he'd lapsed into catatonia. "And a hand."

"A hand," Herman said. "What's the hand doing?"

"It wants to pull me in."

"Demons. If there are demons, there must be angels."

Terry nodded. "There are angels, too."

"Are the demons evil?"

Terry nodded slowly.

"Then the angels must be good."

"The angels are evil."

"The angels are evil too?"

Terry nodded. "I'm afraid it's going to pull me in."

"Into the wall?"

"Yes."

I sat with Terry while Herman went to the phone and called Dorothy. I couldn't hear what Dorothy said, nor most of what Herman said, but finally he said "Yeah" and hung up. He was angry, his mouth pinched, his eyes flat.

He asked Terry to get up and go over to the wooden chair by the staff desk to sit. Herman wanted him to be physically uncomfortable, he told me later. He helped Terry ease himself into it. Then Herman went and sat on the ping-pong table. He looked exhausted. He looked like he didn't know what to do next. He had just opened his mouth to say something when Terry wiped his hand across his face and looked around. Suddenly his pallor was gone and he seemed alert. He looked at me. "Merry Christmas," he said, his standard greeting of late.

We talked with him, Herman and I. Herman wanted to leave—his wife was waiting for him—but he stayed. He wanted to be sure Terry wasn't going to go catatonic again.

Dorothy called. She'd talked to Dr. Arens again. We were not to give Terry any more Paxil. Arens had authorized taking him off it.

I told Herman and he nodded and left.

A couple of hours later he called and asked about Terry. Terry was doing fine. I told Herman how much I appreciated what he had done, and that he'd taught me something. He asked what he'd taught me.

"To trust my empathy," I said. "To go where it tells me to go."

"That's all you *can* do," he said. "I'll tell you something. I didn't know what I was doing. I was really scared."

"So was I."

After all of this, and after we brought the kids out on the floor and I explained to them Terry's reaction to the drug, Stan asked me, "What was going on with that kid who was laying down there?" As if he knew less than I did.

SATURDAY, MAY 17: Daniel Voight called to complain that Terry had called him. Daniel said his lawyer told him not to talk to Terry. This was the first indication I'd had that CPS is doing something. I asked Daniel if he wanted me to prevent Terry from calling him. I asked this several times, but he wouldn't answer. He said Terry was telling lies about him, as he always had. "I've got to get on with my life," Daniel said. Finally I suggested that I tell Terry that he, Daniel, can't talk with him because his lawyer told him not to. Daniel agreed and we hung up.

I told Terry. He guessed, too, that the investigation is proceeding. He asked me if he would have to testify in court. "Probably," I said. "If it goes to court. Maybe they'd let you give a deposition." He's very much afraid of a confrontation with Daniel. He's afraid of Daniel.

MONDAY, MAY 19: I talked with Mary Corning last night. I asked her if she'd ever heard of a kid named Tommy Whitacre. She had.

"What's he doing now, do you know?"

"He's been declined. He's going to be tried as an adult." She didn't know what the charge was. He'd gone to Woodbyrne on a weapons charge, but it wasn't that one. It's something he did after he got out of Woodbyrne.

"He's so anti-authority. He's a sociopath," Mary said.

"No. He wants to die." I told her that Tommy was, is, my favorite kid—the kid, of all the kids I've had on my caseload, I felt closest to. But I was not able to explain my feeling for him except to say that when I think of him I get enraged again at the unfairness of life, that a child could be treated so badly by his parents that life outside of prison becomes closed to him. But it's more than anger at life's injustice: something about Tommy himself touched me deeply.

Mary mentioned a friend of hers, another JPC, who had a kid on his caseload who had witnessed his mother's disembowelment. The JPC said he knew this was a kid who would eventually do the same thing to another woman.

Maybe. But maybe not.

Not everyone tries to replicate the worst thing he's ever seen or had done to him.

THURSDAY, MAY 22: Montague Miller told me a couple of days ago that his math teacher told him not to worry about learning his multiplication tables, just use a calculator. What a thing for a math teacher to tell a kid! Montague was unable to do his homework because we don't have a calculator in the cottage.

Yesterday I talked with Marie Klein, the school psychologist. She said the school would arrange for tutoring if Montague will study.

I assured her that he would. I've found that when he complains about a teacher, it's because he doesn't know how to do the work. But he wants to be able to do it.

Later I told Montague of my conversation with Marie. He thanked me, sincerely, I believe.

Still later, Herman and I found where Montague had drawn stick figures, caricatures, of several staff on the chalkboard in the craft room. By the figure of Herman, he had written: "I have to lose some weight. Or maybe I'm pregnant." By the one of me: "Don't hit women." An allusion to what he's retained of Alternatives to Violence, I'm sure.

WEDNESDAY, MAY 28: Talked with John Parish, Terry's probation officer. He asked me if I believed Terry's story that his father had abused him. I said yes. Parish said he had some doubts now. This was quite a change from his response last February when I told him about Terry's allegations.

He told me, too, that Terry would not be going to Carroll Sanders' place for foster care after all. This, after months of coordinating with and getting assurances from the Sanders! Parish said they had given Terry's bed to another kid, thinking they could get Terry in too by asking DSHS to grant them a waiver on the number of kids they are authorized to care for. But DSHS said no. So Parish placed Terry with somebody named Howard Jackson.

Tonight when I told Terry he would have to go to Howard Jackson's, his reaction was immediate. He said he wouldn't make it there. He had spent a day at Jackson's once and had seen kids openly smoking pot and taking LSD. He'd seen Jackson beat a kid, he said. Jackson was large and muscular like Terry's father, and Terry was afraid of him. He said if we sent him there, he would run.

I asked Michael Collins to relay this to Parish tomorrow (one of my days off).

SATURDAY, MAY 31: Terry was released yesterday, over my weekend. Michael left a log entry to the effect that Parish had dismissed everything Terry had said, but did acknowledge the resemblance between Howard Jackson and Terry's father. He said this was unfortunate, but he had no option other than to place Terry there.

Presumably he is there. But Fred and Kathy, Terry's uncle and aunt, have not heard from him. Kathy said she called Parish, but the office secretary told her he is refusing to accept calls or come to the phone. I advised Kathy to call Terry's parole officer. Terry is on both probation and parole.

WEDNESDAY, JUNE 4: Montague Miller began his tutoring in math and spelling today. He's pretty excited about it.

FRIDAY, JUNE 6: Been thinking about Terry, wondering if he'll run, or if he already has. Wondering if his mental stability will last.

When I talked with Kathy Voight—when? Sunday? Monday? It must have been Monday—I told her that CPS had just informed me that Daniel would not be charged because the prosecutor believed he did not have enough evidence to get a conviction.

"Good," Kathy said. "Anybody looking at Daniel and Sharlo together could not doubt the affection she has for him." Therefore, she implied, Daniel could not have raped Terry.

TUESDAY, JUNE 10: In PC today, Fran went on for twenty minutes, trying to persuade the rest of us to agree to explain to Cory Corson what he did wrong every time he gets a demerit. None of us would agree because we all know that Cory knows why he gets demerits, but that he wants to talk, talk, talk about it every time until staff gets angry. It is a game with him. Once I overheard him telling another kid, "Watch me get Jerry going." Then he went into his "stupid" act, pretending he didn't understand what I was saying.

Rob, who loves harmony, tried to explain to Fran why we would not go along with her, but finally gave up. Fran wanted what she wanted, period.

John Loring, Cory's case manager, laughed through her entire diatribe, until Fran asked specifically for his support. Then he snapped that Cory is playing her, that he knows what the score is and his ignorance is a pretense.

After John refused to budge, Fran turned to me and, out of the blue, asked if William Lee could be in my Alternatives to Violence group. I snapped at her just as John had. "This is the third time you've asked me that, Fran! I told you: he's already completed the group! Other kids are waiting to get in!"

After PC she told me I had offended her in the way I spoke to her. I told her I had had enough of her badgering, that she had already asked me twice and I'd told her no twice, yet she continued to harry me.

She said: 1. She did not understand that I had said no, even though, as she acknowledged, I had said it twice before; 2. She did not intend to badger me. She seemed to feel that because she said she had not intended to badger me, she had, therefore, not badgered me.

WEDNESDAY, JUNE 11: This evening I overheard part of a conversation between Summer Light—yes, folks, that's her name, she chose it herself—and Carl Reid. Summer is working here in a temporary position created by overpopulation. When our population hits nineteen we get an additional staff. We've been at nineteen or twenty for over a month now and expect to stay there. Summer has been with us for about a week. Carl is an intermittent. Both are in their mid-twenties.

Summer: "There are so many Jews in New York."

Carl: "There are more in New York than in Seattle."

Summer: "Whoa! I knew there were a lot, but . . ."

I didn't hear the rest.

This young woman talks a great deal about being a Christian and about being "held accountable" for her behavior by her church. She needs this accountability, she told me, because she had had a drug problem and without the structure her church and beliefs provide, she would fall back into using. I have found her priggish and self-righteous. I suppose expressing her distaste for Jews would be keeping within the limits of behavior allowed by her church and her beliefs.

Earlier in the day I attended a workshop called "Advanced Suicide and Self Mutilation." Of course several of us joked about the title: Are they going to teach us to do it better?

Bob Brown, the program manager for Andromeda Cottage, told us that Andromeda has a girl who pulls her hair out and scrapes the skin off her arms. She puts her hair in one pile on the floor of her room and bloody skin in another pile. The staff has finally gotten used to it but intermittents have a problem. One came out of the zone after checking on her: "She's got a pile of her hair here and a pile of blood next to it. Shouldn't we do something?"

Bob: "No. Would you like some lunch?"

Intermittent: "Oh, no. I ate before I got here."

A good thing came out of the workshop: I met Jack Ralston, Terry Voight's JPC, and Karen Leason, who set Terry up with psychiatric care. They said Terry is doing fine and is already seeing a psychiatrist. Great.

SATURDAY, JUNE 14: I called Terry at his foster care home. He said he's doing okay but still wants to move back with the Sanders. A kid at the Jackson house hit him when they were in a restaurant for lunch the other day. The kid is in custody and charges will be filed against him. Terry doesn't know why the kid hit him.

SATURDAY, JUNE 21: Roy told me that Jim Duckworth at Wolf has been charged with beating up a resident. This apparently happened some time ago. At first, afraid of Jim, other staff tried to cover it up. Finally one of them reported it. Roy says he has all of this "on good authority." It's been so long since I worked at Wolf, I don't even know who the staff are now.

MONDAY, JUNE 23: Ron Lafitte called yesterday from Harborview Medical Center. He was in a car crash last week. He said the driver lost control trying to make a hard turn at the bottom of a rain-wet hill. The three passengers in back were all hurt, Ron the worst, and the driver and passenger up front were not. (I talked with Ron's parole officer today. The crash did occur, but as the culmination of a high-speed chase. Donny Mack, another of our "graduates," was also in the car, but was not hurt.) Ron's pelvis is broken and his bladder "split like a clam shell." That's how the doctor described it to him.

His sister visits him every couple of days, but his homies visit him every day, he said. He's been living with his sister, but when he gets out of the hospital he's going to live with one of his older homies.

I don't believe his homies visit him every day. When he was in Ash Meadow, they didn't even write him. Ron wants so much to be accepted by his homies that he lies to himself about the nature of his relationship with them. They do not give to him, he gives to them.

THURSDAY, JUNE 26: I talked with Summer Light (God—that name!) a few days ago—Saturday, I think. Actually I talked hardly at all. I listened. She was upset because Jesus Haddon ignores her. He does what she tells him to do, but he won't talk to her. If she asks him, "How's it going?" he doesn't answer. She says she feels that he's disrespecting her, but I think she's hurt because she wants him to like her and he makes it clear that he doesn't.

She asked me what I would do. I told her that if I were in her position I would ignore Jesus' lack of response and let him do as he wants, as long as he doesn't do anything punishable. If he does, of course, she should punish him. I did not tell her that he has told me that her persistent moralizing and her insistence on having the last word in any conversation infuriates him, so he tries to avoid her. This avoidance, of course, is what hurts her.

She said that if she ignores what he's doing, then she's playing his game, which is demeaning to her.

I said I didn't think she had a choice.

Summer wants things to be her way, people to be as she wants them to be. She doesn't want anyone to pretend to be something he is not, but to change into what he is not. She wants to make the world over in her own image.

On Monday I asked her what she had decided to do about Jesus.

"Nothing," she said.

We chatted for a while. I asked about the band she's in, which is apparently important to her.

She said it's a Christian band, though it performs some secular music too. I asked if they did any Dylan.

She made a face, said, "What? 'Everybody has to get stoned'?"

I said no, but something from his Christian period.

She wasn't aware he'd had a Christian period.

I said yes, and it was followed by a Zionist period.

She didn't know what Zionism is. This young woman is a graduate of the University of California at Santa Clara. I was explaining Zionism to her when she interrupted: "So he moved to Israel?" That expression of distaste on her face again, the same as when she accused him of encouraging his audience to get stoned. She said she would look up his Christian recordings.

TUESDAY, JULY 1: Dr. Williams, our chief psychiatrist, came down to the cottage during PC. I had not met him before. He informed us that the University of Washington will be sending a team of psychologists to Ash Meadow and that they will be available to us should we want to discuss any of our kids with them. Their role will be to offer advice on managing the kids, not to treat them as clients.

At some point during the meeting I turned the discussion to the issue of Paxil and Terry Voight, and described what had happened (what? six weeks ago?). I used the word "catatonic."

Williams said he did not know anything about what Terry might have experienced, but said, too, that he doubted it was catatonia. I described the symptoms, but while Williams could not or would not put a label on them, he said Terry had not been catatonic. "There's nothing in the literature on that," he said. He shook his head.

"There should be," I said.

I was angry. He was telling me that what Herman and I saw happen had not happened. It could not have happened because no psychiatrist had written about it.

I excused myself and went into the bathroom and splashed water on my face. I stayed in there until I was calm enough to go back into the living room. Williams was just getting up to leave as I sat down. We did not speak to each other.

SATURDAY, JULY 12: New kid on my caseload: Mickey Joyce. Transferred here from Elk Grove. He's fourteen and was the youngest kid there, he says.

He's in prison for Taking a Motor Vehicle Without Permission. This is his second time at Ash Meadow. The charge his first time was also TMVWOP. He says he likes stealing cars. It makes him feel like he knows everything about the car if he can steal it. He doesn't think about getting caught.

When he was here before, he resided in Ram Cottage, where he was in the Survivors' Group facilitated by Doug Little. Mickey says his file contains erroneous information about his having been abused when he was younger. (We do not have his file from Elk Grove yet.)

At Elk Grove, he says, two older boys attempted to rape him in the swimming pool. He described only part of it: one boy held him while the other tried to rape him. He did not try to resist. Afterward the two boasted to other kids about having punked him. Eventually he reported what happened. He did this because his roommate threatened to beat him up if he didn't. He says CPS is investigating.

I suspect he was, in fact, raped. He'll be in Survivors' Group here, too.

TUESDAY, JULY 15: John Loring mentioned that he'd seen Daniel Mallon at that new supermall in Auburn last weekend. Daniel is, was, the kid who had been out in the woods with a rifle and had shot a man who had looked at him funny.[17] When John saw him, he was with his wife and their baby. He was a good ball player when we had him, but he's gotten fat. He'd be twenty-three, twenty-four now. He talked about wanting to go to community college. He didn't seem uncomfortable at seeing John. Just a couple of working stiffs out with their wives, running into each other at the mall.

That wasn't the case at all when I saw Jonas Henson at Larry's Market a few months ago. He was with someone and wanted to pretend he didn't know me. At least he didn't want his friend to know where he knew me from. I, like an idiot, made a big deal about seeing him there. I still feel embarrassed for him.

Tussant Fisher made the papers today, though not the first, second, or third pages. A prostitute brought her trick to a motel where Tussant and another man were waiting to rob him. The john resisted and held a knife to Tussant's throat until his cohorts ran off. Then he let Tussant go. But someone had called the police, and Tussant was caught as he walked out of the motel room.

He was the kid who, when I shined a flashlight into his room during a bed check, began dancing and singing, "I'm in the spotlight now." That was six years ago.[18]

SUNDAY, JULY 20: I got Mickey Joyce's old file from Ram. The one from Elk Grove has not arrived. According to the file, Mickey's mother was deemed incapable of raising him owing to her drug and alcohol abuse. At age seven he was placed in foster care. For at least three years prior to that, he had been beaten periodically by his stepfather. When he was six, he saw his stepfather beat his mother and break her neck. She was not paralyzed.

Mickey was in foster care for four years, during which time he was placed in and ran away from twenty-one homes. Each time he ran he would return to his mother's house. Each time he returned she would force him to leave. When he was twelve he was befriended by Victor Rivas, an adult.

What follows comes from Mickey; it is not in his file. Mickey went to live with Rivas. Mickey says he had sex with him once, at Rivas' request. Mickey does not regard himself as having been abused or exploited by Rivas, as they had sex on only that one occasion and Mickey penetrated him rather than the other way around. Mickey believes Rivas was fond of him and he feels gratitude toward Rivas for taking him in when he was living on the street.

I had talked with Doug Little, who told me Rivas pled guilty to sex offenses against Mickey—Doug didn't know specifically what offenses—and is now in prison. Mickey said this is true.

TUESDAY, JULY 22: In Alternatives to Violence, Eduardo Rojas told us his good friend was murdered a couple of months ago. His set stabbed him when he announced that he wanted to quit them. This is also Eduardo's set.

Even so, Eduardo said he didn't know if he would stay away from them when he gets out. They are his only friends, he said.

But I wonder how much fear has to do with his thinking. Two or three months ago he told me he intended not to have anything more to do with gang life. Perhaps, since his friend's death, Eduardo has become afraid that his set will kill him too if he tries to leave.

Another boy in the group tonight said violence stops being fun when you are the victim. Reminded me of what a former LURP told me of his experience in Viet Nam: war stops being fun when your friends start getting killed.

MONDAY, JULY 28: I asked Eduardo if his uncertainty about quitting his gang owed to their killing his friend. He said yes, because they would kill him too. He said it wasn't a big deal to stay in the gang, "it's just life." I tried to get him to see that a life lived out of fear does not belong to you; it belongs to the people who make you afraid. I gave him the assignment to write at least one page explaining how fear can influence behavior.

I have to say I recognize that I am something of a hypocrite here, as is anyone who talks about living your life unafraid. Everybody who is an employee lives his life, to some extent, in fear of being fired or laid off. Well, I want him to write this essay in order to clarify his thinking about his life. Certainly you can avoid living under some kinds of fear. Whether the fear of being killed by your own gang is one of these, I don't know.

TUESDAY, JULY 29: Summer's explanation for why these kids have done bad things is that they are evil, and evil people do evil things. This line of thinking leads to the idea that the increase in juvenile, and adult, crime in the United States is due to the growth of evil, i.e., the growth of Satan's influence in this country. Summer believes this is true, but that there is nothing to be done about it: the problem is so large and so complicated, and people have become so corrupt. I wonder why she works here.

WEDNESDAY, JULY 30: On the outs, Mickey hung around with Richard Wain, a kid we had here in Swan a couple of years ago. He had a terrific problem controlling his anger, I remember, and we used to let him go to his room when he was angry so he could put his mattress against the wall and punch it.

Mickey and Richard were a team. Mickey would steal a car and Richard would pop the tape deck or stereo and sell it. Then they would buy beer or drugs.

I recall James Pickle telling me, maybe a year and a half ago, that Richard had been stabbed to death. Apparently not.[19]

Mickey also knew Donald Jackson on the outs, but didn't like him.

THURSDAY, JULY 31: Jose Guevara, in Survivors' Group yesterday, said his first sexual experience was at age three when an adult, a neighbor, pulled Jose's pants down and sucked his cock. There was a second episode not long afterward when the neighbor forced Jose to suck his cock.

I brought up the element of power in sexual abuse. Jose did not want to accept this at first, insisting that the neighbor abused him because the neighbor was a pervert. But as the discussion continued, Mickey Joyce argued just as strongly that power is all the abuser is interested in, and Jose grew quiet and finally asked me: "You mean he made me suck his cock so he could feel more powerful than me?"

I said his neighbor had abused him out of a need to feel powerful, but the person, or persons, he wanted to feel superior to may not have been Jose. They may have been Jose's parents, or someone else, so that abusing Jose was a way of getting at someone he feared or hated, even if this revenge or domination occurred only in his own mind.

I wasn't sure Jose was following me; he didn't say anything. But then his eyes filled and he stared across the table we were sitting around. I thought the tears would spill over, but they didn't. He said finally that he wanted to bring up a good memory because this is how he offsets bad memories: he tries to balance good ones against them. He told us about his first crime, which was shoplifting some candy. It was a good memory because the candy, M&Ms, had tasted so good.

After the group had ended, he told me that he keeps having the same bad dream in which he relives these two episodes. He was afraid he was crazy. I talked to him about post-traumatic stress and some of its symptoms, but he wanted only to be told that he is not crazy. I told him he is not.

Postscript: During the session I asked all three boys, Jose, Mickey, and Cory Corson, if they had been abused by more than one person. All three raised their hands. But then they asked if I considered their mothers to be abusers if they knew about the abuse but didn't stop it. This was the situation with all three kids.

SATURDAY, AUGUST 2: Roy Burns transferred to Ram Cottage yesterday. Herman is now the program manager for both Swan and Ram, and he asked Roy to transfer. Herman is trying to establish a core of people there that he knows and trusts. Rob Gorey moved over there last month. The previous program manager took over Wolf Cottage following the revelation that Jim Duckworth beat a kid. The entire Wolf staff was replaced. I'm going to miss Roy.

(Herman asked me last Wednesday if I wanted to take Rob's spot here at Swan. Actually, he didn't ask me so much as invite me to ask for it: he told me it was available and then stared at me until I said something. I said I didn't want it.)

SUNDAY, AUGUST 3: Roy called from Ram. Herman told him that he's going to hire Candy Laine to take Rob's place as Swan's supervisor. I remember Candy. She used to excite the boys here by wrestling with them, then give them demerits when she had enough. She became so obsessed—maybe "infatuated" is more accurate—with one boy on her caseload that Herman finally took him away from her and gave him to me. This boy, after his release, stalked her. He got inside her apartment when she was out and left a note in her underwear drawer. He's in Elk Grove, the last I heard, where Candy has been working for the last two or three years. It was she who—oh, never mind. So she'll be our supervisor.

Herman is also going to hire Steven Ruer to take Summer's slot when her temporary appointment runs out. Steven was fired from Dolphin Cottage because a kid went into another kid's room and beat him up; this happened because Steven neglected to lock their doors after putting them in their rooms. He was hired at Wolf and then fired there because he had not been paying attention to who was going where during after-dinner details, and two kids went into a head and had sex. He's been working as an intermittent since.

I've worked with him a couple of times. Both times he was late coming in to work. In another job this might not be a problem. But when he's late here, someone else has to stay until he arrives. And we like to get out of here on time. He offered no explanation, not even an acknowledgement that he was late. He doesn't do anything unless he's told to do it, though he's worked at Ash Meadow for a year and a half and is expected to be able to anticipate what needs to be done.

And, of course, there's Fran.

This is bad.

MONDAY, AUGUST 4: Herman hired Sue Doggett and Tony Black to fill the position Roy Burns left and another position that's been vacant for so long I don't remember who used to work it. Sue has been working for us as an intermittent for some time. She's conscientious, takes the job seriously. I can count on her to be where I need her to be and do what she has to do. Maybe she'll offset Steven Ruer.

I haven't seen Tony in four or five years. He was a permanent staff in Fox, then left. I don't know why.

WEDNESDAY, AUGUST 6: I told Herman I would like the job as supervisor. He knew I was trying to block Candy's hire, but it's only a temporary position, six months, during which he'll look for someone to hire for it permanently. Herman told me: 1. I have a tendency to overreact; 2. I need to question myself about my ability to get along with female coworkers; 3. he'll let me know. He'd already committed himself to hiring Candy, but he didn't think Elk Grove would release her when he wanted her.

THURSDAY, AUGUST 7: I worked till midnight last night and saw Susan Lesser when she came in to work the graveyard shift. I told her what Herman had said about my ability to work with women. Susan didn't buy it. She said Herman likes to hire women who are needy, so he can feel powerful. He doesn't like her, she said, and they've had a number of confrontations. She reminded me that she was foisted on Herman by Carol Ripito, whom Herman hated.

TUESDAY, AUGUST 12: In Alternatives to Violence we watched a video called *Men's Work*. The best parts are some short skits performed by actors. In one of them a husband comes home and asks what's for dinner. The wife says spaghetti. He complains that they had spaghetti last night and suggests they thaw a couple of steaks and get a bottle of wine. She says she doesn't have time, she's been called back to work at the hospital. He asks her to call in sick but she replies that they need the money. "Oh, so it's my fault," he says. More words, then he calls her a bitch and slaps her.

Seeing the wife slapped and cursed at, the kids were shocked. A few laughed, Jose Guevara among them. I asked, as I always do, why they laughed. Jose said he laughed from the surprise of seeing the woman hit. There are always some kids who say this.

While the other boys were talking, Jose suddenly asked to go to his room. He was obviously upset and I allowed him to go. Later, after the group had ended, I checked to see how he was doing. He told me that seeing the part of the video where the woman is hit by her husband brought on flashbacks of his mother being beaten. He couldn't turn them off, which was why he wanted to go to his room. He apologized.

I said he didn't need to apologize, that it's all right to remove himself when he's having flashbacks.

He said he's getting them more often now and is worried about going crazy.

I assured him that he is not going crazy. I asked him if he had told Fran about his flashbacks. Fran is his staff. He said no, only me, because I am the one who leads Survivors' Group, which he is in, and I already know so much about him.

FRIDAY, AUGUST 15: Steven Ruer told me that Summer Light had been pushing her own brand of Christianity on the kids, some of whom resented her for it. I suspected this, but never saw it.

Steven, who is also a Christian fundamentalist, asked me if he could conduct Bible study with the kids in the cottage. He says they've asked him to do it. I told him Summer should not have been doing it, that she had been told not to, but had apparently continued despite the directive.

Oh, yes. I'm the (temporary) cottage supervisor now, as of August 9.

SUNDAY, AUGUST 17: This morning at the gym Tyrone Wiley assaulted William Lee. I was in the weight room with several kids when I heard "Fight! Fight!" I ran out onto the basketball court and saw Michael Collins rolling around on the floor with both kids. I pressed my alarm, then realized it wouldn't work away from the cottage. Ran back to the weight room, got the radio, called Security, then ran back out on the floor, radio in hand. Michael now was holding William down and trying to keep Tyrone away. At the same time, William was trying to kick Tyrone, who was just hanging on to him, no longer trying to hit him but wanting only to keep from being kicked. I grabbed Tyrone's arm, pulled him away, and started talking at him, distracting him. He didn't resist and William didn't try to kick him.

Several hours later I did a supervisor's review on Tyrone. He was in his room doing twenty-four hours OP. He said William had called him a "fork-ass nigger" when they were down court. This, of course, was an insult against his race, and also demeaned his gang: "fork" is a pejorative for a BGD. So, Tyrone said, he went after William. He said they had fought three times before over William's racial remarks.

I know of one fight in which William went into Tyrone's room and assaulted him. If it was William's racial comment that led to it, it's odd that William went after Tyrone; I would have expected Tyrone to go after William as he did today. Tyrone is known for making racist comments, though William may well be capable of it too.

Three years ago Tyrone came to Ash Meadow on a burglary charge. He was young enough and small enough then to be assigned to Goldfish Cottage. Most of the time he has spent in the institution has been the result of one assault after another, against other kids and staff both. Tomorrow he goes to court to be arraigned for an assault on Rob Gorey several months ago. When he returns he'll go to Wolf for the assault on William.

SATURDAY, AUGUST 23: My duties as Juvenile Rehabilitation Supervisor (JRS) are these: I supervise Stan and Steven Ruer, meaning I meet with each of them monthly, go over their caseloads, paperwork, group work if they conduct a treatment group—neither does—and deal with any problems they might have. Herman will continue to do this for the other staff.

I'm also responsible for payroll and scheduling.

This is a temporary position. I may apply for the permanent job.

My other, JRRC, duties remain in place. I'm being worked to death.

SUNDAY, AUGUST 24: Mickey admitted to me that when he's on the floor he works it so staff send him to his room. This is because he's afraid of getting in trouble on the floor. He's afraid of getting in trouble on the floor because he gets irritated when he's on the floor, and he's afraid he might hit somebody. He doesn't want to take a "self time-out" because he knows he'll leave his door open—because he knows he's not supposed to—and he'll get in trouble for that. So he'll annoy staff until one of us sends him to his room and locks him in.

Mickey is not a kid who is popular with his peers. He says he feels like a racial outcast: white kids don't like him because he isn't like them; they don't consider him white. And black kids call him "white boy." What this boils down to specifically is that he tried to befriend Tyrone Wiley and Robert Holden, but was rebuffed because he's white. Then he tried to befriend William Lee, but was rebuffed because he hadn't "acted white" in trying to befriend Tyrone and Robert.

MONDAY, SEPTEMBER 1: This is for Everett Greimann, connecting us through words, or, as he would say, through worms.

I was at my table at the book fair at Bumbershoot, Seattle's annual arts festival, when Saul came up. He is a wholesaler for herbs and health products. For years he has bought every book I publish, although they have nothing to do with health.

"You heard what happened to Everett." Everett used to do prepress for us, for my books and for Saul's catalogues. He quit when he moved to Alaska.

"No," I said. "I wrote him once but he never wrote back."

"He died. Last February. He thought he had a touch of the flu. Went to bed and died in his sleep." Saul put his hand on my shoulder. "I'm sorry to be the one to tell you."

"No, I'm glad you told me. I didn't know."

About three, Ron Dakron came by so I could take a break. I told him about Everett. I said, "You know, the first thing I thought when Saul told me was, 'Who'll take care of his dogs?'"

"What he didn't tell you was that they found only half of Everett," Ron said.

"God, that's terrible! That's great!"

"Everett would have liked it."

On several nights prior to hearing about Everett's death, I had a recurring dream. In it, I had sent him a package of books to show him what I had been up to, and the package came back stamped "Deceased."

SUNDAY, SEPTEMBER 7: Tyee Horgan called last night. He's in a group home now after spending two years in Elk Grove for blowing up the boys' locker room at school. He wanted to get his homies out of class, he said. It was a joke that backfired. He said he saw "everybody" he knew from Ash Meadow at Elk Grove: Jonas Henson and Reggie Greene, for two. Jonas is getting out soon and so is he, Tyee. He's learned his lessons, he said; no more jokes, no more stealing cars.

MONDAY, SEPTEMBER 22: Mickey says he lost his honor at Elk Grove when he was raped. He didn't resist. He doesn't believe he can regain his honor.

He says his relationship with Victor Rivas included his having sex with Rivas, not Rivas' having sex with him. That was how Mickey termed it: "having sex." What he meant was, he sodomized Rivas but Rivas didn't sodomize him. The one being sodomized is in the female position, Mickey says. So, at Elk Grove, he was made a girl.

TUESDAY, SEPTEMBER 23: Mickey has stolen since he was four years old. He steals, in part, to get back at people he's angry with. But he also steals to please people, because he wants them to like him. So when someone asks him to steal something, he will. But he feels betrayed when he's caught and the person who asked him to steal says nothing to help him.

Rodney Hemming recently accused Mickey of stealing batteries out of his room. I didn't believe Rodney because he said, on the same occasion, that Mickey was refusing to come out of the head—this, while Mickey was locked in his room. Rodney does accuse kids, not only Mickey, of doing things that will get them in trouble with staff. Also, I searched Mickey's room and found no batteries.

But now I wonder if Mickey was telling me, without telling me, that he did take Rodney's batteries and gave them to someone else.

WEDNESDAY, OCTOBER 1: Last Friday, on my weekend, there was an exchange between Oscar Gonzalez and Donny Blocker. According to Eduardo Rojas, Robert Holden and Nathan Dieter moved toward Oscar to back up Donny. Oscar turned to go down to his room and then turned back, saying "Fuck it, I'm not gonna let these niggers punk me." Eduardo, seeing that the three black kids had Oscar surrounded, jumped in and started pushing them away. At that point the floor was cleared.

The next day I could feel the tension in the cottage as soon as I walked in. After reading the log and talking with staff, I called the kids together in the living room and told them that if there was a racial incident, or even a racial slur by any of them, I would lock down the cottage. When I said this, I saw Luis Contreras smile, just a little.

Later I asked him about this smile. He said the black kids have been punking him. He said he wasn't raised to let himself be punked, but he had worked hard for his level and he did not want to lose it. On the other hand, he really did want to beat all of them up, and he was sure he could do it without any help.

Sunday morning Tony Black held a cottage group that ran for two and a half hours, at the end of which kids were hugging each other and shaking hands. Both they and Tony told me about it when I came in in the afternoon. Michael Evans was exposed as having created the problem between the Mexicans and the blacks by going to the black kids and warning them that the Mexicans were going to jump them, then going to the Mexicans and saying the black kids were going to jump them. Michael denied it, but nobody believed him: he has a reputation for doing this very thing.

Then, apparently, Oscar Gonzalez went into Michael's room and hit him. This is what Michael originally said happened. He says now that Oscar came to his doorway and he, Michael, pushed him to keep him out of his room, and that's when Oscar hit him. Michael says he also swung at Oscar. Probably this is not true. Probably Oscar went into Michael's room and hit him and walked out. This is what Oscar says happened and this is what he once did to Michael Biddle. Probably everything Michael Evans says that contradicts this is his attempt to keep other kids from knowing that Oscar punked him.

When I came to work at three, Oscar was off-program, Michael Collins was watching the floor, and Fran and Tony had several kids down at lower court, shooting hoops and flirting with the girls from Peacock and Whale.

When Steven came in at four he questioned why, if there had been a fight—i.e., Oscar hitting Michael—the kids had not been locked down as I had said I would do on Saturday. Tony, returned from lower court, said he didn't think the fight was racial in motivation. But Steven wanted the kids locked down. He seemed to be close to hysteria, so strongly did he feel. I decided to interpret Oscar's thumping Michael as a racial incident in order to calm Steven, and we locked the kids down.

I can't believe I have to work with both Fran and Steven on the same shift. And I don't know what support, if any, I will get from Herman if I make a decision they don't like.

TUESDAY, OCTOBER 14: Abel, in Alternatives to Violence, told this story tonight: "All the clucks was dying down where I lived so I went up to Marysville to sell. I was with three of my homeboys. But after a while nothing was happening so I came back home. I left my homeboys up there. And while I was gone they got into some sort of problem with Big T's little brother and one of them shot him. Killed him, yeh. After that T would try to shoot me when he saw me on the street, or he would try to punk me. You know, he'd stop his car and talk shit and I'd just say "Whatever" and keep on walkin'. Or he'd be selling on my corner and he'd have his homeboys there so I couldn't do nothin' about it. I was about eleven then, yeh. He was about eighteen.

"Finally I heard that he kept a lot of money hidden in his house. So me and my homeboys watched the house until we were sure nobody was there, and then we busted in. We wrecked that place, looking for the money. I even went into the little girl's room and tore up her mattress, looking for it. Nah, she wasn't there. But T's mother was. We thought the house was empty but T's mother was laying in her bed. I guess she was too scared to come out, she was just waiting for us. We didn't do nothin' to her, just tied her up and put tape on her mouth. We got six dollars from her and that was all we got. But we wrecked T's house, and even though we were wearing our hats pulled down over our faces, he knew who did it. That was two years ago when I was thirteen.

"Couple of weeks ago I heard he shot my brother. Killed him, yeh. So now . . . It never ends. It's what keeps us going."

SATURDAY, OCTOBER 18: Back from my weekend, I found a note from Eduardo in my box, telling me he had been transferred to a group home. He thanked me for my help and assured me he would never come back to Ash Meadow.

Unlike so many of the kids we get, I think Eduardo has a good chance of staying out of prison. His parents are together and they are clearly concerned about him. Once, during a visit, his mother started to cry when she thought she saw a tattoo on Eduardo's arm. He does not have one. I don't know what she saw, but her reaction upset Eduardo so that he seems to have made up his mind to give up gang life. This, in spite of his fear that his gang will kill him if he quits, as they killed his friend. Recently, however, he has seemed more confident that he can simply avoid members of his gang without making an announcement of quitting.

MONDAY, OCTOBER 20: I heard another kid alluding to "clucks'" dying as a business problem. It occurs to me that crack sellers' contempt for users is a way of justifying their responsibility for killing them, just as the European colonial powers in Hannah Arendt's discussion manufactured racism as a way of justifying their exploitation of non-white people.[20]

SUNDAY, NOVEMBER 9: Yesterday the noise level in the cottage was unbelievable. It lasted until well past dinner time. I was working with Carol, an intermittent who had been at Ash Meadow for all of a week, and Steven. In Zone 1, Jason Lake and Matt Benson were banging on their doors and they were being answered by Stevie Dorrance banging on his door in Zone 3 and somebody in Zone 4. It was like living in an echo chamber. I asked Steven what he thought we should do. He didn't want to answer, but I stood in front of him, looking into his face. Finally he said, "Ignore them?"

I couldn't help it: laughter just burst out of me. "Ignore them! No, I don't think so." I called Security and had Jason and Matt moved to quiet rooms in Peacock and Ram.

After the kids had done their details and were in their rooms, I spoke with Carol and Steven. I told Carol she was spending too much time in the zones, talking with kids who were in their rooms, when we needed her to help manage the floor. I reminded her that I had talked to her about this earlier, and told her that she needed to do what I asked her to do.

She said it calmed Matt down to be able to vent. It was as though I hadn't said a word. I reiterated and so did she. She spent most of the evening in the zones, talking with kids who were locked down. She refused to answer the phone or to monitor the floor, exactly what intermittents are hired to do. She was absolutely worthless.

After being rebuffed by her, I took Steven into the office and reminded him that he wanted to ignore the racket in the cottage earlier. I told him he needed to be more decisive.

He said he didn't think it was fair that I asked him to make a decision on the spur of the moment. He thought I should have told him first that I was going to ask him to make a decision.

I didn't say a word. What, after all, could I say?

SATURDAY, NOVEMBER 15: Rodney Hemming asked me why people like "stuff," meaning possessions. This question was the beginning of a diatribe against "stuff" and people's desire to get "stuff." This from the only kid in the cottage who owns, and wears, a bathrobe.

Later he talked about how he enjoyed small pleasures, like a good dump. He said he was always careful to clean himself good "back there" because he doesn't like being dirty, especially "there." Sometimes his cleaning left him raw there, "but that's all right."

This child is grooming me.

MONDAY, DECEMBER 1: Walter Cantu and Charles Dietrich finally convinced me that they can't be roommates any longer. They've been telling me this for two weeks but I haven't wanted to accept it. I resisted because I didn't want to move other kids out of their rooms in order to accommodate these two. But I did.

After putting them in separate rooms I brought them into the office. Apparently Walter had been reading aloud parts of *Makes Me Wanna Holler* that talk about beating up on white boys, intimidating Charles. Charles, of course, didn't mention being intimidated. He said the book was racist.

Walter said the book was not racist. He said also that he read to Charles only, or almost only, when Charles asked him to read something to him.

A larger problem resulted when Charles, at dinner, told Richard Kearney, Anthony Demarinis, and Mickey Joyce about the "racist" book. (All are white; Walter is black.) Anthony confronted Walter, who said he would bring the book onto the floor and read it to everybody. Anthony said if Walter did that, he, Anthony, would rip it up.

I talked with Richard, Anthony, and Mickey. They admitted they had not read the book but insisted it was racist. I pointed out that Walter had checked the book out of the school library. Anthony said he would go to the principal and ask her to withdraw the book from the library.

At the end of the discussion, if that's what it was, Anthony said Steven Ruer takes Jason Lake, Robert Holden, and Montague Miller out of their rooms at night to play dominoes after other staff have left. When Anthony asked if he could play too, Steven refused. All of the kids Steven lets out are black. It is a rule at Ash Meadow that when a staff is alone at night, he does not let a kid out of his room for any reason. And Jason Lake is the most dangerous kid we have in the cottage.

A couple of weeks ago, Steven and an intermittent, an African American woman, were teasing Cory Corson about not being able to jump high enough to dunk—an allusion to the film, *White Men Can't Jump*—and Cory accused them of being racist. I took this to be more of Cory's looking for something to complain about. Now I wonder if, at root, Cory wasn't angry at Steven's pulling black kids out at night for dominoes. Cory was in the same zone as Jason and Robert, so he would have heard their doors being unlocked and their talking.

TUESDAY, DECEMBER 2: I asked Steven if he has been allowing kids out of their rooms to play dominoes after other swing-shift staff leave. He hesitated, then said no.

"Some of the kids told me that you do."

Steven let his breath out. "Well, since you know, I might as well tell you." He admitted pulling the three kids out. "But not every night."

I asked if it was true that Anthony Demarinis had asked to play too, but that he had refused to let him.

Steven admitted this had happened.

I asked him why, if he let three kids out, he wouldn't let a fourth out.

He said he thought four were too many for him to manage. He wasn't worried about three, but he thought if something happened he wouldn't be able to handle four. He gave a little giggle, perhaps because he was aware of how silly this sounded.

I asked him if he was aware that all three of these kids had committed violent crimes.

He said he knew, but . . .

I asked if the fact that Anthony Demarinis was white had anything to do with his decision not to let him play dominoes with the others.

"I don't think so," he said, as if he had once considered this as a possibility and had concluded that it was not true.

"Why do you let these three kids out? You knew you aren't supposed to."

"It isn't just dominoes. We're also studying the Bible."

"Dominoes is a lure to get them to the Bible?"

"You could say that."

"Well, is it?"

"Yes."

"You're aware that it's Ash Meadow policy that a single staff is not supposed to let a kid out of his room at night?"

"Yes."

I told him I had no other questions to ask him. He was smiling as he left the office. I've noticed that he often smiles at odd moments. His job could be at stake yet again, and he smiles.

It bothered me, and it still does, that he denied doing anything until he realized I already knew about it. "Well, since you know, I might as well tell you."

I called Herman at home and told him about Steven and about our conversation. Herman asked me what I wanted to do.

"Get rid of him. He's still in his probationary period. It would be easy."

"I don't want to get rid of him."

"Herman, this is the same kind of thing that got him fired from Wolf and Dolphin. You know how dangerous Jason Lake is. Plus, he lied to me. It makes me wonder what else he's lied about. What else has happened that we don't know about?"

"I don't want to fire him. I'll talk to him."

He waited silently while I organized my thinking. How well he and I know each other, at least in some contexts. Finally I said, "Well, that's up to you. Will you let me know what he says? I don't want him letting kids out after the other staff have gone."

"He won't. I'll let you know."

Then Herman asked me to call Candy Laine and set up a time for her to come in for an interview. She's applying again for the supervisor's slot, the one I'm occupying as a temp.

I know I won't be selected for the permanent position. Herman tells me I'm not in a "protected category," meaning my veteran's status will not be of benefit to me. This time the desired categories are Hispanic, Asian, female, and disabled. This is what Herman tells me. Of course, he could be lying.

I called her and set something up. We talked for a few minutes. Actually, I enjoyed talking with her. Whatever demon was in her before seems to have left. She sounded like a mature woman.

WEDNESDAY, DECEMBER 3: Calvin Reed called. He's at a group home up north now. He said he's getting straight A's in solid subjects—chemistry, trigonometry, English, history—and is looking for a job. He has eighteen months left on his sentence. It was good to hear that he's doing well. But he told me, too, that Ron Lafitte is going to be charged with selling crack.

THURSDAY, DECEMBER 4: I dreamed last night that Herman went to a management meeting while we staff were required to remain in the cottage to watch a training video titled *Waxing Grenades in Today's Army*. When I saw the title, black letters on a grainy white background, as in an army training film of the Sixties, I started laughing—in real life, not in my dream—and I woke up. Then I went back to sleep and the dream returned, but the title had changed from *Waxing Grenades* . . . to *Polishing Apples* . . .

FRIDAY, DECEMBER 5: Ron Dakron and I did a reading at Recollection Books in Seattle last night. I read some poems I intend to put in *Prisoners* when it's published. They concern the work I do and some of the kids I've known. At least the kids are the prototypes for many of the characters in the poems.

Afterward a young Mexican woman came up and asked me what a "clique" was. This was her way of beginning a conversation. She said her brother had been murdered and her nephew was in prison in California on a ten-year sentence—a burglary gone awry, with a woman and her children held hostage. Her nephew's idea, and that of his friends, had been to rob a drug dealer. Her story reminded me of Abel, the kid who broke into his rival's house and tied up his mother, and what might have happened had Abel not been luckier than this young woman's nephew.

THURSDAY, DECEMBER 18: Last night I lost it. Stan had told Robert Walden that he had to take off his jacket before he could eat. Robert refused to take it off. He said he wasn't wearing a shirt. Then, when I said I could see his shirt under his jacket, he said he wasn't wearing a long-sleeve shirt and would be cold. I insisted he take his jacket off. He said he wouldn't eat then, and began walking toward his room. I told him that if he went to his room he would be down for the night.

"Fuck you," he said.

"Fuck you, too," I said. I hadn't even thought about saying it, it just rolled right out of my mouth. Immediately I could hear the kids laughing.

"Your mother," Robert said.

And I almost said it back to him.

FRIDAY, DECEMBER 19: Spent yesterday and today in a workshop on domestic violence, sexual abuse, and drug and alcohol abuse put on by the King County Sexual Assault Resource Center. Most of the attendees were public school counselors. Their stories about the kids they contend with were so boring that I wanted to break in with some examples of my darkest humor.

Here's something passed on to me by Roy Burns. It was originally said by Jim Herbold at Ram Cottage. A sex education teacher had conducted a group discussion on sexually transmitted diseases with the kids in the cottage. Afterward, when the kids had been locked down for shift change, Jim, pretending to be one of them, asked the teacher: "If my brother is giving me a blow job and he says something that makes me laugh and the semen comes out of my nose, does that mean I'll get AIDS?"

Getting back to the workshop: It seems to me that there must be some overlap between the kids the school counselors deal with and those I do. But what they describe sounds completely different from what I hear from our kids at Ash Meadow. The counselors talk about the possibility that one of their kids was raped. We're certain that, at a given time, 80 to 100 percent of the girls in our care, and up to 60 percent of the boys, have been raped or otherwise sexually violated. The counselors talk about kids fighting on school grounds. Some of the kids we have have shot other kids.

How did they avoid attracting these counselors' attention? Were they kicked out of school before they could make much of an impact? Probably so, in some cases. But we have kids who attended school, who *liked* school, up until the day they were arrested. Who did their teachers and counselors think these kids were? Were they not paying attention? Or were they purposely avoiding the most troublesome, and troubled, kids?

SUNDAY, DECEMBER 21: It occurred to me this morning that the reason I conduct Survivors' Group is that I'm still trying to heal Cee. And the reason I do Alternatives to Violence is that I'm able, through the kids, to live again the violence of my youth. I've probably discovered this before, but forgot it.

The kid who raped Mickey was to have been tried last week, but at the last minute accepted a plea bargain and pled guilty to fourth-degree assault with sexual motivation. The one who held Mickey while the other boy raped him was not charged. Mickey was at court too, and when he objected to the plea bargain, the prosecutor attacked him as though he were the guilty one. From everything he said, it sounded like she wanted to wrap up the case, and if she had to degrade him in order to do it, she would.

TUESDAY, DECEMBER 23: Robert Walden: "You must be weird."

Me: "Why do you think so?"

Robert: "Because you work here."

TUESDAY, DECEMBER 30: Last night Rob came over from Ram. Herman had told him to talk with me about Sue Doggett. Rob had been over a few days ago and she told him she had discovered a kitchen knife in the staff desk, and that finding it there had scared her because she often finds that drawer unlocked.

It was Fran's knife, of course. She had brought it in to cut up a chicken to make a treat for some of the kids, then had forgotten to take it home. She does often neglect to lock that drawer. But what was I supposed to do about it? She's Fran. She has a special relationship with Herman. "You know the things she's done," I told Rob. "You couldn't fix it when you were here, and neither can I."

"Sorry," he said. "I'm talking to you because Herman asked me to."

I said I know that Sue is unhappy, and perhaps because Fran is a safety hazard unto herself, or perhaps for reasons I don't know, she is intensely angry with Fran. And I know that she is looking for work elsewhere, but again, what can I do about it? And how can I blame her?

Today at PC Sue brought out that Fran has been allowing kids to use her knife to cut up chicken. Fran said Herman had approved this. (Herman was not in attendance.) I told her Herman may have approved her bringing her own cutlery to work and using it herself, but I did not believe he approved allowing residents to handle knives. I told her that if the knife has been taken out of the locked drawer, it must always be in the possession of a staff; the staff may not set the knife down and may not give it to a resident.

Fran objected, saying that other cottages do it and that she monitors the knife's use and lets only the more mature kids use it.

Sue said that our more mature kids are the ones who are doing time for murder.

Fran said she just wouldn't bring the knife in again until after she talked to Herman. She sounded like one of the kids: "I'll just talk to Herman. He'll take off my demerit."

I think Fran will be the one to replace me as supervisor. Herman told me he doesn't feel he can "write around" her. Don Martino told me the other day that the administrators are saying Herman dug himself a pit with Fran and now he has to live in it. Meaning he has given her glowing evaluations and now he can't justify not hiring her. (Candy is apparently out of the running. Herman told me there's some bad stuff in her file.)

When Rob and I talked yesterday he said he's tried to tell Herman that only some people are suited for this kind of work, but Herman insists that anybody can do it.

He believes anybody can be trained, and once trained, will be able to perform competently. Steven and Fran, having received the appropriate training, are therefore able to perform. If they do not perform well, something else, possibly antagonism from other staff, must be preventing them from doing it.

Maybe so, but Herman's failure to take into account individual personality and difference has wrecked the cottage. Because of Steven's indecisiveness and Fran's failure to integrate the most basic ideas of safety and security into her thinking, I see this cottage as an extremely dangerous place to work or to live, with the potential to explode at any moment.

1998

SUNDAY, JANUARY 4: I told Herman a few days ago that Sue is looking for other work. He asked me to find out why she and Fran are not getting along and to try to persuade her to stay on. Gee. I know why she doesn't like Fran: Fran scares her. And Fran also makes it obvious that she doesn't like Sue. Steven told me that Fran told him to be careful not to confide anything to Sue. He claimed he didn't know what Fran meant by "anything."

Anyway, I talked with Sue yesterday. She said she likes Fran personally (uh huh), but has no respect for her on the job. She said she finds it ironic that Herman is asking her to stay just as she's firmed up her plans to leave. She's been offered a job in Portland and she's found an apartment there.

Then she said something I was not prepared for: Steven has her email address—she doesn't know how he got it; she didn't give it to him—and he's been emailing her every day. She told him she doesn't like his writing to her, but he's continued. So she wants to put some distance between herself and him because she thinks he may get more brazen. I offered to talk to him, but she asked me not to, since she's leaving anyway.

TUESDAY, JANUARY 6: Montague Miller was transferred to Elk Grove today. He and Dathan Strait were accused of molesting a girl in one of their classes. I talked with the girl. She said one of the boys touched her thigh and one, perhaps the same one, put his hand inside her pants. One asked her if she had "a fat vagina." One of them placed her hand on his penis and told her, "Jack me off." She said that throughout the incident she asked one or both boys to stop, but they didn't stop.

I do not doubt that everything she said happened did happen. But she was not clear about which boy was doing what or saying what. The boys may have been moving around as well. Apparently Dathan sat by her at first and Montague sat beside her later. Also Dathan told her his name was Montague. When I asked Dathan why he had lied about his name, he said, "Why not?" (And where was the teacher when all this was happening? Pretending that it wasn't?)

Two other boys from our cottage, Miguel Santos and David Warne, said they saw it all and Montague didn't do anything. Dathan went to Wolf Cottage instead of Elk Grove. The administrators think he wouldn't be able to protect himself at Elk Grove.

Both Herman and I were upset and withdrawn. It's interesting that we reacted in the same way. We didn't want to see Montague get the short end of the stick.

SUNDAY, JANUARY 11: I found a set of keys on the staff desk in the office, and the top drawer, where Fran keeps her carving knife, unlocked. I knew the keys would be Steven's; Fran wasn't in today. Sure enough, he said he had unlocked the drawer to get a pair of scissors out of it, then set his keys down and forgot about them.

He did not regard either the keys or the unlocked drawer as a big deal. He said he was glad I had discovered them rather than Sue, as she would be a lot more upset than I seemed to be.

I was amazed he didn't see that I was seething. I was too angry even to ask why the scissors were in the drawer instead of locked up in the tool box.

TUESDAY, JANUARY 13: In Alternatives to Violence tonight, the kids and I got into a discussion of welfare cheats. Cory knows personally of one woman who is a welfare cheat—one out of the millions of women he claims he knows. Michael Evans says he knows two, of the one or two hundred women he has known. Still, both of them railed against the welfare cheats who are impoverishing this country. I had forgotten how conservative these kids' views are. The poor are grist for the mills of demagoguery.

MONDAY, JANUARY 19 (MARTIN LUTHER KING, JR.'S BIRTHDAY, AT LEAST THE DAY WE'RE CELEBRATING IT): When I went in to work today a TV talk show had on something to do with Martin Luther King and civil rights. Andrew Guerin wanted to turn the channel because, he said, discussions of race always bring trouble into the cottage. Anthony Demarinis said kids were told at school that they weren't supposed to watch a talk show unless there was a discussion of it afterward.

The black kids were not watching TV but were playing dominoes in the dining room, so I told the others they could change the channel. Matt Benson, in the dining room, got an odd expression on his face and I asked him if he wanted to come into the living room to watch the talk show, but he said no.

When Tony Black came in for his shift, he announced that he'd brought in a movie for Martin Luther King Day, *Cry the Beloved Country*. Several non-black kids said they wouldn't watch it.

Later, after it was all over, Richard Kearney claimed he said he didn't want to watch a movie about some dead guy, to which Ronnie Williams responded that he would kill Richard and then he'd be a dead white guy. Ronnie's version does not quite match Richard's. According to Ronnie, Richard said he didn't want to watch a movie about "a dead nigger." Knowing Richard, I suspect Ronnie's version is the truer one.

Regardless of what Richard said, I did not hear it. I did hear Ronnie say he was going to kill Richard, and I saw him rush at Richard. This was in the living room. I got in front of Ronnie and yelled at him, but he ignored me except to push me aside. Each time he did this I stepped in front of him again. He is so round that I was unable to get a hold on him. He was not out to fight me, he wanted to get to Richard. He kept looking past me, over my shoulder, at him. At some point I yelled "Clear the floor!" and I could see, from the corner of my eye, kids running out of the living room. But then Fran shouted "No!" and called the kids back. She said later that she did not think there would be a fight, that she could see that Ronnie was upset but believed he would be able to "process" with Richard without hitting him. She said she thought this even though she could see me struggling with Ronnie.

Finally Tony slipped behind Ronnie and put his knees behind Ronnie's. The result was that Ronnie collapsed backward on top of Tony. This is a good time to give some idea about the respective sizes of those involved. All three of us are around five feet ten; maybe Ronnie is an inch shorter. Tony weighs, I would guess, about 140, I weigh 190, and Ronnie 260. So when Ronnie fell backward onto Tony, this was an event of some significance.

Ronnie was now on the floor, cushioned by Tony, so I got down and put my weight against him (and Tony, beneath him) to keep him from getting up, and tried to turn him over by rotating his arm so I could get an arm lock on him. Ronnie, of course, tried to keep me from doing that, and unable to get to his feet, started sliding along the floor on his back, that is, on top of Tony. Ultimately, the three of us slid from the vicinity of the staff desk all the way down Zone 3, a distance of about forty feet, stopping only when we found ourselves wedged in a corner at the end of the zone. As we passed Fran, who was standing with Richard Kearney on a low table in the living room, I shouted at her: "Would you please press your goddamn panic alarm! Can you do that?"

She started to say something, caught herself, then pressed the alarm.

By the time Security arrived I had succeeded in rolling Ronnie over, still on top of Tony, and had gotten a wrist lock on him. As soon as I applied pressure, he started yelling, "Ow! Ow! Ow! I'm sorry! I'm sorry!" I told him I wouldn't hurt him if he stopped struggling and waited for Security to arrive. He agreed. I had completely forgotten about Tony.

The two guys from Security came down the zone. I waited until they had handcuffed Ronnie, then got off him. I started out of the zone, remembered Tony, and went back to help him to his feet. Amazingly, he was not hurt.

Security took Ronnie to Central Isolation and Tony and I sat down at the desk to do the paperwork: the incident report and tracking sheet, the logging, and the police incident report (because Ronnie had put his hands on me). Fran wanted to let the kids out; she'd had to lock them down when Security came. She hadn't a clue as to how shaken Tony and I might be; either that, or she had no concern. I said no, just give them head calls if they need them. After a while she brought me a cup of coffee. I wanted to throw it in her face.

We got Ronnie as a transfer from Andromeda, the mental health unit, about a week ago. I called the unit now. What interested me is that he seemed not to hear me all the time I was yelling at him, at least until I began to hurt him. He may not even have seen me except as an obstacle to his getting at Richard. Also, when we were in the zone waiting for Security, he asked me what had happened. He claimed not to remember any of it.

I don't recall the name of the Andromeda staff I talked with, but she told me that Ronnie has seizures accompanied by black-outs, after which he does not remember what he did. When he had a seizure at Andromeda, she said, everybody just stayed out of his way until it was over.

That's pretty hard to do when he's going after somebody, I said. She agreed it would be.

I asked her if there was a reason why we were not informed of his seizures. She said she was surprised we weren't.

I called the health center and asked if Ronnie Williams was supposed to be taking anti-seizure meds. Dorothy checked his chart and said indeed he was. I told her we have never had meds for him. She said, Well, that explains a lot, doesn't it?

She said she didn't have that med in stock. It would have to be reordered. She'd get the doctor to do it tomorrow. That will be good, I said.

After the paperwork was done, we got the kids out of their rooms. Richard told me he expects to spend a lot of time in his room tomorrow. Ronnie will be back in the unit tomorrow morning.

TUESDAY, JANUARY 20: There was an article in yesterday's newspaper about Willie Gonzalez. He has been killed.[21] He was smoking and drinking with some of his cousins. He took a beer belonging to one of them out of the refrigerator and opened it. His cousin had been smoking marijuana soaked in PCP and shot Willie in the head.

I once asked Willie to imagine himself five years from now—what did he want for himself? He said he expected to be dead by then, though he didn't know how he would die.

I liked Willie. He'd been living with his father, who was devoted to him. I remember his dad telling me that at birth several minutes had passed before Willie started breathing, and that he had been late in developing in some ways.

It was true that Willie was not intelligent. He wasn't stupid—at least I didn't like to think of him that way—but he was slow. Other kids would have picked on him when he was small. His father must be devastated.

WEDNESDAY, JANUARY 21: I talked with Mickey Joyce this evening. A couple of kids from Elk Grove are here in the Phoenix Program, and they've told other kids that Mickey was raped. He's desperate to hide from this third humiliation. (The first was the rape itself; the second was the experience with the prosecutor last month.) He asked me to send him to Wolf, to Andromeda, anywhere away from the general population of Ash Meadow. Of course, I can't transfer him: he's done nothing to warrant being sent to Wolf, and he doesn't have a mental health problem that would put him in Andromeda.

SATURDAY, JANUARY 24: We were giving head calls after supper when Stan let Aaron Sneed out of his room without checking to see if anyone was already in the bathroom. Just as Stan walked past, Stevie Dorrance stepped out. We had been having problems with them, Stevie talking shit, relying on staff to protect him, Aaron looking for an opportunity to get him.

I heard Sue Doggett say "Oh shit!" She was looking into the zone. I had been sitting on the ping-pong table, monitoring the kids doing their details, and I jumped down and started running toward the zone. Kids had clustered around Sue at the mouth of the zone, curious, slowing me just by their presence. I pressed my alarm and shouted "Clear the floor!" Aaron had Stevie down on the floor at the far end. He looked up, saw me, and hit Stevie one more time before I grabbed him.

Herman was right behind me, having run out of his office when he heard Sue shout. I handed Aaron off to him and grabbed Stevie to keep him from going after Aaron. I locked Stevie in his room and went to the staff office after Herman.

He and Stan had already put Aaron in the quiet room. Aaron was yelling, "Why'd I do that? Why'd I do that?" He was hitting his head against the door. Then he said, "Wait a minute! I didn't do it. He hit me first. Hey, staff! He hit me first!" We got out of the office and closed the door before we allowed ourselves to laugh.

It was a pleasure to work with Herman. When I turned Aaron over to him, he immediately put an arm lock on him and took him away. There was no hesitation, no fumbling. I would trust him again to cover me. But two take-downs in five days is more than I want to do. I broke my watch on the one with Ronnie. No damage, to me at least, on this one. Stevie Dorrance's face was beginning to swell when I left work.

TUESDAY, JANUARY 27: Herman told me today that Fran got the JRS job I've been temping for the last six months. I'd been expecting this. He told me again that he couldn't figure out a way to "write around her" that would satisfy the superintendent. Of course, this is because for the last three years he's written evaluations on her that were dishonest.

He said he was going to put me in for Employee of the Year. Then he told me to remind him to do the paperwork which is due on January 31. Sure I will, Herman.

WEDNESDAY, JANUARY 28: It's been a rough week for some of these kids. On Sunday, Matt Benson's dad called and told him he's dying: lung cancer. When I arrived at work they had already finished talking and Matt was in his room. I was on the floor only a few minutes when I heard a crash from Zone 2. Fran laughed and said Matt's been having a hard day. I went to check on him and found him sitting on his bed. His desk had been overturned. He was wearing his black baseball cap; black is his gang color. Ordinarily kids are not allowed to wear their colors, even in their rooms, but I didn't say anything. I sat with him for a while and let him cry.

Then last night Mickey Joyce, after talking with his mother, dropped the phone into its cradle and went to his room. A few minutes later I found him lying on his bed, crying. His mother had told him flatly that she didn't want him back. "What am I going to do?" he asked me. Of course, he'll go back into foster care, and from there he'll probably drift back to the street. But that isn't what he meant. What he meant was, What is he going to do about his heart breaking? If he were on the street, drugs would be the answer.

I don't think I've described Mickey physically in these pages. He's a large kid who has gained enough weight since he's been here as to be able to intimidate other kids if he wanted to, which he does not. Horsing around with him once, I could feel how difficult he would be to restrain if he really wanted to resist. So when he cries "What am I going to do?" it's especially rending because he's a kid who looks like he should be able to take care of himself, but cannot. And this gives bullies a certain amount of pleasure when they're able to punk him. I think something broke in him when his mother gave him up the first time.

I sent in my application for a position as a juvenile parole counselor in Region Four. I also put in a request for transfer to another cottage here at Ash Meadow. I've known since before I finished graduate school that 90 percent of a job, for me, is who I work with. That is, the satisfaction, or even pleasure, I get from working a job depends on my relationships with colleagues. I enjoy my relationship with Stan, but it does not sufficiently offset my dislike for Fran and Steven.

I think, too, that with Fran and Steven on the same shift, something bad will eventually happen in Swan, and whoever else is working that shift will be assigned the blame, because Fran and Steven will stick together, lying if they have to in order to save their own necks.

TUESDAY, FEBRUARY 3: Herman announced at PC today that Fran is the new JRS, starting immediately. Then he told us that he is being investigated and will be going on administrative leave. This means that Fran will be running the cottage. I have no idea what the investigation is about.

TUESDAY, FEBRUARY 10: Fran, in Herman's absence and in her new capacity as supervisor, conducted PC today. She was under some misapprehension about something—I've forgotten what—but nobody said anything to set her straight, though I'm certain we all knew she was wrong. There was no collusion: we hadn't gotten together before the meeting and decided we were going to screw Fran. Rather, it was individual passive-aggression, which is the only kind of aggression you can use if you have no power. Each of us decided, silently and alone, to let Fran encounter the consequences of her mistake on her own.

FRIDAY, FEBRUARY 13: I met Ron Dakron for coffee at Larry's Market. Leaving the market, I ran into Eduardo Rojas, Nathan Dieter, and Luis Contreras on their way to the Oak Tree to see *Sphere*. They looked great! They're all in the same group home. Eduardo will be released to go home in two weeks, Nathan in a month, Luis in August. They were accompanied by a staff member from the group home who was antsy about getting into the theater in time to see the beginning of the movie, so I did not get to talk with them as much as I would have liked. But it was good to see them, and wonderful to hear that they are doing so well.

SUNDAY, FEBRUARY 22: Aaron Sneed, permitted by Fran to watch a movie with the other kids on Tables status, handed something to Lawrence Norby and told him to give it to Michael Evans and tell him "it" looks like Mike. "It" was a photo of a gorilla, torn out of a magazine. Mike crumpled it up and threw it on the floor. When I picked it up and unfolded it and saw what it was—kids were crowding around me to get a look at it—I sent Aaron and Lawrence to their rooms.

Fran talked to Aaron, who told her that Matt Benson had passed the picture to Lawrence, but Lawrence told her it had, in fact, been Aaron. So Fran gave Aaron a minor bust and two hours OP for lying.

When I saw this in the log later, I told Fran that Aaron had been "racial ranking" on Mike. Fran said she thought Aaron was alluding to the gorilla's nose and Mike's nose, which, to her, looked similar. I told her Aaron was making a racial comment by equating the gorilla's face with Mike's, and if she didn't respond to it now, the kids would be throwing it—her failure to respond—in her face later. "I hear you," she said. She changed Aaron's punishment to a major bust with twenty-four OP.

Maybe that's the way to handle Fran: if I want her to do something, make it look like it's in her own interest to do it.

MONDAY, FEBRUARY 23: Region Four called this morning. Someone else got the parole officer position.

SUNDAY, MARCH 1: Steven and I had taken some kids to chapel. After services the congregation was beginning to leave when Lee Buckman from Security appeared at the door and told us that the campus was locked down and we were all to remain in the chapel. Everybody returned to their seats and sat down. Rumors of an escape began to spread.

Dick Peck, our new chaplain, as ignorant as anyone else as to what was going on, began to sing and asked everyone to sing with him. He got the band, musicians from a church group on the outs, playing. Prayers alternated with singing while kids and staff tried to figure out what had happened. Then kids began asking to use the bathroom.

Lee was still at the door. I got up and went over to him and told him we were going to have to start giving head calls. He agreed but said the kids would have to be accompanied by a staff. Then I asked him what was happening. He told me to keep it to myself, but a girl in Whale had killed herself. Without thinking, I looked over at where the Whale contingent was sitting. There were eight or ten girls accompanied by a single staff, Sal Reiver, and he was watching Lee and me.

I returned to Swan's area and told the kids I would take them two at a time to the head. Steven asked me what was going on and I told him I didn't know, but it looked like we were going to be here for a while. I saw Dick coming toward us and I left Steven because I didn't want him to hear Dick and me talking—I didn't trust Steven not to say anything to the kids, and the last thing we needed now was a panic. I caught Dick a few rows away and whispered to him what Lee had told me, and said I was going to start giving head calls. Dick nodded and went up front and announced that we would be giving head calls, one cottage at a time.

I took the first Swan kids and then returned with them and took two more. Then one of the staff from another cottage took a couple of his kids. I sneaked a look at Sal. He seemed mostly concerned with keeping his girls calm. They didn't seem especially active, but they were buzzing like everybody else.

An hour had passed from the time chapel was to have ended when Lee went to the front and told us they were ready to start releasing us to return to our units. They would release one cottage at a time in just a moment. He motioned Dick and me to him. He asked Dick to take charge of releasing the cottages and asked me if I would mind if he held Swan back until all the others but Whale had gone. I thought he wanted to do this because I already knew what had happened. I agreed.

The other cottages were called out, and then Swan was. I sneaked another look at Sal. He knew something was wrong and that it affected his cottage. I could see it on his face, something worse than anxiety but not quite horror.

On the way back to Swan we saw two ambulances parked in front of Whale. One left as we watched, and moved slowly toward the main road. Kids wondered aloud what had happened and one of them asked me if there had been a suicide. I said I didn't know. At the cottage Fran told me there had been a suicide at Whale and we needed to get the kids locked down. I said I knew.

We locked the kids in their rooms and I left. My shift had ended a half-hour earlier. In Seattle I stopped at the Barnes and Noble at University Village. I think I just wanted to be around people and in a well-lighted place. But I bought a remaindered copy of *The Violence of Our Lives: Interviews with American Murderers*. The cashier seemed interested in the book and I started rambling: "Suicide tonight . . . worst thing that could happen . . . Some of the kids I work with have killed people . . . kill themselves . . ." She turned away from me, of course.

I hadn't realized how distraught I was until I heard myself babbling. The kids haven't been told yet. Tomorrow, I suppose.

MONDAY, MARCH 2: I talked with Rick Newton, Mickey Joyce's parole officer. He said he expects to have to put Mickey in a shelter until he finds a home for him.

I talked with Mickey later. I said that sometimes short-term pain has long-term benefits.

He said he has no patience. (He's right.)

I gave him the assignment to list legal activities that he enjoys doing so he can fall back on those things when life on the outs gets hard. We talked about reading and lifting weights. He said he might get back into playing hockey. He'll be paroled at the end of April.

Dean Nader, Ash Meadow's nearly invisible superintendent—there's a story going around that his existence is a rumor started by JRA—came down to the cottage tonight. He said he was going to all of the cottages. He asked me how I was doing. He meant with the suicide. I told him it is the worst thing that can happen, worse even than an assault on staff, but that I'm doing all right. As I was talking, I saw Sal's face as I had seen it when I was leaving the chapel last night, and I started to choke up. But I got through it without breaking down. I don't think Nader noticed anything.

Aaron Sneed asked me later how everything can go on as if nothing had happened. There's school, we give meds, we have supper, gym time, and so on. I told him that we don't know what else to do.

One of the boys feels guilty because when he was in the Phoenix Program with Sandi, the girl who killed herself, she had begged him to go out with her and he had refused.

WEDNESDAY, MARCH 4: As I was unlocking Zone 1 after quiet time, one of the kids told me Aaron Sneed was stuck between the shelves in his room. Unable to imagine that, I shouted at Aaron to hurry up out of his room, and went on to unlock Zone 2. When everyone was seated in the living room, Stan and I counted heads and came up one short.

"Aaron's stuck in his room," one of the kids said. He seemed to be serious so I went into Zone 1 again and looked into Aaron's room. I didn't see him and was about to clear the floor, thinking we had an escape, when I changed my mind and walked into the room. There was Aaron, lying in the fetal position, on one of his clothing shelves.

"Get out of there," I said.

He started kicking his legs—he looked like a dog wagging two tails—but didn't come out.

"I can't," he said.

I started to laugh and so did he. I could hear the kids in the living room laughing too.

"I don't believe this," I said.

Stan came into the room.

"What's he doing in there?"

"Aaron," I said, "what are you doing in there?"

"I was looking for something."

"He was looking for something," I said. "Did you find it?"

"No."

Stan was laughing.

"We'd better lock the kids down while we figure out what to do," I said. "We may have to cut his legs off."

"Cut my legs off!"

"I'll get the ax."

"You can't cut my legs off!"

"Aaron, chill. I was just kidding."

"Oh."

"No I wasn't."

"Hey!"

Stan and I put the other kids back in their rooms—they didn't complain at all—and returned to Aaron's room.

Stan tried to pull him out by his legs, but that didn't work. I felt around in the space surrounding Aaron to try to figure out how he was positioned. He was lying on his left side. His right palm was on the shelf supporting his weight. His left hand was at the lip of the shelf above him. This lip overhung the shelf he lay on.

"It's really hot in here," he said.

"I'll get the ax," Stan said.

"No!"

I asked him what his right hand was doing.

"Nothing."

"What's your left hand doing?"

"Pushing."

He was pushing himself toward the wall at the far end of the space, thinking he was pushing himself out. What a metaphor for this kid, I thought.

I didn't know if he knew the difference between his right and his left, so I placed my hand on his left one and told him to do nothing with that hand. Then I put my hand over his right one and told him to push with that hand when I said to.

"Push?"

"When I tell you."

I held his legs so their weight wouldn't hang off his hips and twist his back when he came out.

"Now. Push."

He slid out.

"I ought to give you OP," I said.

"Why? I didn't mean to get stuck."

"You were looking for weapons." A year or two earlier Charlie Lewis told us there were carpenter's nails hidden behind the shelves in this room. Charlie said another kid told him he put them there. We tore the shelves out, looking for them, but found nothing but a report card and some bits of plaster from the wall.

"No I wasn't. What weapons?"

"You start rooting around in there again, I'll give you twenty-four OP. Understand?"

"Yes. But I wasn't rooting. Pigs root."

We went out to the living room and I sat with him while Stan let the other kids out.

SUNDAY, MARCH 8: As soon as I walked into the cottage to start my shift I sensed something unusual. It was quiet. Michael Collins told me that Aaron Sneed had been moved to Wolf. The decision to move him was made yesterday after John Loring took him down twice and Aaron destroyed his room—pulled the light socket out of the ceiling, broke his window, etc.

I knew Aaron would be moved after his performance yesterday, but I hadn't expected it to happen this soon. I assumed we would be stuck with him until the administrators got around to putting their imprimatur on his transfer.

MONDAY, MARCH 9: Mickey Joyce is anxious about leaving Ash Meadow. He says he's certain he can keep from committing more crimes, but he thinks he'll probably drink again and skip school.

I told him he needs a plan in case he does start drinking again: he should ask his parole officer if he can call him if he finds himself slipping.

TUESDAY, MARCH 10: Heard a frog for the first time this year. Spring will be here soon.

SATURDAY, MARCH 14: Rodney Hemming, after I told him other kids had said he'd left the TV on in the craft room: "They couldn't know. I was the only one in there."

Mickey has been working on a prevention plan. I told him to try to anticipate problems he's likely to run into, and then find realistic solutions. I told him to be honest with himself, both in defining the problems and in coming up with solutions. He says it's the hardest work he's done here so far, being so honest with himself.

SUNDAY, MARCH 15: I've been feeling sad lately, as though seeing the world through a darkening lens. My sense is that my machine is simply closing down.

TUESDAY, MARCH 17: At PC we got into a discussion about what our psychiatrists do. Someone said they are interested only in experimenting with drugs. I noted that psychiatrists do not employ "drugs," but "medications." If it's legal, it's a medication; if it's not legal, it's a drug. I think one of the kids pointed this out to me. Or maybe John Loring did on another occasion. Or maybe I said it to him.

Are we cynical, or what?

MONDAY, MARCH 23: Mickey has been working on his prevention plan but is stymied. He's written out six scenarios in which he encounters conflict, but he "resolves" each one by running away. In each scenario the conflict is brought on, in part, by using drugs again. He becomes afraid that he'll fail a UA or that his mother will shout at him, and he runs. He knows that his drug use and his drinking are also ways by which he avoids dealing with his unhappiness.

WEDNESDAY, MARCH 25:

To: Fran Sikora
From: Jerry Gold
Subject: Steven Ruer's performance

This memo concerns Steven Ruer's performance on the evening of March 23, 1998.

Steven, during after-dinner details, told Michael Evans to go to his room. When Mike asked why, Steven said Mike had been "mean-mugging" him. Mike denied this, but Steven insisted. The two walked down Zone 3 side by side, Mike objecting that he hadn't been mean-mugging, Steven saying he had. (The information on the exchange between Steven and Mike came from Mike. I did not hear Steven say this. Everything else recounted here I saw or heard.) At no time did Steven or anyone else put a hand on Mike. There was no physical coercion of any kind. The two walked side by side, arguing. This is an important point, because on the incident report Steven wrote that Mike refused to go into his room. Mike did not refuse. I had followed them down the zone because I could see that Mike was upset and I thought the presence of a second staff might keep the situation from getting out of hand.

At the door to his room, Mike stopped and continued to plead his case, insisting he had not mean-mugged Steven. He had begun to cry. Steven told Mike that if he didn't go into his room he would get a minor bust. Mike did go into his room, again without physical coercion. Steven locked Mike's door and we left the zone together. Soon, Mike started to kick his door.

After Security moved him to Ram's quiet room, I checked his room for damage and found none. The room was not trashed, not even disordered, yet Steven wrote on the incident report that Mike had trashed his room.

You may recall that after Mike was moved, the three of us, you, Steven, and I, put our heads together to determine Mike's punishment. Steven wanted to give Mike a major bust. I objected that his kicking his door warranted his being moved to a quiet room, and possibly a minor bust, but there was no room damage, therefore no reason to give him a major bust. Recall that a major bust means the loss of Mike's level and a reduction to Tables status.

At this point, Steven said Mike had called him an Uncle Tom. Steven did not say when this occurred. It did not occur in the zone. And Steven did not write this on the incident report or in the log. However, we—you and I— acquiesced before Steven's insistence that Mike get a major bust, based on his alleged use of racial epithets.

There are a couple of points I want to make which are hinted at above.

1. Steven's relationship with the residents. I have heard from other staff that some residents have a problematic relationship with Steven. Matt Benson told Sue Doggett that he does not feel safe when Steven is on shift. Sue and I took this to mean that Matt feels, because of Steven's frequent inattention (with which all the staff are familiar) to what is happening in the cottage, that he might be beaten up and Steven would not notice. But I wonder now if Matt feels unsafe because Steven targets him. Walter Cantu does feel that Steven targets him, but I do not know why. John Loring told me that Walter disclosed to him, too, his apprehension concerning Steven.

As you know, many of the residents treat Steven with contempt. When I was acting supervisor, I counseled Steven on what he does, if not to encourage their contempt, then not to discourage it either. I suspect now, however, that Steven is not entirely passive in his relationship with the residents. I have wondered, for example, why almost all of the demerits he gives out are given after I leave for the evening, when he is the only staff on duty.

2. Steven's informing, or misinforming, other staff about what occurs when he is on duty. I have already indicated that Steven's description of what happened on March 23 is at variance with what I observed. Someone who had not been present, reading Steven's account, would get the impression that Mike physically resisted when, in fact, he did not. I am afraid that Steven so frequently distorts information that I, for one, am never certain when he is telling the truth and when he is not.

On one occasion I told him he could bring out a resident for counseling after I left for the evening. He brought out three, not for counseling but to play dominoes. When I learned of this later, I confronted him on his deception. He insisted that I had authorized his bringing out three residents. Not so.

Sue Doggett also complained to me that Steven had asked if she would mind if he got a resident out of his room. When she agreed, he again brought out three, again to play dominoes.

Steven's judgement is flawed, to put it politely, and he is dishonest. I do not think he should be retained in Swan Cottage.

It has been extremely unpleasant for me to write this memo. I consider it an act of conscience.

There were some things I did not put in the memo, one of them being my own response to what happened between Steven and Mike. I was sick about it, seeing Steven close himself off to Mike's pleas for an explanation. I felt humiliated on Mike's behalf. And I realize now that I was ashamed because I did not intervene. Was there something I could have done other than simply observe? Not without subverting Steven's authority in front of the kids.

And there, more than anything else, is the rub. A bad staff corrupts everybody associated with him. In not opposing this staff's influence, we succumb to it. In not speaking against him, we end up serving him.

Clearly Steven had a personal interest in punishing Mike, though he has yet to say what it was—I do not believe the Uncle Tom business. I would bet we will never know what it was.

I also did not mention in the memo that Steven brought kids out of their rooms at night not to play dominoes, but to conduct Bible study—dominoes were just the bait to draw them to the Bible. (But this may be another of Steven's lies: I haven't heard anybody mention Bible study with Steven, only that he takes kids out of their rooms for dominoes.) I didn't put this in the memo because after I give it to Fran she is required by regulation to pass it on to Don Martino. And Don Martino, I know, is a deeply religious man who might be tempted to overlook a security problem if he thought it served a higher cause.

THURSDAY, MARCH 26: I gave the memo to Fran yesterday. She passed it on to Martino, who told her to investigate.

I also gave her a copy to give to Herman. I knew from Rob Gorey that Herman was working on Steven's evaluation and I didn't want to embarrass him.

Fran said she had no contact with Herman. Certainly she is not supposed to as long as he is on administrative leave from Swan.

"Well, if you do happen to run into him, you can give it to him," I said.

Late in the afternoon Fran told me Herman was furious about the memo. He had wanted to promote Steven to JRRC but the memo will kill that.

Good.

1:30 P.M. Cee called me here at home a few minutes ago. She mentioned the suicide at Ash Meadow. I think she was asking out of concern for me. I told her how I found out about it at chapel and how we arranged to dismiss the cottages one by one, leaving Whale for last so Dick could talk with them to prepare them. I got to how Sal's face looked as he was beginning to understand that it was bad—it was his last week at Ash Meadow before leaving to get married and moving to California—and I started to cry. Then I couldn't talk anymore and I had to hang up. I hadn't even been aware that I felt anything about it since the first night after the suicide. This must be why I've been so depressed lately.

SUNDAY, MARCH 29: Steven sent Michael Evans to his room tonight a little before his actual bedtime. Mike didn't know why. I didn't, and don't, either. On the way to his room he asked if he could talk to me. He said Steven seems to have it in for him and Matt Benson and Andrew Guerin. Mike thinks Steven must be afraid one of them will tell Herman that he lets kids out at night after other staff have left; by being mean to Matt and Andrew and him, he is letting them know they have something to lose if they tell.

This doesn't sound accurate to me. Obviously Steven has singled out Mike, and maybe others, for some nasty treatment, but I don't know why and I don't think Mike knows either.

But apparently Steven is still bringing kids out at night after I've gone, even though Herman cautioned him against it. Or maybe Herman lied to me. Maybe he didn't tell Steven to stop as he told me he had. In any event, there's nothing I can do; Steven will do as he pleases.

TUESDAY, APRIL 7: Fran asked me to write a special program for Mickey Joyce and Michael Evans, who tore their rooms up last night. They've taken a lesson from Aaron Sneed; he was the first in our cottage to do that kind of damage. Mike broke his desk apart and used one of the legs to break out all of his windows. Mickey tore the light fixture out of his ceiling.

This was to be an In/Out program, allowing the two kids to be out of their rooms only to go to school and to use the bathroom. Fran said it had to be in to Don Martino tomorrow for his signature.

I went in the staff office and began to write. A couple of minutes later she asked me if I wanted to take some kids to the gym to play volleyball. I told her I could not write the program and take kids to the gym at the same time.

She said if Stan took the kids I'd have to come out on the floor. I said if I had to cover the floor, I wouldn't be able to write the program.

The next thing I knew, Stan had a list of kids who were going to the gym. He said Fran asked him to take some kids up.

"What kind of shit is this!" burst out of my mouth.

But before Stan could leave the cottage, a couple of other kids went off and he had to stay back.

"You're lucky," Fran said. "You can get off the floor now."

This is her style of revenge. I wonder what she's getting back at me for. Or maybe it's Herman: maybe he's retaliating for my blowing the whistle on Steven.

Coming to work these past few months, my gut just knots up every time I pull into the parking lot. I loathe working with Fran and Steven.

MONDAY, APRIL 13: This morning Sheryl Bunch, the program manager for Whale Cottage, called me at home. "This is your lucky day," she said, and offered me a job in her cottage, Fridays and Saturdays off.

I accepted.

She asked me if I had any doubts about my ability to work with girls. They are different from boys, she said. I told her I trusted my ability to adapt.

She said she would let Herman know and they would make the arrangements for my transfer.

My entire life is about to change. I'm not certain what I feel.

TUESDAY, APRIL 14: Roy Burns called from Ram last night to tell me that Mark Robinson had died in an auto crash; it was in the paper. I found the article. It was a high-speed chase in a stolen car, and he drove it into a tree.

After quiet time we assembled the kids in the living room. I asked who knew Mark Robinson. I felt I owed it to his friends to tell them about his death. Only a couple of kids raised their hands, though I knew more must have known him. He had been released less than a year ago.

Someone asked if something bad had happened. I said yes. Someone else asked if he was dead. I said yes. I started to tell them how he had died, then just read the article to them. Gerald Bardot suddenly bent in half, sobbing. Mark had been his best friend, he said. He had jumped Mark into his gang and later Mark had jumped him out.

Gerald was in a bad way. When he tried to sit up, his stomach muscles contracted and bent him over again. Finally I got him straightened up in his chair, but he complained of cramping. I pulled up his tee-shirt and saw his abdominal muscles contracting, first the left side, the contractions running up his torso in a line, one bunch of muscles after another, and then the same thing on the right side. Gerald saw this too and began screaming that he was being possessed by Satan and that he was going to die. Afraid that the other kids would be infected by his hysteria, I cleared the floor, but put my hand on Gerald's shoulder and told him to stay where he was.

I told Steven not to bother locking the kids down, but had him watch Gerald while I called the health center. Dorothy was on duty and she lectured me about the kids not drinking enough water and getting dehydrated and stomach cramps were one of the things that happened when you didn't get enough water and no, she was not going to see Gerald.

By now the contractions were lessening and Gerald and Steven both were watching Gerald's abdomen, fascinated. A few minutes more and his body had relaxed and he was calm. I told him I wanted him to go to his room and lie down, and he agreed. I locked him in, then got the other kids out. I told Steven we needed to check on Gerald every fifteen minutes.

At about eight-thirty, Lawrence Norby and Walter Cantu in Zone 2 began pounding and kicking their doors. Steven was in Zone 1, giving head calls. We still had some kids on the floor and I was monitoring them. To me, the noise coming out of Zone 2 sounded like another kid knocking for a head call. Steven yelled at them to stop banging or he'd give them a minor bust. They kept it up and Steven came out of Zone 1 and went into Zone 2, angry.

I started toward the staff office. I was going to start giving out the evening meds. I thought I heard someone call my name, but I wasn't sure and I didn't know where the sound had come from. Then I heard it again, from Zone 2. Steven was in Ronnie Williams' room. Ronnie was on his bed, lying on his stomach. Steven couldn't wake him up. I asked if he was breathing. Steven said yes.

I left the zone to get the radio to call Security. Coming out of the office, I decided my body alarm would get Security here faster. I yelled "Clear the floor!" and hit my alarm. Immediately Steven yelled out that I should call Security and tell them it was a false alarm. I did as he wanted: I called Security on the radio, said it was a false alarm, and returned to the office and put the radio back in the charger.

I went back to Ronnie's room and saw him lying on the floor. His eyes opened, then closed. "What the hell are you doing, Steven!" I shouted even as I was running out of the zone. I got the radio, called Security on my way back to the zone, Steven all the while yelling at me not to call them. Speaking into the radio, I told Security that we had thought we had a suicide, that it was not a suicide, but that the kid was not responding to us as he should, and I wanted them to come down to the cottage.

Lee Buckman and another security officer, I've forgotten who, arrived, lifted Ronnie to his feet and forced him to walk to the quiet room. He wasn't fully conscious, and each man held one of his arms as he shuffled along, moving as though he'd been drugged. At the quiet room they treated him as an attempted suicide. They told him to strip. He objected, but did it. They took his socks and underwear and gave him yellow heavy-duty pants and shirt to put on.

After Ronnie was safely tucked in in the quiet room and Security had left, I went into Zone 2 and talked with Lawrence and Walter. They said Ronnie, on the way to his room at his bedtime, had told them he had nothing to live for now. The two boys, already locked in, tried to persuade him that he did, Walter telling him to put Mark's death out of his mind and get on with his life. Ronnie said good night and went into his room. Then I came down and locked his door. After I had gone, Lawrence saw him in his window with something green around his neck. Lawrence told Walter and the two of them began banging on their doors.

I told them they had done the right thing and that I appreciated their persistence even after Steven threatened to bust them. As I was talking to them I suddenly flashed back to J.P. Prince coming out of his unlocked room to tell us that Peter Chaple had broken his window. Peter had been in Room 5, Ronnie's room now, and J.P. had been in 7, which Lawrence now occupied.[22]

I talked with Ronnie. He said he had fallen and hit his head. That was why he was woozy: "I always get woozy when I fall and hit my head." Remember that this kid has an I.Q. of fifty-eight.

I called the O.D. and explained what had happened. We agreed that I would put Ronnie on SPL III. I called the health center and notified Dorothy. She said she would have to see him. Security came back and took Ronnie up there. Dorothy said he was fine, physically, and Ronnie was returned to our quiet room. After he signed a commitment not to try to kill or otherwise harm himself, and to tell staff if he felt like doing either, he asked me to close the office door. I don't know why he didn't want Steven, the only other person on the floor, to hear him; I didn't ask. Ronnie admitted he had tried to strangle himself with his shirt. He had wanted to die out of grief at losing Mark.

Throughout all of this Steven seemed utterly bewildered. After Security arrived the first time, he became passive, sitting in the chair beside the staff desk at the edge of the living room. He watched me go from one task to the next, but did not offer to help, and said nothing at all.

WEDNESDAY, APRIL 15: Mickey told me that once when he was younger his mother stuffed cigarettes in his mouth and slapped him. He, in turn, punched her and knocked her down.

I told him I thought his mother was afraid of him. I had seen fear on her face when she visited him on Saturday.

He said he felt both proud and ashamed.

We talked about my leaving Swan next week. He's upset, even though he'll be leaving only a few days after I do. He said he wanted to think of me as doing the things I'd always done when he knew me. If I stayed at Swan, he would still be able to think of Swan as his home.

Part Three: Whale and Bull

For almost a year, I did not so much enter descriptions and commentaries in my journal as notes to myself that I thought might cohere, one with another, later. I was, I think, a little thrown off by the sudden difference in my life that came from changing cottages. But also, later, something happened that so troubled me that I could barely write about it. I have written this section and the next, then, based on the notes I did take.

On my first day at Whale I asked Wayne, a small, soft-spoken man I would work with three days a week, how girls were different from boys.

"They're quieter," he said. After some thought, he added that he couldn't define the other differences, but they were there.

One of the girls cried at chapel that night. Apparently religiosity had nothing to do with it: she'd spotted a boy from Ram Cottage who had recently broken up with her. A Swan or Ram boy in the same situation probably would have ignored the girl, then bad-mouthed her to his friends when they returned to the cottage.

A couple of days later I came up with this: When a girl shows emotion other than anger, other girls provide support, at least for the moment. When a boy shows emotion other than anger, most other boys will make fun of him. (When either a girl or a boy is angry, their peers must take into account the possible danger to themselves before deciding what to do.) Though simplifications, as all dichotomies are, I think these statements are more or less accurate.

The female staff at Whale insisted that girls harbor grudges where boys explode. 'Tisn't so. Boys hold grudges too. After all, there would be no retaliation, which is much of what gangs are about, if boys simply went off and then felt at peace. Compare these two stories.

In the van on the way to Ash Meadow from detention, a girl exposed her breasts, then her pubic hair, to Lucas Carne, a Ram kid coming back from an arraignment. Back at Ash Meadow, he told other boys what she had done, saying too that she had given him a blow job. She was humiliated, of course, when word of what Lucas was saying got back to her. When someone at school told her Lucas had said she performed oral sex on him, she denied it, saying his dick was so tiny you'd need a tweezers to find it. As one might predict, Lucas was infuriated when he was told what she had said.

Story number two: Lucas (again) learned that Mickey Joyce had been raped while at Elk Grove, and said something about it in a class they had together. A month later, in the same class, Mickey called him an immigrant, an allusion to Lucas being Canadian. Lucas, so worried about fitting in with his peers, was again incensed.

Similar situation, similar response: gender had nothing to do with holding or acting on a grudge.

But there were differences in boys' and girls' cottages aside from the noise levels, and emotional support or the lack of it. Most girls, having free time, sat in the living room and talked or watched television. Boys more often played ping-pong, or basketball, or dominoes, or cards.

In Whale I did not hear war-storying, that is, the glorification of crimes one has committed or heard about. Neither did I see girls pretending to be firing Uzis or MAC-10s or shotguns. In Swan there was a nervous, even muscular tension in the cottage that I did not feel in Whale. In fact, after a couple of months of working with girls I found that I missed the tension, the low-level anticipation that something violent may erupt at any time. (I did miss the boys at Swan and some of the staff, Stan and John Loring especially, but when I thought of Fran and Steven my gut twisted and churned as it used to at the beginning of each shift I worked with them.)

By the end of my first week or so at Whale, I realized that boys were not liked at Ash Meadow, not when compared with the girls, and certainly not by most female staff and administrators. Since Swan was out toward the southern end of the campus while most cottages were clustered around lower court at the northern end, I had lived away from the greater part of activity at Ash Meadow for almost five years. Whale offered a different view of what the campus was about. Jewel Larson, the cottage director at Serpent, another girls' cottage, greeted me with "Welcome to the girls' part of campus" when she heard I'd transferred. One of the administrators, who had never worked in either a boys' or a girls' cottage, told me I'd like Whale better than Swan. A staff member in another cottage, a woman who had two sons, told me, "Nobody likes boys." She was talking about Ash Meadow, but also about the larger society. In Whale one of the staff, Caroline Bloodworth, alluded to "Herman and his thugs," meaning by the latter, at least on the surface, the residents of Swan and Ram. Below the surface, I was certain she included me because I had come from a boys' cottage.

Caroline did not like me, and she did not like Kathy Creeley, who was also relatively new to Whale. It was Kathy who had found Sandi dead in the shower and had tried to revive her. At PC meetings Caroline bullied her and dismissed her ideas as not worth talking about. Once Caroline came into the office where Kathy and Kaylee, a girl on Kathy's caseload, were talking and started screaming at the girl, accusing her of driving a wedge between staff, meaning, presumably, between Caroline and Kathy. Caroline had moved right up against Kaylee, her fists clenched, but Kaylee would not back up and yelled back at her. Kathy had to place her own body between them because neither was listening to her pleas to stop. She finally grabbed Kaylee by the arm and pulled her out of the office.

Caroline treated me differently: she took reports I was working on out of the file cabinet drawer I kept them in, so that I had to write them over. I discovered this only because I noticed a bit of paper with my handwriting in her mail bin and found it was one of my case notes. Beneath it were other case notes and a treatment report that I had not completed. This began within a week or two after I came to Whale.

I told Brian Meara, the cottage supervisor, about it, but he said it was a problem I needed to work out with Caroline. I tried several times to approach her but she always told me she didn't have time to talk to me. We did make an appointment to talk once, but she called in sick that morning.

She went after the kids on my caseload as well as those on Kathy's. She put Darlene Lauder on Tables, telling me that Darlene had manipulated me "big time" so that I would allow her to tape a photo on her wall in which kids were throwing up gang signs—except they were not gang signs; the kids in the photo were using the Hawaiian sign for "okay" or to signify something positive. And she changed Jennifer Lessing's phone list without consulting me, so that the girl could not talk to her aunt, her only adult living relative. Caroline was not liked by other staff, but she had been at Ash Meadow since the early Seventies and was unassailable.

If girls received more sympathetic attention on campus than the boys, and generally they did, they had problems boys did not have. In early May we learned that the Bible-study group that came to campus had been asking the girls whether or not they were virgins. Finally a girl complained and Don Martino said he would talk to the Bible people about avoiding certain topics.

At PC one day, Caroline told the rest of us that the nurses at Ash Meadow were pro-lifers. She said it as a blanket statement, as though not even one or two of them might be pro-choicers. Until the last few months, a pregnant girl would request an abortion and the nurses would stall about making the referral until it was too late.

This happened to one of our girls. She was thirteen when she came to Ash Meadow, she was pregnant and knew she was too young to be a mother, and she asked to have an abortion. The nurses ignored her until she was in her sixth month, then told her it was too late. She became a very reluctant four-teen-year-old mom. Her daughter was placed with a foster care family, then given up for adoption.

Yet this changed—I don't know why—and within the three months prior to Caroline telling us about the nurses, two Whale girls had abortions.

Inside the institution, we saw some problems as specific to boys and others to girls, but to some on the outside, boys and girls were simply inmates who themselves were problems. Martino came to PC one day. He had recently spoken to the legislature about the needs of the juvenile institutions, and one of the legislators had asked him when we at Ash Meadow were going to start hanging residents. Martino said the guy was serious.

Another said residents should not be educated past the eighth grade. Martino said that that made sense only if kids are never going to be released. I said that what this legislator may want is to turn residents into slaves.

Except for prostitution, the crimes the girls were locked up for were the same as those the boys had committed. (Some of the boys had been prostitutes, but, to my knowledge, none had been prosecuted for prostitution.) Among the girls who were on my caseload were one imprisoned for armed robbery, one for indecent exposure, one for assault with a deadly weapon, and one for murder.

Marie, with whom I used to talk, although she was not on my caseload, had been a prostitute. She said she felt bad about it now, about having used men, especially one man she manipulated into spending everything he had on her, though she slept with him only once. His wife had died recently and he was grieving, so it was easy to string him along. When his money was gone, she dumped him. He was twenty-three and he went into the army afterward and she didn't hear from him again.

She was addicted to heroin, as was her mother. In fact, she had been kicked out of the Phoenix Program after her mother brought heroin into the cottage and the two were caught snorting it in the bathroom. Marie said she wanted to use whenever she was stressed, or tired, or hungry, or experiencing just about anything that was unpleasant. What she really wanted, she said once, was a man to make her life easier, to protect her.

The cottage had a full-length mirror on the door of the cottage director's office, and Marie and Carmen, another resident, spent a lot of time making themselves up in front of it. I, and other staff, believed that if we allowed it, they would spend all day, every day, in front of the mirror.

Carmen had also been a prostitute, but was in on several charges of molesting smaller children. She had been sold by her parents to a man who used her in child porn, then put her on the street when she was older. He threatened to kill her if she refused to do what he told her. She, like Marie, appeared to have internalized the idea that women are always sexually available.

Once, after I unlocked her door at the end of quiet time, Marie came out of her room and slid her hand down my arm as she walked past me. It was clearly provocative, yet she could deny her intent if accused of coming on to staff.

I mentioned this to Brian. He said it was not a matter of if, but of when, a male staff working in a girls' cottage would be accused of being sexually inappropriate toward a resident. He warned me that things could easily turn so that I, or any male staff, could be accused of doing something the girl actually did—or something that was made from whole cloth. He himself had not been accused of anything yet, but he regarded this as simply good luck.

As I had at Swan, I read *The Gifts of the Body* to those residents who wanted to be read to. As at Swan, I usually got six or seven.

In one chapter the narrator talks about applying salve to the sores on the torso of a man dying of AIDS. Erna Hernandez raised her hand. I called on her and she asked if "torso" meant penis. After I defined torso, the girls broke out laughing. Erna too, though she was embarrassed. The girl who laughed hardest and longest—in fact, for a while she seemed unable to stop herself—was Carmen.

After *The Gifts of the Body*, I read a novel, *Why Me?*, by Patricia Dizenzo. It's about a girl who has been raped and how she deals with it, and how people she knows deal with it. Toward the end of the story, Jenny, the protagonist, finally works up the courage to tell her mother what happened to her, but insists her mother not tell her father. I asked the girls, Why not? Why would she be afraid of her father's finding out?

All of the girls said Jenny was afraid he would blame her. It was also the reason she delayed telling her mother: fear that she would blame her. I was amazed that, among the seven girls sitting around me, there were no exceptions to this thinking.

Later, I decided to read one of Primo Levi's books. I thought it might be inspiring, that he might provide the girls a model for retaining hope when life threatened to overwhelm them. Also, he wrote short sentences.

Almost immediately I realized that they didn't know the Nazis were Germans. The girls thought Naziism was an American invention, a variety of American racism. They didn't know when World War II was fought, nor which country fought on which side. They hadn't heard of the Holocaust and did not know of the mass murder of Jews.

I asked them at what point their history courses ended, what era? They said they had never had a history course. I said that surely they had to have had something that was called History. Some said they had, and in that class they learned how government worked and talked about what was in the newspaper. Others said they had not had that class.

I told them I could not read this book to them. I would have to teach them something about European history first, and I didn't have the time to do that. They pleaded with me to make the time, to start, to start now, but I felt too discouraged to try.

Yet the next day I found myself saying, and meaning it, "There is nowhere I would rather be at this moment than here with you." The occasion was Dick Peck's campus Grief-and-Loss group. Through the work I had done with kids in Alternatives to Violence, I had come to think that underlying all anger, at least chronic anger, is a prior experience of grief. I wanted to understand the latter emotion so I could better understand violence, and I had arranged with Dick to sit in on group meetings. It was during a "feel-ings check-in" at the beginning of this week's session that I said "There is nowhere I would rather be at this moment."

I had brought Alternatives to Violence to Whale with me. Some of the girls were in, or had been in, gangs. Also, I had expanded the group to include a module on domestic violence, and nearly all, if not all, of the girls had grown up in households where violence was a constant threat.

One evening, in group, Darlene Lauder said that if she found a homie beating a female, she would intervene because a man shouldn't beat up a girl. Instead, Darlene would beat her up.

I asked whose work she would be doing, her own or the work of the boy who was beating the girl.

She said she identified with the man, but didn't believe he should beat a girl, even if the girl deserved it.

Kristin Booker agreed with her, even to the point of saying she also would beat the girl herself.

Darlene said she knew her own thinking was twisted, "but that's how it is."

I said: "If I stop a rapist, should I then rape the victim myself?"

My question produced an immediate and collective howl from almost all of the girls, as though it had released something primal in them. "Have you ever been raped!" Kaylee shouted.

"No."

"Then you can't talk!"

"Jerry, knowing what you know about me, how can you even use that word!" Darlene screamed.

I don't think I understood what a violation rape is, even after working for so long with Terry Voight and Mickey Joyce, until I saw and heard these young women's reactions.

But it was Darlene saying she would beat a girl herself if she saw a homeboy doing it that I ruminated on over the following weeks. I thought about the character Kurtz in *Apocalypse Now* who said you have to befriend Death, meaning you have to submit to Him, ingratiate yourself with Him. In my novel, *Sergeant Dickinson*, I held that you have to become Death. You have to possess Him, make Him your own. This, so you can control Him, domesticate Him, make His effects predictable. It is in your fear of Death that you become Him. And in becoming Him, you find yourself doing His work. The result, of course, is that you become the exact opposite of what you intended. Instead of becoming Death's tamer, you become His servant.

Either view may be accurate. The difference between Kurtz and Dickinson is where they start. Whether you strive for friendship or ownership, you end up serving Death. Which brought me back to Darlene, who would beat a girl so that her homies would not.

Which brought me back to Viet Nam. My love of war owed to the threat of death, which I found stimulating and which required me to focus all of my attention on thwarting it. It was this, rather than the love of violence, that attracted me to war.

But I could find no moral justification for war (unless it would be to protect a weaker party, and then only in particular circumstances). War delivered death to combatants and noncombatants, the old and the young, regardless of how they felt about it. It was one thing to seek death or its threat, it was another to try to hide from it and have it find you anyway.

How could I love it, at least aspects of it, when it did such horrible things? Yet I did love it, in spite of its effects rather than because of them. I loved war not only for its threat of death but because it could, and sometimes did, compress the entire emotional experience of living into a single, intense moment that would stay with you for the remainder of your life.

Which brought me back to Darlene.

She told me once that she was experiencing grief for the person she used to be, and who she still wanted to be. (She actually used the expression "experiencing grief," and I thought she must have been talking with Dick Peck.) But she knew she could not be that person again unless she wanted to return to prison. She felt so powerful, so in control, when she was able to take what she wanted, when no one could stop her. She was describing the sensations of violently dominating someone, or of using the threat of violence to intimidate someone into submission. She was not thinking, I'm sure, about how she had been raped, twice, the second time by four boys.

She said she thought sometimes that she'd been brainwashed into accepting values—society's values—that she didn't really believe in. She used to think that the best job in the world would be as an assassin in the pay of the government. She missed all the violence she used to know, she said, but admitted she did not like to come out on the losing end of a "conflict."

The day after the Alternatives to Violence session in which Darlene and

Kristin had said they would beat up a girl on behalf of their homeboys, we watched a "Nightline" segment about girls in gangs. Diane Sawyer kept referring to gang girls as "they." Kristin said Sawyer made it sound as if "they" were animals or something. Darlene said she regarded Diane Sawyer as "they."

One part of the program showed boys being beaten by their set for having violated discipline, for having "broken the rules." Watching the beatings, Darlene seemed almost happy, and I asked her why she was smiling. She said she had not realized she was.

A couple of months before her release, we talked about her father. He had been found in a coma on the street the day before. He had been beaten. (He died a few weeks later.) She said her emotions regarding him were in "conflict"—she did like that word. When she first heard about him she thought about when she was "Daddy's little girl," how she had tried to please him, and how proud he was of her, and the grades she got in school, and her athletic ability. Then she remembered how he had beaten her, and how, after her mother left, he would leave her alone for days at a time while he went off drinking with his buddies.

She was released early in September on her twenty-first birthday. She was nervous. Her stomach hurt so that she complained of being hungry, though she had just eaten breakfast. She'd been at Ash Meadow for seven years.

I took her to the bus station. She had a few hundred dollars and a place to stay in Seattle. She could hardly keep from smiling and she couldn't keep from fretting.

A few days later when I came to work, Brian greeted me at the door by asking if I'd heard about Trent Nguyen and Penny Davenport. I thought he was going to tell me they'd gone AWOL, but he said Penny was pregnant, Trent was the father, and she had gotten pregnant in Swan Cottage. Caroline said she didn't remember another instance in which a girl had gotten pregnant at Ash Meadow. Trent had been sent to Elk Grove, Penny to Wolf Cottage. Someone, Caroline or Brian, said Penny's parents would be suing Ash Meadow.

I had anticipated that something would happen at Swan, but I thought it would be a fight in which somebody got badly hurt, or a suicide. There would be an investigation, of course. I guessed the administration would try to hang Fran. They would have gone after Herman, but he'd been on administrative leave from Swan since February. Penny got pregnant in May. I left Swan in April—a good thing, or Fran would have tried to hang me.

This could be the best thing that ever happened to Penny, I thought. Her parents would sue for support of the child until it reached adulthood, settle for a large sum, and Penny, if she was smart, would never want again. What a lovely irony. But it was a sure thing that Ash Meadow's unwritten policy of allowing kids to visit each other at their respective cottages was going to change.

Later that week I worked with an intermittent who had just finished a shift at Andromeda. She said the staff there were having a name-the-baby contest. Some said it would be named "Herman," others said "Fran." I broke up when she told me that; it was the hardest I'd laughed in years.

In early October I ran into Stan MacEvoy coming out of the Administration Building. The Trent-Penny thing was falling on him. He said Penny told someone—he didn't know who—that she and Trent had cut holes in their sweat pants and screwed in the foyer while Stan and Steven were on shift. He didn't know what, if anything, was going to happen to Steven. Steven was claiming he didn't know anything about it. Stan said everyone—administrators, Fran—was ducking. He was probably going to get a lawyer.

Sheryl announced at the beginning of June that she would be leaving for a position at JRA headquarters, and Ralph Purple, the cottage director for Goldfish, would be leaving there to manage both Whale and Bull. None of us line staff knew anything about him other than that he had a beard and owned a real estate company that he ran out of Goldfish. A staff there once counted forty-six calls Purple made or received during a two-hour PC meeting.

We did not see him until mid-July when he showed up at PC to inform us that treatment reports we did on the kids were going to be replaced by "competency reports." The major difference was that the treatment reports required the case manager to write a narrative describing the kid's progress, or lack of it, in a variety of treatment categories—managing his impulse to be aggressive, developing empathy for the victims of his crimes, learning negotiating skills to get what he needs or wants, to name three—and the competency reports would require only that the case manager check boxes. In certain areas, at our discretion, we might add a short statement, not more than one or two sentences.

I pointed out that this kind of report lent itself well to statistical surveys, but it would prevent us from conveying information about the kids to their parole officers. JRA might be pleased with it because it would help them when they requested money from the legislature, but it had nothing to do with our doing our jobs.

Purple responded by saying this job was not for everyone and I might be happier if I went into a different line of work.

I was stunned. I could think of nothing to say. Everyone else was quiet too.

After Purple left I asked Brian what that was about. He had no idea.

Brian had just written my six-month evaluation. He told me he had no criticism of me. He said he particularly appreciated my having introduced Alternatives to Violence to the cottage and my reading to the girls during quiet time. He liked the idea, too, that I was attending Grief-and-Loss group so that I could become familiar enough with it to start a similar group in the cottage.

Six days later, immediately after I arrived at work, Ralph Purple called me into his office. I had not seen him in three months. Kirsten Ford, the supervisor at Bull Cottage, was there, seated beside Purple's desk. Purple pointed to the chair he wanted me to sit in. I sat down. He sat facing me. Kirsten was to my right. As Purple spoke, Kirsten watched my face. Purple did not look at me, but read from a text typed onto several sheets of paper he held in his hands.

As he went on, my eyes started to close, and it was only with some effort that I could keep them open. Every time I willed my eyelids apart they would begin to close again. My face felt swollen with heat. I heard Purple's voice as a distant echo of itself. I thought of killing him, of leaping on him and beating him to the ground and kicking him to death. I visualized his face coming apart, his skull collapsing under my boot (though I was not wearing boots, but running shoes). His voice went on and on.

Kirsten asked me if I was all right. I said no. Purple looked up. He seemed surprised.

"This won't take much longer," he said. He went on reading. He read word for word: when he stumbled, he backed up and reread the passage. When he was done he told me I had been reassigned to Bull Cottage while the investigation was going on. I was not to speak to any of the staff or residents of Whale Cottage during this period. My days off would be Wednesday and Thursday. What I had to do now, he said, was go with Kirsten.

I told him I needed to get my belongings out of the staff office.

Again, that quizzical look on his face. "You can leave them here. This won't take more than a week or two."

I thought to ask him if he was only pretending to be stupid, but did not. I had seen this happen to other staff: once you were removed from a cottage, you did not return.

"This will take forever," I said.

Purple decided I could get what I needed out of the office. He warned me again not to talk to anyone on my way there. As I walked from his office to the other one, staff and residents on the floor stared at me. Kathy Creeley was sitting behind the desk on the floor. Caroline Bloodworth was standing beside her, but now moved away toward the craft room. Half a dozen kids were on the floor, as immobile as if woven into a tapestry. Nobody spoke. I could not tell what they knew, if anything, or if they were responding to what must be on my face.

I followed Kirsten to Bull, gripping by its carrying handles a large paper sack filled with books and videos I had used in Alternatives to Violence, and my own copies of reports I had written. In Bull's staff office, Kirsten began to tell me what would be expected of me there. I stopped her.

"I'd like to go home," I said.

At home, I called in sick for the next day, too.

I had been accused of using unprofessional language when talking to one of the residents. The previous Sunday one of the girls had come out of her room wearing pants tight enough to show that she was not wearing anything under them. She had been a prostitute, and when she came to us from county detention a month earlier she was wearing the clothes she had been arrested in: a top, a short skirt and a thong under it that showed her buttocks when she bent over. In school at Ash Meadow, kids complained that no matter what the topic of discussion, she turned it to sex.

Now, when she came out of her room, I called her over to where I was standing by the staff desk. Some of the other girls had visitors and I did not want them to hear us. I told her her pants were too tight; they were "not appropriate" for the cottage and she needed to change. She objected, demanding to know what was inappropriate about them. She said that yesterday another girl had worn pants that were tighter than hers and staff didn't say anything to her. I said I wasn't here yesterday and couldn't speak about what other staff were willing to tolerate, but I considered her pants to be too revealing.

She demanded to know what I meant by "revealing." She was not being coquettish. She was angry and her voice was growing louder. I said, "Okay, I'll be blunt. Your pants are too tight. They show your vaginal lips and make you look like you're not wearing panties." She said she was wearing a thong. I told her again that she had to change clothes.

She went to her room and came out wearing looser pants. She asked if she was dressed appropriately now. She emphasized "appropriately." I said she was.

When her staff came in at two o'clock, she buttonholed her and the two of them went into the office. After a few minutes, the girl came out and walked past me to her room. She was angry again. Jane followed her out of the office, her hand over her mouth, trying to suppress her laughter. "Thank you, Jerry. She needed to hear that, especially from a man."

"Well, I'm sorry she feels bad."

"It's good for her. I wouldn't worry about it."

I wrote in the cottage log about the encounter I'd had with the girl. I was worried that she might accuse me of using a slang term for "vaginal" and I wanted what I had actually said to be on record.

It was the logging that came back on me. Caroline saw it the next day and showed it to Purple. And months later, in a hearing, Don Martino, responding to the union steward's request simply to drop the matter, said that the problem was that I had written about it in the log. "It's a legal document," he said, referring to the log. And that meant the administration had to do something about it.

1998–1999

Looking over my journal entries for the three and a half months I spent at Bull, I find almost nothing pertaining to the kids or the job. One entry quotes a boy: I asked him, "What do you want to do with your life?" He replied, "Get a new one." I thought that was hilarious. "Funny as hell," I noted.

A month later I wrote that I'd seen Stan MacEvoy on his way down to his cottage as I was on the way to mine. He was coming from his hearing on the Trent-Penny flap. He didn't want to talk, but said Martino, who had presided over the hearing, had been pretty rough on him and had given him a PCR.

Shortly after arriving back at Swan, he had a heart attack.

A few days later I ran into Steven Ruer at chapel services. He also had been PCR'd.

In November Martino conducted the hearing on my case. He found me guilty of misconduct. Corrective or disciplinary action would follow. He would make his recommendation to the superintendent, who would make the final decision.

Ralph Purple was there. He offered what he must have thought was a sympathetic smile.

In January we locked the cottage down for a day because a boy's mother had passed him a ball of marijuana during a visit. Another boy stole it from him and hid it. Two others told us about it, but we couldn't find it.

Mostly I was bored during my time at Bull. The boys there did not seem to be driven to dominate other boys, a major difference from the boys at Swan. I attributed the difference to their being a year or two older at Swan, and to Swan being a cottage for gang kids. In Bull, when a kid put on gang colors—gang colors were permitted at Bull, but not at Swan—he looked silly, he looked like a kid out of his league.

At Whale, as much as I had enjoyed the company of the girls, they did not as a rule convey the sense of tragedy that the boys did. At Swan the kids who most stimulated me were those who had lived with violence on the outs. At any time they would account for the majority of the cottage. In Whale there were only a couple of girls who had known the kind of violence that can take you close to rapture. In Bull, I realized that I had been bored since I left Swan.

Late one afternoon toward the end of January, Martino came down to Bull and handed me a packet. I had received a Letter of Reprimand, which I had expected, but there was also a notification that I was being transferred to Wolf Cottage. My days off would be Tuesday and Wednesday.

Martino said, "The cottage director is looking forward to having you there."

"Which one?" I knew Ralph Purple would be happy enough to get rid of me. Which was it, the first or the second time I saw him after he took over as Whale's director that he told me I should consider another line of work?

After a moment's hesitation, Martino said, "Jan." She was Wolf's program manager.

"This is really shitty," I said.

"What?"

"This is really shitty."

He turned away from me. He did not say anything.

Finally I said, "All right." What I meant, really, was to acknowledge having received the packet and to indicate that I had nothing more to say. But Martino said, "Thank you." I was surprised.

After he left I called Whitney Lynch, one of the union stewards. She came over at nine-thirty after she got off shift. She agreed that the Letter of Reprimand was to be expected. We both believed that the administration was using me to fill a slot that nobody wanted in a cottage nobody wanted to work in.

"I hate feeling like a slave," I said.

She looked appalled, as though wondering how I could still be so innocent after all these years.

"I know, we're all slaves," I said, "but this really brings it home."

I said I thought Martino felt some guilt when he handed me the packet of bad news. She said, "No, he didn't. He didn't feel anything."

She wanted me to despise Martino. I did.

She would file a grievance on my behalf the next day.

I heard from one of the Recreation staff that Stan had come back to work. The administration had dropped its charges against him since his heart attack. I ran into Steven Ruer again and learned that the PCR on him had been dropped too. He said his prayers had saved him.

On the last day of January I worked with Lissa Blocker, an intermittent I used to work with at Swan. She showed me a news item about Larry Street shooting a McDonald's manager after forcing him to open the restaurant's safe. Shot him four times, but didn't kill him—surely an accident that he didn't kill him. Larry had worked there until a couple of weeks before the shooting.

On Monday, February first, I had my grievance hearing. Martino presided. Nan Brown from Personnel took notes.

Whitney's argument was that the transfer to Wolf was overkill: a reprimand plus a transfer was too much. Others had been reprimanded without being transferred. Also, my using the words "vaginal lips" was debatable in terms of whether or not I deserved disciplinary action.

Nan put in that I had not received disciplinary, but corrective, action. Disciplinary action was defined by the loss of money—for example, through a demotion. I hadn't been demoted.

Whitney ignored her. She said it was very common for staff throughout Ash Meadow to speak as I had. She gave as an example: "Your breasts are falling out of your bra. Go change it."

Martino said he hoped she was wrong, that "this type of abusiveness is not being practiced widely. It's hard for me to accept that there's such a difference in perception between management and labor."

I don't think my mouth fell open. At least Martino didn't respond to anything that may have been on my face. But immediately the words came into my mind: What planet do you live on?

I said I had learned last night from someone at Wolf that the position I would be filling had been vacant for a year and a half. Obviously nobody wanted it.

Whitney said I was being used unfairly to fill a slot that the most desperate job-seeker wouldn't take.

Martino denied this. He said I was being transferred to "an enriched cottage"—that is, one that had more staff (because it was maximum security)—so that the supervisor would have time to supervise me.

I knew that Wolf's supervisor, with whom I had talked last night, would be on sick leave for the next five weeks, but I knew, too, that Martino was not going to change his mind. I had learned that when he fell back on bureaucratese in his speech, he had stopped listening. As far as he was concerned, the hearing was over.

He had one week to respond to my grievance. Then, assuming his decision went against me, as I was certain it would, I would have two weeks to file an appeal at Secretary—i.e., Headquarters—level.

One more note and then I'll let it go. At one point during the hearing Martino complained about staff deviating from what he called "professional norms."

"It's leadership!" I almost shouted. "You've got one program manager on administrative leave and another who runs a real estate business out of his office. And their supervisor is hardly ever to be seen on campus." Their supervisor, of course, was Martino himself. I gave out a contemptuous laugh; Nan laughed with me.

Later that week Kirsten told me she'd heard that Caroline Bloodworth was the one who had gone to Ralph Purple about my log entry on the girl in Whale. I already knew this. I asked her how she knew, but she wouldn't say. She did say that Purple felt he had no choice but to give me a PCR.

That same day Martino gave me his response. I called Whitney and asked her to file the appeal.

Part Four: Wolf

1999

WEDNESDAY, FEBRUARY 17: Well, if I missed the paranoid tension of working at Swan, I have more than I want of it at Wolf. I began working here on February eleventh. Spent the major part of Sunday and Monday dealing with Justin Barrows—especially Monday because the other two staff, Anita and Margareta, spent most of the shift in the kitchen preparing soul food in celebration of African-American History Month, leaving me alone on the floor with sixteen kids including Justin who was on SPL III and talking suicide half the time and denying any intention of it the other half.

There is another character, Ryan Helmsley, who apparently believes it is his mission in life to violate cottage norms in small ways, then to deny he has done anything wrong. Of course, this petty wrongdoing is a sign of defeat, an implicit admission that he has lost authority over himself, that it has, in fact, been taken from him. An example: Allowed out of his room for a head call, he walked out of his zone, grabbed a Teddy bear off the TV cabinet, laughed, then put it back and returned to his room. What he is trying to tell himself is that he can be a pain in staff's ass. What he is telling me is that, at most, he can be a pain in staff's ass.

Then we have Abdul Burton, a small fourteen-year-old on my caseload. He is frustated because we—I, in particular, being his case manager—don't

231

treat him as an individual. "There's only one Abdul. There's no other Abdul here," he says. Rather, we treat him as someone whose needs and desires are not important to us.

He's kind of right. The problem is that I have no time to attend to him because I have to cover for Margareta, who avoids working the floor. She's tremendously overweight and sits down whenever she can, usually behind the staff desk. Dick Teale thinks she's inconsiderate, and this may be so, but her weight must be a problem for her.

Remember Dick Teale? He's the one who encouraged me to apply at Ash Meadow eight years ago. But, hell, I don't hold it against him. He's on the staff at Wolf now, too. This is the first time we've worked together.

SATURDAY, FEBRUARY 20: Driving to work today, I just hated the idea of going in. I consoled myself with knowing that I had the Steve Erickson book, *Days Between Stations*, to look forward to after I got off. Then I told myself that maybe the shift wouldn't be so bad. How long ago was it that I said "There is nowhere I would rather be at this moment than here?" October. Four months.

The idea that human beings can live without distraction from our lives as we experience them daily, that we must confront the human dilemma unremittingly, as Camus would have us do, does not hold water. I am better at it than anyone I know, yet the world overwhelms me, too, at times.

MONDAY, FEBRUARY 22: Talked with Jan Herve and Herman Boats this afternoon. He was visiting her. Each, for different reasons, has been PCR'd.

Jan had her first hearing yesterday. The superintendent, Dean Nader, was there.

Nader is roundly despised on campus. At the union-sponsored picnic last September, I saw counselors turn their backs on him and walk away when he went up to them. There has been an exodus of senior staff from Ash Meadow and it is difficult not to think that they have been forced out by Nader and his thugs in administration, given how freely they are tossing around PCRs.

MONDAY, MARCH 1: Beginning this month, my days off will be Sunday and Monday. One of the staff transferred to Crane Cottage. I'm taking her slot. I'll also be Wolf's liaison to the psychiatry team, which meets on Tuesday mornings. I'll work day shift on Tuesdays, Thursdays, and Saturdays, swing shift the other days. I can't say I like it, but it's better than Tuesdays and Wednesdays off.

THURSDAY, MARCH 18: At PC today—Wolf's PC is on Thursdays—Jan was talking about Employee of the Year awards and how some staff got them. Her point was that she was going to start putting us in for awards too. She mentioned that Caroline Bloodworth got one for reading to the girls at Whale Cottage.

"She what?" I said.

"She got an award for reading to the kids in Whale."

"She didn't do that! I did that! I used to read to them during quiet time."

"Maybe she read to them too."

"No. The girls told me they asked her to and she refused."

"Well, she's taking credit for it."

Caroline. Fucking thief. She must be holding something over Ralph Purple's head.

THURSDAY, MARCH 25: Rob Gorey came over during PC today to talk about what is happening on campus. Just as the kids in maximum security are isolated from the rest of the campus, so are we, the staff who attend them.

Rob believes that Nader believes everything is fine at Ash Meadow. Yet almost everyone else, including administrators, sees Ash Meadow as a disaster.

According to Rob, the administrators see the problem at Ash Meadow as systemic; there is understaffing as a consequence of the legislature's under-financing the institutions. We counselors, of course, look at the world in more personal terms. We are the ones on whom other people's neglect falls.

FRIDAY, APRIL 2: Lyle Munson. Out for a head call after bedtime, he delayed returning to his room. I told him to go back to his room and he turned and punched the craft room window. (He didn't break it.) Then he waited for me. I yelled "Clear the floor!" and in a moment Layton Calder came over and Lyle walked to his room ahead of us, slamming his door behind him.

Twelve years old. A pudgy little jailhouse lawyer trying to goad me into making a mistake. Yesterday Layton and I had to handle him to get him back into his room.

His mother and grandmother visited him last Saturday. Charlie Patterson, Lyle's case manager, says the mom has fetal alcohol syndrome, as does Lyle. Lyle is the oldest of six children. Grandma is the one trying to maintain the family. She was the one who asked us questions and provided information. A tragic situation, no matter how you look at it.

TUESDAY, APRIL 6: Received a letter from the union's area representative, informing me that the Secretary-level hearing on my grievance is scheduled for June fifteenth.

MONDAY, APRIL 19: Dick Teale, who has a friend in high places, told me that Ralph Purple has been invited to resign for taking time off from his job without using either vacation time or sick leave. As though nobody knew about it until now. I deserve some credit for getting rid of him. If I could prove it, I would bet that my outburst during my hearing in February about Purple running his real estate business out of his office here had something to do with getting him fired.

TUESDAY, APRIL 27: Fran invited me over to Swan to say goodbye to Stan, who is retiring. May first is his last day. I went over after I got off shift. Others from outside the cottage were there too. Martino showed up to attend PC, apparently not knowing this was an occasion for Stan. Actually, the Swan staff were also unaware that they were going to have guests; Fran hadn't told them.

Stan made a number of allusions to the heart attack he suffered after his PCR hearing. They seemed to go over Martino's head, but I suspect he was putting on a front of indifference. Stan told me later, after the coffee and cake, that it was the heart attack that made him decide him to leave. He said he didn't want the kids to see him if he had another one.

I walked out with Dr. Arens. He said it was smart of Stan to leave now, what with his health problems. He was referring to something other than Stan's heart. I hadn't known Stan had other problems. Arens said he himself would be retiring soon.

SUNDAY, MAY 30: I've been reading Susan Griffin's *A Chorus of Stones*. She talks about an episode of rage she experienced when she was nine years old. Angry with her grandmother for having punished her unjustly, she imagines herself beating her grandmother, torturing her. "I have tied her up and I am shouting at her. Threatening her. Striking her. I batter her, batter her as if with each blow, each landing of my hand against her flesh, I can force my way into her . . . I can grab hold of someone inside her, someone who feels, who feels as I do, who feels the hurt I feel, the wound I feel, who feels pain as I feel pain. I am forcing her to feel what I feel. I am forcing her to know me."[23]

This passage reminds me of Terry Voight, who, as he tortured cats, would see, imposed on their faces, the faces of his cousins who had raped him, and say to them, "Now how do you like it?"

It also reminds me of my reaction to Ralph Purple's informing me that he was giving me a PCR.

TUESDAY, JUNE 1: Received a letter from Nan Brown informing me that my grievance hearing has been rescheduled from June fifteenth to August fourth.

WEDNESDAY, JUNE 16: Martino buttonholed me on my way down to Wolf to begin my shift and asked me to come into his office. He said he was writing my yearly evaluation for 1997-1998 since Herman hadn't done it, and he wanted to know about my work at Swan.

I told him I had integrated a module on negotiation into Alternatives to Violence. For the gang kids, I created a scenario in which two gangs, weary of killing each other—or, perhaps more accurately, weary of having their own members killed—want peace and are willing to give up something to get it. Negotiation at a peace table is a way by which they might be able to stop killing each other, I said.

Martino said negotiation might also help them in business. I'm sure he was thinking of legitimate business rather than selling crack or marijuana or stolen auto parts. I didn't say anything.

He mentioned, seemingly in passing, that the United States is one of the few countries in the world that opts for punishment of criminals over restitution: he didn't know why. I was not aware of this—I assume he's correct—but I think I know why it would be true: if you believe in evil, if you believe that it exists and that it manifests itself in people you find frightening, or in those you have exploited (making your social evil their spiritual evil), you will want to destroy it. If you cannot destroy it, you will want at least to brutalize it so that it will fear you more than you fear it. We do have an aggressive national religion and the belief in evil is an integral part of it.

We talked amiably about how this kind of work changes your life. Both of us have learned that women, at least those we know on the outs, do not, seemingly cannot, accept that girls are capable of doing the things some of them have done, or that women can be sexually abusive to children.

I told him that I do not share the values of most men I know, that, to me, the work and the people I work with are more important than money or status. He said this was true for him too, but I did not believe him. After all, if he loved this type of work he would be doing what I do.

He asked me to make some notes, if I have time, on "personal challenges" counselors might have to deal with in doing this work. He's going to be speaking to a new group soon and would like to incorporate my notes into his presentation.

Then he spent the next five or ten minutes lauding me, telling me what a great asset I am to Ash Meadow, how insightful I am, how innovative, and so on. He said repeatedly that he would be glad to have me work for him again. He seemed sincere, but how can anyone trust him? He did not admit to having a hidden motive in praising me, but I'm certain there was one. I'm not going to make any notes for him.

TUESDAY, JUNE 22: Well, I think I understand now why Martino wanted to talk to me last Wednesday. Jan told me today that he selected Regina Cromwell from Andromeda to be the new cottage director for both Swan and Ram, instead of Rob Gorey, who has been the *de facto* director since Herman was placed on leave more than a year ago. This must be crushing for Rob.

I wonder why Martino chose Regina. Her only experience is in the mental health cottage. The rumor is that she was not even on the Cottage Director register, but that he sought her out and invited her to apply for the position. Perhaps he, like many male administrators, prefers to have women as his immediate subordinates. But maybe the issue was Rob. Maybe he didn't want Rob because he's the union local's president and he's active in advocating for the membership.

I think Martino must envision turnover at Swan and Ram, since morale will dive. Also, my grievance hearing is coming up. I'm accusing him of "double discipline," in that 1. he gave me a Letter of Reprimand and 2. he transferred me to Wolf. His solution at the hearing may be to offer me a transfer out of Wolf to Swan or Ram. Returning to Whale is out of the question. I wouldn't want to work with Caroline again, and Martino seems to really believe that I shouldn't work with girls.

WEDNESDAY, JUNE 30: We have a Nazi in the unit. He claims to be in Aryan Nations. He's from Spokane, of course. All of our Nazis come from Spokane. I assume this is because of its proximity to Hayden Lake, home to Richard Butler and Aryan Nations. The kid's name is Andrew Walters. A wiry blond kid. He told me his father served three tours in Viet Nam in the Marines' Force Recon. But he also said his father is thirty-six or thirty-seven now, which would make him too young to have been in Viet Nam. Either the boy is wrong or lying about his father's age, or he's wrong or lying about his father's military experience. My guess is he's lying about the military experience.

A couple of days ago Andrew's mother notified him that his father had had a heart attack. The father is a straight arrow who won't allow Andrew to live with him until he's straight, too. The racism comes from his mother and her boyfriend. We allowed Andrew to call his dad in the hospital. Andrew was very remorseful. Too distraught to conceal his tears, he apologized to his father for the unhappiness he's caused him. When he got off the phone he apologized to a couple of black residents for calling them niggers. (He did not apologize to me for calling me a kike. Maybe he considers staff fair game.)

This is a boy who desperately wants to please the adults closest to him in whatever way he can. His father's heart attack may be the best thing that ever happened to him.

THURSDAY, JULY 8: At Ash Meadow, the only institution in the state that houses girls, we have seen that the girls' offenses are generally more serious, and often more violent, than the boys'. Although girls have always been a minority of the population here, they consistently account for the majority of the murders our residents have committed, and a proportionately higher number of the other more serious offenses than those committed by boys.

Kathleen Foreman, to whom Jan reports, said at PC today that the reason girls' violence is so much more extreme than boys' is that girls don't grow up using it. So when at last they do use it, they don't know how much is enough.

Maybe. But it sounds too simplistic to me. Kathleen likes simplistic answers;

she equates this kind of academic reductionism—she used to be an academic—with abstract thought, which she believes is good. (She tells me I think
too concretely, which means, in her eyes, that my thinking is inferior to hers.)

SATURDAY, JULY 10: I pointed out to Lin Jerris, our new staff, that while
three girls had visitors today, only one boy did. She said that boys aren't
loved. Just like that—no affect, a statement of fact. She said she'd noticed in
other cottages also, when she was an intermittent, that boys don't get as many
visitors as girls. There are currently ten boys and six girls in Wolf.

I went over our visitor records for the last eight visiting periods, or four
visiting days, to determine the number of visitors for female and male residents. [A visiting period is from 1:00 to 2:45 p.m. or 3:00 to 4:45 p.m.] Here
are the results.

FEMALE RESIDENTS	MALE RESIDENTS
4	0
4	2
4	1
4	2
1	2
2	1
3	0
3	2

Conclusion: Girls are better connected to family and other emotional and
material resources on the outside than boys are. If I ever go for another graduate degree, I'll use this as my thesis (he said, sarcastically).

WEDNESDAY, JULY 28: Lyle Munson went off tonight. Ripped the light fixture out of the ceiling in his room. Jon, the intermittent we were working
with, went into the zone to check on him. It was dark in Lyle's room, of
course, and Jon said he could smell something electrical burning. I went into
the zone and I smelled it too. I called Security.

I warned them of a possible electrical fire, though there was no sparking
or flame that we could see. Warned them, too, that Lyle tore his light out of
the ceiling. I waited out by the staff desk with Jon and Margareta and Jan,
who was working late. Little sound came out of the zone; Lyle was not

resisting. After a few minutes, they came out with Lyle in handcuffs. He had on that odd smile of his that connotes both happiness and insolence. One of the Security guys said, "We found your electrical fire. Be careful not to step in it." Lyle giggled. Then they took him out of the cottage.

I took a flashlight and Jon and Margareta and I went down to Lyle's room. Just inside the threshhold was a turd between nine inches and a foot long. Obviously Lyle had wanted to lure us, or Security, in so that we would step on it.

When I turned, Margareta was gone. I went out on the floor again and told Jan what we'd found. "Somebody's going to have to clean it up," I said.

"It's not in my job description," she said, and started for her office.

"It isn't in mine either," I said.

"I'll do it," Jon offered.

"No, I'll get it." I hate to give intermittents the most unpleasant tasks. They get shit on enough anyway. So to speak. What I mean is, they work the least desirable hours, sometimes sixteen or more at a time, and they're usually given those tasks that the regular staff don't want to do.

"You hold the flashlight," I told him.

So I pulled on a pair of plastic gloves and took some paper towels and a plastic bag and Jon and I went back to Lyle's room. During all of this I still hadn't seen Margareta.

As I was picking up the turd, Jimmy Waller, in the room next to us, said, "Why don't you have Lyle do it?"

"Lyle's going to spend the night elsewhere. Do you want to live with this smell until he gets back in the morning?"

"No."

"All right then."

I put the shit and the paper towels in the plastic bag and dropped my gloves in after them. Jon tied the bag. "We'll let Lyle mop his floor when he gets back," I said.

Coming out of the zone, I saw Margareta and Jan standing together at the staff desk. "Where the hell were you?" I said.

"I had to take a head call. The smell of human waste always does that to me."

"Don't lie!" Jan said. "You were hiding behind the desk!"

Both women thought that was very funny.

"I have no excuse," Margareta said.

THURSDAY, JULY 29: New kid on my caseload: Lawrence Smith. Fifty-two to sixty-five weeks for Violation of the Uniform Controlled Substances Act. Prior offenses include two counts of assault, fourth degree; burglary, second degree; theft, first degree. He says he began to commit crimes when he was nine. He's fourteen now.

His father died before Lawrence was born. His mother is an alcoholic. He was placed in foster care at age ten because his mother beat him. At ages seven and eight he would hang out around a police station at night, afraid to go home, until he thought his mother had gone to bed or passed out.

In detention he was assaultive toward both staff and peers. He has not been assaultive here, though he says he has had to make an effort to keep from hitting Lyle Munson, whom everybody has difficulty with. When angry, he may hear voices or hallucinate. While potentially assaultive, he is also personable and seems to want to please. He is thoughtful and intelligent, with an IQ of 148.

His file says that he wets his bed, but he says he has stopped. He has nightmares but does not remember what they are about. I talked to him about Survivors Group. He says he was not sexually abused but can tolerate listening to other kids talk about their experiences without being repulsed by them.

He is gang-involved, a Crip.

TUESDAY, AUGUST 3: At the psychiatry meeting this morning, Whale's new director, reading from a referral one of her staff had written, said the mother of one of her girls worked in "adult entertainment." This brought laughter from those sitting around the table. Martino said, "It doesn't say what she *does* in adult entertainment." I saw only two who did not laugh: Doctors Williams and Christopher, both of whom are black, in fact the only African Americans at the table.

Later, drawing again from the referral, the cottage director—I didn't get her name—noted that the woman has sickle-cell anemia. This was the only allusion to her being black. Nobody laughed.

Can these people's lives be so different from the one I know? Was I so ignorant of the way other people live when I was in academia, when I lived as one of the middle class?

WEDNESDAY, AUGUST 4: Had my Secretary-level hearing this afternoon. Present were Dean Nader, Don Martino, Sara Thompson from State Personnel, Helen Geertz, the area representative for the union, and a guy named South—I've forgotten his first name, if he told it to me—who presided over the hearing and who said he was impartial, but if the case progressed to mediation or arbitration, he would represent management. Uh huh.

The meeting began with a stunner: Helen announced that she was going to have me present my own case because no one knew it better than I did. Then she was silent. She had given me no indication she was going to do this. What it meant, of course, was that she had not read up on my case. And, because she had given me no warning, I was not prepared to present it myself.

I did what I could. I asked that the Letter of Reprimand be removed from my file. I pointed out that although I had been instructed by Nader, via Martino, not to communicate with female residents, I had been transferred to Wolf, a coed cottage.

Nader responded that his restriction on communication applied only to the period of investigation, which ended with my transfer to Wolf. Martino added that they really did not expect me to commit misconduct again, that they had no problem with my communicating with female residents now.

I might have asked then, but did not, why I was transferred to Wolf instead of being sent back to Whale. I didn't ask because I wanted to remain in Wolf. More accurately, I did not want to return to Whale, where I would again come under Martino's authority. I said I was withdrawing my request to return to Whale, and regardless of how this case turned out, I would like to continue working in Wolf.

South said that in my grievance I had asked to return to Whale Cottage, but now I was saying I wanted to stay in Wolf. He said, too, that I had not mentioned anything in my grievance that challenged my being given the Letter of Reprimand. (I had pointed this out to Whitney when she was composing the grievance. She told me the challenge was implied.) Now I was asking for the letter to be removed. He said I was not asking for remedy in accordance with my grievance.

It looks certain that I will lose this round. If I continue with mediation or arbitration, I'll need to emphasize management's inconsistency in transferring me to Wolf: at no time was I informed that I was not to communicate with female residents *only* during the period of investigation. (Of course, I have communicated with girls in Wolf all along. You can't work in a coed unit without communicating with the girls in that unit.) And I'll have to try to persuade whoever represents me—or is pretending to—to look at other management decisions about disciplining employees for similar so-called infractions, though I doubt there are similar cases. But I'll probably drop the whole thing now: management is despicable, yes, but the union is either incompetent, uncaring, or both.

When the hearing ended, Helen left the room ahead of me. She was waiting in the corridor when I came out. She said again that she had thought it would be best if I spoke for myself since I knew my case better than anyone. I said nothing but walked away and down to Wolf to finish my shift.

FRIDAY, AUGUST 6: I'm not going to ask for mediation or arbitration. You can't trust JRA, but you can't trust the union either, and it isn't worth it to me to hire a lawyer.

THURSDAY, AUGUST 12: Newt Smith was bringing Lyle Munson back from the health center, where they had checked his blood pressure—he's on a new med—and Lyle was mouthy, as usual. They were in the foyer. I hadn't been paying much attention, but I caught a flash of movement and then Lyle was on the floor and Newt was hunkered down over him. I went over from the staff desk and saw Newt applying a wrist lock, a "gooseneck," as we call it, to him. Lyle was yelling and Newt was yelling over him, "Don't you put your finger in my face! Don't you *ever* put your finger in my face!"

Newt took him to our quiet room and strip-searched him, probably to demean him rather than because he suspected Lyle of concealing something. All the while Lyle screamed, "Ho! Bitch! Motherfucker!" over and over. After he locked Lyle in, Newt said—to me? to anyone in particular?—"No kid is going to put his finger in my face! No! No! I'm not going to let *any* kid do that!" We were in the office, with the door open.

Outside, sitting in the living room, was another kid. His hand was over his eyes so that he couldn't see what was going on. I can imagine what this kid experienced when he was younger.

When Newt went to get his key out of the foyer—he had just unlocked the door when Lyle jabbed his finger at him—we found it still in the lock, bent at a ninety-degree angle. He had moved so fast he'd swept it flush against the mortise.

As soon as he left, Lyle, in the quiet room, went off, yelling that he had cut himself, though he hadn't. Two guys from Security, but not Newt, came down and put him in a three-point restraint: handcuffs chained together for a strait-jacket effect. The rest of the shift, Lyle was even more obnoxious than usual, trying, I'm sure, to reconstruct his illusion that what he does is important to us.

One of the paradoxes about life at Ash Meadow is that while we staff encourage kids to gain control over their lives, we often punish them when they try to do it. In Lyle's case, of course, his feeling of control comes with victimizing other people. But even with kids who question strenuously—I do not mean as a way to intimidate, but, for example, as a way of objecting to a cottage or institutional policy—staff may punish them for "arguing," that is, for challenging authority. We want to empower the kids, we say, but, really, not too much.

THURSDAY, AUGUST 19: Fleshing out some of what Lawrence Smith told me a few weeks ago: when he was three, he and his mother were in a car acci-dent in which she was almost killed. He still doesn't like to think about it.

From age four to age six, he was often beaten by his mother. She was not drunk or high, but beat him because he misbehaved, Lawrence said. Once she beat him so brutally that he thought she was going to kill him. Once she stabbed him with a fork.

He has seen his uncle beat his mother. His uncle is currently serving time for murder.

He sees shadows at the edge of his vision whenever he's at rest. The shadows resemble people moving very fast.

When he's angry, he hears a voice from the side telling him to hit someone or otherwise hurt someone. When he looks, there is no one where the voice came from.

When he was six, a fourteen-year-old tried to rape him. He punched the older boy and ran away.

TUESDAY, AUGUST 24: Stopped at Whale Cottage after work to say hello to Rob Gorey. He transferred there after Regina Cromwell became the pro-gram manager for Ram and Swan. I warned him about Caroline Bloodworth. He said he had her pegged; he would watch his back.

THURSDAY, SEPTEMBER 2: Lawrence Smith transferred to Ram Cottage today. He's done well here, in that he has been able to manage his anger. He has not hit anyone, though he has wanted to; there has not been even a rumor of his trying to intimidate someone.

SATURDAY, SEPTEMBER 11: Sam Hopps disclosed to me that when he was nine his babysitter forced him to put his flaccid penis in her vagina. He said he had never told anyone about this before. As he talked, he became angry. In the middle of his disclosure, he suddenly said, "This is how I felt when I raped my cousin!" It was, I believe, a true epiphany, all the more convincing because I hadn't coached him in any way. I was doing his MAYSI and asked him the question about whether or not he'd ever been raped. It was as though the answer and what it signified were there waiting for the question to be asked. He said he was glad now that his cousin had told on him.

I remember an occasion when I was doing Survivors' Group with Carol Ripito. Charlie Lewis disclosed that his babysitter, a teenage girl, had done things to him when he was five—I don't remember now what the things were, or even if he told us—and then had passed him on to her girlfriends. The other boys in the group had laughed and told him how lucky he was, and Charlie had laughed, too. But then he slid his chair back against the wall and pulled his cap down so the visor hid his eyes, and for the rest of the session, immense tears rolled down his face without let-up. He made no move to wipe them away and did not respond when someone spoke to him. The things that happen to these boys. The girls, too, but also the boys.

THURSDAY, SEPTEMBER 16: We're getting Lawrence Smith back. He was on my caseload before, he'll be on my caseload again. At Ram, we're told, he tried to intimidate a couple of small Asian kids, as well as staff. He also tried to persuade a female staff to unlock his door after the other swing-shift staff had left.

At The Rivers a few years ago, a lone female staff was tricked into leaving her locked booth—The Rivers' architecture is different from ours—to help a boy who said he was sick. She was attacked and nearly killed by three kids who were trying to escape.

FRIDAY, SEPTEMBER 17: Lawrence admitted that he threatened staff at Ram, at least implicitly, by refusing to go to his room when told and forcing them to clear the floor, and by telling one of them that he, the staff, didn't look like he could fight. This was Tom Hopkins, a small, lean guy whom I personally like. But I could picture Lawrence, who probably outweighs Tom by twenty pounds, saying this, and Tom's reaction—Lawrence said Tom just went off, yelling about all the fights he's been in—and I started laughing. This surprised Lawrence.

After I collected myself, I asked about his intimidating two Asian kids, as we had been told he did. He seemed perplexed. He said there were no Asian kids in Ram. There was a Samoan kid he had had a problem with on the outs, but the Samoan is bigger than he is. I know the Samoan kid. Lawrence is right. I'll call and ask Ram about any smaller kids.

What about his trying to get Josefina to unlock his door?

He said she had unlocked another kid's door to talk with him. Lawrence thought they were talking about him and he wanted to talk with her too, to present his side. When she refused to open his door, he talked to her through the crack between the door and the jamb.

I called Ram and talked to Josefina. She got huffy, accusing me of accusing her of having unlocked a resident's door when she was the only staff in the cottage. I asked to talk to Roy Burns and she—gladly, I think—handed the phone to him. Roy said they didn't have any Asian kids, but there might have been a problem between Lawrence and a small Mexican kid; he wasn't sure. He offered to ask around but I told him it wasn't important.

WEDNESDAY, SEPTEMBER 22: Sam Hopps did his committing offense group tonight. We had it in the classroom with only the more mature kids in attendance, that is, those least likely to break their commitment to honor confidentiality. This means that seven of the fourteen kids in the cottage were there.

Sue Royce bore right in when Sam admitted he had raped his cousin. Sam is back at Ash Meadow, not for this charge—he's already served his time— but for violating parole by not attending sex offender group meetings. Sue accused him of not going to the meetings because he didn't want to acknowledge himself as a sex offender. She said that, as a small child, she had been raped repeatedly by adult relatives, and that because of this she hated men now, which she regretted, and that she wasn't going to let Sam go until he acknowledged what he was.

Sam tried to evade her but she persisted, growing angrier, insisting that he admit, now, to everyone present, that he is a sex offender. Finally, crying, Sam did admit that he is a sex offender and that he had not gone to his meetings because he was too ashamed. He did not want to put himself in the company of other sex offenders, because as long as he did not, he could tell himself that he was not one of them.

Melanie Roberts, who went off on Sam even more than Sue did, said that what Sam did to his cousin had been done to her by her cousin. She said she had hidden her head in the pillow as she was being raped, and had tried to make herself believe it was a dream.

Thinking about these two young women now—when she was fifteen, Sue stabbed a woman, intending to kill her; Melanie is in for armed robbery—and remembering Darlene Lauder, who had stabbed a woman to death, and seeing that all three had intended robbery without going beyond that, I posit this: that rage I have perceived in some of the boys who have been raped is present also in girls. With the boys, it can be released in gang-sanctioned or other intended violence; with the girls, it is more often released, unplanned, during the commission of another crime.

Neither Darlene nor Sue originally intended to kill anyone. The murder Darlene committed and the one Sue attempted were both done on impulse after their respective robberies were botched. Melanie was involved in robbing a store. Following the robbery, the clerk was pistol-whipped, although not by Melanie.

Perhaps girls' violence is a result, not of their not knowing how much is enough to accomplish what they want to accomplish, as Kathleen Foreman would have it,[24] but of its lying dormant, then being released through the commission of another anti-social act. I think I'm right.

THURSDAY, SEPTEMBER 23: I asked Melanie today if she attributed her anger to anything in particular. She said there was a lot in her history that she was angry about, even if maybe she shouldn't be, but she couldn't think of anything that was more important to her than other things.

I told her of my experience with boys in Survivors' Group, how I sensed a kind of rage beyond anger, the kind of rage that makes a person see red, literally. Perhaps it is a kind of madness of the moment, I suggested.

Melanie agreed. When she robbed the Seven-Eleven, it was as though she were outside herself, watching herself from somewhere above, almost disinterested. And again, once when she beat up another girl, she was kind of outside herself.

I asked if she thought it—this rage, if that's what it is—pertained to her having been raped. She didn't think so; it was a single act when she was nine, and she'd put it away in her mind and only recently had she mentioned it again. The first time she said something about it, she told her mom what had happened and her mom told her she was lying, so she didn't say anything about it again for several years. Then when she was in Whale Cottage it came out, and then during Sam's committing offense group.

I wonder though. Recall that yesterday she said that when she was being raped she tried to make herself believe it was just a dream. What she was describing now, the detachment from her body during the robbery, and again when she beat up that girl, is reminiscent of how she responded to that first trauma (if it was her first. This kind of disassociation, or the sense that you've left your body, is often experienced during sexual abuse. I wonder if there really was only one occasion, as she recalls). Even her manner in telling me of these events, the way in which she recalls observing them from outside herself, and how she recounts being raped—as if the memory of it appears of its own volition, as if it surprises her when it does appear—may harken back to that first terrifying experience.

FRIDAY, SEPTEMBER 24: On Wednesday Lawrence got twenty-four hours OP for having an inappropriate picture in his room. He complained that the picture was in a magazine he got from Wolf's bookcase. And when he picked the magazine out, Lin looked through it and approved his taking it to his room.

It was Layton who supposedly found the picture. He said it had been torn out of the magazine and hidden under Lawrence's mattress. Layton said Lawrence also had a rubber glove in his room.

I asked Lawrence what the hell he was doing with a rubber glove. He said he hadn't had a rubber glove. He looked genuinely bewildered.

What about the picture? Even if it was legitimate, you're not supposed to tear the pages out of the magazines. Lawrence said he hadn't torn anything out of a magazine; he had had the magazine in his room, that was all.

I went to Jan and told her Lawrence denied having the glove. Jan said he was lying, that Layton had taken it out of his room.

Layton, too, told me he had taken the glove out of Lawrence's room, as well as the picture.

But then Dick Teale said in PC yesterday that he had put the rubber glove and an ad he had torn out of a magazine in my box. The ad shows a woman in an evening gown; her shoulders are bare. This is the "inappropriate" picture we've been talking about. Dick had meant it as a joke. But then Layton apparently took them out of my box and said he'd found them in Lawrence's room. Dick did not know until yesterday that Layton had used them to set Lawrence up. Interestingly, neither Jan nor anyone else said anything to Layton about it, at least during PC. Jan moved us on to discussing other topics.

It's apparent that Jan and Layton and, it seems, Margareta and Mary, have a personal dislike for Lawrence. When we got him back from Ram he was placed on an in-and-out program in which he was allowed out of his room only when other kids were not on the floor. The purpose of this program is to protect others from an assaultive kid or to protect a kid from those who intend to assault him. Lawrence has not been a danger to anyone in Wolf, and no one has threatened him. But to say this to Jan or Mary would be like pissing in the wind.

(About Lawrence's intimidating Asian kids when he was in Ram: although he did not do it—there were no Asian kids in Ram—this story has followed him back to Wolf. I have no idea who originated it. It makes no difference that I tell staff it isn't true; they believe it is true.

Until this minute, as I was writing the last sentence, I had forgotten that one of Mary's sons is half Korean, and that Layton's son is Vietnamese. This, I think, explains a lot, though not everything. And, of course, it is not something I could bring up in Lawrence's defense.)

SATURDAY, SEPTEMBER 25: I asked Lawrence about his gang activity here at Ash Meadow. I was fishing. Roy Burns, when I talked to him last week, had alluded to some gang stuff, but didn't know anything specific. Lawrence said he hasn't been involved in gang stuff. I think he meant it: he didn't see what he did as gang activity because it didn't pertain to colors, to Crips or Bloods or Folk.

What he told me is this: A kid from Goldfish Cottage was rumored to be gathering some homies together to beat up a Ram kid named Michael. Lawrence said he couldn't let that happen so he volunteered to cover Michael's back. A second rumor had it that the Goldfish kid was gathering still more homies, so Lawrence began to organize more kids to back up Michael. But his zone mate at Ram, who is the Goldfish kid's cousin, blew the whistle. This was apparently at the root of the problem he had with this kid.

I asked Lawrence if he understood how easily a situation like that could get out of control. Even now, I said, with you in Wolf and the attack against Michael apparently called off, some kid may not have gotten the word and may take it on himself to do something that will get people hurt.

Lawrence said he didn't know what else he could have done. You should have informed staff what was going on, I said.

Of course he said he didn't want to be a snitch.

I told him again how seriously staff regarded this kind of situation, and told him too that even if he was not involved in it, but knew about it and didn't tell staff, he would be punished.

He took this to heart. He said if somebody was doing something that would get him, Lawrence, in trouble, then he would tell me or Charlie or Lin; he didn't trust other staff enough to talk to them.

TUESDAY, SEPTEMBER 28: Sue Royce told me that Ron Lafitte, released from Elk Grove, where he had done two years for dealing drugs, was shot in a gang incident and lost part of his leg. It's plastic from the shin down now.

Jimmy Mills also went to Elk Grove on a drug charge. He got out, started selling again and using it himself. Crack. He's skinny now, Sue said. I remember him when he was fifteen, about five feet ten, 215 pounds, built like a wall. I remember him telling me how he had seen his mother cut his father's throat. Jimmy wrote her all the time she was in prison. He felt his father deserved to die for having brutalized her as he had. But he did not die, although his brain no longer worked as it used to. Jimmy wrote him also.

Jan knew Jimmy when he was at Wolf. That was before my time here. She's talked about him a number of times. He was her favorite kid. I'm not going to tell her what Sue said.

THURSDAY, SEPTEMBER 30: A bad thing happened yesterday. A little before supper, Layton had four kids outside: Juan Barajas, Gilbert Boyce, Justin Sears, and Sue Royce. Three were in their rooms, six were at Tables, and two were in the living room. I was in Zone 1, talking with one of the kids. I had locked his door and was on my way out of the zone when a panic alarm went off. As I ran out onto the floor, kids were just beginning to get up from their seats at Tables. Margareta was walking into the dining room from the direction of the door leading to the recreation yard. I couldn't make sense of the alarm: there didn't seem to be a problem and nothing was happening in the zones. Margareta had apparently just come in from outside, or from looking outside, and did not seem perturbed. I hadn't realized, until I thought about it later, how much we rely on reading other staff's reactions in order to figure out what is going on. Margareta's standing in the dining room, doing nothing, threw me.

Then I thought that maybe my hearing was tricking me—maybe what I was hearing was the fire alarm. I yelled "Clear the floor! Get the kids outside!" I told Margareta to get Lawrence out of his room and outside while I got the kids out of Zone 1.

Jan meanwhile came out of her office, saying something about turning off the alarm, and I thought now that probably what had happened was that somebody had bumped a panic alarm, that it had not been the fire alarm after all. I noticed now, too, that the fire doors to the zones had not closed as they would have if the fire alarm was sounding.

I followed the kids from Zone 1 outside. Layton had his knee on Gilbert's back. The boy was handcuffed and lying on his stomach, blood flowing out of his mouth, water from his eyes. Juan was on his stomach nearby, and beyond him was Justin Sears. Twelve other kids, those we'd sent outside, were lined up against the far fence. It was obvious that Juan had hit Gilbert. Layton was the only staff there.

I went down the stairs and over to Juan. I told him to put his hands behind his back and I handcuffed him. I asked Layton if Justin was involved. Layton said no. I told Justin to get up and go over to the fence with the others. Sue Royce told me later that Layton had yelled at Juan, "Hit the deck!" and Juan had, but Justin also had flopped down. He bounced twice, Sue said. He's not the brightest kid we have.

Security arrived, and three or four staff from other cottages, in response to the panic alarm—they'd had to wait for Jan to open the front door because their keys don't fit our new lock. Security took Juan to Central Isolation, Gilbert remained with us.

When I first went outside, I noticed that the AM/FM radio that the kids had been listening to on the porch was off; Margareta had turned it off after Layton hit his alarm. She had to have seen Layton out there, but she came back inside and pretended she didn't know what was going on. Dick and Charlie told me today that she'd run away from kids' fights before, leaving other staff to take kids down alone. This time Layton already had the kids down, and I, not knowing what to make of Margareta's actions, followed fire-alarm procedure and got all the kids outside where any of them could have assaulted Layton or the kids lying on the ground. It was a bad, bad situation. Margareta has since pleaded confusion, but no one except Jan, possibly, believes her. They have been friends for twenty years.

This evening I told Layton that, especially when we work with Margareta, we need to watch out for each other. I said I would always cover his back and he said he would always cover mine.

SATURDAY, OCTOBER 2: In Alternatives to Violence, when I ask, "Who are the victims of violence?" one of the categories the kids almost always bring up is the disabled. These kids know that anybody who cannot defend himself is a potential target.

Who was that kid . . . I remember we had a kid who, when in county detention, punked a crippled kid so he could get his food at mealtimes. Even his homies asked him not to do that, but he was hungry, so he kept doing it. I don't remember his name now.

TUESDAY, OCTOBER 5: Lawrence said, "They want to like me, but they can't." He was referring to Jan and Mary, but also others he's known. I asked if this was true of his mother. No, he said, she can't help but love him, even if she doesn't want to.

A couple of days ago Bernie took him down. Lawrence's description of what happened is that he was rewinding a video when Bernie told him to go to his room. (Lawrence didn't say why Bernie told him to go to his room. Bernie told me there was some verbal back-and-forth between Lawrence and another kid and he, Bernie, decided to end it.)

"I'm rewinding the movie for Layton," Lawrence said.

"Just head to your room," Bernie told him.

Another kid—the one he'd been having a problem with?—said, "That's okay, you can go to your room and I'll rewind it."

"No, just sit there and I'll do it," Lawrence said. The kid's saying that made him angry, but when Bernie told him to head down again, Lawrence decided to do it. As he walked by he pushed Bernie, and Bernie immediately took him to the floor. He pushed Bernie, Lawrence said, because he was trying to be playful, and he wanted to be playful because he was angry and he wanted to relieve his anger "in a good way."

Bernie and I do not think Lawrence intended to hurt him, but to diminish him so as to build up his own status; he had just lost face by being sent to his room in front of Sue Royce and Melanie Roberts, with whom he had been having some difficulty over the last few days. Lawrence is driven to dominate and to keep from being dominated, and the two girls are currently the dominant residents in the cottage.

Today in P.E., he and Melanie ran several laps together, running fast and encouraging each other. Now Lawrence feels he can trust her more. He still distrusts Sue. I have been watching their interactions, and while I don't think she is trying to punk him, she will not allow him to punk her, either.

SATURDAY, OCTOBER 30: I told Lawrence that he has something going for him. He burst out with: "Hah! What?" as though not believing it.

"Your intelligence," I said.

He asked what good it was: it had never benefited him.

This exchange was part of a larger discussion we were having about his education. He did not know until I told him that there are colleges in Seattle besides the University of Washington. He thinks the University of Washington is not for him because he's black.

THURSDAY, NOVEMBER 4: Andrew Walters is back with us on a parole violation. He says he can no longer live in the Aryan Nations compound at Hayden Lake because he was caught shoplifting. When he talks about Aryan Nations, it's obvious that it's given him a sense of belonging. Racism, of course, helps him to define himself in terms of who he is not, and may even give meaning to his life.

Andrew says he "disowned" his father for his refusal to approve of Andrew's beliefs. If it's true that he has disassociated himself from his father—or, more likely, that his father has disassociated himself from Andrew—this is significant. It means that there is no one in Andrew's life now to influence him so that he will want to return to mainstream society.

He's been antagonizing a couple of the African-American residents by calling them niggers. He is safely locked in his room when he does this, of course. And he told Josie Fells that they can't be friends anymore because she's black. They've known each other since they were small children. She was crying, off and on, all day today.

What a sweet child our little Nazi boy is.

FRIDAY, NOVEMBER 5: Lyle Munson was transferred to Dolphin Cottage. Dolphin is the boys' mental health unit now. Andromeda is exclusively female. There is federal mental health money available, so the institution has increased its mental health care.

WEDNESDAY, NOVEMBER 10: Received a memo from Jan telling me that she has monitored my interaction with female residents over the last eight months and has found that I relate "well and appropriately." She has assigned a female resident to my caseload.

THURSDAY, NOVEMBER 11: Yesterday Lawrence nudged an intermittent in the same kind of move, though not as forceful—a forearm against the body—he used on Bernie a month ago. Jan asked me at PC today what I thought our chances of fixing Lawrence were. By "fixing" him, she meant making him into somebody we wouldn't mind living beside on the outside.

I've put a lot of effort into working with Lawrence, and I personally like him, but I'd be surprised if he didn't resume gang life when he gets out. I said I thought we would fail—the damage his mother did to him runs too deep. Of course, long-term therapy would help, but where would he get therapy, either inside or outside the system? Our own psychiatry component has refused to accept him as a patient. Williams, the chief psychiatrist, told me Lawrence wasn't interesting enough for him.

Jan commented that everybody blames the father, but in her experience, it's the mother who, if she abuses the child, does even more damage. I was reminded of something Carol Ripito told me years ago, that a boy—that is, a boy who is a sex offender—whose mother had sexually abused him was practically untreatable, whereas in treating other boys, she always had hope.

The antipathy that most of the female staff—Jan, Margareta, Mary (Lin wasn't at PC)—feel toward Lawrence came out again. I have no doubt that they are afraid of him, though none say why. I suspect they don't know why. Whatever it is they sense in him probably pertains to his relationship with his mother.

TUESDAY, NOVEMBER 16: Jan talked with Fred Thoele. He's going to transfer Lawrence to Elk Grove within two weeks. It makes me sick. It's so rare to get a kid who works this hard, who wants so to turn himself around. With the exception, maybe, of Reggie Greene (who did not, after all, go after his sister's killers), I don't think I've had another kid on my caseload who worked so hard.

But Jan and Mary say they don't want Lawrence in an open unit where he might hurt a young, inexperienced, female staff. There is no evidence, not even a rumor, that he has ever assaulted a woman or a girl, although he has been angry with some of the girls and truly dislikes Mary, whom he sees as responsible for his being held to a higher standard of behavior than the other residents and for his being treated more severely when he screws up. It's true, she is responsible, but Jan is also. They have acted out of fear, and the fear is unreasonable. Until he goes, I will continue with him as I have been doing.

WEDNESDAY, NOVEMBER 24: Andrew Walters was released to parole today. He'll live with his mother and her boyfriend. They'll be proud of him for having maintained his sense of racial superiority under trying circumstances.

SATURDAY, NOVEMBER 27: On November 17, after four months or more of talking about a no-confidence vote against Dean Nader, Ash Meadow's superintendent, the union went ahead and did it. The votes have been counted and, according to the local's newsletter, 84.5 percent of the membership voted No Confidence, 14.5 percent expressed Confidence, and .0172 percent abstained. Well, we'll see what happens. Rumor has it that the deputy director of JRA asked the union officers if it is Nader alone who is the problem. They said no, and pointed the finger at the entire administration—i.e., the superintendent and the four associate superintendents: Don Martino, Celia Barney, Kathleen Foreman, and Fred Thoele. I suspect this will just make us appear peevish.

SUNDAY, NOVEMBER 28: Went to a Volvo repair shop that was advertising used Volvos. Saw the sign on the side of the road and stopped. The shop owner said he'd bought a particular car at an auction for his brother's daughter and had repaired it, but now she didn't want it. He's a large, fleshy man from Ukraine. While he was talking, building up the car and complaining about the Americanization of his niece, I suddenly comprehended the murderousness of people who are devoted to family—a murderousness usually, but not always, directed outward, away from those they love, as though human beings are unable to love without an accompanying rage.

This is a theme that keeps recurring to me: it's in my essay, "How I Learned That I Could Push the Button"[25] and makes up part of my view of gangs.

Speaking of which—Lawrence got cute with Charlie Patterson yesterday, telling him, among other things, that his concerns about the safety of the cottage "mean nothing to me." He essentially punked Charlie.

I pulled Lawrence into the staff office, where he told me that Jeremy West and Bert Gabel are talking gang mess to him. Jeremy called him a "crab," which is a derogatory term for Crip. Lawrence is angry with these two but he's taking his anger out on staff, including Charlie, even though he likes Charlie. Lawrence said that being unable to retaliate against those kids makes him feel trapped. The only thing he can think to do to make himself feel better is to punch somebody. It does no good to exercise or punch his mattress. He says he gets so angry he can hardly stand it.

But he does stand it. Kind of. The anger leaks out in relatively small ways, but he hasn't assaulted anyone here at Ash Meadow. Oddly, he believes— he's said this—that he's "in control." I'm not sure what he means by this. He must realize that he's not in control of Jeremy or Bert. He wasn't in control of Andrew Walters, who spouted his crap about Aryan Nations from the safety of his locked room.

He asked me yesterday why staff think he has a problem with women. He's picked up on this on his own, or else one of the other staff mentioned it to him; I haven't spoken to him about it. The question was so specific, I suspect somebody else, probably Charlie, said something to him. Charlie often talks out of school.

I told him that staff know he was badly abused by his mother, so they expect him to transfer his anger toward his mother to other women.

He said: "I love my mother."

I said I would expect him both to love and to hate her.

He nodded yes, then said he used to hate his mother, but "I got through that."

SUNDAY, DECEMBER 5: Sasha Crow, a girl I knew at Whale, is back on a parole violation. A UA indicated both marijuana and cocaine use. She denies using crack, says she wasn't even selling it, but she helped her boyfriend— maybe not her boyfriend, she said, but he's the father of her second child—cut it up, and she absorbed some through the skin on her hands.

She's ashamed of being here again. She was in Ash Meadow for two years for robbery, then was out for three months, and now she's back. She has two children she doesn't want, and is ashamed of not wanting them and of being a poor mother. What she wants is a real boyfriend. The only boyfriend she's ever had is the father of her younger child. (Her first child is the product of a rape.) She's never been to a movie. She'd like a boy to ask her to go to one on a date, but the only men she meets are those she sells to, and they're interested only in crack. (I realized that she contradicted her earlier denial that she had been selling, but I didn't have the heart to point this out to her now.)

Her mother has been in and out of prison all her life, and Sasha is afraid she'll follow in her mother's footsteps.

FRIDAY, DECEMBER 10: Sasha was transferred to Peacock Cottage today before I came in. I had given her the assignment to set some goals for herself for after she leaves Ash Meadow. She left me this:

"1. I just want to get of [sic] parole without coming back to jail.

"2. Stay alive.

"3. Have a place to rest my head that I can call my own."

After talking with her and reading this, I honestly feel despair.

In return for Sasha, Peacock gave us Cassandra Martin. She'll replace Sasha on my caseload. I don't know her. According to Peacock, Cassandra told another girl, "I'll murder your face into the ground." She also tried to intimidate staff and had a desk calendar with some staff home phone numbers on it, as well as other phone numbers she should not have had. Peacock said, too, that she had been staff-bashing on the calendar, meaning, I assume, that she had written things on it that were critical of staff.

SATURDAY, DECEMBER 11: I talked with Cassandra for the first time today. She told me this: Staff had asked her to attend PC last Tuesday. There, the program manager and other staff told her they considered her intimidating because she was big, she was loud, and she was outspoken.

I was stunned. Cassandra is a large, imposing young woman, granted. And she may be loud and outspoken, I don't know. I haven't seen her like that here yet. But to criticize her for her size and the way she carries herself? What do they want from her? Not to be big? Christ, don't add to the girl's already feeling stigmatized. (I believe Cassandra's account because I read a letter she wrote to Peacock's program manager, telling her how hurt she was by what staff had done to her and what they'd said. The emotions she conveyed sounded genuine.)

She said she had not tried to intimidate anybody and had not threatened anyone. Peacock had a new staff member, she said, a small woman only three or four years older than Cassandra, who may have been frightened by her because she said what she thought when she disagreed with something. She said, too, that there were a couple of girls in the cottage who did not like her and whom she did not like. She did not know if it was one of them who had accused her of threatening to "murder your face into the ground."

Regarding the calendar, Cassandra said she had not done any staff-bashing on it. All she had written on it were comments staff had made that were critical of her. Her idea had been to improve herself, and she had written their comments down so she would have a record of them. She said she had not written any phone numbers on it, and how would she even know staff's personal phone numbers anyway?

Her competency report, dated three weeks ago, says she has almost completed her GED and holds two jobs on campus. It calls her a leader among the cottage residents. It describes a young woman who has turned her life around. So what happened? Her case manager at Peacock, when I called her, said she did not know. She was on her weekend when Cassandra was transferred to us. It was a complete surprise to her. She said she would have opposed it, had she been there.

So here we are.

The calendar was not with Cassandra's belongings that were sent to us. I called Peacock and asked them to send it.

FRIDAY, DECEMBER 17: Jan told me that Lawrence would be going to Elk Grove on Monday. I had intended to tell him tomorrow night. I would not tell him what day, only that it would be some time next week. We—that is, the institution—have a policy not to inform kids that they will be leaving campus, even for medical appointments or court appearances, until the last minute. It's a security issue: at least once in the past, some kids tried to force a transport vehicle off the road in an attempt to snatch their homie. Also, you don't know how a kid will react when he's told, so you don't want to give him a lot of time to dwell on it before he leaves.

But tonight Dr. Gilbert, our new M.D., told him. She must have learned about it from one of the administrators, called Lawrence up to the health center, and told him he was going to be transferred and on what day and at what time. She had been seeing him once a week with my concurrence, because both she and I recognized that he has psychological problems that have been neglected by the psychiatric staff. She has been another person for him to talk to.

I don't know if she understood the significance of what she did. When Lawrence came back to the unit, he was frightened and angry. And we staff did not know why, because he wasn't ready to talk and Gilbert had not informed us about what she had done. Finally he asked me if it was true that he was leaving, and I had to tell him.

I said that Ram does not want him back, and while we could insist that they take him, both Jan and I feel that at the first sign of trouble, they would send him back to us. Our choices, then, were to keep him in Wolf indefinitely, which would not be fair to him, or to send him to a different institution, where he would at least have the chance to get out of maximum security.

But, although I put as good a face on it as I could, sending him to Elk Grove isn't good. Lawrence has been working hard on himself and has progressed tremendously. He's been more open and relaxed with people, less intimidating. And, after having worked so hard, after having bent over to please us staff and having won the affection of most of us—it's rare to have a kid who is bright enough to feel frustrated at the obstacles the system puts in front of him and to know why he is frustrated, and yet to want badly enough to succeed, not on his terms but on ours, that he surmounts or finds a way around these obstacles—he gets no reward, but is punished anyway.

Elk Grove, I've been told by our school psychologist, is a warehouse for kids. Each cottage houses sixty-four kids instead of the sixteen ours are designed for. They are understaffed and staff morale is bad, bad, bad, worse even than here at Ash Meadow. It is a prison.

TUESDAY, DECEMBER 21: Lawrence was transferred to Elk Grove yesterday.

WEDNESDAY, DECEMBER 22: Andrew Walters called Margareta from Spokane to cry on her shoulder. It will be six months before he can go to live with his mother, who has moved to Idaho; first he has to serve out his parole in Washington. It's interesting that he called Margareta for support, given his attachment to Aryan Nations and Christian Identity–Margareta is

African American. He once told her that she is less human than he because she's black and he's white.

TUESDAY, DECEMBER 28: Mary told me she's found another job. She'll be on campus but will be leaving Wolf. A few seconds later she said she and her husband had separated and she's going to file for divorce. I didn't know what to say. I commiserated with her.

2000

SUNDAY, JANUARY 2: I had breakfast with Leah at Elliott Bay Book Company this morning. She asked me why I do the work I do at Ash Meadow. Without thinking, I said, "Because I want to know about people!"

It's true. All of my searching for a reason—my sense of guilt at not having been closer to my own children, my sadness at having missed out on so much of their childhood, my desire to provide something of value for other people, my pleasure in the low level of paranoia, the "hypervigilance" I feel at Ash Meadow—all of this is true, but the base reason is my search for knowledge. A student for life. I feel silly, having said this, but there it is.

THURSDAY, JANUARY 6: There were two swans on the pond behind the cottage today. I'm certain words like "stately" and "regal" have been used to describe them before, but they do apply. Visions like this one make me glad, sometimes, that I work here.

There have been no raccoons here for months. I'd be willing to bet that the institution has poisoned them without telling anyone, at least without telling cottage staff. If there was a reduction in their population, I'd look for another explanation. But nobody has seen one in quite a long time. They were pests, of course. They would get into the trash bins and even sneak into the cottages, looking for food. But complete extermination rather than thinning them out, perhaps by relocation—that's what happens when institutionthink prevails.

Well, another month or so and the frogs should be out. I remember once, when I worked at Swan, the frogs were so loud the kids couldn't sleep.

"Jerry, make them stop," one of the kids, his hands over his ears, begged.

I went to the door and shouted out, "Stop!"

Then I came back in and told the kid, "They won't listen."

He was so miserable he didn't even laugh.

We have deer year-round. Small blacktail, with big ears. A type of mule deer. It's a kick, seeing some of the kids get so excited the first time they see them. Some of them never saw a deer outside of a movie before. Some mistake them for cows or horses.

Our campus is one of their feeding grounds. As far as I know, none has ever been taken by a mountain lion, at least on campus, though we have seen mountain lions on or near the grounds. Three or four years ago, I was driving to work one morning and had just turned off the interstate and onto the highway that takes you to the feeder road that leads to the institution, and I looked in my rearview mirror and there, twenty or thirty yards behind me, was an adult lion bounding across the highway.

FRIDAY, JANUARY 7: In Alternatives to Violence, Jeremy West and John Matafa talked about how angry they felt when people they loved died—in Jeremy's case, a brother and a sister; in John's, a favorite uncle. John said he wanted to smash someone but talked with his homies instead. Jeremy said he went crazy at his sister's funeral, embarrassing his mother: "I started tearing things up." I was reminded again of how often grief lies at the heart of our anger.

Then Allen Joiner said that the source of his grief was the death of his daughter. But he also feels glad, he said, because she's better off dead than she would be growing up with him as her father. He's fourteen.

FRIDAY, JANUARY 14: When we lose someone we love, the world becomes incomprehensible. Any sense of justice we might have is tossed aside. Why should my brother/sister/uncle/daughter die? They did nothing to deserve death. Whatever evil I have done is as nothing compared to this sorrow. We rage at the world, at God. But God and the world are too large for us to devastate them. So we take our rage out on other human beings upon whom we know we can have an effect. We tell ourselves they are responsible for our melancholy, our pain, thereby making the world comprehensible again and allowing God to appear merciful.

My father told me today that he's wearing diapers now. He's become incontinent. He pissed himself at a movie. He's eighty-three.

SUNDAY, JANUARY 16: Cassandra Martin told me that while she does not intend to sell crack again, she doesn't regret having sold it, except for the fact that she was caught. She says staff tell her that she should empathize with her victims, but she sees them as victimizing themselves: nobody forces them to use drugs. Staff tell her to consider the addicts' children, but she says, "What about my children! I've got a daughter to support too."

We've created this underclass, left them without hope or resources by which to gain entry into the middle class, and then we punish them for being poor and adapting to the life of the poor. Hell, it was our CIA who introduced them to crack cocaine in the first place!

Cassandra has been in Wolf for over a month now, and every week since she's been here I've called Peacock to ask them to send me the calendar she purportedly wrote staff's home phone numbers on. Finally, yesterday, the calendar arrived in the campus mail. It has not a single phone number on it. There is not a single instance of staff bashing, though Peacock has all along insisted the calendar was filled with it.

MONDAY, JANUARY 17: I briefed Jan about Cassandra and showed her the desk calendar. Neither of us could think of a reason for Peacock's wanting to destroy this girl. Her jobs—she held two, and there are only a handful available to residents on the entire campus—her high status in the cottage—all of this was taken from her in a moment and she was placed in maximum security without any kind of explanation that makes sense, either to her or to us.

Jan called her into her office and talked with her for close to an hour. She told me after Cassandra went back to her room that a lot of that time was spent simply sitting with her while she cried.

We and Cassandra are just going to have to accept that she's here, even if we don't know why, Jan said. She'll get hold of Bev Gorey, Peacock's program manager, and try to get some information out of her, assuming she knows why all of this happened. Jan thinks Bev was on leave when Cassandra was sent to us.

SUNDAY, JANUARY 23: Had coffee with Mary last night. Talked about Wolf. She said she wasn't acculturated to violence as men are. Immediately after she said that, she said she had had to defend herself against violent, drunken, or drugged men several times in her life. One man she had shared a house with tried to kill her. While he was strangling her, he told her he had done this to other women. She learned later that he had been abused by his mother when he was small and had been taken away from her.

As she was talking, it occurred to me that this was the root of her fear of Lawrence, that someone with a past similar to his had tried to kill her. I wish I hadn't been so intolerant of this fear when she worked with us.

FRIDAY, JANUARY 28: Jan told me that Herman Boats—Remember him?—settled his suit against Ash Meadow. They had demoted him to JRRC even after CPS determined there were no grounds for punitive action—Remember the investigation that began two years ago? He has been reinstated as a cottage director and he'll get back pay. He'll get Goldfish Cottage.

SATURDAY, JANUARY 29: Jonas Gardiner is a severely retarded sex offender. He's small, with a poorly developed musculature. He's thirteen. He drools almost constantly, a side effect of the meds he's on.

This morning Jonas cheeked his med. Why did he cheek it? Maybe he doesn't like its taste or effect, or maybe he wanted to give it to another kid to win his favor. Last week he invited a boy to go into the head with him so he could put his penis in the boy's butt; Jonas is very direct about what he wants. He didn't persist when the other kid told him, "That might cause a fight."

Lin, who had been distributing meds, asked me to come into the office. I have a good relationship with Jonas and she thought I might be able to persuade him to swallow the med. I couldn't. He denied having cheeked it, but also refused to let me look in his mouth. I wanted to get him out of the office in case we had to handle him, so I told him to come out into the living room and sit down. He obeyed without resistance. I stood beside his chair and told Lin to call Security. We were working with Tony Dangerfield, an experienced intermittent, and I signaled him to lock the other kids in their rooms.

Jonas complained that he was feeling dizzy. I told him to lean back. Instead, he flopped forward out of the chair onto the floor. The seats in those chairs are canted upward under the legs, so it required some effort to fall out of it. He was lying on his stomach, his face turned to the right, his eyes open. I moved around to his side and could see his eyes tracking my shoes as I walked.

"Jonas, are you all right?"

He closed his eyes and did not respond.

"Let me give you a hand." Tony and I helped him back into his chair.

"I want to go to my room," he said.

"Not until you give us your med."

He stood up and started for the door leading to the fenced court, our rec yard, behind the cottage. Tony placed himself in his way. Jonas turned, started for Zone 4 where his room is. I stepped in front of him. Then the pill just rode out of his mouth in the flow of his drool. He bent to pick it up but I grabbed his arm and spun him around and put an arm bar on him. Tony came over and locked his other arm while Lin, stopping first to grab some tissue paper off the staff desk, scooped the med up off the floor.

Tony and I took Jonas to his room and put him face-down on his bed. Tony handcuffed him and I crossed his legs one over the other so he couldn't kick. Jonas was hysterical. He was absolutely terrified. His screams, the depth of them, reminded me of a boy Rob Gorey and I once took down: we had bent him forward over a chair and that was when he began to scream.[26]

Security arrived. Newt Smith uncuffed Jonas and sat beside him, patting his back, trying to calm him. Finally it became obvious that Jonas was crying now only to gain our sympathy. We moved him to our quiet room.

Tony and I felt terrible. But Lin was laughing about Jonas' pretending to faint and my being so solicitous of him—"Jonas, are you all right?" She was certain he had taken me in.

Layton, Jonas' staff, came in to work about the time we took him out of the quiet room. When he saw Layton he went over to him and put his face against Layton's chest and began genuinely to cry again. "I got in trouble," he said.

Layton put his arm around him and walked him down to his room. He talked with Jonas for a while, then locked him in.

TUESDAY, FEBRUARY 1: Jonas Gardiner transferred to Dolphin Cottage, which, as of the first of the year, is the boys' mental health unit.

THURSDAY, FEBRUARY 3: Cassandra Martin was transferred to Whale today. Caroline Bloodworth will be her case manager. Sigh.

FRIDAY, FEBRUARY 4: In Alternatives to Violence this evening, I gave the boys a scenario: they are with their friends, their "set" or "clique"—when I said these words, Brendan Perris and John Matafa looked at each other as if to say, "What's this old white guy think he's talking about?"—and they come upon an enemy set. They fight and at the end of the fight they've driven their enemy off, plus they've captured one of them. Their friends want to torture him until he dies. What should they—the kids I'm talking to, the kids in Alternatives to Violence—do? If they oppose their friends . . . well, after all, these guys are homies, people they've grown up with who may still be their friends after the event has passed.

John said he'd go along with what his friends wanted to do.

Brendan said that if you don't kill him, he'll come back with his set and maybe kill you.

I said that the issue is not killing somebody outright, but torturing him until he dies.

Stephen Cork said he'd just walk away.

Paul Durnham didn't say anything.

Randy Fulton said if you don't go along, your friends will kill you.

Then Brendan said he would stand up against his friends if they wanted to torture this guy.

John said he would oppose torturing the guy because his, John's, culture would not allow him to attack a helpless person. He could see one on one, but not nine on one. (I don't know where he got the number nine.)

Randy said again that they would kill you if you didn't go along.

Brendan shrugged and said he would still try to keep them from doing it.

John said he would oppose it because he wanted his culture to be proud of him. He wanted his mother to be proud of him.

MONDAY, FEBRUARY 7: This afternoon on the way to work—clouds rising out of the mountains like vaporous snakes.

WEDNESDAY, FEBRUARY 9: Ran into Brian Meara on my way down to Wolf. He's the program manager for Dolphin now. He said Jonas Gardiner had indeed been raped. I had told Brian of my suspicion based on Jonas' hysteria when Tony and I took him down. Someone who had been Jonas' counselor on the outs had shown up and given Dolphin this information.

FRIDAY, FEBRUARY 18: Mary told me that there really is a list of cottage staff the administrators want to get rid of. A number of senior staff have suspected this. I did not believe it at first. But I believe Mary. She says the list is composed of those who have expressed disagreement with the administrators at some time.

Yet I haven't felt any pressure to leave. I thought for a long time that the PCR I received was the first salvo. But there wasn't a second.

THURSDAY, FEBRUARY 24: Jan told us at PC that Sue Royce, whom we released some time ago, is selling drugs. She is also running a stable of girls. This information comes from Kathleen Foreman. I don't know Kathleen well enough to be able to tell when she is lying and when she is not.

FRIDAY, FEBRUARY 25: Several girls will to be transferred to Woodbyrne on March first, and Cassandra is going to be one of them. This issue of a transfer has come up before, and Jan had an agreement with Kathleen that Cassandra would stay at Ash Meadow until she could go to a group home. This was so she could remain geographically close to her daughter, who is living with Cassandra's mother. But now all bets are off, for reasons no one is confiding to me. Kathleen told Jan to get Cassandra to buy into it because it's inevitable. Why Jan? She isn't Whale's program manager. But she has a good relationship with Cassandra, who doesn't trust anyone at Whale.

Speaking of which, Caroline Bloodworth called me last week. She asked if I thought Peacock staff had been justified in sending Cassandra to Wolf. I didn't know what to say: I don't trust Caroline not to twist whatever information I might give her so she can use it against Cassandra, or against me. But before I could say anything, Caroline said, "I hate to say anything about other staff, but I think they framed this girl."

I said, "I think you're right."

Caroline loves to badmouth other staff, and now Peacock has provided her an opportunity.

It's interesting whom you find yourself in bed with on occasion. Alliances are constantly shifting.

WEDNESDAY, MARCH 1: I start working a different schedule this month. I'm taking Margareta's shift: Fridays and Saturdays off. She's gone on medical leave for diabetes and a host of other physical problems.

Dick, for one, won't miss her. She was consistently late coming in to work. There was always a question as to when she would show up, or if she would.

When Dick complained to her about not getting here on time—he couldn't leave until she arrived—she told him, "You're lucky I come in at all."

Then, of course, there was the time Layton pressed his panic alarm while trying to stop a fight, and she ran away. You don't forget something like that. I don't. Layton doesn't.

Jan told me she finally persuaded Margareta to go on medical leave after two months of talking to her. Jan must have been under terrible pressure to get rid of her, both from the administration and from her own staff. She and Margareta have been friends for many years. She said she doesn't think Margareta will ever come back to Ash Meadow.

Layton will be taking Mary's place as supervisor beginning now.

THURSDAY, MARCH 2: Cassandra didn't go to Woodbyrne yesterday. She needs surgery, and care afterward that Woodbyrne can't provide. Ovarian cysts.

WEDNESDAY, MARCH 15: Lyle Munson was released today. This morning when he went to the office to get his Clonidine, Ryan Renton was there, waiting to be given his meds. Lyle punched him in the mouth, then ran to his room and sat down on his bed. We'll charge him with assault.

SATURDAY, MARCH 18: What continues to trouble me most about these kids is that, though many of them have done terrible things, almost all of them were the victims of terrible things first. While they are being punished for what they have done, indirectly they are being punished for what has been done to them. For these kids, life isn't a matter of getting into the right university, it's a matter of dealing with the memory—and the consequences—of seeing your mother beaten to the ground, or your father stabbing someone, or having his own throat cut. Life is goddamned unfair, but we all know that, don't we?

SUNDAY, APRIL 2: The word is that Lyle Munson is back in the system with new charges. I suggested to the other staff that when he comes back to us he should suffer the consequences for having punched Ryan Renton.

SUNDAY, APRIL 9: Allen Joiner is back with us on a parole violation. He's the one who, telling of his daughter's death, said she was better off dead than to have him for her father.[27]

He told me today that his daughter was shot in a drive-by. She was walking with his brother and the shooters killed them both. They mistook his brother for him. He himself was attacked recently by the kids who killed his daughter and brother. He was stabbed in the head with a screwdriver but it didn't penetrate the skull.

I asked him what he's going to do when he gets out this time. He laughed and swung his arms as though fighting. "Get even."

I told Ron Dakron about him. "I'm glad I don't live around that," Ron said. "But you do. It's all around you. You just don't see it."

TUESDAY, APRIL 11: Training today on DBT (Dialectical Behavior Therapy. I always want to substitute "Diabolical" for "Dialectical" when I try to recall what the initials stand for). Boring, boring, boring. And if I'm bored, think how bored the kids must be when they are trained in it. It's designed for suicidal women with borderline personality disorder, but it's being imposed, at least here at Ash Meadow, on everyone, boys and girls of every age, whether they are talking suicide or not. Somebody is making a career for himself on this.

But I saw Mary Corning there. It was good talking with her again. She's running a group home now.

She asked me why I haven't gone into administration. I told her I've never seen my job as a career, and I like doing what I'm doing. I didn't tell her, because I didn't want to offend her, that I believe only line staff know what is going on, because we are closest to the action. All you have to do is listen to the administrators talk about the kids to realize how little they know. And what I want most of all is to understand the world, at least the part of it I live in.

TUESDAY, APRIL 18: At the psychiatry team meeting this morning, the doctors spent the first ten minutes of what promised to be a very long meeting talking about what it means that Microsoft's stock is tumbling. Every one of them was absorbed in the discussion, reassuring one another that Microsoft would bounce back. I started laughing. I looked over at Shelby MacIntyre from Goldfish Cottage and she was laughing too.

Doug Little from Ram was sitting across the conference table from me. He is known, and I know him, for his patient, insightful abilities with kids. I asked him, "Doug, are you rich yet?" I expected him to make some sort of gesture or signal or say something that would indicate . . . what? the absurdity? the irony? of our sitting here listening to the shrinks, so many of whom are ever so quick to point out that they, not we, are professionals, obsess about money.

Instead, he said, "Well, I have my money in Starbucks and it's doing pretty well." He started telling me about the virtues of Starbucks, catching the doctors' attention. They had been listening to him for perhaps thirty seconds when Dr. Williams decided to get on with talking about kids.

TUESDAY, APRIL 25: I asked Malcolm Isley if I reminded him of someone else. He's been antagonistic toward me since shortly after he arrived in the cottage last month and I could not think of anything I had done to warrant his hostility.

He shook his head no, but said yes even as he moved his head. Then he said he didn't want to talk about this other person, but that I am about his age and "You look like him. You laugh like him."

Malcolm said he was at the man's trial when the judge sentenced him to twenty-five years. The man laughed and the judge changed the sentence to life. Malcolm described the man's face as falling with shock then. On Malcolm's face I saw something like satisfaction. Malcolm hates this man, but didn't say why. I can guess.

SATURDAY, MAY 13: Met Leah and Ron for coffee last night at Elliott Bay Book Company. I started thinking about Tommy Whitacre from . . . what? four years ago? five? and how I didn't want him to confess to a murder because I couldn't stand the thought of him spending his life in prison. You never know if you're doing the right thing, or what the consequences of what you do will be. I think now that I should have allowed him to confess, that he felt the need to, and that I prevented him from doing it out of my own need.

Throughout all of my thinking about Tommy last night, I carried on a conversation with my daughter and my friend, laughed with them and told funny stories. I wonder if they detected anything of what was going on inside me.

TUESDAY, MAY 16: Had a workshop today, "Working with Juvenile Female Offenders," conducted by Kathleen Foreman, Jan's boss. This was the third time I've had this workshop, and I resisted going again, especially as I do not like Kathleen. But she insisted that Wolf be represented, so Jan selected me.

She said she wants me to try to understand Kathleen since we have to work with her. The workshop was very superficial, as is Kathleen.

When I went down to the cottage for lunch, Dick and Bernie told me Casey Fairchild had "broken out" of our quiet room this morning. About six-thirty, Katrina Person at Crane called and asked if we had all of our kids. "Katrina, don't fuck with me," Bernie said. Katrina said we had better count heads because there was a little blond-haired kid running around outside her cottage.

Bernie checked the quiet room and found nothing wrong, except Casey wasn't there. Bernie said he felt the shit running down his leg—probably an exaggeration. Then one of the Fox staff called and said Casey was jumping up and down outside his window. Eventually Security returned him to us.

Apparently the quiet room door leading to the outside had not been locked. Casey pushed it open, closed it behind him, and took off. Question of the hour: who unlocked it, or did not lock it? We have a new staff, Frank Payne, who was working graveyard: he denies having unlocked the door. Security also has a new officer who was working graveyard and he, too, denies unlocking or failing to lock the door. My money says the Security guy did it. Casey spent the night in somebody else's quiet room. Security brought him back about six. Did he put him in our quiet room from outside or from the staff office? If he did it from outside, that would mean Security was the last person to open that door.

TUESDAY, MAY 23: Cassandra Martin called to tell me she's going to a group home tomorrow. She thanked me for everything and told me she wouldn't forget me. Awfully sweet of her to say that.

She finally got her GED. A few weeks ago she was accused of stealing a sweat shirt from the commisary where she was working and lost her job because of it. At her GED graduation ceremony, the girl who actually stole the shirt confessed in front of everyone and apologized to Cassandra.

I asked how things finally came together for her. "What do you attribute it to?" I thought she might say that she discovered something inside herself that gave her the strength to persevere.

"God," she said.

TUESDAY, MAY 30: I ran into Caroline Bloodworth at the psychiatry team meeting this morning. Afterward, she briefed me on Cassandra's life at

Whale. She had earned a high level again and gotten a job on upper campus, as she had when she was at Peacock. But then Kathleen Foreman accused her of having tried to intimidate the interviewer from Woodbyrne who had come to talk with her by telling her that she would go off if she was selected to go there. Cassandra's level was taken from her again and she was placed on Tables. It was Anna, Whale's new program manager, who did this to her, under Kathleen's direction. Caroline heard Kathleen tell Anna: "I want her on Tables." Then Kathleen went on vacation.

In her absence, Caroline persuaded Anna to call Woodbyrne. The woman who interviewed Cassandra said she had not tried to intimidate anyone and had not threatened to go off: Cassandra had been turned down because she needed surgery.

Even so, Anna did not give her back her level. "It's bad enough when they treat staff like this—and they do—but there's no excuse for treating kids like that," Caroline said. Anna did find the courage to allow Cassandra off Tables.

It's easy to see why the administration has worked so diligently to get rid of experienced counselors and program managers. Inexperienced managers like Anna do not resist when faced with implementing cruel decisions.

During the psych meeting, Casey Fairchild's name came up. I said I didn't understand why he was on the list to be reviewed since Harry Grass, the psychologist Ash Meadow recently hired, Don Martino, and Kathleen Foreman had all said that Casey is not a mental health case.

Dr. Williams said, "Jerry, if your point is that we don't know what we're doing, I agree with you. But we all know that Casey is crazy."

"That wasn't my point," I said, "but I'll accept yours."

Actually, my point was that Casey does not belong in maximum security, but in the boys' mental health unit. He is in Wolf because he wasn't responding to DBT—Dolphin has given itself over entirely to DBT, and has eschewed any other kind of treatment. So, since Casey represents a failure for them, and proof that DBT does not work for everyone, as Harry and the administrators claim it does, they want to get rid of him. But if he is a mental health case, he should be in a mental health unit.

The solution? Change the label. Call him recalcitrant, or "oppositional defiant," anything but mentally ill, and ship him to Wolf. Simple. It's as if reality exists only in the writing of it.

WEDNESDAY, MAY 31: One of the girls was ragging on Layton and me today. She asked Layton if he wore dentures. He didn't say anything. Then she asked me. "I do," I said, "but I wear my real teeth to work." Layton laughed but the girl looked like she was considering my answer. Finally she said, "Oh, that's interesting."

WEDNESDAY, JUNE 7: Got a call from Reception this evening: a sow bear and two cubs were seen on campus. Staff are to be careful going to their cars. Okay.

SATURDAY, JUNE 10: I woke up so sore this morning, I might have had the flu but for the lack of a fever. I feel as though I've been beaten up. Today is the second day of my weekend, my "Sunday." I usually feel this way on my "Saturdays" and have recovered by "Sunday," but Thursday was an especially rough day.

I did Survivors' Group in the evening. After beating around the bush for a while, all three boys, one after another, disclosed their abuse, in greater or less detail. Malcolm Isley pushed the others to tell their stories first, but they would not allow him to be last. They compromised by agreeing that Malcolm would go second, after David Savitch.

David said he was raped when he was eleven. A friend, a boy he had known since he was three, enticed David over to a neighbor's house, where they watched porn videos. Both boys were given drugs—David did not say what they were—and the man told David's friend he could watch, and then raped David. Afterward, David said, his friend laughed at him. That was the worst part. Apparently his friend had an ongoing sexual relationship with the man that David had not known about.

The man served two years. He now lives only a mile from David's house in a small town in the eastern part of the state.

I told David that his mother told me she thinks he reoffended—this is his second time at Ash Meadow—so he would be sent back here because he's afraid of this man. David said this was true.

Malcolm said that when he was eleven years old he was kidnapped. He was yanked by his hair off the street where he was walking and into a flat where he was tied up and then raped.

Another kid the man had done this to eventually told. At the trial, Malcolm admitted to having been molested, but said he had not been raped: he was too ashamed. The worst part, he told us, was that this was the second time this happened to him. He said he couldn't talk about the first time yet.

He apologized to me for treating me badly early in our relationship, but I looked and sounded just like the man who raped him. I accepted his apology and assured him he had every right to be angry, and *should* be angry.

Suddenly he started chattering about things entirely unrelated to his abduction and rape: what we'd had for dinner—he hadn't liked it—the kinds of food he especially liked. The other boys stared at him, then they too started talking about food.

I asked Malcolm how he felt now that he had told others about what happened to him. He said he was trying to think about good things, to put the bad out of his mind.[28]

Leon Anderson also disclosed, but I must have been shutting down because I can't remember anything he said.

All of the boys had been reluctant to tell their mothers—none have fathers at home. Malcolm still hasn't told his mother that he was raped. All feel guilty, as though the responsibility for being raped were somehow theirs. All are worried that they might do this to someone else. "That's why I wanted to be in this group, so that I won't," Malcolm said. And, of course, they're worried about their own sexuality. Malcolm is fourteen, the others thirteen.

Later in the evening I went over to Goldfish to do Alternatives to Violence. Several weeks ago Herman asked me to train Shelby MacIntyre, so I've been going there on Thursday nights. The plan is to do one complete cycle with Shelby assisting me.

Tonight we talked about domestic violence. Brendan Perris, whom we transferred to Goldfish in April, said he would never hit a woman, but he might shake her—he mimed gripping someone's upper arms and shaking her—"to show her what's what."

"What's what, Brendan?" I asked.

"You know—what's what."

"I don't know. Tell me what you mean by 'what's what.'"

"You know. So she'd know who's boss."

While Brendan and I were sparring, another boy, Henry Jones, was growing visibly agitated. He was squirming and his face had gone from sorrow to annoyance to anger. Finally he said there's never a reason to hit a woman.

Brendan said that if she just kept dogging him and wouldn't get out of his face, she'd have to be taught. She couldn't just think she could do that and get away with it.

Henry said, "That's stupid! There's never any reason to hit a woman!"

Brendan stood up, said "Suckah!" and then said something else I didn't catch or don't remember. Shelby and I got between him and Henry, who was also on his feet now, and she took Brendan to his room while I watched the other kids.

I asked Henry if he wanted to go to his room. He had sat down again. He didn't speak but took immensely deep breaths, filling his chest with every one, one after another, until tears finally came. Other kids were telling him, "Don't be trippin'." They were not sure where this was going to lead or what it might mean for them.

Shelby came back and we continued with the group, Henry silent for the rest of it. Another boy, Marlin, talked about his cousins who shot up that tavern in south Seattle last year. When the police were closing in on them, the older brother shot the younger, then himself. Marlin was going to say something about "the killing fields" in Cambodia, but said instead, "I don't want to think about that." He's Cambodian.

After group was over and we put the kids in their rooms, Shelby took Henry into the office. He told her he had seen his father beat his mother, and when Brendan was talking, he saw his father's face superimposed on Brendan's.

I don't know if it's such a good idea to do Survivors' Group and Alternatives to Violence on the same night. It's very hard on me.

FRIDAY, JUNE 16: Had Aggression Replacement Training (ART) this past week. Its purpose was to learn to train kids in techniques to replace their impulse to act on their anger, or their desire to be aggressive, with more socially acceptable behavioral skills. It sounds pompous and academic, the way I've just described it, but actually I was impressed.

Initially I had not wanted to attend this training—the flyer advertising it made it sound dull—but I found it stimulating. And I was impressed by the apparent honesty of Chris Hayes, our instructor. He said ART reduces recidivism by as much as 35 percent, but neither he nor the originators of ART know why.

Herman Boats was at the training as well as Shelby MacIntyre and another staff from Ash Meadow and two from Elk Grove. The Rivers did not send anyone. At lunch one day Herman entertained me with tales of staff transgressions at the various institutions: a cook selling crack at The Rivers, two female counselors there having sex with a resident, one of the support staff at Ash Meadow leaving his wife and running off with a former resident, and, of course, the counselor at Ash Meadow who beat up a resident and threatened to shoot any staff who informed on him. I had already heard about almost all of these, but enjoyed listening to Herman tell about them again. All of them occurred over a period of five or six years. I assume other things have happened that neither Herman nor I have heard about.

THURSDAY, JUNE 22: I was awakened this morning by a man shouting outside: "I just got out of prison! I have no money! I can't find a job! Freedom! Freedom! Freedom! Is this freedom?" Then he laughed. In the laughter was rue.

FRIDAY, JUNE 23: Casey Fairchild is back in Dolphin Cottage and is not doing well. Harry Grass, our resident psychologist, is talking about returning him to Wolf for "a short period"—he suggests a week—"for aversion therapy." This would involve isolating Casey as much as possible, so he would eat in his room, he would not go to school, he would be out of his room only when other kids are not on the floor. In addition to isolating him, we staff would taunt him by reminding him of what he is missing by not being in Dolphin: no swimming during recreation, no school on upper campus, no interaction with other kids.

Last night I noticed Layton ostentatiously pinching his nose as he went into Zone 3, the girls' zone. He was performing for Josie Fells, who was laughing at Zora, a new girl who has a bad bowel problem. She is sometimes incontinent and almost constantly farting. So what's going on with Layton? I've never seen this kind of cruelty in him before.

SATURDAY, JUNE 24: I've been thinking about the situation Casey Fairchild, or Harry Grass, may be presenting us with. I've decided that I'm not in the business of tormenting children. When staff makes things unpleasant for them, by putting them off-program, for example, we do this because they are threatening or assaultive or not in control of themselves. Even then, I, and most staff, make it a point to treat them with some consideration for the difficulties they are having.

I imagine Harry believes that isolating and taunting Casey is best for him, but what I see is applied sensory deprivation à la the Russian model, or something near to it.

I'm going to tell Jan that I will not participate in mistreating Casey. But I'll frame it in this way: by doing as Harry wants us to do, we will be violating those regulations concerning staff's treatment of residents. And who will authorize an exception to JRA and Ash Meadow regulations?

Another issue: we have three new, inexperienced staff. They are unknown quantities, at least to us. Will one or more of them see the requirement to taunt Casey as an opportunity to bully him?

If Harry wants Casey mistreated, why not have the staff at Dolphin, the cottage where Harry spends most of his time, do it? Why should Harry foist this off on us? I'll say this to Jan, too.

This I will not tell Jan: if the requirement to torment Casey comes down, I'll blow the whistle, and not only to JRA; I'll go outside the system.

LATER: I had coffee with Ron Dakron tonight. I told him about the Casey Fairchild/Harry Grass problem. Ron said something that has been at the back of my mind throughout: Who is being studied? Is it Casey, or is it staff?

TUESDAY, JUNE 27: We've not got Casey yet. I told Jan of my concern—that was how I couched it: it's a "concern"—about our violating JRA regulations if we treat Casey as Harry wants us to.

She said nobody is going to violate JRA regulations. But she said, too, that she would bring up the issue of staff's "inadvertently" bullying Casey at the next meeting on what to do about him.

End of discussion.

WEDNESDAY, JUNE 28: Malcolm Isley, in Ram Cottage now, attempted suicide last night. He made up a concoction of cleaning agents, toothpaste, and I don't know what else, and drank it. One of the guys from Security told us.

At the psych meeting yesterday, Doug Little said staff at Ram think Malcolm has been depressed for two or three weeks, sleeping for long periods, refusing to eat, etc.

I was about to leave, having presented on Josie Fells, when Doug started talking about Malcolm. I put in that Malcolm is really raw now, having disclosed in Survivors' Group a great deal about what had happened to him, and that there is some stuff he has not disclosed yet, that he says he's not ready to talk about.

This explained a lot, Doug said. Meg Bellardine, our Mental Health Coordinator—a dumb title, but she's a very decent person, generous with her time and open to staff's concerns—said that, coupled with Malcolm's participating in Grief-and-Loss Group, his experience in Survivors' Group may be simply too much for him. I suspect she's right. I hadn't known he was in Grief-and-Loss, and Doug hadn't known he was in Survivors' Group. Cottages don't compare notes on kids unless the kid presents a major problem, as Casey does.

THURSDAY, JUNE 29: Called Doug. Malcolm is on SPL III. His room has been stripped, he's checked visually every ten minutes, and he has a denim sleeping bag instead of bedding, no mattress. Doug said Malcolm threw a book at him when he asked how he was doing.

"Well, at least he has enough energy to throw a book," I said. Doug laughed. Doug is one of the best therapists on our little island. I would trust his judgement on any kid he deals with.

MONDAY, JULY 3: Every time I see one of those cross-country rigs on the interstate, I think of that girl we had who wanted to drive one. I don't know what became of her.

For weeks now, maybe longer, I have suddenly and unpredictably become tearful. I have, once or twice, had to break off from conversation or change the subject, to keep from breaking down. Sometimes, when alone, I will even start sobbing.

What seems to set me off is hearing or reading about an act of kindness or mercy. Exactly what this means, I do not know, but I'm certain it relates to my job. I think I have numbed myself, at least the surface of my emotions, but the kitsch—and it is only kitsch—that breaks through threatens to overwhelm me.

It's time to leave this job, I think. But even if I do leave, I know I will not recover from it.

TUESDAY, JULY 11: At the psych meeting today, Mark Conley, one of the psychiatrists, talked about his daughter. She's eighteen, has left home, and is living with her boyfriend. Conley was obviously in pain. I've been contemptuous of him for his arrogance, and his insistence on having the last word in any discussion (except with Dr. Williams, his boss). Gave me a different take on him. I was quite touched.

THURSDAY, JULY 13: I met with Matt Hall, a JRCC—i.e., a parole officer—to talk about teaching ART to residents of Wolf. He's been trained in it also and we're going to teach it together. Matt is a kind of liaison between the institution and the parole system and has an office here at Ash Meadow.

WEDNESDAY, JULY 19: Nader was at the cottage this afternoon. He asked me if all of the residents in maximum security wore orange jumpsuits. He was serious. He really did not know. How many years has he been superintendent? How many times has he been in this cottage? I said yes, they all wear orange.

WEDNESDAY, AUGUST 2: One of the kids in Alternatives to Violence said this: "I think pain is all in the mind, because when my cousin got shot—Wait . . . we were in that park on Twentieth and Yesler, we were walking through that park, my cousin and me, and when we came to the street we heard this car like they do"—mimics the screech of tires—"and we began, you know, running this way and that, zigzagging, even before we heard the bullets popping, and it wasn't until we got to the other end of the park that I saw my cousin was bleeding, he had blood on his side coming out through his shirt and he didn't know it until I told him and that's when it began to hurt and I called 9-1-1 and we went to ER and they decided to leave the bullet in, it wasn't doing no damage to him except for the pain and he wouldn't have even had that, at least not right then, if I hadn't told him he was bleeding. That's why I think pain is all in the mind, because he wouldn't have even felt it if I hadn't told him."

THURSDAY, AUGUST 3: Kathleen Foreman came to PC today to brief us on four girls we're going to get from Purdy, the women's prison, as part of an agreement between DOC and JRA. The girls are juveniles who have been convicted as adults. State law requires that they have the opportunity to finish their schooling, and Purdy cannot afford to hire tutors, so, because we have a school on campus, we get them.

We were discussing how to recognize them when they go to upper campus, as they'll be wearing their own clothes then instead of the orange jumpsuits they'll wear while in Wolf—we assume they'll eventually transfer to another cottage, and having longer sentences than most of our other kids, they may be more easily tempted to try to escape—when I suggested that Ash Meadow tattoo "DOC" on their foreheads, as adulteresses in New England were once branded with the letter A. I was being outrageous.

Kathleen, sitting beside me, immediately shot back: "Next you'll want to put yellow stars on their shirts!"

There were three or four "Ooh!"s from other staff and Jan shouted over them: "And you're the diversity person!" Kathleen is responsible for diversity training for both staff and residents at Ash Meadow.

For the remainder of the meeting she tried to downplay her error, touching me on the arm, play-socking me, but I ignored her.

WEDNESDAY, AUGUST 9: Wolf won't be getting the DOC girls. Serpent will. Fred Thoele objected to their taking up four beds in maximum security.

SUNDAY, AUGUST 20: I haven't been able to write about this until now. About a month ago my son Jack was in L.A. visiting some of his mother's family and my father. He called me at work from his cousin's house. He said Dad had fallen and could not use his left leg. Jack was with him at the time and he thought Dad had had a stroke. He refused to go to ER, saying he wanted to talk to his own doctor first. But his doctor did not return his calls. Dad had also antagonized the staff at his assisted care residence, so they were reluctant to look in on him.

I called Dad. Jack was right: Dad wanted to talk to his own doctor before going to a hospital. I talked with one of the facility administrators. She said he'd sent away an ambulance she had called to take him to ER. She told me this almost as soon as I identified myself. The implication was that she was not going to put herself out for him again.

I called Dad back and persuaded him to go to the hospital. Then I called the administrator and asked her to talk with him again to reinforce his decision to go. She agreed. She said, too, that his doctor's nurse said she had called him three times, but no one had answered the phone.

I told this to Dad and he said, "That's a crock of shit. No one called me."

Later, my sister told me that, in fact, his doctor was not on call, a colleague was, and the latter's nurse had called the assisted-care home and left a message with the same administrator I had spoken with. The nurse had not tried to call Dad directly.

THURSDAY, AUGUST 24: Contemplating acts of kindness or mercy makes me weep. I think I said that recently. Yes, I did. On July third.

THURSDAY, SEPTEMBER 14: Lyle Munson is back. A two-and-a-half-year sentence for TAMVWOP and Assault Four. He's a little taller. His voice hasn't changed yet.

SUNDAY, SEPTEMBER 24: For the past several months we've been getting girls back on parole violations who are detoxifying from coke or heroin or meth or crack cocaine. Dorothy Moon has been back half a dozen times. She's eighteen, looks thirty-five. She likes speedballs, a heroin and cocaine concoction. Geraldine Cage is a sweet young woman with a clean-and-sober boyfriend who seems to love her. She's twenty; she can't stay away from meth. Shari Woods is with us now for the second time. Right now she's sleeping away the crack in her system.

MONDAY, OCTOBER 2: Frank was in Zone 1 for several minutes, long enough that I went to see what was going on. He was talking to Darryl Connors at Darryl's door. Frank looked at me and said, "He won't go in his room." I shouted "Clear the floor!" and waited while James, another of our new staff, and Frank locked everyone in. Then Frank and I went into Zone 1 where Darryl had remained, waiting for us. He refused to go into his room and I sent Frank to call Security. While he was out of the zone, Darryl went into his room and I locked the door.

That was last night.

Tonight Frank spent almost the entire evening at the computer, writing a report over and over—Jan calls him a perfectionist—instead of monitoring the kids, even though Jan has told staff (at my request) that when we are on the floor with the kids, we are to pay attention to them, not to busy ourselves with the computer. [The staff computer is at the staff desk on the floor, but is positioned so that if you are looking at the monitor you cannot also watch the floor.]

At seven-fifty, Frank took some of the kids outside for a few minutes of recreation before they had to go to bed. Almost as soon as they were outside,

James told Darryl, who had stayed inside, to go to his room; I don't know why. Darryl refused and James cleared the floor. Frank came inside, alone; that is, he left the kids outside unattended. I told him to go back outside, then called Security on the radio and asked for assistance. After setting the radio down, I turned and found Frank inside the cottage again. Again I told him to go outside. He said he could watch the kids from where he was, near the doorway. But he wasn't at the doorway. He had come into the cottage and his back was to the door leading to the recreation yard.

Meanwhile Darryl was starting to roam. I was reluctant to escort him physically to his room because he is a big kid and I didn't know how he would respond if I took him by the arm, because I didn't know what James knew about handling a resident, and because Frank continued to wander into the cottage. As often as he came inside, I told him to go back out. And as often as I told him to go outside, he objected that he *was* outside, though obviously he was not, or that he could see the kids outside from where he was. Once when he said he was outside he was standing in the middle of the cottage not ten feet from me. So I limited myself to blocking Darryl's attempts to go into the kitchen or the mudroom. When, through the kitchen window, he saw Security pull up, he went to his room. I had Security move him into our quiet room. It has its own toilet, so we wouldn't have to let him out for head calls later.

About nine o'clock I gave him his med. He stepped out of the quiet room to take it, swallowed it down with water, then refused to go back in. I told him twice to step back but he shook his head no. I shoved him so hard he fell back against the far wall of the quiet room. He looked at me in absolute surprise, but didn't say a word. I made certain to look directly into his eyes before I closed the door.

Frank Payne is the guy who was working graveyard when Casey Fairchild escaped.[29]

TUESDAY, OCTOBER 3: I talked to Jan about what happened last night. I emphasized Frank's coming into the cottage, but telling me he wasn't in the cottage, and I brought up also the time he spent on the computer, leaving the floor work to James and me.

Jan said she told him, told all the staff, not to work at the computer when kids are on the floor—as if telling Frank not to do something will make him stop doing it. She said she couldn't understand how he could be inside but believe he was outside. Then she decided that there must be "a communication problem" between Frank and me.

Immediately I was on my guard. This is what she says when she doesn't want to deal with a staff problem. This is what she said when other staff complained about Margareta's habitually coming in late to work and her refusal to do floor work. I think, too, that this phrase about a communication problem has deeper significance. It means that Jan feels sorry for Frank. It means that Jan will toss back at me anything I might say about him that is negative.

WEDNESDAY, OCTOBER 4: For weeks I've had a recurring fantasy of wrestling a kid to the floor, and while I'm trying to restrain him, Frank is leaning over me, telling me the kid has a phone call and asking if he should let him take it.

Matt Hall told me the other day that Frank is different from the rest of us. The way he put it was: Other staff are constantly watching what's going on; no matter what else we are doing, we are watching the kids. Frank, on the other hand, is looking only inside himself.

I think Matt meant more than that Frank is simply unobservant. Regardless of what Matt meant, what I and other staff need from Frank is for him to do his job so we can do ours. What we need from him is to adhere to the same norms and observe the same rules the rest of us do. But Frank does what he wants. Each staff is allocated "off-the-floor time" each week to do paperwork. Frank frequently goes into the office just before another staff is scheduled to be off the floor, then says he needs this time more than the other staff, or simply refuses to leave the office. When he began doing this, I thought I was the only one he was stealing time from, but other staff are complaining about him too—complaining to each other, that is; nobody is going to say anything to Jan.

THURSDAY, OCTOBER 5: Chatting while we were waiting for PC to start, Clare said she couldn't imagine what she would feel if one of the residents killed himself. This was part of a larger conversation about the graveyard staff who did not log on Darryl last night; Darryl is on SPL III.

I started to tell her about my reaction to the suicide in Whale a couple of years ago, how I would start crying at odd times, though I hadn't even known the girl. And then, as I was talking, I started to cry again. It never goes away, this sorrow. It just hides so you don't know it's there, then shows itself when you least expect it. I think it must be related to that Rhadé boy we lost when I was in Viet Nam.[30] I don't know what else it could be.

Speaking of Darryl, he's been shadowing me like a puppy since Monday, wanting to talk with me about nothing in particular, just trying to win my attention. I don't know how many times I've seen this: after you've taken a kid down, he becomes your best friend. It was Rob Gorey who pointed this out to me. Of course, I didn't take Darryl down, I only pushed him. Hard.

FRIDAY, OCTOBER 6: Talked with my father today, his birthday. He's eighty-four. He sounded old—old. Bonnie called later. His doctor says he's deteriorating fast—Parkinson's Disease. His hands tremble now. When I talked with him, I asked if he'd seen Bonnie lately. He said no. She told me she took him out to lunch yesterday.

TUESDAY, OCTOBER 17: We've had a girl with us for a couple of weeks now on a parole violation. She's a young woman, actually; she's eighteen. Something about her reminds me of Ron Lafitte. I finally asked her if she knows him. Indeed, she does: they're cousins. She says he's doing fine. He's been out of Elk Grove for about a year. He has a good job, he has a child he's devoted to and has become a committed Muslim, going to the mosque on Fridays and Saturdays. She said he had not been shot (Sue Royce told me he had).When her brother was jumped a few months ago, Ron's impulse was to retaliate, but she talked him out of it, telling him to stay away from the gang stuff. He agreed that he should, but also acknowledged the temptation to take revenge. He doesn't want to go to prison again, and is soured on his gang because none of them wrote him when he was in Ash Meadow or Elk Grove. He told her that prison was the best thing that ever happened to him because it removed him from Seattle's Central District and gang life. He's still writing rap, she said. I asked her to give him my regards when she sees him again.

SATURDAY, OCTOBER 28: Got back to Seattle last night. Bonnie called me on Monday to tell me she'd gone to visit Dad, but was unable to wake him and called the paramedics. I flew down on Tuesday. On Thursday he had an MRI, and yesterday we learned he's had several recent strokes. It's the strokes, not the Parkinson's, that has degraded him. The MRI also showed "cerebral atrophy," meaning his brain has deteriorated, both in function and in size.

What I noticed was that, while he sometimes speaks gibberish, he often uses words now in a way that, I think, indicates he's struggling to say exactly what he means. His working vocabulary has actually grown larger.

He's been talking with his mother, who died about forty years ago. He told Bonnie about a dream in which he was a child in a hotel room with his mother. He was hungry and wanted to have Room Service bring him something to eat. His mother said, "All right, but you'll have to get a job to pay for it."

He did not remember this dream or having told it to Bonnie, and when she repeated to him what he'd reported, he said, "You're describing my mother as being witty. I don't think she said anything witty in her entire life."

But what Bonnie had meant to say was that his mother had told him *she* would have to get another job to pay for Room Service. And when Bonnie corrected herself, Dad responded bitterly: "You mean you can't get away from money even after you die?" When I saw him on Friday, he laughed. I don't remember now what he thought was funny, but it was wonderful to see him laugh. There was no malice behind the laughter, no hidden meaning. It was just laughter, as pure as clear water, and he appeared, as a child would, to delight in the laughter itself. It was as though he were laughing for the first time in his life, as though he had only now discovered it.

Just before leaving to return to Seattle, I kissed his forehead and told him I loved him. "I love you, too," he said. Walking out of the room, I turned to wave goodbye. His eyes contained such warmth, and knowledge of the bond that connects us and has since he was young and I was a child, that I was reminded too of that bond, seemingly prehistoric, and I was so glad I had seen him these last few days.

SUNDAY, NOVEMBER 5: I have a thirteen-year-old girl on my caseload now: Norah Joines. She's in on a six-year sentence for attempted murder.

An abusive, neglectful, alcoholic mother. When Norah told her she had been raped by her mom's boyfriend, Mom accused her of lying, of trying to break up her relationship. An old story; I've heard it a thousand times. I still get angry every time I hear it.

A few months later, Norah's mother lost custody of her children because of her drinking. Norah and her sisters went to live with their father. Three years later he had a stroke—he remains in a nursing home—and the girls were placed in separate foster care homes. Norah went to live with Louise

Keyes. Louise was too busy with other children to care for her, and Geraldine, Louise's twenty-three-year-old daughter, "kind of inherited me."

Geraldine, Norah says, smoked weed and drank with her. She taught Norah to drive and, even though Norah was still too young to drive legally, sent her on errands.

About six months ago, Norah was raped by a friend of Geraldine's. He was drunk, Norah said, and she also had been drinking. When Norah told her that her friend had raped her, Geraldine got her brothers to beat the guy up. They didn't beat him up badly enough, Norah said. Now the guy and his homies are looking for Geraldine's brothers.

When Geraldine would get angry with her, she would say to Norah, "I hope somebody kidnaps you and beats you and rapes you and kills you." Norah and Crystal, another girl in the house to whom Geraldine said these things, made a plan to beat Geraldine up. It was not an impulsive act. Crystal testified against Norah in return for a reduced sentence.

TUESDAY, NOVEMBER 7: Matt Hall said that someone at JRA headquarters—he wouldn't tell me who—told him we shouldn't go too far with the ART stuff because if we're too successful we'll wind up putting people out of work. He or she was serious.

THURSDAY, NOVEMBER 9: I went with Matt and Herman Boats to The Rivers to attend a conference on Aggression Replacement Training. We had lunch in the cafeteria, where I saw several kids I'd known at Ash Meadow, including Ryan Helmsley, who was in Wolf when I first transferred there, and Matt Benson, whom I knew at Swan. Both Ryan and Matt are in on new charges.

WEDNESDAY, NOVEMBER 15: Tonight in Alternatives to Violence, as we were watching the tape of the Maury Povich show with Bill Cosby and Deborah Prothrow-Smith talking about gang violence, Paul Grise grew quiet. He usually chatters constantly, to the extent that other kids have threatened to beat him up if he doesn't shut up, but tonight he was withdrawn and said not a word. In the audience on the Povich tape were several young paraplegics who had been shot by gangsters, and a young mother whose son had been murdered by gangsters.

During our discussion after the video Paul described how a homie he had loved was killed by a rival gang. They had caught him on the street and, from bravado, he threw one of their rags on the ground and stomped on it. In turn, they shot him.

Paul organized a drive-by; he knew his homie "would want his set to ride for him." But when it came time to shoot, he didn't, because he didn't want to spend twenty years in prison. And those with him didn't shoot either. And now he feels guilty that he didn't. He said he'd never minded violence—he had, in fact, liked it until his homie got killed. But since then he hasn't liked it.

War is fun until your friends start getting killed, or until you're wounded.

THURSDAY, NOVEMBER 16: Talked with Norah Joines. She asked me if I wasn't afraid of being with kids who had murdered people or done other "terrible things." We were in the staff office, sitting in chairs facing each other as we talked. But she wasn't looking at me. She was staring at her hands in her lap as she asked this question, which must have been very hard for her.

I said no, the nature of a kid's crime didn't frighten me; I didn't believe that because a person had done something terrible, she was always getting ready to do it again.

She said that when the judge sentenced her, he told her he was giving her the longest sentence he could because he wanted to protect society from her as long as possible. She asked me if I thought she was evil.

"No, Norah, you're not evil. The judge was probably angry with you and wanted to hurt you, and he did. I see you as having made a bad mistake, but I don't see you as evil."

She did not say anything more about being evil. Instead, she began talking about Geraldine Keyes, about how Geraldine is a bad person. The implication, of course, is that Norah was justified in assaulting her. Yet I think she truly regrets what she did and, at least sometimes, has a hard time believing she did it. She has flashbacks of the attack, and dreams about it. What she focuses on when she talks about it is the amount of blood that came from Geraldine: she hadn't expected there to be so much of it. She probably hadn't thought about blood at all before she attacked her.

Last week I asked her to write a short autobiography; that is, to answer questions about her life that I listed on a sheet of paper. She hasn't turned it in yet. I asked her tonight if she was having a tough time with some of the questions. She said she was. I told her to skip the questions that are hard for her and do the others.

She said she didn't like to think about her life, and the questions make her think about things she wants to forget. Then she said that after her mom's boyfriend raped her, she thought about killing herself with her father's gun—she had gone to live with him by then—because she was so afraid her attacker would get out of prison and come after her. He had threatened to kill her if she told anyone what he did to her.

I said that I thought she was very angry with her mother, that while she may care for her mom—she told me that her mother is always asking if she loves her, but the most Norah can say is "I care about you"—she was also angry with her for having allowed her to be raped and then for having accused her of lying about it. I said, too, that her assaulting Geraldine was done out of anger at Geraldine, yes, but also out of anger at her mother, that this anger hadn't gone away.

Norah didn't say anything. Her features began to puff up, but she didn't allow herself to cry. She was in county detention for six months before she came to us and she cried there every day, she told me once.

Finally she said that Geraldine was really mean. She said Geraldine once told her to take the car to get some cigarettes, then called the police to report her car stolen. Norah didn't know why Geraldine did this—her explanation was that Geraldine is cruel—but she was arrested and spent the night in detention. Geraldine committed other betrayals too, and about a year ago Norah tried to kill herself by overdosing on Valium because she felt so trapped.

She likes to read—mythology and poetry. I'll get her some books.

SUNDAY, NOVEMBER 19: Gave Norah an anthology of poetry and a copy of Judith Roche's *Myrrh*. The latter will be too advanced for her, I imagine. Still, she may get something from it.

TUESDAY, DECEMBER 19: I was thinking about Lyle Munson today as I drove to work. What most irritates me about him is his "junior staffing," his insistence that his peers follow procedure as he understands it: setting up the kitchen counter to serve meals in a particular way, doing what your job description calls for—e.g., mudroom, kitchen, dining room details—neither more nor less. His drive to control the activities of other people, staff as well as peers, reflects what he has learned by watching staff. We are his models. We've raised him. He's been in and out of Ash Meadow for four years; he came here when he was ten. He's our creation. Looking at him, we see our-selves, although with some distortion, I hope.

I said something like this at the psych meeting this morning. Dr. Williams said I was being too hard on myself.

WEDNESDAY, DECEMBER 20: Norah has been dreaming about her father. She dreams that he is dying and that she won't be able to see him again. She says if he dies, she'll want to die too; he's the only person who has "been there for me." Yet he's been in a nursing home for years.

She tells me she's been trying to write about her life, but when she gets to the part about being taken away from her mother "and all the other things," she can't write about them. She can't write about herself beyond the time "when everything went bad."

She believes people—her mother, her sisters—have left her because she's been bad. She knows she's being unreasonably hard on herself, but she can't help it. On the surface she appears to be a cheerful little girl—she is small, not much over five feet, and gives the impression of vulnerability. But beneath the cheery facade lies depression. She says she cries in bed at night, from sadness and fear of losing her father.

THURSDAY, DECEMBER 21: I've probably written this before, but coming out of Ash Meadow—that is, returning to the outside world after work and on weekends—is like returning to the United States from Viet Nam in the Sixties. Everybody has an opinion, nobody who has not been there knows what he is talking about, and those who were there but were not in the field—in the Ash Meadow context, the administrators—are just as ignorant.

SUNDAY, DECEMBER 24: I have not been able to write about this until now. (Somewhere in this journal I have written that same line. Yes, on August 20, this year, when I talked about trying to get Dad to a hospital.) A month ago, Nader, Ash Meadow's superintendent, assured Jan and me that after Norah had spent forty-five days in maximum security, she would be transferred to another cottage, provided her behavior remained acceptable.

She was eligible to be transferred almost two weeks ago. Serpent had a bed for her and was ready to receive her. All they, and we, needed was for the administrators to sign off. But they did not, and they did not respond to our inquiries about their delay. Last Tuesday, Jan emailed Nader, reminding him that he told us Norah would be moved, and informing him that Serpent had agreed to the move.

Finally, on Wednesday, he emailed her back to say that the administrators had decided that, because of the severity of her crime and the length of her sentence, Norah will spend at least the next five to six months in Wolf. There was no mention of his earlier promise to move her and no mention of the Ash Meadow regulation that provides for transfer after forty-five days in maximum security. Prior to getting his email, Jan and I polled the administrators—all but Celia Barney, who has never worked in or overseen a cottage, but has made her career by pushing paper—and all said they had no objection to Norah's transferring.

Norah has lost only one behavior point in the nearly two months she has been with us—other kids lose, on average, two points per week. The point she lost was one I took from her to see how she would react. I don't remember now what excuse I used to take it, but it was for something that was in a gray area: I could as easily have let it go as take it.

One morning Norah went into the mudroom and found the outside door wide open. Apparently the graveyard staff had gone out to empty the trash and had not closed the door when he returned. Norah stepped back into the living room, closed the inside door behind her and stood in front of it so no one could go in. She waited there until she could get Bernie's attention, and he went and locked the outer door. Another kid may have run—there's no fence around the campus. We have the example of Casey Fairchild running from this cottage when he found a door unlocked. But Norah doesn't want any more trouble in her life.

About Celia Barney: another administrator inadvertently (or not) let it drop to Jan and me that Celia had objected to transferring Norah. Her reason: Norah had lost a point some weeks earlier. Her real reason: I can only guess that something about Norah's offense resonates with something in Celia's past. Celia may not even be aware of it; it doesn't matter. Of course, this other administrator, for his own purposes, could have lied to us. But I don't think he has the imagination to concoct a story, no matter how simple.

I broke the news to Norah on Thursday. Jan wanted to get Celia down here and coerce her into telling Norah, but I believed it would be better for Norah if I told her. I thought about telling her on Wednesday evening after Jan showed me Nader's email, but Norah has trouble sleeping, and I did not want her to take this to bed with her.

When I came in on Thursday afternoon, I called her into Jan's office—Frank was at the computer in the other office—and told her. She wears the sleeves of her sweat shirt pulled down over her palms; she immediately brought her sleeved wrists to her eyes so I couldn't see her face. She asked why. She said they had told her she'd be moving on Friday; then, if not on Friday, for sure the following Monday or Tuesday; then, when those days had passed, for sure later in the week.

All of this is true, but it was I, not "they," who told her. And I had told her because Nader had assured Jan and me that this would happen, and both Jan and I believed him. After all, he's the superintendent. I had not known that he does not recognize an obligation to honor his word. This is an old story, of course: accepting the assurance of someone in authority only to have him betray you. It's especially hateful when you are the one played for a fool, and worse when you have persuaded someone with no recourse and no ability to defend herself to have faith, only to have her trust betrayed, too.

"Why are they doing this to me, Jerry?" Norah asked.

I said I didn't know, but it didn't have anything to do with her personally—

"Obviously it does."

—but the administrators had their own reasons which they did not confide to me.

She began crying, hard, almost convulsively, the sobs taking over her body. It was terrible. I don't think I've ever had a worse experience at Ash Meadow. Jan started to come into the office but turned and left without speaking.

Norah asked if they had ever done this to anyone else. I told her no, no Ash Meadow resident has ever been kept in maximum security for such a long period. I told her again that I had no explanation for why they were doing this.

She cried. "I've worked so hard. I've done everything they wanted me to do. Why won't they let me go?"

"I don't know, Norah."

We sat together until she stopped crying. When I was certain she had regained some control over herself (or was simply too exhausted to cry any more), I told her I was going to have to put her in her room—it was time for PC. Leaving the office, I saw the rest of the staff sitting in the living room, waiting to go in. After talking with Norah for a moment at the door to her room, reassuring myself that she would manage all right for the next couple of hours, I returned to the office. Jan said again that we should have made Celia tell Norah.

"No. It had to be me."

Jan said that when she came into the office and saw Norah like that, she could think only of getting out. If she had stayed, she would have broken down herself.

2001

TUESDAY, JANUARY 2: Last night Lyle Munson was sent to a quiet room in another cottage for going off in his room and trying to incite other kids to go off. This morning, after he was returned and had taken a shower, he wanted to know who had stripped his room.

We had done this as punishment: he has been going off regularly and swearing at staff. He has targeted Frank particularly, ignoring his instructions, maddogging him, essentially punking him, as the kids say. By stripping his room, we were reminding him that we, not he, control the cottage.

I told him "staff" had stripped his room. He demanded to know who. He had walked into the office, where I was preparing to give out the morning meds.

I told him to get out of the office.

He told me not to shout at him.

I told him again to get out of the office.

He told me again not to shout at him.

We went back and forth like this as I moved toward him, sheparding him out.

He picked up the trash can and threw it into the living room, then threw his towel at me. Bernie bounded across the living room and grabbed Lyle by the arm and walked him to his room, Lyle yelling the while that he was going to punch me in the mouth the next time I shouted at him. He's been refusing his Thorazine. (Again I was surprised by how fast Bernie moves.)

An hour later I went to the psych team meeting where I mentioned what happened. Dr. Williams said he was sorry Lyle hit me with a towel—he laughed here—but, in his experience, Lyle acts out when he feels unloved.

I couldn't believe Williams said this. I couldn't believe he could be so banal. The child feels unloved. I told Williams that the towel incident in itself means little, but it does indicate an escalation in what Lyle is willing to do. He had not assaulted staff before, even symbolically.

Williams shrugged his shoulders as if to say he was no longer interested, and we went on to talk about another kid.

When I got back to the cottage I told Dick and Bernie what Williams said. We had one of the great laughs of the new century. Poor baby. He takes a sledge hammer to his mother's car because he's unloved, then does the same thing to his grandmother's car. Well, Williams is probably right, but so what.

After lunch Lyle threatened me again, telling me he was going to break my glasses. Bernie took him to our quiet room.

Later this afternoon Lyle went back to taking his Thorazine.

TUESDAY, JANUARY 9: I have a new kid on my caseload: Davis Peters. He's Nez Perce, grew up in Idaho. We got him from Ram, where he went off and destroyed most of his room. We've already noticed that he stays to himself rather than mixes with other kids. Jim Herbold says Davis did the same thing at Ram. He preferred to associate with gang kids, but there weren't that many in Ram, so he'd often just stay in his room.

Davis told me he has trouble sleeping. I called the health center and asked for a med to help him sleep.

SUNDAY, JANUARY 14: Anticipated the worst today—on Thursday we learned we would be getting Casey Fairchild back from Dolphin as well as keeping Lyle Munson, whom we had hoped to exchange for Casey—but it turned out to be a good shift. Both kids were fairly undemanding. When you're prepared for the worst, it doesn't happen. All that anxiety goes for nothing. But when you don't anticipate it, everything turns to shit.

THURSDAY, JANUARY 18: Davis Peters. Offenses include residential burglary, car theft, disorderly conduct and malicious mischief. Tests at third- and fourth-grade levels in math and spelling, respectively; in reading, at third-grade level. Began drinking at age eleven or twelve, began using crank and cocaine at the same age. He's been smoking marijuana since he was nine. He's thirteen now.

He doesn't know his biological father. Mom's boyfriend at the time of Davis' birth calls himself Davis' father, and Davis also refers to him as his dad.

Mom and stepdad are heavy drinkers. When Davis was three, his aunt filed a CPS report alleging that Davis' mother was beating him. Mom admitted slapping and yelling at him. Within a year after that there were four more CPS reports alluding to mom's drinking and neglect.

When Davis was eight he went to live with his aunt, but returned to his mother and stepfather. Both Davis and his aunt say his stepdad made him live alone in a shed behind the house. When he was nine he was placed in foster care, and at ten he went back to his mom and stepdad.

Here in Wolf he says he does not like any of the other residents. In treatment groups, at recreation, in one-on-one counseling sessions, he will ask to be locked in his room or will suddenly get up and go to his room without asking permission. Staff believe he is trying to avoid acting out on the floor. In his room he has gone off several times in the ten days he has been here.

SUNDAY, JANUARY 21: This evening I was giving meds while James and Frank were managing the floor—getting kids out of their rooms to do their routines, get their clean jumpsuits off the laundry table, toss their dirty ones into bins, etc. About eight-fifteen I heard something unusual—a raised voice, something—and I came out of the office. Lyle Munson had come out of the zone, walked past Frank, and was seating himself on the brick platform where the fireplace used to be. I had told Frank earlier not to allow Lyle past the edge of the zone because, unless we wanted to handle him, he was a pain to get back into his room. Now Frank was telling him to go back to his room and Lyle wasn't budging. James was at the mouth of Zone 2, watching; Norah was folding clothes at the laundry table; a kid was at the drinking fountain; one or two others were on the floor. It was obvious that Lyle was not going to go to his room unassisted.

I cleared the floor. James went into Zone 3 to lock it down. Frank looked at me, then back at Lyle, and headed for Zone 2. I yelled at him to come back on the floor. He stopped at the edge of the zone, looked at Lyle again—What was on his face? He wasn't thinking, but responding to something visceral. His eyes were crazy—and disappeared into the zone, leaving me alone with Lyle.

Lyle, fortunately, was content to sit tight. James came out of Zone 3, then Frank came out of Zone 2. I called Security to take Lyle to our quiet room. Lyle waited for Security to arrive, then did as they told him.

This episode is especially troubling because I had drilled Frank and James repeatedly on what to do on a clear-the-floor: one staff locks kids in, two stay with the kid. James did all right: he saw two staff on the floor and went to lock the kids in. But Frank did exactly what he should not have: he ran, leaving me alone with the kid. (The craziness in Frank's eyes, I believe, was fear, uncontrolled fear.)

All of this is bad, too, because last Friday Lyle picked a pair of scissors up from the kitchen counter where the art teacher had set them and raised them as though to stab James. James and Charlie took him down, and James pried the scissors out of his hand. A week earlier he tried to hit Gil, our newest staff, with a flashlight he snatched from the staff office when Gil was giving meds.

So we know Lyle is dangerous and Frank is worthless in a jam. What to do? If I go to Jan, she will tell me again that I have a problem communicating with Frank. But I'd be remiss in my obligation to staff as a whole if I don't.

I confronted Frank after Security left, telling him he had done precisely what I had drilled him not to do. He didn't say anything. He just grew red.

TUESDAY, JANUARY 23: I told the psych team that Lyle had threatened staff with a scissors. Williams wasn't there. I wish he had been. I had intended to say "Lyle must not be feeling loved" to needle him about his comment three weeks ago that Lyle acts out when he's feeling unloved.

WEDNESDAY, JANUARY 24: I did not tell Jan that Frank ran away. She was so upset Monday that the administration had foisted Casey Fairchild off on us that I didn't want to say anything that would trouble her more.

The original plan was that we would house Casey until we could transfer him to Elk Grove. Nader told Jan he would do everything he could to get Casey out of Ash Meadow as soon as possible. (The Rivers is not a possibility for him. He's too small to defend himself against adult-sized kids.) This week Elk Grove said no. They have two very dangerous kids in maximum security now: Justin Barrows, whom we knew here,[31] and a kid I hadn't heard of. Justin beat up a female staff there and will go to trial soon. They anticipate transferring him in March. Then, Elk Grove says, we can talk about Casey again.

Casey, the psychiatrists say, is retarded and has Asperger's Syndrome. He belongs in Dolphin. But he does not respond to DBT, and DBT is all they do there.[32] So the administration gave him to us. It's a real screw job and everybody knows it. But why Jan, or anybody else, would believe anything

Nader says is beyond me. By trusting him, they set themselves up for their own betrayal.

So, as I said, I did not talk to Jan about Frank. But on Monday night Lyle came out of the zone again, again walked past Frank, and again sat down on the fireplace platform. I cleared the floor, James locked the kids down, and Frank *did not* leave the floor, but waited with me and Lyle for Security to arrive. Maybe he's learning. I suspect he feels he has to make up for Sunday night, which is good.

Tonight Layton and I moved Lyle into the quiet room instead of allowing him to do his routine. His behavior had been bad enough to justify it. This may be a model for dealing with his disruptiveness in the evening—pre-empt him.

I told Layton that Frank ran off the floor last Sunday.

THURSDAY, JANUARY 25: Wolf feels now like a town under siege. We respond to assaults by kids against other kids, try to limit their opportunities for assault by keeping apart the most violent of them, and try to anticipate the worst case, which would be Lyle and Casey going off at the same time, either on the floor or at school. (Oddly, this has not happened. I've noticed that when one kid goes off, whether it's Lyle, Casey, Davis or someone else, the others become quiet. It's as though they comprise a single organism that can permit only one of its parts to go off on a given occasion. The exception occurs when one kid incites others, or when several conspire together.)

Our main disadvantage is that the initiative lies with the kids. They decide when to assault someone; we can only respond to their decision. We've tried to recapture the initiative by suspending privileges and activities during which residents interact. This has not worked: the number of incidents occurring has remained the same. We can lock down entirely, but Nader probably wouldn't authorize it, and, frankly, several of us staff wouldn't like it, as it would punish the well-behaved along with those who are misbehaving. Another possibility would be to return privileges to those kids who have earned them. Maybe this would encourage some of the others to return to the straight and narrow.

FRIDAY, JANUARY 26: Last night Norah and I talked again about the length of time she has to spend in Wolf. She said she is getting depressed, but is trying not to. She knows the administration has singled her out for harsh treatment. She's asked me before if any other resident has ever been treated this way. Now she asked me again, and I told her again: No, none.

"Why are they doing this to me?" she asked.

The only explanation I can offer is the one Nader provided—"because of the nature of her crime and the length of her sentence"—but, when you consider that kids who are in for worse crimes and who have even longer sentences have not had to spend half a year in maximum security, this only reinforces the idea that she has been singled out. All I can say honestly is, "I don't know."

She believes she'll never be happy, that whenever something happens to make her happy, something else will happen to take her happiness away. "I'm always victimized," she said. But I've watched her handle her peers, verbally and by body language, and she's very adept at avoiding trouble. She's learned a lot from living with her mother, and from living with Geraldine. And from the street.

I asked her if she had ever assaulted anyone besides Geraldine. She said yes, and described a couple of incidents involving gang retaliation that she was involved in. She sees the victim of retaliation as deserving what he gets. Yet, while her attack on Geraldine could be considered an act of revenge, and while she despises Geraldine, Norah expresses genuine remorse—I and other staff are convinced it is genuine—for having beaten her.

SUNDAY, JANUARY 28: I called in sick today. I'm emotionally exhausted and the thought of working with Frank tonight is more than I can stomach.

WEDNESDAY, JANUARY 31: Jan said that Nader told her—verbally, not in writing—that after Norah has spent five or six months in Wolf, Wolf staff may determine her eligibility to be transferred to another cottage. This is a change in that he had said earlier that Norah would have to stay in Wolf for five to six months in addition to the two months she had already been with us.

Jan sent him an email telling him what she understood him to say. This was an effort to get a written commitment from him. He hasn't responded, of course.

This morning, before I came in, Norah was so depressed that she did not go to school. She got up, did her mudroom chores, and returned to her room. In the evening I talked with her about life in general, joked with her about some of the other kids, then told her what Nader said, but cautioned her not to count on anything.

"I know better than to count on anything. I've learned my lesson," she said.

As I was locking her in her room after our talk, she said, "I love you." I pretended I hadn't heard.

I hope I haven't made a mistake by encouraging her to hope again. But she's been so unhappy—I've been afraid for her.

THURSDAY, FEBRUARY 1: Casey Fairchild attempted to escape this morning. Frank was taking him to a doctor's appointment off campus when Casey, shackled but not handcuffed—Why hadn't Frank handcuffed him? Who knows. Maybe even Frank doesn't know—began kicking the side of the van, finally kicking one of the windows out. Frank pulled over to the side of the road, got out and pushed Casey back inside as he tried to climb out through the broken window. A motorist stopped and asked if he could help and Frank asked him to call the police. Frank had a cell phone on him but didn't think to use it. He said the police arrived in about a minute and a half.

He says now that he learned a lot. He says he realizes that if Casey had had a knife or a gun, Casey could have killed him. Well, I suppose so, if Casey had had a knife or a gun.

What went wrong, aside from Frank's judgment?

It should not have fallen on us to take the kid to an off-campus appointment. That's Security's job. They were short-handed, but assigning one of our staff to be a driver left us short-handed.

The van should have had its own cell phone, or a radio could have been signed out from Security. Even if Frank would not have thought to use it, another driver would have.

There should be no loose tools in the back of the van, i.e., a jack, as there was this time. (Wait: Frank didn't handcuff Casey, and also didn't check the van for potential weapons? No, worse yet: Frank didn't cuff Casey, and did check the van, and did see the jack lying out in plain sight, and did leave it there.)

What set Casey off in the first place? Casey says Frank had country-and-western on the radio and refused to change the station. Frank says he had a country-and-western station on and wanted to listen to the music.

Anyway, Frank is a hero now for having survived an attempted escape while alone with the would-be escaper. Jan put him in for some sort of special recognition. The rest of us, and Security staff, shake our heads and laugh.

THURSDAY, FEBRUARY 8: One of the kids told me he thinks it's cool the way I cut my hair really short on top but let it grow on the sides. He said he's going to do that when he gets out.

I told him that I am bald. He said he still likes it. He was serious.

FRIDAY, FEBRUARY 9: I asked Norah yesterday where, on average, she would place herself on a scale ranging from one to ten, one being least angry. "Eight and a half," she said. "Sometimes six."

I was stunned. No other kid has ever said more than six unless they were psyched to fight. But she was adamant. "I hate the world because it's treated me so bad."

She said she had money—her father's, that is—when she was younger. He was rich, and when she had money she associated with other girls who had money and ignored the girls who did not have it. She adopted a kind of willfully silly, affected style of speech and gesture she had learned from older girls and from television. (She demonstrated it for me.) She lost all that when her father had his stroke, and she went to live with Geraldine and Louise and was no longer rich.

She had been a pretty, intelligent, upper-middle-class little girl whose mother was an alcoholic, abusive and neglectful, whose mother's boyfriend raped her, and whose father appears to have been a thoroughly decent man. If fate were a little less twisted, she might have been born to a different mother and been, if not happy, then certainly less unhappy than she's become.

SATURDAY, FEBRUARY 10: Still thinking about my conversation with Norah Thursday night. She said that at one point in her life she lost her voice and had to go to counseling to learn how to talk again. She listened to tapes that taught her pronunciation.

I said I'd wondered how she had acquired such a large vocabulary and such clear enunciation.

"It was the tapes. I listened to them for years."

I'm guessing that this must have been after she was raped by her mother's boyfriend. He had threatened to kill her if she told, and when she did tell, her mother accused her of lying.

THURSDAY, FEBRUARY 15: I talked with Norah tonight. We had nothing special to talk about, and just joked about boys and gossiped about other residents. That is, she gossiped; I listened.

She said she had a dream in which she assaulted Daniel Lyons, one of the boys in the cottage, while Jan and I laughed. At one point during the fight, Daniel wrapped his arm around her beneath her breasts, and I yelled at him to watch where he put his hands. He apologized and then he and Norah resumed fighting, quitting only when they were tired. She wasn't upset by the dream. I know that she and Daniel are attracted to each other.

She told me her feelings about staff. She likes Layton, Dick, Clare, and me, but doesn't trust some of the others. She thinks Jan and Bernie are all right, but doesn't feel close to them. She doesn't like James or Gil or Frank, James because he jokes too much at kids' expense, Gil because he's mean, and Frank because he doesn't know what he's doing.

She's felt depressed and irritable most of the week without knowing why. She said she often doesn't know what she is feeling or thinking until long after she has stopped feeling particular emotions or thinking particular thoughts. But people want to know what she is thinking or what she is feeling, and when she says "Nothing," they accuse her of trying to hide something.

She thought she might be feeling depressed because she's starting her period and she often gets severe cramps just prior, and is "snappish." Her boyfriend on the outs knew to stay away from her when her period was starting. But she thought also that she may have been especially depressed this week because Layton has been gone. (I have to say that when she said that, I felt jealous.) She told me not to go away for a week like Layton has, particularly if he is gone too.

She's been skipping meals, she said, because the food is so rich in calories and she's afraid of getting fat. (I'm going to have to start monitoring her food consumption. If anything, she's too thin now.)

SUNDAY, FEBRUARY 18: Davis Peters and I went over his misdeeds since he's been in Wolf. I told him he'll be on Tables until later in the week for having refused to go to his room, forcing staff to clear the floor. I told him he needs to gain control over himself.

He said he realizes he's not ready to leave Wolf.

I asked him why he wants to be on the floor now. The first few weeks he was here he preferred to be in his room when the other kids were out.

He said he's comfortable with the other kids now that he knows them better. He said it takes him a long time to get to trust someone.

Then he said that some time before he came to Ash Meadow his stepbrother was murdered, shot to death at a party. After he told me this, he gave a sigh.

I asked why he made that sound.

He said he felt better, having said it. The sigh was the release. After Gus died, Sean, Davis' stepfather, saw an eagle circle their house. Sean and Davis felt that the eagle was taking Gus to heaven. Davis thought that was good.

Then, abruptly, he said it's hard for him to express his feelings against whites, because whites have treated his family so badly. He said sometimes his feelings build up inside him and then they explode and get him in trouble.

I said he could punch his mattress instead of his wall or his door when he's angry, and staff will not punish him.

He agreed to try this.

I said I would make up a sign to tape to his door, saying:

—If I do this, what will happen?

—Do I want this to happen?

—If I don't want it to happen, what can I do instead?

Davis agreed to consider these questions when he's thinking about doing something wrong, and said he would try not to tear the sign off his door when he gets angry.

TUESDAY, FEBRUARY 20: I talked about Norah at the psych meeting today for the first time. Among those present were Dr. Williams and Don Martino. I mentioned her depression and said that after she, and the cottage, had been led to believe she would be transferred last December, Nader changed his mind. This had the effect of throwing her into a sudden and, at least for staff, frightening depression.

I was looking at Martino as I said this. He shifted his eyes so as not to look at me and I remembered that this was what he did at Stan MacEvoy's retirement party when Stan alluded to the heart attack he'd had after his meeting with him.

I had expected Martino to challenge me, but it was Williams who stopped me. He asked me the reason for the psychiatric referral. I said again that it was for Norah's depression. Then he said she had probably been kept in Wolf owing to the severity of her crime.

I said Norah had met Ash Meadow's requirements to be transferred out of maximum security. She was eligible for transfer in December. By keeping her in max, the administration had violated its own regulations. Having said this, I stood up and walked out of the room.

THURSDAY, FEBRUARY 22: I asked Norah about her depression. It hasn't been as bad as it was, though she would like something to help her sleep. The health center has not responded to my requests for Benadryl for her.

She asked if I thought she would ever leave Wolf. I said I hadn't heard anything to indicate she wouldn't.

MONDAY, FEBRUARY 26: After I got to work, I hadn't even taken my coat off when Dick buttonholed me. He was laughing and choking on his words at the same time as he told me what happened. Casey escaped again, this time from Central Isolation. He kicked his cell door off its hinges; it's a steel door weighing around three hundred pounds. Casey said it was poorly made and all he had to do was touch it and it fell down.

Security, on a vehicular patrol, found him in the parking lot near the Maintenance shops, looking for a car to steal. (The easiest would have been the Suburban he kicked almost to death a few weeks ago: it has no glass in its side windows.) Security had no idea he had escaped, which is interesting: Central Isolation is in the same building as the Health Center and is supposed to be monitored, by TV camera, by the nurses. Yet apparently no one noticed the door lying in the corridor or heard the sound it made when it fell. If a door falls in the health center and no one hears it, has it really fallen?

WEDNESDAY, FEBRUARY 28: Earthquake today. Radio says it was 6.2 or 6.4, depending on which station you're listening to.

I was walking through an alley on my way to the post office in the University District, and had just stepped into a narrow space between a stopped van and the rear steps of a church when the truck began to rock from side to side. For a moment I thought the driver was playing some kind of game with his clutch and brakes, but then the ground began to roll under me. I felt as though I were on a boat again.

A group of people had gathered in the alley behind the Vietnamese restaurant. One of the men pointed at the high-tension lines directly above them, but nobody moved.

People were going back into the post office when I got there. Lots of talk and edgy laughter about their initial reactions to the quake. I went to University Book Store afterward. Apparently not everyone had gone outside when they felt it. The speaker system announced after I was there for a few minutes that, should there be another quake, the store would be evacuated. The voice was peevish.

THURSDAY, MARCH 1: Suicide at Peacock Cottage tonight. She's still alive, but not expected to pull through. Charity Miles. Thank God I didn't know her.

After Administration called to tell us, we locked all the kids down according to procedure. Three hours later, Don Martino and Fernanda Lyons (no relation to Daniel), one of the cottage directors—apparently they are Ash Meadow's Crisis Response Team—came in to explain to the kids why they'd been locked down. We got the kids out of their rooms and had them sit in the living room. Except for Ginny Bell, they didn't seem too upset. But you can't tell. They'll be thinking about it for weeks, or longer. Lyle Munson wanted to know how the girl had done it. Fernanda, who was doing the explaining, put him off.

Ginny knew Charity from when they were in detention together. She started shaking and crying and asked to go to her room. Martino said Dick Peck was on campus and I got hold of him by radio and asked him to come in to talk with Ginny. I don't know how close Ginny was to her, but she was crying hard when she was talking to Dick.

This is Ash Meadow's second suicide in three years, our third in ten years. How am I doing? I seem not to feel anything. We'll see.

SUNDAY, MARCH 4: Charity Miles did not regain consciousness. Her family authorized the hospital to pull the plug yesterday.

The kids talk more about the earthquake than the suicide, perhaps because they feel more threatened by the possibility of another earthquake. Or perhaps they are more threatened by the suicide.

TUESDAY, MARCH 6: I talked about Davis Peters at the psych meeting this morning and told him so afterward. He seemed pleased that someone outside the cottage is taking an interest in him.

I told his psychiatrist that Davis adjusts to change with more than usual difficulty. Dr. Williams said we—i.e., Wolf staff—should be careful where we transfer him. As though we have a choice.

By and large, Davis has shown improvement. He's made a few friends among the more marginal and the gang-involved kids. He has suppressed his anti-white feelings, but lets them show when he talks with me alone.

Norah is worried about her father. She's left messages on his answering machine, but he hasn't returned her calls. He's seventy-six years old and has not been in good health.

THURSDAY, MARCH 8: I attended a Quality Assurance meeting for ART in Olympia yesterday. Several of the other attendees asked how staff at Ash Meadow are doing—that is, relative to the suicide. Amanda, who chairs these meetings, said the suicide was three years to the day since our last one. I hadn't thought about it, and I don't know that it has any significance, but she's right.

I seem not to feel anything about it. But I don't believe it. Sooner or later I'll find myself bawling, and it will be a complete surprise to me until I remember what happened. I'm beginning to know myself.

FRIDAY, MARCH 9: I heard frogs last night for the first time this year. I guess spring has arrived.

I haven't seen a raccoon in a year and a half or longer. I mentioned this to one of the maintenance guys a couple of weeks ago. "They got rid of some of them," he said, but others died from some disease that affects only raccoons. Sounds suspicious to me. I wonder if the disease was poison. And how did "they" get rid of the others?

SUNDAY, MARCH 11: Norah has been withdrawn for the past few days. She says that every few months she feels she has to do something bad in order to release the anger that builds up in her. She's mentioned this to me before. Here at Ash Meadow she's handled this feeling by pulling into herself and sometimes crying. She says her judgment is affected at times like these so that she stops caring about the consequences of what she does. She's done things she's ashamed of, she says, and which she will never tell anyone about.

I asked if her assaulting Geraldine happened when she felt like this. She didn't know.

She says she stopped trusting people or regarding them with anything but contempt when she was small.

I asked if anything in particular had caused her to re-evaluate her life, as apparently she's been doing. Nothing she knew of, she said. She's just been doing it.

I told her I'd be on vacation for the next four days. She accepted this.

MONDAY, MARCH 26: This morning Charlie took Lyle Munson down when he tried to push past him to get out of the zone; Lyle apparently confused Charlie with Frank. Tonight I took him down.

He was out for his routine and started bad-mouthing James, calling him a turd. Then he threw a pencil at Frank, grazing the top of his head. (Frank had his head down, reading the log instead of helping James and me with routines. Serves him right.) He had returned to his zone to go to the head and Frank went over to chastise him for throwing the pencil. Lyle turned and walked around him while Frank was talking and came out of the zone, as he's done many times to indicate his contempt for Frank.

He headed for the office but I got in front of him, and then he went toward the kitchen, but I blocked him there too. Finally James and I boxed him in, and he sat down on the fireplace platform and dared us to call Security. I told Frank to call. Lyle said something to me—I don't recall now what he said—and he started jabbing his finger at me, and I grabbed his arm. He pulled away and I grabbed his leg and pulled him off the bricks, then twisted his leg so that he rolled over on his belly and then James held his shoulders to the floor until Security arrived and took him to Central Isolation. While all of this was going on, I was telling Frank over and over to lock the other kids in. He was just standing off to the side, watching the action.

Ordinarily I feel sorry for a kid after taking him down, but this time I felt good. I was still angry afterward, but I felt good.

TUESDAY, MARCH 27: Jan told me the administrators would discuss Norah's transfer at their April fourth meeting. I haven't said anything to Norah.

WEDNESDAY, MARCH 28: Rough morning. Paul Grise had to be taken down, and apparently somebody else. For some reason, the latter incident wasn't logged, but Bernie mentioned it to me.

This afternoon Bernie thought he might be having a heart attack. He had pain over his heart and in his shoulder. He asked me if I've ever had one. I haven't, but Matt Hall has. Matt and I were getting ready to go down to the classroom for ART. He said that chest pain is one of the symptoms. Bernie said then that he was all right. He didn't seem to have any other symptoms. He's about thirty.

I think I'd be dead by now if I didn't run regularly. It's as if a steady drip of adrenalin starts into my blood from the moment I come through the doorway into the cottage to begin my shift. Sometimes when it rushes and I can't do anything to relieve it—that is, when I prepare myself to take a kid down, but then he does not require it—the sensation is almost unbearable. My hands and arms go numb, my skin tingles, and the pressure in my chest feels as though a basketball has inflated inside it. What I want to do is run at someone, but I don't permit myself to do it. But I did it once, a couple of days ago, with Lyle Munson.

Speaking of whom. He was on edge all day today. Jan stayed late and when Lyle came out to do his routine and get his snack she agreed to talk with him. When he left her office he turned suddenly and threw his pear against her office window, then sat down on a chair in the living room. I was the only male staff on duty, and neither Jan nor Clare are very large. I stood in front of him so he couldn't get out of his chair and I hit my body alarm. Security arrived and put him in our quiet room. Apparently what set him off was Jan's telling him that she was disappointed in the way he had been behaving lately.

THURSDAY, MARCH 29: Bernie seems to be okay today. He looks healthy, as usual.

Dick told us at PC that he discovered yesterday that Casey had dug through his wall into Paul Grise's room using a toothbrush and some plastic spoons Paul had given him. Both kids were moved to Central Isolation until their common wall could be repaired. They were returned this morning, Paul going into Room 15 instead of 2.

Casey dug an inch into the newly plastered wall with another toothbrush before being found out again. Again we moved him to Central Isolation. An amazing child. There isn't a building on this campus that can hold him. But how did he get a second toothbrush in his room? I'll bet Frank gave it to him this morning to replace the one he'd ruined, then forgot to get it back after Casey brushed his teeth. That, or he's afraid of Casey and decided not to try to get it back.

FRIDAY, MARCH 30: Norah said something interesting last night. She said Daniel Lyons is really nice to girls unless Lyle is around. If Lyle is there, Daniel will belittle girls. Daniel, by the way, was transferred to Ram yesterday. Norah said she already misses him. He made her laugh.

She told me that boys with whom she's had relationships have sometimes hit her. I remembered that when my daughter was Norah's age, she said once, after having seen a boy hit a girl, "Maybe she deserved it," and I asked Norah now if she thought she deserved to be hit. She said she usually did because she got mouthy with them and then they would hit her.

I asked who had the right to decide that she deserved to be hit. After some waffling, she said she didn't know. Anyway, she said, if her boyfriends hit her, she would hit them back. She wouldn't let anyone get away with hitting her.

If I were married I'd look into the possibility of adopting her. She's become as important to me as Tommy Whitacre was. Maybe, as with Tommy, I sense her despair and want to fix it. Knowing I can't, I still want to.

So this is why I'm here: to try to fix kids' despair. Knowing I must fail, but trying anyway. What a fucking brave guy I am. But hell, maybe I win sometimes, even if I don't know when or with whom.

SATURDAY, MARCH 31: Bonnie called at six-thirty this morning. Dad died at one-fifteen last night. After the call, I felt relief—for him. His body had become such a burden to him: Parkinson's Disease, diabetes, gangrene, urinary tract infection, calcification and atrophy of his brain.

When I saw him a couple of weeks ago, he didn't wake up. I saw him twice and both times he slept through my visit. I don't think he knew I was there, but who knows.

SUNDAY, APRIL 8: Returned from California—my father's funeral. Went over his accounts with Bonnie while I was down there. Notified his insurer that he'd died. Called in sick for today. I'm not sick, just need some time to myself.

I didn't start feeling anything about him until I was on the airplane back to Seattle. Then sadness. I've been thinking about my mother too. She died twelve years ago. Twelve years and three months.

MONDAY, APRIL 9: Waiting for me at work was an email Jan had forwarded from Marty Biggs, who had sent it to her. He's our new administrator, replacing Kathleen Foreman, who resigned a couple of months ago. The email says the "Administrators"—note the upper case A in Administrators; Marty wrote it that way—have approved the transfer of Norah Joines out of Wolf Cottage, to happen on April twenty-fourth. The email says, too: "Thank you for the good work and of course the willingness of Norah to invest in herself, we were able to accomplish this request [sic]."

Fuck you, Administrators. In the upper case. Fuck you, too, for taking credit—the "we"—where none was due. And fuck you most of all for your duplicity.

Norah already knows. Layton told her. You can see that she's happy, but also that she's afraid to trust them, the Administrators, capital A. I don't blame her for distrusting them, of course, but I'm glad she's happy.

Meanwhile, Lyle Munson has put together a little coalition made up of himself, Casey Fairchild, Lawrence Strong, and Merle Nielson whose goal is to beat up certain people. Norah is at the top of their list. Below her is another resident whose identity we don't know, then a staff whose identity we also don't know.

Why? Well, it's common for kids who are not doing well to try to bring down those who are. So we might have expected Lyle and his friends to try to bring Norah down. But usually kids in Lyle's position will try to set up kids in Norah's to make it appear that they've done something wrong when they haven't, or the Lyles of Ash Meadow will try to goad the Norahs into actually misbehaving. This is the first time I've encountered a situation in which kids intend to assault another kid for doing well.

THURSDAY, APRIL 12: Norah will be moving to Serpent Cottage in less than two weeks. She is pleased to be moving at long last, although at one point as we talked she became tearful. She is apprehensive about leaving Wolf and staff she knows and likes. But she is also determined to do what she must to get out of Ash Meadow as soon as she can, and she knows she cannot get her minimum sentence as long as she is in maximum security, or transfer to a group home without first having lived in an open unit. She believes still that if she obeys the rules at Ash Meadow and overcomes the obstacles she encounters, she will succeed.

Davis Peters believes the devil tries to get at him through his dreams. The devil does this because Davis has so much bad in him, owing to the things he's seen. He gave as an example his mother's overdosing. Describing it, he mimicked her convulsions, probably without realizing what he was doing. He said he's afraid of the dark sometimes. I told him he could have his light on until he falls asleep. He said he'd like that.

His meds, Serozone and Vistaril, are helping him, he says. Ritalin makes him angry, and he didn't understand why he was angry until his psychiatrist told him that Ritalin could affect him like that.

We talked about what his life will be like after he leaves Ash Meadow. He said he would like to dance in powwows, but he would have to give up drinking and drugging and he's reluctant to give them up. He said that when he's sober his brain "can't get up"—he can't be like other kids. Only when he's drunk or drugged does he feel normal. He acknowledges that he uses drugs and alcohol to escape from thinking about the bad things he's seen and lived through.

MONDAY, APRIL 16: At eight o'clock we were getting ready to put the kids in their rooms and start routines. The kids were lined up at the edge of their zones and we started herding them toward their rooms. Frank had Zone 1, James Zone 2, I had Zone 4, and Jan was covering the floor with Zone 3, waiting for a staff to get free to lock them in. In Zone 1, Ezekial Hall accidentally bumped into Casey Fairchild, who turned and shoved him. Frank yelled "Clear the floor!" Lawrence and Merle started out of Zone 2, but saw James coming toward them and turned back. In Zone 4, Lyle turned to see what was going on, hesitated, then went on to his room.

These are the four residents who have been talking about beating up other kids. I suspect Ezekial is one of their targets, and Casey triggered something the others weren't ready for. We got them all locked down without a problem, but it could have been bad. Staff was scattered through the cottage. A fight in a zone would have to be handled by a single staff until another could get the kids in his zone locked down and then go to help the first staff. If the fight began in Frank's zone, as it seemed it was going to, he would not have been able to contain it until James or I arrived to help him; he probably would not even have tried. If Lyle and the others had been better coordinated, they could have accomplished something.

Forty-five minutes later, all four of them went off in their rooms, yelling and pounding and mule-kicking their doors. Lyle was screaming that he was going to beat Norah's ass, while the others were shouting insults and threats at staff, mostly James.

Norah is afraid of Lyle. Smart girl. The last time Lyle was here he assaulted a kid on the very day he, Lyle, was paroled. Lyle believes he'll be transferred to Elk Grove when he turns fifteen, and he may be right. He'll be fifteen on April thirtieth. Norah is scheduled to leave on April twenty-fourth. I expect him to try to assault her before she goes. If he doesn't, then he'll go after someone else.

MONDAY, APRIL 23: Stayed late to talk with Norah. She was tearful about leaving tomorrow. She said she wished I worked at Serpent.

She's afraid of having to tell people she doesn't know well about her life. Apparently Serpent requires its new residents to write an autobiography and to read it to the others in the cottage. She doesn't want to leave herself vulnerable by revealing what has caused her pain.

I tried to reassure her, telling her she would do fine. But secretly I don't blame her one bit. I'm going to miss her.

TUESDAY, APRIL 24: Transferred Norah to Serpent at nine this morning. I allowed her to wear her regular clothes instead of the orange jumpsuit she's been wearing for six months. I was supposed to transfer her in her jumpsuit, but I didn't. I don't know why I didn't, but I didn't. I may hear about it later, but so what.

In any event, she was overjoyed to be leaving, and in her own clothes! She was running all around, searching for a place to look at herself—no mirrors in Wolf—and finally settled on the window looking into Jan's office. "I'm cute!" she squealed. "And I know it!"

Bernie and I were delighted to see her so happy.

Went to the psych meeting at nine-thirty. Talked about Norah for the last time. From now on, it will be up to Serpent to present her. I mentioned that she had just been transferred after six months in maximum security. It was as if these people had never been told that Norah has been in Wolf forever, longer than any other resident we've had. Someone, one of the psychiatrists, asked why so long, and before I could reply, Marty Biggs said it was because she's a high-profile resident. I was immediately angry, but let it pass as just another instance of the administration's mendacity.

Later in my presentation, I said Norah is estranged from her mother and had learned from her uncle only last Saturday that her mother has cancer.

Mary, the school psychologist, said Norah hadn't had contact with her

PART FOUR: WOLF □ 309

mother in years. I corrected her, saying that Norah hadn't seen her mother in several years, but until four months ago she had talked regularly with her.

What happened four months ago, I said, was this: Norah had been told she would be transferring to Serpent Cottage on a particular date in December; I didn't remember the date now. The superintendent had told Jan and me that this would happen, and I had told Norah. That date passed and she was not transferred; we were not told why. In fact, none of the administrators even answered our emails or phone calls. Finally the superintendent told us the other administrators had dissuaded him from allowing Norah to transfer out of Wolf. The administration had simply changed its mind.

I told Norah. She called her mother to tell her. Her mother told her that she, Norah, must have done something wrong or the administration would have allowed her to move. In fact, Norah had done everything right and everyone knew it, but this was her mother's response.

I was looking at Marty when I said this, and his response was silence.

Of course, I went on, her mother's response was the same Norah had met with after her mother's boyfriend raped her, when her mother said that she was lying after Norah told her what had happened.

"Invalidation," one of the psychiatrists said.

"Yeah. Invalidation. I have nothing else to say," I said, and left the meeting.

SUNDAY, APRIL 29: For a year and a half, as my father inched his way toward death, I waited for the call from my sister telling me he had gone. Now that he is gone, I continue to wait, checking my answering machine each evening upon returning home for the blinking light that will signal the message that my father has died.

WEDNESDAY, MAY 2: Lyle Munson was transferred to Elk Grove today just before I came in to work. He was fifteen on Monday.

Dick and Layton removed everything from the top of the staff desk and the bookcase behind it, likewise the table where the kids' jumpsuits and sweat pants and shirts are folded and set out. They stripped Lyle's room of everything movable. Then Security came down and Dick called Lyle up from school.

He came up and Layton told him he was being transferred. He looked around—Dick said he could see the wheels spinning in Lyle's head—but did not go off. He just gave a little laugh. He was given a set of his street clothes and told to go to his room to change. He laughed again when he saw his room.

Dick and Layton had wanted to have Lyle out of the cottage before the other kids returned from school, but the vehicle from State Transportation was late in coming down and the kids were coming back, so Dick decided to have a goodbye group for him. Everybody said something encouraging until it was Paul Grise's turn. He said, "Don't bend over when you're in the shower."

Lyle asked Layton why he was being transferred when he's been good lately. Layton said he'd been good for a few days, yeah, but this good period followed several weeks of terrible behavior, and we know him well enough to know he'll be terrible again.

Life will not be the same without him. For real.

SUNDAY, MAY 6: I saw a young girl at the Safeway today who reminded me of Tim Silver's daughter. Then I realized I hadn't seen Tim in what? nine years? His daughter would be sixteen or seventeen now. And then I thought: "If she's still alive."

It isn't the sort of thing you ordinarily think when you think about a young person. But I've been at Ash Meadow for a long time, and I've learned that kids die, too.

MONDAY, MAY 7: A new kid asked me yesterday, "Who's Lyle Munson? I see his name all over." By which he meant, I'm sure, he saw it scratched into the tile in the head, etched into the walls and bed platforms of the rooms Lyle lived in, and in most of the quiet rooms on campus.

Perhaps it's because he asked about Lyle that I thought about him on my drive to work this afternoon. I think I owe Lyle something. As quick as I've always been to pick up on other people's moods, to skirt the obvious and focus on what lies beneath, my dealings with Lyle have honed these abilities to an edge sharper than it's ever been. I feel something near to satisfaction now when I look at a kid and toss around in my mind the possibilities of horror and trauma, the emotional barriers of defense and assault he may experience, and which he may surmount or by which he may be defeated.

This very moment, as I write this, I feel such an eerie clarity of perception—it's as if the gods have given me a special power. The things I could do to a vulnerable person if I chose to—the things Lyle did.

TUESDAY, MAY 8: The talks Davis and I have often turn to the spiritual. He's very interested in his culture's religious beliefs and practices. He was put off last Friday by "the chapel lady" who comes to the cottage. She said that all magic is evil. His grandmother practices good magic, he says, and he doesn't believe she's evil. (Wolf has chapel services on Friday evening since the kids in max are not permitted to attend Sunday services at the campus chapel. As I don't work Fridays, I have not observed these services, but from what I've been told by both staff and kids, the people who come down to the cottage to conduct services are fundamentalists who are not only anti-magic but also anti-Catholic.)

Davis himself sees spirits almost every day, some of which scare him; he does regard these as evil. He said he had a dream the other night in which he and his cousin were chased by a demon. He was quite frightened by this dream. He believes he has bad dreams because he's seen or done bad things.

I asked him if his grandmother ever has bad dreams.

He said she does.

"But she's good, isn't she?"

"Yeah, she's good." He could not explain how she could have bad dreams if she was good, but he knew she was good.

I told him that I believe his grandmother is a good person and that the chapel lady could be wrong.

"She *is* wrong," Davis said.

I said he could stay in his room during chapel services if he wanted to; he didn't have to attend.

He said he didn't like to be in his room when the other kids were out.

I suggested he think about something else, something pleasant, when the chapel lady says something that upsets him.

He said he would try to do that.

Davis is retarded and suffers from FAE (fetal alcohol effects), PTSD, and ADHD. He's a kid who wants to be like other kids, but says, "I know everybody else is smarter than me."

After we talked he thanked me for saying his grandmother is good.

THURSDAY, MAY 10: Brian Meara interviewed Davis for possible transfer to Dolphin Cottage.

MONDAY, MAY 14: Davis was transferred to Dolphin this afternoon. I'm glad it happened when I was here, so I could say goodbye. He was nervous but didn't act out.

TUESDAY, MAY 15: Ash Meadow is in the midst of an epidemic of attempted suicides. At the psych meeting this morning, Dr. Williams said there had been seven attempts in the last two weeks. "Make that nine," Meg Bellardine said, seating herself at the table. There had just been two more this morning.

WEDNESDAY, MAY 16: Meg caught me as I was starting down to the cottage to begin my shift this afternoon. She asked me how I was doing, then said, before I could answer, that I didn't look so good. Actually it was she who looked terrible, stress lines creasing her forehead, her nose red and swollen as if from crying.

She wanted to give me a heads-up, she said. Belinda Fish tried to kill herself last night. Layton cut her down. He was having flashbacks about Viet Nam now, but otherwise he was all right. Meg was worried about Clare though; she was so young and inexperienced.

At the cottage Layton and I went out on the back porch to talk. He said what Meg had said: he was flashing on Viet Nam, but he expected that to pass in a couple of days. He was more concerned about Clare than about himself. She was pretty shaken last night. Here's what happened:

Dick Peck had just finished his grief-and-loss group. Some of the kids were already in their rooms and Darrell Pound, the intermittent working with us, was delivering supper trays to them. He opened Belinda's door and screamed. Then he froze. Dick cleared the floor and Layton ran into Belinda's room. She had fashioned a noose from a bed sheet she had looped through the frame of the air vent in the ceiling. There was a hole in the plaster next to the frame and she had worked the sheet through that. She was hanging from the vent.

Layton lifted her up and got his fingers between the sheet and her neck, easing the tension, the while yelling for someone to get him a knife. Clare brought the knife and Layton cut the sheet away and then lay Belinda down on the floor. Suddenly her body jumped almost off the floor and she began to tremble. She was breathing again. When he described how her body jumped, Layton's own body mimicked hers. It reminded me of Davis Peters mimicking his mother's convulsions after she overdosed.

Later in the evening I stood with Clare where Layton and I had talked on the porch, watching the kids play basketball.

"It's more than just a job, isn't it?" I said.

She nodded yes.

"Have you tried to tell your friends on the outs what it is you do here?"

She nodded again. "They don't have a clue. I didn't have a clue when I started. I didn't have a clue until last night. I keep thinking about what could have happened if Darrell hadn't been delivering trays just at that time."

Once when I was in Viet Nam—I always begin my war stories with "Once when I was in Viet Nam"—I was asked to help debride a child and his mother who had been burned in a gasoline fire. I could not. It looked so bad, the charred flesh, the fused bone, and they were in such pain, crying even under the morphine, I felt I was only adding to their pain. Finally the medic told me to go outside, and after a moment he came out and sat with me on the concrete steps leading into the infirmary and we smoked cigarettes. It was wonderfully kind of him, I thought then, and I still think so. It has been years since I thought of them, the infant boy and his mother, a Jarai woman, herself not more than fourteen or fifteen.

When I came back from Viet Nam I wanted to have many children. I had three and I wanted more, but my wife did not. I think now that I wanted so many children because I had seen so many die—or perhaps I saw the same one dying over and over—and those I could father would be a kind of cosmic compensation for those who had died. Perhaps that is why I do the work I do: I'm trying to save the children, most of all those who have already died.

I did not tell Clare much of what I wrote in the last two paragraphs. I told her enough to let her know she was not alone in her suffering, but, hopefully, without diminishing the import of what she was going through. Also, I wanted her to know that others had disappointed themselves, that I had disappointed myself. When Layton was yelling for a knife, she panicked and forgot where we kept them and had to go to him to ask where they were. This ate up time; she had been embarrassed.

SATURDAY, MAY 26: Had suicide prevention training Thursday and Friday. Isn't this typical of Ash Meadow? After the crisis has passed, we get training to prevent it. I'm not sure I learned anything I didn't already know, but judging from the kinds of questions that were asked, and the responses to some of what Meg Bellardine and Don Martino, our trainers, were saying, it's apparent that all of us who have worked here at Ash Meadow for at least a few years are suffering from chronic trauma.

Meg said she'd been involved in over fifty attempted suicides, mostly in Andromeda. She'd recently taken up motorcycling "to relieve stress." When she said this, laughter broke out of me like an explosion.

It does appear that our "suicide epidemic," as we came to call it, is over. We suppressed it by borrowing staff from other institutions to take over the mundanities of cottage life—answering the phone, helping to set up for meals, fetching toothpaste or shampoo for kids who had run out—while we regular staff dealt with the kids and their fears on a more intimate level, mostly by making ourselves available to them when they wanted to talk.

SUNDAY, JUNE 10: Earthquake this morning at six-twenty. Does this mean we'll have another suicide? Sick humor.

SUNDAY, JUNE 24: Doug Little worked with us today. Dick was out sick and there aren't enough intermittents to fill all the open shifts. We talked about kids we knew five, seven, eight years ago. Russell Guerra—I don't know if I've written about him before—called him recently. He just got out of prison, an adult facility, after having served seven years for murder. He killed the guy with whom he committed the crime that got him sent to Ash Meadow. The guy had cooperated with the police in return for a reduced sentence.

Russell said he'd spent almost all of his sentence in maximum security. Every time he was released to the general population he would do something to get sent back to max. That was how he kept from being raped.

Doug said he'd always liked Russell. I had too—rather, I had felt sorry for him. He was a small kid who was afraid and was trying to live up to his father's idea of manliness. His father had also served time for a murder, which Russell had witnessed.

"I always felt that Russell had a good heart, despite what he did," Doug said. He said he distinguished between kids who he perceived to have evil hearts and those he felt had good hearts. He tried to avoid the former, thugs who were involved with gangs, who did violent things and who liked doing them, and to get good-hearted kids, needy, immature kids, on his caseload. He knew that Russell did bad things, but felt that he did them out of fear of his father rather than for the enjoyment of doing them.

I was astonished that he used the dichotomy of good and evil, and told him so.

He said it helped him decide where he wanted to put his energy. He just preferred to give it to those he could sympathize with, and write off the others or leave them to someone else.

I said I preferred working with those he called thugs. I said I didn't see them as enjoying doing violent things; what appeared to be enjoyment was usually a mask for fear or grief. Although, I said, some felt genuine pleasure in what they did.

We were both in a nostalgic mood. Doug said he has nineteen paychecks to go until he retires. And, while I didn't tell him this, I intend to quit within the next three or four months.

WEDNESDAY, JUNE 27: Rumor has it that Lyle Munson is not doing well at Elk Grove. He's in maximum security, locked down twenty-three hours a day, smearing his shit on the walls of his room. The rumor comes from Dick Peck.

TUESDAY, JULY 3: At the psych meeting Dr. Williams said he is concerned that Wolf is caught in a squeeze, by which he meant kids come in but do not transfer out. His concern was professed in response to Swan's refusal to accept back a kid they sent us months ago. He is not the first kid a cottage refused; it's become more the rule than the exception that kids come to Wolf and stay. I said it was a real morale killer for kids and for staff, too, not to be able to give residents something to look forward to. I reminded him that we are supposed to have kids thirty to sixty days, but we've had them up to six months.

Williams said his concern—he liked that word today—is that Ash Meadow is creating mental health problems in our residents by not giving them the opportunity to transfer out of maximum security.

When I brought up this same issue as it pertained to Norah, he brushed me off. But I didn't mention that now. Instead, I told him I was glad to hear him say that because I felt as he did. I'm certain all of this is a reaction to the suicide and the rash of attempts we had, although only one occurred in Wolf.

WEDNESDAY, JULY 4 (INDEPENDENCE DAY): I visited Norah at Serpent tonight after I got off work. We talked for about an hour. Not long enough. As I was leaving, Yvette, her staff, told me, "She really loves you."

I don't know what I'm going to do about her, about my feeling for her, when I quit. I wish I could adopt her.

FRIDAY, AUGUST 10: Casey Fairchild was transferred to Elk Grove on Wednesday. We had not wanted to tell him he was going to be moved until shortly before it was scheduled to happen, but the administration insisted we tell him immediately after we were informed. In the week before he left, he assaulted Security, twice, and a teacher. When he left, he was crying.

Yesterday Marty Biggs came down to the cottage during PC and congratulated us for managing Casey as well as we had for the past seven months. Then, to everybody's surprise, he bestowed congratulations on himself—"And congratulations to me"—for arranging Casey's transfer. He said it had been very difficult to accomplish. This was followed by a verbal attack on Wolf staff generally and on Jan specifically. He said we were not communicating with other cottages and that we have a terrible reputation on campus—this after we had just received, for the second consecutive year, the Best-Staff-Team-On-Campus award, or whatever it's called. Jan was so upset she began to cry and left the room.

It is our—Wolf's—opinion that the administration is trying to get her to resign, or to create a scenario for firing her. This, we assume, is probably related to Herman Boats' bringing suit against them for harassment. They are trying to get at him by getting at her.

SUNDAY, AUGUST 19: Bernie told me he's applied for a position with parole. He said he made up his mind to leave after seeing Marty humiliate Jan.

FRIDAY, AUGUST 24: Norah told me last night when I was visiting her at Serpent that a student from a Bible college had spoken at chapel on Sunday. He said he'd been a resident of Ash Meadow some years ago and he mentioned a staff at Swan Cottage named Jerry. Jerry once said something that came to mean a lot to him. But Norah couldn't remember what he said I'd said, or what his name was.

Dick Peck was in the cottage talking with some other kids, and Norah asked him if he remembered who the Bible student was. Dick did remember: it was Rodney Hemming.[33] Rodney had graduated from community college and now he was in Bible college. Rodney didn't know if I was spiritual or not, Dick said, but I'd said something to him that he considered spiritually important.

Actually, I remembered what I'd said, though I had not regarded it as anything spiritual. Rodney had asked me why I work at Ash Meadow. One of the other staff had told him that I had a PhD, and Rodney wondered why I was not doing something that carried more prestige or more power. I told him that when I die, if I have time to reflect, I don't want to regret not having done something. I want to be able to look at my life and feel that what I did had meaning, for myself and for others. And one of the ways to create meaning is by giving of yourself to others. The kind of work a PhD can buy, academic or managerial, only provides a way to pass through life with some comfort; beyond that it means nothing to me. (Rodney did not ask why I got a PhD in the first place, the answer to which would have led in a different direction altogether.)

Dick thought Rodney recalled my saying something like that, but not quite that. Of course. Rodney would make it his own, would change it to suit his own needs. And perhaps I had not said it quite like that either. But it is something I decided when I was an adolescent, even if the vocabulary I've used to express it has changed over the years.

It's interesting that Rodney is one of only a few of all the kids I've known at Ash Meadow that I did not like. It had nothing to do with his offense, though it was a bad one. Rather, I did not like him because I did not trust him. I thought he was without empathy. Perhaps I was wrong, though I do not think so. Perhaps his sense of empathy developed after he left Ash Meadow. That is possible. But, empathy or no, I doubt that he will harm anyone again as he did once.

Release

I did not leave Ash Meadow in the fall of 2001, as I had fantasized doing. I did not leave for another four and a half years. There was always a reason not to go, although nothing I told myself seemed to me to get at the real reason. A year and a half after I discovered I was at Ash Meadow to try to save children, I wrote, "I realized suddenly why I do the work I do. I'm trying to save the lives of those I lost thirty-some years ago in Viet Nam. All the other reasons I've come up with over the years—raising other people's children because I couldn't raise my own, making Cee's pain go away, etc.—all of these are valid, but the core of it is my trying to resurrect my dead by trying to save others."

I felt as if I had never had this thought before, though I had, several times. It sounded good and I thought it was true, and still do, but it wasn't enough, because it didn't take me to the single, incontrovertible truth that I insisted must be there, even if it wasn't.

And three years after that, I woke up one morning with the sudden understanding that I did the work I did in order to try to answer the question: Who are we? But that question can lead in a variety of directions, and I wasn't sure what I meant by it. In any case, I had asked it before, but had not been able to answer it then, either.

My anger toward Ash Meadow's administrators for the way they had treated Norah did not diminish. It made no difference, of course—my anger. Norah's six months in maximum security was only the beginning. Later we had a boy for twenty-seven months. For years I kept a letter of resignation in my wallet.

If I had decided to use it, all I had to do was date it and hand it to Jan. My loathing for the administration was a lump in my gut, yet I did not leave.

In July 2001, we again voted no confidence in the superintendent. Eighty-eight percent of the union membership voted against him. But life on campus went on as though nothing had happened.

In December, Norah transferred to a group home.

In August 2002, a man in Seattle's south end shot and killed a two-year-old boy, shot a six-year-old girl but did not kill her, and shot to death a twenty-year-old man. Police shot and killed the killer, who was "shermed out." That is, he'd been smoking sherm every day for ten days. He did not know the children; the man he killed was his friend. The little boy he killed was the son of Ron Lafitte, who had been on my caseload five years earlier.

In January 2003, Carol Ripito retired after thirty years as a state employee. Later in the year Lyle Munson beat up a staff at Elk Grove and was tried and sentenced as an adult. He got ten to fifteen years, according to one source; twenty-six years, according to another. The following year Casey Fairchild was also in the adult system.

In 2004 Andrew Walters fire-bombed a synagogue in Oklahoma. He was sentenced to thirty-nine years in prison.[34]

Herman Boats accepted Ash Meadow's offer to settle his harassment suit. The state of Washington paid him an undisclosed (to me) amount. He left state service.

In March 2005, in Alternatives to Violence, the kids came up with these conditions that make for violence in people:

1. Single-parent families: the parent does not have time to supervise her children.

2. The parent is addicted to drugs or alcohol, so neglects her children.

3. Violence in the household or neighborhood.

4. Drugs in the household or neighborhood.

5. The acceptance of violence as normal.

6. The lack of jobs, leading to theft and robbery and the violence employed in committing these offenses.

I had not coached the kids in any way: the list came from their own experience and observations.

That year I had a dream in which I was charged and convicted of violating the terms of a contract in which I had agreed to be a slave—to whom or to what, I didn't know. Now, in the dream, I was waiting in Wolf Cottage, a prisoner myself, to be transferred to an adult facility. Bernie was waiting with me. It was daytime, and sunny outside. Bernie and I kept looking out the kitchen window, waiting for the transportation van to arrive. It was late. "Maybe it won't come," Bernie said. But I knew it would, and he did too.

Early in 2005 my red-leafed trees were cut down to make room for the truck parks and heavy equipment needed in a cottage renovation project. But later in the year staff were seeing raccoons again. Once I saw one bounding toward the lake. Another time I saw two scramble out of a dumpster and up a tree.

In April Norah was released to parole from her group home.

In July one night after I left work, my car wouldn't start. I turned the key and nothing happened—no lights, no sound, not even a "click." I had it towed to a garage in north Seattle.

On the way, sitting in the cab with the driver, we talked. He said he'd had some friends who went to Ash Meadow when he was younger, though he himself had not.

I asked him how they were doing now.

"Not too good. One's in and out of jail." He asked how long I'd been working at Ash Meadow.

"Fourteen and a half years."

"Maybe you know them." He said a name. It was unusual and I knew it immediately. It belonged to a kid who'd been at Swan when I was an intermittent.

"I knew him. What's he doing now?"

"He's serving life."

"That's too bad. I remember hearing he'd been shot."

"Shotgun. That was in middle school. You ever hear of"—he said another name. It was familiar, but I couldn't attach a face to it.

"People remember"—he said the first name again—"because of his last name."

We were silent. After a while he said, "I did everything they did, but I never got caught. The police would be chasing us, and they'd go one way and I'd go the other, and the police always went after them. I don't know why."

"Luck," I said.

Silence again.

"I got stabbed and I got shot once," he said. "I decided I didn't want that life anymore."

More silence.

"My father was a pastor," he said. "People think that because your father's a pastor, he's always there for you. What people don't realize is that because he's a pastor he's a father to five hundred other people too. I didn't feel he was there for me. I felt he was too busy with everyone else to have time for me. We're close now."

He'd worked for a large communications company that eventually went bankrupt. "I was making two hundred thousand dollars a year. Now I'm driving a tow truck. You have to be prepared for life to change. Sometimes you have no control over it. But you have to accept it, whatever it brings. But sometimes you do have control. Whatever you do, it will come back on you."

When he got out of the truck and unstrapped my car, I could see that his left arm was useless. It hung at his side. If he needed to reposition it, he grasped the wrist with his right hand and moved the arm where he wanted it. I hadn't noticed this before.

In September, Norah completed her parole. A few weeks later she left the state.

Five months later, I left Ash Meadow for the last time. I had stayed years too long.

Notes

1. Edwin Chen, "You're going to be scared," *Seattle Times*, February 16, 1991, p. A2.
2. Actually, rehabilitation, or at least something about the prison experience in Washington state, may well work. Barnoski and Aos found that twelve months after release from prison, 67.3 percent of juveniles had not committed another felony. (See Robert Barnoski and Steve Aos, "The Effects of Parole on Recidivism: Juvenile Offenders Released From Washington State Institutions," Washington State Institute for Public Policy, March 2001, www.wsipp.wa.gov.)

    Sex offenders have a lower recidivism rate. Karen Kersting ("New hope for sex offender treatment," *Monitor on Psychology*, July/August 2003, Volume 34, No. 7, www.apa.org/monitor/julaug03) cites a 2002 article by Karl Hanson in *Sexual Abuse: A Journal of Research and Treatment* (Volume 14, No. 2) as showing sexual recidivism rates of 9.9 percent for treated offenders as against 17.3 percent for untreated offenders.

    In Washington state, Washington State Institute for Public Policy ("Sex Offender Sentencing in Washington State: Recidivism Rates," August 26, 2005, www.wsipp.wa.gov) found that only three percent of sex offenders released from prison, jail, or a Special Sex Offender Sentencing Alternative (SSOSA) program were convicted of committing another sex offense, felony or misdemeanor, five years after release, although 10.3 percent committed another type of felony and 11.4 percent another type of misdemeanor.
3. Peter Matthiessen, "The Blue Pearl of Siberia," *New York Review of Books*, February 14, 1991, p. 42.
4. See Glossary: Minimum/maximum release dates.
5. The first time we talked, Dean told me that the gun was not his, but his friend's, and his friend was playing with it when it fired; it was supposedly unloaded. See my journal entry for May 18, 1994.
6. As far as I know, there are no statistics on female sex offenders. Of the boys I've known who were raped or sexually molested, I estimate that 40 percent were victimized by teenage girls or adult women. According to Carol Ripito, therapists estimate 20 to 50 percent of sex offenders are women.
7. See journal entry, September 19, 1994.
8. See journal entry, December 1, 1991.
9. This resident did not remember having told me part of this "dream" or "flashback" where he represented it as a memory. See journal entry for January 9, 1996.
10. Years later, another boy told me that he came home one time and went into his room and there was a clock radio his grandmother had bought him. A card was propped against it on which she had written "Happy 14th Birthday." "Am I only fourteen?" he thought. "I felt so old," he told me.
11. See journal entry, May 1, 1996.

12. This was meant literally. If a young gangster wants to go from one place to another in the city, for example, he may have to pass through an enemy set's territory. As he would likely be on foot, or dependent on buses on which his enemies also travel, he may not be able to leave his own neighborhood by any convenient means, or he may have to go so far out of his way in order to avoid enemies that he could not accurately predict when he would arrive at his destination.

13. See Glossary.

14. Gary Webb, "Cocaine pipeline financed rebels," *Seattle Times*, August 22, 1996, pp. A1, A6-A7; "Drug king free, but black aide sits in jail," *Seattle Times*, August 23, 1996, pp. A1, A10.

15. See journal entry, June 11, 1996.

16. Joanna Catherine Scott, "An End to Dreaming," in *Coming Down From Bataan*, (Hamilton, Ontario: Unfinished Monument Press, 2001), pp. 18-23.

17. See journal entry, December 1, 1991.

18. See journal entry, June 28, 1991.

19. See journal entry, December 20, 1995.

20. Hannah Arendt, *The Origins of Totalitarianism* (New York: Harcourt, Brace & World, 1973).

21. See journal entry for December 20, 1995: Rob Gorey told me then that Willie Gonzalez had been killed, and James Pickle said that Richard Wain had been stabbed to death. Neither report was true.

22. See journal entry, May 22, 1994.

23. Susan Griffin, *A Chorus of Stones* (New York: Doubleday, 1992), p.147.

24. See journal entry, July 8, 1999.

25. Collected in Jerome Gold, "How I Learned That I Could Push the Button," *How I Learned That I Could Push the Button* (Seattle: Black Heron Press, 2003), p. 37.

26. See journal entry, December 14, 1993.

27. See journal entry, January 7, 2000.

28. See journal entry, July 31, 1997 for another boy who used this technique.

29. See journal entry, May 16, 2000.

30. See Jerome Gold, *Sergeant Dickinson* (New York: Soho Press, 1999), p. 30-31.

31. See journal entry, February 17, 1999.

32. See journal entry, May 30, 2000.

33. See journal entries, September 23, 1997; November 15, 1997; March 14, 1998.

34. See journal entries, June 30, 1999; November 4, 1999; November 24, 1999; December 22, 1999.

Glossary

AA: Alcoholics Anonymous.

ART: Aggression Replacement Training.

ARVN: Army of the Republic of Viet Nam; i.e., the South Vietnamese army.

AWOL: Absent Without Leave. Adjective: e.g., "He is AWOL," or has escaped. Noun: e.g., "He is an AWOL." Verb: to go AWOL, or escape.

BGD: Black Gangster Disciples: a gang. BGD has undergone several transformations, including name changes, over the years. It traces its lineage back fifty years. It has a hierarchical structure and is organized as a corporate body. As compared with most other gangs of the Nineties, whose reach was local or regional in scope, BGD operated on a national as well as a local level. It was, and is, a part of Folk, an aggregation of gangs.

Book: to run away.

Case manager: a counselor.

Central Isolation: isolation cells located in the same building as the Security Office and the Health Center. These cells are monitored by closed-circuit television and are specially constructed to withstand physical abuse.

Cheeking meds: a resident's concealment of a medication pill or capsule in his mouth while pretending to swallow it. This is done in order to give it away later, or exchange it with other residents for their medications or something else of value, or to hoard it with other medications of the same type in order to take them all at once to get high. A resident may give his medications away to ingratiate himself to another resident, or as a favor to someone he cares for, or because another resident has intimidated him.

Class I/Class II: school punishments. A Class I is given for a minor infraction such as not paying attention or distracting the class, despite the teacher's admonitions. A Class II is given for something more serious, usually aggressive behavior, such as swearing at the teacher or slamming a door.

Clear the floor: a command shouted by cottage staff with the purpose of getting residents into their rooms, or otherwise away from a scene of trouble, as quickly as possible.

Cluck: a contemptuous term used by residents to refer to someone who uses crack cocaine. The word is said to have originated with the idea that a crack user is as stupid as a chicken.

CO group: Committing Offense group. A group attended by staff and residents wherein one resident discloses the details and repercussions of the crime he was convicted of. In Swan Cottage, the resident must do his CO group before obtaining his Level 1.

Committing offense: the crime a resident was convicted of committing, as opposed to other crimes he may have committed, but with which he was not charged.

Complaint form: a form filled out by a resident wishing to have his complaint reviewed by the program manager.

Consequence: may be used as either a noun or a verb. A euphemism for "punishment" or "punish."

Cottage director: see program manager.

CPS: Child Protective Services.

CR: carpet restriction. A behavior level. Residents on CR must stay in the day area, or living room, unless they obtain staff's permission to go elsewhere.

Cue: warning.

Cycle: pattern of behavior. An offense cycle is a pattern of behavior leading to the commission of a crime.

Day sheet: a form, made up daily, showing residents' status: their behavior levels, their work details, their individual bedtimes, whether or not they had a telephone call, whether or not they took a shower, and any notes staff made about them.

DBT: Dialectical Behavior Therapy.

Decline: to sentence a juvenile as an adult, usually owing to the severity of the offense of which he has been convicted, or to an extensive criminal history.

Details: chores.

DOC: Department of Corrections. The state agency that oversees the adult prison and parole systems.

DSHS: Department of Social and Health Services. Juvenile Rehabilitation Administration's parent organization.

Feedback group: a meeting of cottage staff and residents, convened to provide verbal evaluations of how a particular resident is progressing in terms of behavior and treatment. In Swan Cottage, a feedback group was held when a resident applied for a higher level. Immediately following feedback, cottage residents voted for or against awarding the applicant his level. Staff usually accepted this vote as determining level "move-up," as attaining the next level was called, though they sometimes overrode the vote.

Floor work: monitoring the activities of residents in the common areas of the cottage: the living room, the dining room, the kitchen. Interacting with residents: talking, playing board games or card games, chess and checkers.

Folk: an aggregation of certain gangs. See BGD.

Group home: a residence housing juvenile offenders under the supervision of adult counselors. Living in a group home, residents may hold jobs and attend public school.

Head: bathroom.

High profile: a resident who meets all of these criteria: 1. His offense is one of the following: murder in the first or second degree; first-degree manslaughter; first-degree assault; first-degree rape; first-degree robbery; first-degree arson; first-degree kidnap. 2. The minimum length of his sentence is eighty weeks or more. 3. His offense has a "high impact" on the community. 4. Community response to his offense is high.

Huff gas: to inhale the fumes from gasoline in order to induce a feeling of euphoria.

Intermittent staff: a substitute for counselors and security officers on vacation or sick leave, or who fills in when a permanent position is vacant.

JPC: Juvenile Parole Counselor; parole officer. See JRCC.

JRA: Juvenile Rehabilitation Administration. The state agency overseeing juvenile institutions and the juvenile parole system.

JRC1: Juvenile Rehabilitation Counselor 1. See JRCA.

JRC2: Juvenile Rehabilitation Counselor 2. See JRRC.

JRCA: Juvenile Rehabilitation Counselor Assistant. The JRCA has the same duties as the JRRC, but fewer of them; e.g., the JRCA in most cases has a smaller caseload than the JRRC. The JRCA classification came into use in the mid-1990s. It is approximately equivalent to the earlier classification JRC1. See JRRC.

JRCC: Juvenile Rehabilitation Community Counselor; parole officer. This classification came into use in the mid-1990s, replacing the classification JPC, or Juvenile Parole Counselor.

JRRC: Juvenile Residential Rehabilitation Counselor. This classification came into use in the mid-1990s. It is approximately equivalent to the earlier classification JRC2 (Juvenile Rehabilitation Counselor 2). The JRRC's duties include managing a caseload, floor work, and other duties as required, such as conducting treatment groups and performing various housekeeping or administrative chores. See JRCA.

Jumped in (also called "beaten in"): initiated into a gang. A prospective member is beaten by those already in the gang. Less common since the beginning of the twenty-first century.

Jumped out (also called "beaten out"): beaten by other gang members when a member decides to leave his gang. A ritual rather than punishment.

Level: a position in a hierarchy—the level system—that, upon their attaining it by good behavior and progress in treatment, rewards residents with specific privileges.

Life story: a list of questions about his life and the commission of his offense that a resident in Swan Cottage must answer in order to move from Level 1 to Level 2. The questions are similar to those he must respond to during his CO group. The life story, however, is told individually to each staff member rather than to a group.

LURP: the pronunciation for LRP, Long Range Patrol. A LURP was a soldier assigned to a US Army Long Range Patrol unit during the Viet Nam war.

MACV: Military Advisory Command Vietnam.

Maddogging: staring at another person with hostility. Also called "Meanmugging."

Major bust: see Minor bust/Major bust.

MAYSI: Massachusetts Youth Screening Instrument. Questionnaire given to all residents within thirty days after being assigned to a cottage. When completed, it provides an idea of the emotional state of the resident.

Meanmugging: see maddogging.

Meds: medications, usually in pill or capsule form.

Minimum/maximum release dates: in Washington state, the sentence range awarded by the court to a juvenile convicted of a felony. The minimum date is the earliest a resident may be paroled, the maximum date the latest. The length of his sentence is linked to his behavior while incarcerated.

Minor bust/major bust: punishment awarded by Swan Cottage for the more serious infractions. Lying, for example, warranted a minor bust, including a minimum of four hours off-program and a reduction of level. A major bust warranted twelve to twenty-four hours off-program and a reduction of level to Tables status. Infractions meriting a major bust included fighting, inciting others to fight, and making racist comments.

Monroe: location of a men's prison.

NA: Narcotics Anonymous.

Norteños: Mexican-American gang.

NVA: North Vietnamese Army

OD: 1. Officer of the Day. The OD is responsible for specific administrative duties in the absence of other administrators, i.e., after business hours, on weekends and holidays. 2. overdose of a drug or drugs.

ODD: Oppositional Defiant Disorder.

Off program: see OP.

OG: Initially, the initials stood for "original gangster," but have since come to indicate "old-time gangster" or "old gangster."

On the floor: situated so as to perform floor work; being present in the living room or dining area of a cottage.

OP: off program. A resident's confinement to his room for having committed behavioral misdeeds.

Panic alarm: body alarm.

PC: Program Committee. 1. cottage staff. 2. the weekly cottage staff meeting. Most cottages hold them on Tuesday afternoons, beginning while the residents are still in school. When residents return, they are locked in their rooms until the meeting is over. Meetings last two to three hours.

PCR: Personal Conduct Report. It usually involves disciplinary or corrective action against an employee.

Permanent staff: Staff employed to work full-time, with full benefits.

Phoenix program: residential treatment program, located at Ash Meadow, for drug and alcohol abusers.

Phone list: list of names of persons a resident is permitted to call, or from whom he can receive calls.

Program manager: the person responsible for the operation of a cottage. The lowest level of management in the institutional system; also known as cottage director.

Psych meeting: a weekly meeting of Ash Meadow's psychiatry staff and, usually, a representative from the administration, to which each cottage sends a liaison to "present on," or bring up for discussion, residents the psychiatrists will be seeing that week.

PTSD: post-traumatic stress disorder.

Punk: to demean another person by intimidating him.

Purdy: location of Washington Corrections Center for Women. The only women's prison in Washington state.

Quiet room: euphemism for isolation cell.

Quiet time: from approximately 6:00 to 6:30 pm. Beginning after supper when cottage details are completed and residents are locked in their rooms, and ending thirty minutes later. This period is considered staff's break time, but is usually used to try to catch up on paperwork, to conduct individual counseling with residents, or to do housekeeping chores. It is also the time residents most commonly attempt suicide.

Rec: recreation.

Resident: a prisoner. Often used interchangeably with "student."

Routine: the resident's brushing his teeth and washing his face and hands before being locked in for the night. Time is set aside for routines only in Wolf Cottage.

Set: a subset of a gang. In this sense, a gang may be regarded as an aggregation of sets.

Sherm: a marijuana or tobacco cigarette soaked in formaldehyde, allowed to dry, then smoked. Also called "wet."

Shift change: a period of time, usually thirty minutes, during which residents are locked in their rooms while staff getting off duty brief staff coming on. This time is also used to catch up on paperwork or to do housekeeping chores.

60-percent board: a meeting of a resident, his counselor, and an administrator, held soon after 60 percent of the resident's minimum sentence had been served, to establish the date on which he would be released from the institution to the parole system. In 1998, the 60-percent board was eliminated.

SO: sex offender.

Social: a party, heavily chaperoned by staff, usually hosted by a single cottage. Occasionally, as for Halloween, a campus social may be sponsored by the Recreation Department.

SPL: Suicide Prevention Level. For most of my time at Ash Meadow, there were three levels of SPL: I, II, and III. A resident on SPL I required constant observation, a counselor with him at every moment. A resident on SPL II required a counselor to observe him every five minutes, and a resident on SPL III, every fifteen minutes. Later in my tenure, a fourth level, SPL IV, was added. Now SPL I's, II's and III's require the observing counselor to log on the resident under watch every five, ten, or fifteen minutes, respectively; a resident on SPL IV does not require special logging, only a heightened awareness by staff as to where the resident is at any time and what he is doing.

Strap: a handgun.

Student of the Week: Each week in Swan Cottage, Student Government nominates candidates for Student of the week. Of the candidates nominated, staff, at their weekly PC meeting, select one to be Student of the Week. That resident is given a level advancement for one week and has the privileges of the higher level during that time. To be eligible for Student of the Week, a resident must have had three days during the previous week in which he did not get a demerit or have a major or minor bust.

Supervisor: assistant to the program manager, usually responsible for clerical and other routine duties and for the operation of the cottage in the program manager's absence.

Sureños: Mexican-American gang.

Tables: one of the most restrictive of cottage punishments. On Tables status, a resident is required to spend all of his free time sitting silently and alone at a table in the dining room, while residents not on Tables may watch television in the living room, play table tennis, or go outside.

Take down: to physically restrain a resident. This usually involves wrestling him to the ground and, in Wolf Cottage, handcuffing him.

Talking mess: also called "talking shit" or "talking trash." Trying to humiliate or intimidate another person through insult or threat.

Talking shit: see "talking mess."

TAMVWOP: Taking A Motor Vehicle Without Permission.

Telephone privileges: In most cottages, residents are permitted to call their parents or other close relatives on their phone list once a week. If their parents are separated or divorced, residents may call each once a week. Residents may receive one call per day from their parents or others on their phone list. Calling hours vary from cottage to cottage, but generally they are from 6:30 to 8:30 or 9:00 pm and, on weekends and holidays, from 1:00 to 5:00 pm.

The outs: outside of prison.

Treatment plan: a plan for rehabilitating the offender. It might include drug-and-alcohol counseling, keeping a journal, participating in certain treatment groups—e.g., Alternatives to Violence, Victim Awareness, Male Survivors of Sexual Abuse—and whatever else a resident's case manager, with the approval of his program manager, may think necessary. Ash Meadow's campus-wide adoption of Dialectical Behavior Therapy (DBT) at the turn of the millenium served to standardize treatment plans, and, therefore, treatment. Administrators forbade grief-and-loss counseling, for example, because, in their view, the empathy shown by counselors to residents during grief-and-loss group encouraged residents to act out.

Treatment report: a report written by a case manager documenting a resident's progress and indicating the direction rehabilitative treatment should go in the future.

UA: urinalysis. An examination of a person's urine to determine whether or not he has recently used drugs.

VA: Veterans Administration.

VC: Viet Cong.

Visiting hours: the period during weekends and holidays that residents may receive visitors. There are two visiting periods each of these days: 1:15 to 3:00 pm and 3:15 to 4:45 pm.

Yellow suit: yellow short-sleeve pullover and pants worn by residents who, based on recent behavior, staff judged were likely to present further behavioral problems.

Zone: Each cottage has four "zones," or corridors, radiating out from the living room, dining room, and kitchen, which are located centrally. Zones are numbered 1 through 4. From the front door, facing into the cottage, Zone 1 is to the immediate left. Then, counting clockwise, there are zones 2, 3, and 4. As the cottages are rectangular in shape, Zones 1 and 2 are located to the left of the common areas, Zones 3 and 4 to the right. Each zone has four bedrooms, each room having a unique number in the cottage. Zone 1 is composed of Rooms 1 through 4; Zone 2, Rooms 5 through 8, and so on. Each zone has one bathroom, or "head," shared by the residents of that zone.

Cast of Characters

Ash Meadow Staff

Anita—Wolf Cottage counselor

Anna—Whale Cottage Director

Dr. Arens—Resident medical doctor

Celia Barney—Associate Superintendent

Meg Bellardine—Mental Health Coordinator

Bernie—Wolf Cottage counselor

Beth—Bull Cottage counselor

Marty Biggs—Associate Superintendent

Bill—Swan Cottage counselor

Tony Black—Swan Cottage temp

Lissa Blocker—Intermittent

Caroline Bloodworth—Whale Cottage counselor

Herman Boats—Swan Cottage, Ram Cottage Director

Bob—Goldfish Cottage counselor

Bob Brown—Andromeda Cottage director

Nan Brown—Director of Personnel, Ash Meadow

Lee Buckman—Security officer

Sheryl Bunch—Whale Cottage Director

Roy Burns—Swan Cottage, Ram Cottage counselor

Layton Calder—Wolf Cottage counselor, Supervisor

Candace—Nurse

Carol—Intermittent

Cherry—Wolf Cottage counselor

Dr. Christopher—Psychiatrist

Clare—Wolfe Cottage counselor

Michael Collins—Swan Cottage counselor

Dr. Mark Conley—Psychiatrist

Kathy Creeley—Whale Cottage counselor

Regina Cromwell—Swan Cottage Director

Tony Dangerfield—Intermittent

Dennis—Wolf Cottage counselor

Sue Doggett—Swan Cottage temp

Dorothy—Nurse

Jim Duckworth—Wolf Cottage counselor

Essene—Intermittent

Felicia—Eagle Cottage counselor

Kirsten Ford—Bull Cottage Supervisor

Kathleen Foreman—Associate Superintendent

Dan Fried—Teacher

Guido—Wolf Cottage counselor

George—Crane Cottage counselor

Gigi—Swan Cottage counselor

Gil—Wolf Cottage counselor

Dr. Gilbert—Medical doctor

Bev Gorey—Peacock Cottage Director

Rob Gorey—Swan Cottage, Ram Cottage Supervisor

Jake Gorman—Ram Cottage counselor, Serpent Cottage Supervisor

Harry Grass—Psychologist

Jim Herbold—Ram Cottage counselor

Jan Herve—Wolf Cottage Director

Deirdre Holser—Chaplain

Tom Hopkins—Ram Cottage counselor

James—Wolf Cottage counselor

Jane—Whale Cottage counselor

Lin Jerris—Intermittent, Wolf Cottage counselor

Jerry—Intermittent; Swan Cottage, Whale Cottage, Bull Cottage, Wolf Cottage counselor

Jon—Intermittent, Wolf Cottage counselor

John—Intermittent

Josefina—Ram Cottage counselor

Marie Klein—School Psychologist

Kris—Andromeda Cottage counselor

Candy Laine—Swan Cottage counselor

Lani—Swan Cottage temp

Jewel Larson—Serpent Cottage Director

Susan Lesser—Swan Cottage counselor

Hedda Levy—Group home counselor

Summer Light—Swan Cottage temp

Doug Little—Swan Cottage, Ram Cottage counselor

Lollie—Andromeda Cottage counselor

John Loring—Swan Cottage counselor

Whitney Lynch—Goldfish Cottage counselor; shop steward

Fernanda Lyons—Serpent Cottage Director

Mary MacDonald—Wolf Cottage Supervisor

Stan MacEvoy—Swan Cottage counselor

Shelby MacIntyre—Goldfish Cottage counselor

Margareta—Wolf Cottage counselor

Don Martino—Associate Superintendent

Brian Meara—Whale Cottage Supervisor, Dolphin Cottage Director

Mick—Wolf Cottage counselor

Mike—Intermittent

Ruth Monroe—Wolf Cottage, Whale Cottage counselor

Dean Nader—Superintendent

Nels—Ram Cottage counselor

Julia Park—Intermittent

Charlie Patterson—Wolf Cottage counselor

Frank Payne—Wolf Cottage counselor

Dick Peck—Chaplain

Katrina Person—Crane Cottage counselor

Paul Pitchess—Recreation counselor

Darryl Pound—Intermittent

Ralph Purple—Whale Cottage, Bull Cottage Director

Angel Ramsey—Intermittent, Swan Cottage temp

Raquel—Goldfish Cottage counselor

Carl Reid—Intermittent

Sal Reiver—Whale Cottage counselor

Carol Ripito—Associate Superintendent

Robert—Wolf Cottage counselor

Roberta—Wolf Cottage counselor

Benny Roche—Wolf Cottage counselor

Steven Ruer—Swan Cottage counselor

Ronnie—Intermittent

Shirley—Wolf Cottage counselor

Fran Sikora—Swan Cottage counselor, Supervisor

Newt Smith—Security officer

Stasha—Intermittent

Swampman—Security officer

Dick Teale—Wolf Cottage counselor

Fred Thoele—Associate Superintendent

Wayne—Whale Cottage counselor

Sara Willey—Swan Cottage counselor

Grant Williams—Youth Group facilitator

Dr. Wilton Williams—Chief of Psychiatric Services

Jim Wilson—Peacock Cottage counselor

Yvette—Serpent Cottage counselor

Others in an official or pseudo-official position

Amanda—Chairwoman of ART Quality Assurance committee

Debby—Palm Springs CPS worker

Helen Geertz—Union area representative

Shannon Gore—CPS worker

Matt Hall—Parole officer, ART trainer

Wilt Jones—Tommy Whitacre's parole officer

Karen Leason—Community mental health coordinator

Rick Newton—Mickey Joyce's parole officer

John Parish—Terry Voight's probation officer

Matthew Plumber—Volunteer

Jack Ralston—Terry Voight's parole officer

Mr. South—Presided over author's Secretary-level hearing

Sara Thompson—JRA personnel officer

Residents

Abel
Albert
Amelie
Leon Anderson
Ricky Arden
Tom Ballou
Juan Barajas
Carmen Barclay
Gerald Bardot
Justin Barrows
Bobby Beal
Danny Beck
Ginny Bell
Matt Benson
Jack Bergeron
Ronnie Berry
Michael Biddle
Julio Bitford
Donny Blocker
Rick Blue
Willie Bolles
Kristin Booker
Gilbert Boyce
Brendan
Joe Brown
Tony Brown
Johnny Brunson
Derek Burk
Philip Burl
Abdul Burton
Geraldine Cage
Caitlin
Walter Cantu
Carmen
Lucas Carne

John Cash
Peter Chaple
Alberto Chavez
Cindy Clausen
Darryl Connors
Luis Contreras
Stephen Cork
Cory Corson
Sasha Crow
Penny Davenport
Anthony Demarinis
Nathan Dieter
Charles Dietrich
Stevie Dorrance
Donnie Dorset
Paul Durnham
Eamon
Earl
Michael Evans
Ezekiah
Casey Fairchild
Josie Fells
Belinda Fish
Tussant Fisher
Felton Ford
Jacob French
Michael Fuentes
Randy Fulton
Paul Gabbard
Bert Gabel
Jonas Gardiner
Jorge Garza
Oscar Gonzalez
Willie Gonzalez
Ben Green

Reggie Greene
Paul Grise
Russell Guerra
Andrew Guerin
Jose Guevara
Jesus Haddon
Ezekial Hall
Ryan Helmsley
Rodney Hemming
Jonas Henson
Erma Hernandez
Charlie Hicks
Beanie Higham
Bernie Higham
Martin Hill
Charity Hoary
Robert Holden
Hollis
Sam Hopps
Tyee Horgan
Don Hoskins
Tony Hunter
Malcolm Isley
Donald Jackson
Jimmy Jackson
Cindy Johnson
Allen Joiner
Norah Joines
Henry Jones
Royal Jones
Mickey Joyce
Kaylee
Richard Kearney
Robbie Kelso
Tomas Lafarge
Ron Lafitte
Jason Lake

Darlene Lauder
William Lee
Jennifer Lessing
Charlie Lewis
Johnny Longtree
Louie
Daniel Lyons
Martin Lyons
Terry MacArthur
Donny Mack
Daniel Mallon
Anthony Manning
Marie
Marlin
Cassandra Martin
John Matafa
Anastacio Merced
Peter Mertz
Michael
Charity Miles
Montague Miller
Jimmy Mills
Dorothy Moon
Lyle Munson
Nels Nelson
Trent Nguyen
Merlin Nielson
Josh No Bear
Lawrence Norby
Vincent Oldham
Pang-li
Brian Parker
Theodore Patterson
Tim Pendleton
Brendan Perris
Davis Peters
James Pickle

Curt Prince
J.P. Prince
Richard Quiroga
Raquel Ramirez
Juan Reece
Cal Reed
Ryan Renton
Melanie Roberts
Willie Robinson
Les Rogers
Roy Rogers
Eduardo Rojas
Sue Royce
Sandi
Miguel Santos
Dean Savage
David Savitch
Justin Sears
Billy Shawn
Jamie Small
Lawrence Smith
Aaron Sneed
Bethna Spalding
Terence Starbuck
Dathan Strait
Larry Street
Lawrence Strong
Justin Swallow
Tatyana
Travis
Dusty Trudow
Colin Turner
John Tyler
Vicente
Terry Voight
Joe Voit
Richard Wain

Robert Walden
Jimmy Waller
Andrew Walters
David Warne
Eric Warner
Jeremy West
Tommy Whitacre
Tom White
Tyrone Wiley
Will
Kent Williams
Ronnie Williams
Dan Wilson
Shane Winn
Shari Woods
Morris Workman
Zora

Persons known to residents from the outside

Mike Carter—former resident of Swan Cottage

Crystal—Norah Joines' co-offender

Mario Guerra—Russell Guerra's brother

Gus—Davis Peters' stepbrother

Margarite Jackson—Donald Jackson's stepmother

Michael Jackson—Donald Jackson's brother

Richard Jackson—Donald Jackson's father

Shannon Jackson—Donald Jackson's grandmother

Josiah—former friend of Ron Lafitte

June—Reggie Greene's girlfriend

Geraldine Keyes—Norah Joines' victim

Louise Keyes—Norah Joines' foster mother

Marion Lafitte—Ron Lafitte's brother

Marlon Lafitte—Ron Lafitte's brother

Victor Rivas—man with whom Mickey Joyce lived

Mark Robinson—former resident of Swan Cottage

Carroll Sanders—Terry Voight's foster father

Sean—Davis Peters' stepfather

Knute Turner—Colin Turner's brother

Cindy Voight—Terry Voight's stepmother

Daniel Voight—Terry Voight's father

Fred Voight—Terry Voight's uncle

Kathy Voight—Terry Voight's aunt

Sharlo Voight—Terry Voight's half-sister

Morgan Whitacre—Tommy Whitacre's brother

Earl Winn—Shane Winn's brother

Loretta Winn—Shane Winn's mother

Shannon Winn—Shane Winn's sister

Persons known to the author from the outside

Bonnie—author's sister

Cee—author's friend

Mary Corning—friend

Ron Dakron—friend, writer

Tony Deacon—friend

Freida—a regular at Burgermaster

Everett Greimann—friend

Hector—Tony Deacon's friend

Laurel—a regular at Burgermaster

Roy MacCready—friend

Judy North—childhood friend

Robin—friend

Sharon Ruykeyser—cocaine addict

Saul—friend

Tim Silver—friend

Marilyn Stablein—friend, writer

Victor—father of a former Ash
  Meadow resident

About the Author

JEROME GOLD is the author of ten books, including *Sergeant Dickinson*, which was based on his experiences in the US Army Special Forces during the Vietnam War. He is also the publisher of Black Heron Press.